C000051053

New Security Challenges Series

General Editor: **Stuart Croft**, Professor of International Security in the Department of Politics and International Studies at the University of Warwick, UK, and Director of the ESRC's New Security Challenges Programme.

The last decade demonstrated that threats to security vary greatly in their causes and manifestations, and that they invite interest and demand responses from the social sciences, civil society and a very broad policy community. In the past, the avoidance of war was the primary objective, but with the end of the Cold War the retention of military defence as the centrepiece of international security agenda became untenable. There has been, therefore, a significant shift in emphasis away from traditional approaches to security to a new agenda that talks of the softer side of security, in terms of human security, economic security and environmental security. The topical *New Security Challenges series* reflects this pressing political and research agenda.

Titles include:

Jon Coaffee, David Murakami Wood and Peter Rogers
THE EVERYDAY RESILIENCE OF THE CITY
How Cities Respond to Terrorism and Disaster

Tom Dyson
NEOCLASSICAL REALISM AND DEFENCE REFORM IN POST-COLD WAR EUROPE

Christopher Farrington *(editor)*
GLOBAL CHANGE, CIVIL SOCIETY AND THE NORTHERN IRELAND PEACE PROCESS
Implementing the Political Settlement

Kevin Gillan, Jenny Pickerill and Frank Webster
ANTI-WAR ACTIVISM
New Media and Protest in the Information Age

Andrew Hill
RE-IMAGINING THE WAR ON TERROR
Seeing, Waiting, Travelling

Andrew Hoskins and Ben O'Loughlin
TELEVISION AND TERROR
Conflicting Times and the Crisis of News Discourse

Bryan Mabee
THE GLOBALIZATION OF SECURITY
State Power, Security Provision and Legitimacy

Janne Haaland Matlary
EUROPEAN UNION SECURITY DYNAMICS
In the New National Interest

Michael Pugh, Neil Cooper and Mandy Turner *(editors)*
CRITICAL PERSPECTIVES ON THE POLITICAL ECONOMY OF PEACEBUILDING

Brian Rappert and Chandré Gould *(editors)*
BIOSECURITY
Origins, Transformations and Practices

Brian Rappert
BIOTECHNOLOGY, SECURITY AND THE SEARCH FOR LIMITS
An Inquiry into Research and Methods

Brian Rappert *(editor)*
TECHNOLOGY AND SECURITY
Governing Threats in the New Millennium

Lisa Watanabe
SECURING EUROPE

New Security Challenge Series
Series Standing Order ISBN 978-0-230-00216-6 (hardback) and ISBN 978-0-230-00217-3 (paperback)

You can receive future titles in this series as they are published by placing a standing order. Please contact your bookseller or, in case of difficulty, write to us at the address below with your name and address, the title of the series and the ISBN quoted above.

Customer Services Department, Macmillan Distribution Ltd, Houndmills, Basingstoke, Hampshire RG21 6XS, England

Neoclassical Realism and Defence Reform in Post-Cold War Europe

Tom Dyson
Lecturer in International Security, Department of Political, International, and Policy Studies, University of Surrey, UK, and Alexander von Humboldt Foundation Research Fellow, International Security Research Division, Stiftung Wissenschaft und Politik, Berlin, Germany

First published 2010 by
PALGRAVE MACMILLAN

Palgrave Macmillan in the UK is an imprint of Macmillan Publishers Limited, registered in England, company number 785998, of Houndmills, Basingstoke, Hampshire RG21 6XS.

Palgrave Macmillan in the US is a division of St Martin's Press LLC, 175 Fifth Avenue, New York, NY 10010.

Palgrave Macmillan is the global academic imprint of the above companies and has companies and representatives throughout the world.

Palgrave® and Macmillan® are registered trademarks in the United States, the United Kingdom, Europe and other countries

ISBN 978-0-230-24623-2   hardback

This book is printed on paper suitable for recycling and made from fully managed and sustained forest sources. Logging, pulping and manufacturing processes are expected to conform to the environmental regulations of the country of origin.

A catalogue record for this book is available from the British Library.

A catalog record for this book is available from the Library of Congress.

10   9   8   7   6   5   4   3   2   1
19   18   17   16   15   14   13   12   11   10

Printed and bound in Great Britain by
CPI Antony Rowe, Chippenham and Eastbourne

Dedication......
To my father, Kenneth, with love and gratitude

Contents

Acknowledgements

In working on this book I have acquired a number of debts of gratitude, in particular, to my family – my wife Denitza, mother, father, and brother, Ann, Kenneth and Charles Dyson, mother-in-law, Dorina Bobeva and grandmother-in-law, Baba Denka – whose advice and support has been of immeasurable value. I would also like to thank my friends Daniel Brinkwerth and Christopher Wollin and my colleague and friend Theodore Konstadinides for the many interesting conversations which have fed into this book and crucially, for helping me to keep a sense of perspective about my work.

I am very grateful to Professor Theo Farrell, Professor Chris Flood, Professor Klaus Goetz and Professor Adrian Hyde-Price for their support. I would also like to thank my colleagues at the Department of Political, International and Policy Studies at the University of Surrey and at the University of Potsdam's Chair of German and European Politics and Government for providing a stimulating and enjoyable working environment. The empirical research was funded by the Alexander von Humboldt Foundation and involved numerous semi-structured elite interviews across the British and German Ministries of Defence. I would like to thank my interviewees for their openness and generosity with their time. Finally, my thanks to Rui Alves, Babken Babajanian, James Cook, Tony Ereira, Lars Houpt and Hendrik Kraetzschmar for their support and friendship during the research and writing of this book.

List of Tables

List of Abbreviations

4GW	4th Generation Warfare
ACCIS	Allied Command Europe Automated Command and Control Information System
ACCS	Air Command and Control System
ACF	Advocacy Coalition Framework
ACT	Allied Command Transformation
AG JACOP	Joint Command Operations Working Group
AGS	Alliance Ground Surveillance
AICCS	Allied Command Europe Automated Command and Control Information System
AJCN	Advanced Joint Communications Node
ALTBMD	Active Layered Theatre Ballistic Defence System
ASTOR	Airborne Standoff Radar
AU	African Union
AutoFue	Automatic Command Communications Network
Autoko-90	*Automatisiertes Korpsstammnetz*
AWACS	Airborne Warning and Control System
BALTBAT	Baltic Battalion
BALTDEFCOL	Baltic Defence College
BALTNET	Baltic Air Surveillance Network
BALTRON	Baltic Naval Squadron
BAO	Air Land Bubble
BDC	Baltic Defence Cooperation
BMVg	*Bundesministerium der Verteidigung*
BOA	Air-Land Bubble
BTC	*Bundeswehr* Transformation Centre
BWB	Bundesamt fuer Wehrtechnik und Beschaffung
C2	Command and Control
C2IEDM	Command and Control Information Exchange Data Model
C2IS	Command, Control and Information Systems
C3	Command, Control and Communications
C3ISR	Command, Control, Communications, Intelligence, Surveillance and Reconnaissance
C4	Command, Control, Communications, Computers
C4ISR	Command, Control, Communications, Computer, Intelligence, Surveillance and Reconnaissance
CACD	Commander's Appreciation and Campaign Design
CAESAR	Coalition Aerial Surveillance and Reconnaissance

CAPAZUB	Study on the Capacities Necessary for a Combined Arms Task Force to be Deployed Within Urban Areas
CBRN	Chemical, Biological, Radiological and Nuclear
CCDP	EDA Comprehensive Capabilities Development Process
CD&E	Concept Development and Experimentation
CDEF	*Centre de Doctrine d'Emploi des Forces*
CDU	Christian Democratic Union
CEE	Central and Eastern Europe
CEEB	Combined Communications Electronics Broad
CEERAT	Army Intelligence Study and Training Centre
CEMA	*Chef de l'etat Major des Armies*
CENZUB	Military Operations in Urban Terrain Training Centre
CEREX	Army Exercises and Operations Feedback and Assessment Centre
CHG	Civilian Headline Goals
CICDE	*Centre Interarmees de Concepts, de Doctrines et D'Experimentation*
CJTF	Combined Joint Task Force
CNAD	NATO Conference of National Armaments Directors
COBRA	Counter-Battery Radar
CoC	Code of Conduct on Defence Procurement
COE	NATO Centre of Excellence
COIN	Counterinsurgency
CPCO	Centre for Planning and Conduct of Operations
CPG	Comprehensive Political Guidance
CREDAT	Army Doctrine Centre
CRT	Civilian Response Teams
CS	Copenhagen School
CSEM	Higher Military Education Staff Course
CSU	Christian Social Union
CSW COE	NATO Centre for Excellence in Confined and Shallow Waters
CVF	Future Carrier
DARPT	Defence Acquisition Reform Project Team
DBK	Dominant Battlespace Knowledge
DCDC	Development, Concepts and Doctrine Centre
DCDS	Deputy Chief of Defence Staff
DCI	Defence Capabilities Initiative
DCMO	Defence Crisis-Management Organisation
DE&S	Defence Equipment and Support
DfID	Department for International Development
DG	Director General
DGA	*Delegation Generale Pour L'Armement*
DII	Defence Information Infrastructure

DIS	Defence Industrial Strategy
DLO	Defence Logistics Organisation
DLoD	Defence Lines of Development
DOC	Directorate of Operational Capability
DoD	Department of Defense
DPA	Defence Procurement Agency
DSACEUR	NATO Supreme Allied Commander in Europe
DSG	Defence Strategic Guidance
DWP	Defence White Paper
EAC	European Airlift Centre
EADS	European Aeronautic Defence and Space Company
EAI	European Amphibious Initiative
EBAO	Effects-Based Approach to Operations
EBO	Effects-Based Operations
ECAP	European Capabilities Action Plan
ECE	East Central Europe
EDA	European Defence Agency
EGF	European Gendarmerie Force
ELINT	Electronic Intelligence
EMF	*Etat Major des Forces*
EMFE.IA	Joint Staff for Forces Training
EMU	European Monetary Union
EPC	European Political Cooperation
ERRF	European Rapid Reaction Force
ESA	European Space Agency
ESC	European Satellite Centre
ESDP	European Security and Defence Policy
ESG	War College
ESS	European Security Strategy
EU	European Union
EUFOR	European Union Force
EUMS	European Union Military Staff
EUROFOR	European Operational Rapid Force
EUROMARFOR	European Maritime Force
EUSC	European Union Satellite Centre
EUSEC	European Union Advisory and Assistance Mission for Reform of the Security Sector in the Democratic Republic of the Congo
FAO	Foreign Area Officer
FAUST	Tactical Command Provision System
FCO	Foreign and Commonwealth Office
FCS	Future Combat System
FDP	Free Democratic Party
FLN	*Front de Liberation Nationale*

FM 3-24	Joint Army/Marines Counter-Insurgency Doctrine Field Manual
FPU	Formed Police Units
FREMM	Franco-Italian Multi-Role Frigate
FRES	Future Rapid Effects System
FSAF	Future Surface-to-Air Anti-Missile Family
FueInfoSys H	Army Command System
GAST	Common Intelligence Analysis and Evaluation System
GDA	*Délégation générale pour l'armement*
GDP	Gross Domestic Product
GEODE	Optimised Electronic Management System
GEOINT	Human Geographical Intelligence Branch
GMES	Global Monitoring for Environment and Security Programme
GO-CO	Government Owned; Contractor Operated
GPS	Global Positioning System
HERO	Army Command and Control System for Digitally Supported Command of Operations in Staffs
HHG	Helsinki Headline Goals
HHG2010	Helsinki Headline Goals 2010
HTS	Human Terrain System
HTT	Human Terrain Team
HUMINT	Human Intelligence
IAB	Investment Approvals Board
IAGFA	Integrated Working Group for Capability Analysis
IED	Improvised Explosive Device
IFOR	The Implementation Force
IMINT	ISR Imagery Intelligence
INTERFET	International Force East Timor
IO	Information Operations
IPPR	Institute for Public Policy Research
IPT	Integrated Police Teams
ISAF	International Stability and Assistance Force
ISL	Franco-German Research Institute
ISR	Intelligence, Surveillance and Reconnaissance
ISTAR	Intelligence, Surveillance, Target Acquisition and Reconnaissance
JAPCC	Joint Air Power Competence Centre
JDCC	Joint Doctrine and Concepts Centre
JFCOM	United States Joint Forces Command
JIP	Joint Investment Programme
JIP-FP	Joint Investment Programme on Force Protection
JIP-ICET	Joint Investment Programme Innovative Concepts and Emerging Technologies

JSS	Joint Support Service
JSTAR	Joint Surveillance and Target Attack Radar System
JTAC	Joint Terminal Air Controller
JtMWCap	Joint Medium Weight Capability
KFOR	Kosovo Force
KSK	German Special Operations Division
Link 11	Tactical Digital Information Links
LOI	Letter of Intent
LPM	*Lois-Programmes Militaries*
LTO	DGA Battle Lab
LTV	EDA Long-term Vision for European Defence Capability and Capacity Needs
M&S	Modelling and Simulation
MACS	Maritime Airborne Surveillance and Control
MAJIIC	Multi-Sensor Aerospace-Ground Joint ISR Interoperability Programme
MC	NATO Military Committee
MCCE	Movement Coordination Centre Europe
MCO	Major Combat Operations
MIB	Ministerial Investment Board
MIC	Multinational Interoperability Council
MIDS	Multifunctional Information Distribution System
MIP	Multilateral Interoperability Programme
MoD	Ministry of Defence
MPFSEE	Multinational Peace Force South Eastern Europe
MPMP	Multilateral Interoperability Programme Management Plan
MTR	Military Technical Revolution
MUSIS	High Resolution Optical Satellite Programme
NATO	North Atlantic Treaty Organisation
NC3A	NATO C3 Agency
NC3TA	NATO Technical Architecture Initiative
NCO	Non-commissioned Officer
NCW	Network Centric Warfare
NEB	*Numerisation de l'espace de Bataille*
NEC	Network Enabled Capabilities
NetOpFü	*Vernetzten Operationsführung*
NGCS	NATO General Purpose Communications System
NGO	Non-Governmental Organisation
NMEC	NATO NEC Project
NOA	New Operational Art
NORDCAPS	Nordic Coordinated Arrangement for Military Peace Support
NRF	NATO Response Force

OCCAR	Organisation for Joint Armaments Cooperation
OFT	Office of Force Transformation
OGD	Other Governmental Departments
OOTW	Operations Other Than War
ORFEO	Optical and Radar Federated Earth Observation Satellite
OSCE	Organisation for Security and Cooperation in Europe
OTD	Operation Training Detachments
PAAMS	Principle Anti-Air Missile System
PACE	Performance, Agility, Confidence and Programme
PCC	Prague Capabilities Commitment
PfP	Partnership for Peace
PGM	Precision Guided Munitions
PJHQ	Permanent Joint Headquarters
PMESII	Political, Military, Economic, Social, Information and Infrastructure
PSC	Political and Security Committee
PSO	Peace Support Operations
PSYOPS	Psychological Operation
PUS	Permanent Under Secretary
QDR	Quadrennial Defense Review
R&D	Research and Development
R&T	Research and Technology
RAF	Royal Air Force
RDO	Rapid and Decisive Operations
RITA 2000	Radio Programme and Automatic Transmission Integrated Network
RMA	Revolution in Military Affairs
RoE	Rules of Engagement
RPR	Rally for the Republic
RTB	RTO's Research and Technology Board
RTO	Research and Technology Organisation
SAC	NATO Strategic Airlift Capability
SACEUR	Supreme Allied Commander Europe
SAD	Strategic Affairs Division
SAIM	Multi-Source Interpretation Assistance System
SALIS	Strategic Airlift Interim Solution
SAR	Synthetic Aperture Radar
SCC	Sealift Coordination Centre
SCF	Future Contact System
SDR	Strategic Defence Review
SFOR	Stabilisation Force in Bosnia and Herzegovina
SHAPE	Supreme Headquarters Allied Powers Europe
SHIRBRIG	Multinational Standby High Readiness Brigade for UN Operations

SIGNIT	Signal Intelligence
SOD	Systemic Operational Design
SPD	Social Democratic Party
STANAG	Standardisation Agreements for Procedures and Systems and Equipment Components
TCAR	Trans-Atlantic Cooperative Radar
TIES	Tactical Imagery Exploitation System
TIPS	Transatlantic Industrial Partnership for Surveillance
TLCM	Through Life Capability Management Programme
TMD	Theatre Missile Defence System
TOPSAT	Tactical Optical Satellite
TPG	Transformation Planning Guidance
TRADOC	Training and Doctrine Command
UAV	Unmanned Aerial Vehicles
UCAV	Unmanned Combat Aerial Vehicle
UDF	Union for French Democracy
UKDA	United Kingdom Defence Academy
UN	United Nations
UNFIL	United Nations Interim Force in Lebanon
UNPROFOR	United Nations Protection Force
UNSOM II	United Nations Operation in Somalia
UOR	Urgent Operational Requirement
VPR	*Verteidigungspolitische Richtlinien*
WEAG	West European Armaments Group
WEAO	West European Armaments Organisation
WEU	Western European Union
WMD	Weapons of Mass Destruction
ZFGO	Joint Operations Centre

Introduction

The empirical research questions, theoretical approach and contribution to the literature

This book asks to what extent the militaries of Britain, France and Germany have been converging or diverging across the main axes of defence policy during the post-Cold War era (1990–2009):

(i) Defence policy objectives (from territorial defence to a new form of 'forward defence' that seeks to meet the threats to international stability at source through low/medium/high intensity expeditionary crisis-management operations);
(ii) Defence policy instruments (reforms to military structures, capabilities and doctrines);
(iii) The institutional forums of defence policy (prioritisation of EU/NATO; tri-bi-pluri-lateral initiatives or national strategic autonomy)
(iv) The temporality of reforms (temporal location, sequencing and pace)[1]

If convergence is taking place, it leads to the central question of around what model – to what extent are Britain, France and Germany emulating post-Cold War US Military Reforms and the 'Revolution in Military Affairs' or converging around their own innovation in military practices. It also raises the question of whether the patterns of convergence/divergence identified (not least complementarity/competition in institutional forums) are indicative of the emergence of the EU as a potential military rival to the United States, or of Europe seeking to carry a greater burden within (and therefore reinforce) the Atlantic Alliance. These issues will have a crucial bearing upon the extent to which Europe is both *willing* and *able* to cooperate with the US, through NATO and the UN, over a set of pressing security concerns – including avoiding and dealing with state failure, international terrorism and the proliferation of weapons of mass destruction, whose resolution will be dependent upon US/European cooperation (Cottey, 2008: 73; Hyde-Price, 2007: 112).

1

The main focus in public and academic debate has been on the nature and form of European military power projection in the context of unipolarity and the changed configuration of security threats in the post-Cold War world; on the trans-Atlantic relationship and the relationship between ESDP and NATO. Hence the monograph's empirical focus differs from existing accounts, as it is not only on the development of ESDP and its relationship to NATO and other bi-pluri-lateral force generation/capability procurement initiatives (competition/complementarity in the institutional forums of defence policy) and the convergence of defence policy objectives,[2] but on military reform. The study pays close attention to convergence in policy instruments – military structures and capabilities – both within Europe and between European states and the US, in addition to examining the temporality of defence reform. In short, the book offers a systematic examination of armed forces reforms in the three main European states by asking whether these reforms constitute military convergence, if so, around what, and at what speed, pace and temporal location? In doing so, the study also examines the nature and impact of the 'transmission belt' by which international pressure is translated into domestic policy responses. These issues will determine the extent to which Europe is able to effectively pool its military resources and develop autonomy from US assistance in areas like intelligence, logistics, air transport and intelligence, surveillance and reconnaissance capabilities in expeditionary power projection operations (Moens, 2003: 27). The book answers these empirical questions by conducting a thorough review of existing literature, through the analysis of official documents available in the public realm and through semi-structured, elite interviews, conducted with the support of the Alexander von Humboldt Foundation.

Crucially, the book explores how patterns of convergence and divergence within Europe and between Europe and the United States can be explained, by systematically testing cultural and realist approaches to the sources of military change and stasis. There are several monographs analysing the convergence of defence policy objectives and institutional forums in the context of the development of ESDP. The works of Christopher Meyer (2006) and Jolyon Howorth (2007) are at the forefront of cultural approaches to this phenomenon, emphasising normative convergence and the development of 'European strategic culture',[3] whilst Adrian Hyde-Price (2007) and Seth Jones (2007) offer neorealist accounts of the rise of European security cooperation, prioritising the role of systemic imperatives and international structure.[4] The book differs from these accounts by analysing the domestic processes of defence policy reforms, providing an in-depth examination of the impact not just of systemic factors, but also of the domestic political factors determining the temporality of military innovation/emulation and policy convergence amongst the three major European military powers of the EU/NATO.[5]

The book also employs a new theoretical approach to the subject area. The work seeks to build upon Adrian Hyde-Price's notable corrective to the neglect of power politics in European security by demonstrating the utility of neoclassical realism as a framework to conceptualise defence policy convergence and military innovation and emulation (Hyde-Price, 2007: 2).[6] The monograph captures the important intervening role played by domestic material power relationships and 'executive autonomy' in determining the temporality of changes to the objectives, instruments and institutional forums of defence policy.[7] As Hyde-Price (2007: 167) notes: '[structural] realist international relations theory is thus a necessary but not sufficient tool for "turning the soil of ignorance" about the post-Cold War security system'.

By developing realist theory in the context of new and contemporary case studies, the study also contributes to the literature analysing military change across history. It builds, in particular, upon the contributions of Barry Posen (1984) who applies neorealism to case studies of military reform in Britain and France in the interwar period, Joao Resende-Santos (2007), who develops neorealism as a framework of military change in the context of military emulation in South America in the late 19th century and the edited volumes of Theo Farrell and Terry Terriff (2002) and of John Glenn et al (2004).[8]

The core argument: defence policies between international structure and executive autonomy

The book argues that it is possible to identify increasing levels of convergence in the objectives, instruments and institutional forums of British, French and German defence policies.[9] It uncovers, however, significant divergence in the temporality of reform processes. These patterns of convergence/divergence cannot be explained through a focus on the mediating role played by 'national strategic cultures' – 'culturally-bounded' and 'institutionally-embedded' norms that 'predispose societies in general and political elites to certain patterns of behavior' (Berger, 1998; Duffield, 1998: 27). They cannot be understood through an examination of the role of 'political/ norm entrepreneurs' within the core executive or actors within the wider security policy subsystem,[10] in reshaping the three layers of belief systems (peripheral, operational and central beliefs) of which strategic cultures are composed (Dalgaard-Nielsen, 2006: 13).[11] Nor is an examination of the impact of civil-military relations on the organisational culture of defence ministries and military establishments a sufficient account of policy change (Kier, 1997: 4). 'Culture' emerges not so much as a cause of action (Farrell, 1998: 408) as a tool, resource and instrument for policy leaders concerned with the domestic political and temporal management of reform (Dyson, 2005, 2007; Johnston, 1995: 39–41; Klein, 1988: 136).

The analysis finds that 'international structure' is the key source of change and convergence in the objectives, instruments and institutional forums of defence policy (Barnathan, 2006; Jones, 2007; Posen, 1984, 2004, 2006; Waltz, 1979). However, neorealist accounts neglect the impact of domestic political factors in constraining the autonomy of the core executive to respond to systemic power shifts over the short-medium term and cannot adequately account for temporal divergence in defence reform amongst states of broadly comparable relative material power capabilities and 'external vulnerability' (Taliaferro, 2006: 479).[12] Hence neoclassical realism, that emphasises the primacy of 'international structure' – but also integrates the intervening role played by 'unit-level variables' such as domestic material power relationships and strategic leadership – emerges as the most convincing account of convergence/divergence in defence reform (Rose, 1998: 152; Rynning, 2001–2).[13]

As Zakaria (1998: 9) argues: 'Foreign policy is made not by the nation as a whole but by its government. Consequently what matters is state power, not national power. State power is that portion of national power the government can extract for its purposes and reflects the ease with which central decision-makers can achieve their ends'. Jeffrey Taliaferro (2006: 465–8) also highlights how states which are confronted with the same threat vary in their ability to extract and mobilise resources from domestic society: unit-level variables – state institutions, ideology and nationalism – affect whether and when states choose innovation, emulation or the continuation of existing military strategies. This book responds to the research agenda outlined by Sten Rynning (2001, 2001–2: 116), and Gideon Rose (1998: 169) by focusing specifically on the impact of different state structures and domestic material power relationships on the extraction and deployment of national power by state leaders and by testing neoclassical realism against cultural approaches to strategic adjustment (Taliaferro, 2006: 495).

In his work on French military reform, Rynning (2001–2) posits that the key unit-level variable in explaining temporal divergence with systemic power shifts is the ability of policy leaders to successfully manage domestic reform processes. However, whilst it is important to analyse the impact of specific instances of policy leadership, in order to fully understand the root causes of temporal divergence, we must look instead to the domestic material incentives that determine the initial choice of leadership role. The level of 'executive autonomy' in defence policy, resulting from the institutional structure of the state (the degree of centralisation), the formal constitutional powers of the core executive over defence policy and nested and interlinked policy subsystems (defence/budgetary/social policy) incentivises or discourages political entrepreneurship by policy leaders on behalf of 'third-order'[14] change and the 'timely' translation of systemic power shifts into military reform (Irondelle, 2003b: 168; Rose, 1998: 169; Rynning, 2001/02: 115–16).

The study argues that high levels of 'executive autonomy' in defence policy help explain the temporal location, sequencing and pace of military reform in the UK and France.[15] However, the case of *Bundeswehr* (German armed forces) reform highlights that whilst policy over the long-run is dictated by the threats and opportunities presented by the international system (Rose, 1998: 151), deficits in 'executive autonomy' can lead to the active promotion of 'stasis' and 'first-order change' in military reform over the short-medium term (Hall, 1993: 278–9).

Within such a context 'culture' is used selectively by policy leaders as a resource with which to legitimate policy stasis as part of the domestic political and temporal management of reform (Dyson, 2005, 2007). This preoccupation with 'balancing domestic power' and the domestic political ramifications of convergence with systemic change, rather than the 'national interest', also impacts upon the anchoring of defence policy within EU/NATO 'allied cooperation' and determines whether this will reflect systemic imperatives or domestic interests over the short-medium term (Dyson, 2007: 173–7; Rynning, 2001–2: 90). Hence 'executive autonomy', rather than strategic culture or specific instances of policy leadership, forms the decisive causal variable in explaining temporal divergence in defence reform.

The book attempts, therefore, to respond to the neoclassical realist research agenda set out by Ripsman et al (2009: 292–9) by systematically testing neoclassical realism against neorealist and cultural approaches to defence reform. The study also undertakes an analysis of how unit-level factors – including the impact of individual policy leadership, state structures, the relationships between policy subsystems, nationalism, ideology and culture – interact with systemic factors such as the balance of power and threat to determine the capacity of states to generate military power. In addition, the book examines the impact of organisational politics between the Single Services on concept development and experimentation (CD&E), military doctrine and defence capability acquisition and explores the mechanisms through which civilian actors within Defence Ministries have attempted to channel military input to defence planning. Furthermore, the monograph explores the issue of secondary states' responses to the uni-polar world and examines the relative impact of systemic domestic-level variables in explaining the policy positions adopted by the European Great powers towards the key international forums of defence policy in Europe (NATO, ESDP as well as bi-pluri-lateral force generation/capability procurement initiatives).

Ripsman et al (2009: 298–9) do not identify the issue of parsimony as one that should be of grave concern to the field of neoclassical realism. One of the main purposes of theory should, however, be to make sense of a complex set of variables and deliver a succinct explanation of the key forces driving the content and timing of policy change. This study develops a strongly materialist approach to neoclassical realism that emphasises the role played by material forces at both the systemic and domestic levels of analysis in shaping the content and timing of policy. In doing so the book seeks to strike a balance between what some view as the 'foolish parsimony' of neorealism (Byman and Pollack, 2001: 146) and a more nuanced approach that accounts for the transmission belt through which changes in the international system are translated into domestic policy responses.

The book begins by examining the empirical evidence of convergence in British, French and German defence policy around a partial and selective emulation of the US-led Revolution in Military Affairs. It proceeds by outlining the core premises of cultural and realist approaches to convergence and by testing their utility through case studies of the reform processes in each of these three states.

Section I

Context: The Case for Convergence

1
Europe's Partial and Selective Emulation of the US-led Revolution in Military Affairs

Patterns of convergence and divergence in defence reform: The objectives, instruments, institutional forums and temporality of defence policy

According to Colin Bennett (1991: 19) policy convergence represents 'a process of "becoming" rather than a condition of "being" alike...there must be movement over time to some common point. In comparative research...the essential theoretical dimension is temporal rather than spatial'. Christopher Knill (2005: 768) offers a more substantive definition, arguing that policy convergence is 'any increase in the similarity between one or more characteristics of a certain policy...across a given set of political jurisdictions...over a given period of time. Policy convergence thus describes the end result of a process of policy change towards some common point'.[1]

Building upon these broad definitions this study distinguishes between convergence in British, French and German defence reforms along four dimensions: defence policy objectives (the shift from territorial and alliance defence to low- medium- high-intensity expeditionary crisis-management operations in support of meeting threats to international instability at source); policy instruments (military structure, doctrine and capabilities); the institutional forums within which defence policy is anchored (national strategic autonomy or the embedding of defence policy within the EU/NATO or bi-pluri-lateral initiatives) and finally, temporality (the temporal location, sequence and pace of reform) (Schedler and Santiso, 1998).

During the Cold War West European defence policies displayed strong convergence in their objectives: the principles of deterrence and territorial/alliance defence stood at the centre of British, French and German defence policies. The policy instruments of these three states (armed forces) were also convergent, taking the form of heavy armour, mass armies, designed to undertake the forward defence of NATO and resist a Warsaw Pact advance across Germany (see Table 1.1). Divergence was apparent in institutional forums: whilst Britain and Germany prioritised NATO, French defence policy was characterised by the Gaullist principles of 'national sanctuary' and 'strategic autonomy', following its withdrawal from NATO's integrated military structures in 1966, leading to a 'semi-detached' defence policy (Gordon, 1992: 57; Menon, 1995: 19).[2]

The end of the Cold War, however, led to dramatic changes in the international security environment: a shift from a bi-polar to a uni-polar world, uni-lateral changes in US behaviour, the rise of new security threats and challenges such as failed states, humanitarian emergencies, international terrorism, organised crime and the proliferation of weapons of mass destruction (WMD) (Cottey, 2008: 73; Hyde-Price, 2007: 112; Krahmann, 2005).[3] The following two chapters make the empirical case for convergence in the military policies of the West European Great Powers and illustrate how, within this changing context, longer-term convergence patterns in the objectives, instruments and institutional forums of British, French and German defence policy are evident. At the same time, significant divergence in the temporal location, pace and sequencing of convergence is identified.

This chapter begins with an examination of post-Cold War armed forces reform in the US: the country of greatest military capability in the international system. It demonstrates that the US-led Revolution in Military Affairs (RMA) and force 'transformation' has formed an important template for post-Cold War reforms to the militaries of the West European Great powers. The chapter will, however, highlight how European emulation of the RMA is only partial, and has proceeded in a selective and temporally-uneven manner. The second chapter of this section, Chapter 2, focuses upon convergence and divergence in the institutional venues of defence policy. It sheds light on the increasing functional complementarity of the core institutions of European defence (NATO and the ESDP), bi-/pluri-lateral force generation and capability procurement initiatives outside the frameworks of the EU and NATO. The chapter highlights, at the same time, a significant level of geographical and temporal differentiation in European defence cooperation.

US defence policy in the post-Cold War era: 'Revolution', 'transformation' and 'second-order' change

The revolution in military affairs: Extending the 'uni-polar moment'

Post-Cold War US defence reform has been guided by the concept of the Revolution in Military Affairs.[4] The origins of the RMA lie in late 1970s Soviet military thought and the work of Marshal N.V. Ogarkov. Following the emergence of battlefield sensors and guided weapons during the Vietnam War and the development of US capabilities aimed at the obliteration of Soviet forces in the event of their advance across Germany, Ogarkov identified an emerging military technical revolution (MTR) sparked by US dominance in the electronic battlefield (Cohen, 2004: 396, 399; Morgan, 2000: 133).[5] The RMA draws upon the Marxist-Leninist tradition of revolutionary discontinuity in historical development. It rests upon the assumption that whilst warfare develops in an evolutionary manner, at certain periods, revolutionary advances in technology and ideas can offer the prospect of significant military advantage, recalibrating the global balance of power in favour of those able to take advantage of new developments (Metz, 2006: 3).

As John Stone (2004) notes, the ideas which underpin the RMA can be traced back to the work of Carl von Clausewitz.[6] Clausewitz posited that in seeking to compel an adversary to one's will through the destruction of his armed forces, war would escalate to its 'pure' or absolute form: 'an explosion of uncontrolled violence'. Clausewitz identified, however, two intervening factors – political and technical – which act to temper the process of escalation. Technology can impede the escalation of violence by enabling the rapid and decisive defeat of the enemy, whilst the political context of a conflict can also obstruct escalation, as the level of violence in war is directly proportional to the political aims on behalf of which a conflict is fought (Howard, 1983: 25–6; Stone, 2004).

Following the failure of attempts to reach a political settlement with the North Vietnamese as a means of limiting escalation during the Vietnam conflict, both the US military and its civilian leaders have been committed to the decisive defeat of its enemies: to 'fighting to win' and avoiding the stalemate and attrition of the Vietnam War (Stone, 2004: 417). Consequently, the RMA was taken up enthusiastically by a group of influential US strategic planners in the early 1990s, such as Andrew Marshall,[7] Director of the Pentagon's Office of Net Assessment (1973–Present) and Admiral William Owens, Vice-Chairman of the Joint Chiefs of Staff (1994–96). Although the 1991 Gulf War was viewed by proponents of the RMA as a 'Transitional War', involving a ground campaign and only a limited use of precision-guided munitions, it demonstrated the apparent potential of stand-off[8] precision strike air power and satellite-guided, automated command, control and communications (C3) in facilitating swift and decisive victory (Bratton, 2002: 88; Morgan, 2000: 133; Mahnken and Fitz Simonds, 2003: 121).[9] The RMA seemed to offer the opportunity to maintain and extend the uni-polar 'moment' by facilitating global high-intensity power projection to tackle the core security threats identified by the first Quadrennial Defence Review of May 1997: the threat of 'force-on-force' conventional war against rogue states such as Iran, Iraq and North Korea (Metz, 2006: 5).

In short, technological advances presented the promise of revolutionising warfare in favour of the US.[10] The networking of sensors, shooters, command and control systems offered not only an increase in combat power, the ability to destroy enemy weapons systems and greater protection and chance of survival (Betz, 2007: 235); they also seemed to facilitate attacks against the sources of national power of dictatorial regimes without significant averse effects upon their populations (Frank, 2004: 71). For the administrations of President Bill Clinton (1993–2001) and particularly President George W. Bush (2001–9), the adoption of the RMA as the guiding concept for military reform appeared to herald renewed possibilities for the use, or the threat of military force as a tool of foreign policy. The attractiveness of the RMA lay in its potential to permit the US to dictate the terms of conflict and control the process of escalation through the execution of rapid and decisive operations (RDO), whilst minimising the cost to US life and resources.[11] Moreover, the RMA was perceived not just as an opportunity, but as an imperative that would have to be seized to ensure sustained US power and influence and increase its relative power; for if the US did not embrace the RMA, its competitors would (Kagan, 2006: 217).[12]

US military 'transformation' as second order change

The RMA was formally integrated into US defence policy in the 1997 'Joint Vision 2010' that placed 'full-spectrum dominance' at the heart of US military planning. The Joint Vision 2010 involved the utilisation of networking and information technology such as global positioning and stand-off capabilities to enable worldwide complex simultaneous operations (Metz, 2006: 6). By the late 1990s, however, the notion of a sudden 'revolution' began to give way to one of 'transformation'; a term implying complete change in US force structure, doctrine and capabilities in order to exploit the RMA (Kagan, 2006: 311). Transformation was first invoked by the National Defence Panel's Report of December 1997 and was defined by the Department of Defence (DoD) as: 'A process that shapes the changing nature of military competition and cooperation through new combinations of concepts, capabilities, people, and organisations that exploit our nation's advantages and protect against our asymmetric vulnerabilities to sustain our strategic positions, which helps underpin peace and stability in the world.' (Neal, 2003: 78; Reynolds, 2006: 435)[13]

The use of the term 'transformation' to describe the process of change that has taken place within the US military is, however, something of a misnomer. Peter Hall defines three levels of policy change: 'first-order change' in which the settings of policy instruments are changed, while the overall goals and instruments of policy remain constant; second-order change in which both the instruments and settings of policy are altered, while the goals of policy remain unchanged and finally 'third-order change', in which all three components of policy (settings, instruments and the hierarchy of goals) are transformed (Hall, 1993: 278–9).[14] As this section will demonstrate, post-Cold War military reforms in the US are a case of 'second order change', rather than transformation. West European armed forces had focused upon the forward defence of NATO territory during the Cold War. By virtue of their geographic position this task necessitated large, standing, mass armies which required radical reform to deal with the expeditionary challenges of the post-Cold War era. After the Vietnam conflict, the US, had, in contrast, developed a substantial capacity to deploy expeditionary power (including two million active duty personnel supported by conventional, as well as nuclear, capabilities) in order to contain potential Communist expansion across the globe (Boot, 2006: 324–35). Post-Cold War reforms have built upon these capabilities through incremental change to the 'settings' and 'instruments' of policy in a bid to harness the technological advances associated with the RMA. However, the overall goals of policy: high-intensity expeditionary warfighting operations against state-based opponents have until more recently (post-2005) remained largely constant.

Nevertheless, as Metz (2006: 8) highlights, whilst there was a general consensus that future operations would involve expeditionary force projection, during the early mid-1990s contesting visions of defence transformation emerged within the US military. The Air Force promoted long-range precision strike airpower and the concept of 'Effects Based Operations' (EBO). EBO initially stemmed from thinking within the US Navy and Air Force about how to achieve strategic effects through air strikes in an attempt to refine the military tactics and strategy employed by the US in the 1991 Gulf War (Betz, 2007: 235; Farrell, 2008: 4). Although Operation Desert Storm had focused on the attrition and annihilation of Iraqi field forces, it also involved the targeting of strategic assets to destroy the infrastructure of the state (Kagan, 2006: 164–6).[15] Following this operational experience the concept of EBO began to gain wider currency within the Navy and Air Force, as a framework that would enable the military to better 'understand how and where to apply precise force in order to achieve a rapid and decisive victory' (Ho, 2005: 172).

Influenced by figures such as Vice Admiral Arthur Cebrowski (President of the Naval War College 1998–2001 and Director of the Office of Force Transformation between 2001–05), the Navy had been a forceful proponent of the RMA throughout the 1990s (Dahl, 2002: 1–2; Kagan, 2006: 258–9). The Navy promoted a shift away from naval combat to power projection from the sea a stronger role for littoral combat ships, close liaison with the Marines and an exploitation of the opportunities provided by 'network-centric warfare'. Although linked to the Sea Services, the Commandant of the Marine Corps, General Charles Krulak argued in favour of developing the ability to deal with 'three block warfare'. This concept encompassed the idea that US forces would be most likely to encounter the rapid emergence of simultaneous humanitarian, peacekeeping/post-conflict reconstruction and high-intensity warfighting operations in urban environments as small as 'three blocks' (Ho, 2005: Metz, 2006: 7; Terriff, 2007). Under its Chief of Staff, General George Sullivan (1991–95), the Army emphasised the challenge posed by asymmetric threats and 'Operations Other Than War' (OOTW) (humanitarian and peace-keeping missions), in addition to conventional warfare and the necessity to retain the ability to deploy force on land in order to consolidate the gains achieved by air and naval power (Kagan, 2006: 166–7; Metz, 2006: 7). The RMA was, however, central to Army planning. The technological advantage of the US would deliver the capacity to 'engage the enemy over the horizon' and 'mass effects not forces' (Jordan et al, 2008: 111; Kagan, 2006: 169). As General Sullivan argued: 'smaller or fewer units will be able to produce decisive effects because of the vast array of weaponry they have at their disposal' (Kagan, 2006: 169).

It took the intervention of US Defence Secretary Donald Rumsfeld (2000–6), who enjoyed the full-backing of President Bush, to foster a more coordinated reform process by instigating a 'transformation' defined as adherence to the virtues of 'speed, agility and jointness' (Metz, 2006: 9). The 'transformation agenda' finally coalesced in the US DoD 30 September 2001 Quadrennial Defence Review. The Review appeared to represent an important break with previous US defence policy, by recognising the necessity of tackling non-state threats and the problems associated with failed states and that this would require the development of new capabilities. Hence the 2001 QDR outlined a shift from a 'threat-based' to a 'capabilities-based'[16] approach (Kagan, 2006: 279). Instead of assuming that the capabilities necessary to tackle 'rogue states' or 'near-peer competitors' could be employed against non-state actors, the QDR sought to ensure that the military would invest in capabilities which would be able to guarantee the security of the US in a broader set of future conflict scenarios emanating from increasingly uncertain international security environment.

The 2001 QDR charted six core operational goals for the 'transformed' US military (Kagan, 2006: 284–6; Metz, 2006: 12).[17] Firstly, protecting critical bases of operations (home and abroad) and defeating chemical, radiological, nuclear and explosive weapons and their means of delivery. Secondly, assuring information systems in the face of attack and conducting effective information operations. Thirdly, projecting and sustaining US forces in distant anti-access or area denial environments and defeating anti-access and anti-denial threats. Fourthly, denying enemies sanctuary by providing persistent surveillance, tracking, and rapid engagement with high volume precision strike, through a combination of complementary air and ground capabilities, against critical mobile and fixed targets at various ranges and in all weather and terrains. Fifthly, enhancing the capability and survivability of space systems and supporting infrastructure. Finally, leveraging information technology and innovative concepts to develop an interoperable joint Command, Control, Communications, Computer, Intelligence, Surveillance and Reconnaissance (C4ISR) architecture and capabilities that includes a tailorable joint operational picture.

In short, the 2001 QDR attempted to instigate a transformation process that was ongoing; a state of 'permanent revolution' designed to take full advantage of the RMA and tailor it to the requirements of the post-Cold

War security environment. The fundamental goals and pillars of transformation were given 'institutional protection' within the DoD through the creation of the Office of Force Transformation in October 2001.[18] The OFT, whose work was imbued with greater gravitas after September 11 and the inadequacies of US 'off the shelf' plans for tackling Afghanistan, was charged with the task of coordinating and evaluating transformation amongst the four services of the military in order to ensure that they conformed with the six operational goals, and to lead the shift towards network centric capability (Boot, 2006: 364; Corum, 2007: 400).[19]

Following the success of long-range precision air strikes, combined with special forces support for indigenous forces in the Afghanistan Campaign of 2001 (the 'Afghan model')[20] and the initial success of the more conventional campaign fought in Operation Iraqi Freedom of 2003, Rumsfeld felt emboldened to accelerate and widen the transformation agenda (Kagan, 2006: 308; Sapolsky et al, 2009: 104–5). In April 2003 the Secretary of Defence released 'Transformation Planning Guidance' (TPG) that outlined in bold terms the creation of a network-centric military by 2010. Prefaced by the quotation of George Bush that heralded: 'a future force that relies...more heavily on stealth, precision weaponry, and information technologies', it was a document that represented the apex of the 'technological determinism' that had been the hallmark of the US military reform in the post-Cold War era.[21] TPG emphasised the explicit goal of grasping the 'historical opportunity'[22] to place the US at the forefront of the transformation from 'an industrial age to an information age military'[23] and the achievement of 'fundamentally joint, network centric, distributed forces capable of rapid decision superiority and massed effects across the battlespace',[24] through the acceleration of C4ISR procurement programmes.

Whilst Rumsfeld's vision of transformation acted to foster greater coordination between the Air Force, Army, Navy and Marines, around speed, airpower, precision-guided munitions and information dominance, it also reinforced and confirmed many of the plans which the services had developed in the late 1990s (Metz, 2006: 15–16). This reflected the nature of 'transformation', not as a process of radical and 'revolutionary' 'third order' change, but the further development of thinking that had arisen during the mid-1980s, concerning the existence of a military technical revolution and the ability of the technological lead of the US to deliver the capacity to control the process of 'escalation' (Bratton, 2002: 88). These ideas had been embodied in Cold War strategic scenarios such as the Air-Land-Battle, Follow on Forces Attack and Maritime Strategy (Bratton, 2002: 88). The implications of 'transformation' were therefore largely ones of 'second order change' to the instruments and settings of policy: the adaptation of existing military structures and capabilities to meet the goal of attaining rapid and decisive victory over state-based opponents.

Consequently the Air Force was given the green light to push ahead with net-centric precision strikes and EBO – though with greater emphasis upon global strikes, mobility, persistent attack, agile combat support and a shift away from manned combat aircraft to unmanned aerial vehicles (UAVs). The Navy, whilst continuing with its plans to develop a large aircraft carrier, was instructed to focus more strongly on the development of surface action groups and arsenal ships, rather than carrier battlegroup operations and an emphasis on the role of the Littoral (coastal waters) Combat Ship in support of expeditionary operations. The Marines became the lead organisation in the war on terror and were integrated within the Joint US Special Operations Command.

TPG signaled far-reaching change for the Army in a bid to improve its flexibility, speed and agility. The document strengthened the hand of General Eric Shinseki, the Army Chief of Staff who, following the difficulties the Army faced during the Kosovo conflict in mobilising its forces, developed the concept of the 'Future Combat System' (FCS) in October 1999 to guard against the Army's marginalisation by the Air Force and Navy (Kagan, 2006: 243; Reynolds, 2006: 448). The FCS is a 'system of systems' involving manned and unmanned ground and aerial assets that, as Reynolds (2006: 448) notes: 'when fully fielded will rely on superior intelligence and battlespace awareness, lightweight and strategic mobility, speed and agility on the battlefield and over the horizon target acquisition and precision engagement'. The FCS underpinned Shinseki's vision of a medium-weight Army capable of deploying a 5,000 troop combat brigade at any point across the globe within 96 hours, the deployment of a division within 120 hours and five divisions within 30 days. Hence following TPG, change within the Army involved the replacement of heavy, armoured mechanised divisions with a medium-weight force utilising lighter weapons systems, dispersed formations and more rapidly and globally deployable weapons systems, supported by intelligence and information dominance (Mahnken and FitzSimonds, 2003: 113).

The three pillars of US 'transformation': Modularity, network centric warfare and effects based operations

By 2003, the RMA and the consequent US military 'transformation' had coalesced around three main features. Firstly, the development of expeditionary forces characterised by modular command structures and a Joint Force Headquarters (Jordan et al, 2008: 110; Reynolds, 2006: 458). Modularity involves 'the creation of modular combined arms maneuver brigade combat teams' in order to 'improve force packaging, sustainability, battle command and situational awareness whilst retaining the same lethality as the larger, task-orientated brigade combat teams'.[25] This shift in command and force structures reflected the influence of Admiral William Owens, who had been a strong proponent of moving away from corps division units towards the development of a joint command spanning all three services and placing all support units under central organisation (Bratton, 2002: 90; Jordan et al, 2008: 110; Kagan, 2006: 212–17; Owens and Offley, 2000: 224–36).[26]

Secondly, the networking of forces and a move away from weapons platforms to knowledge-empowered networked forces capable of exercising increased agility, skill and precision in the application of attritional force. NCW is associated with hardware and the improvement of the technology of military equipment – command and control systems, IT and computer networking and the three 'grids': the sensor grid, command and control grid and engagement grid.[27] NCW is, however, also associated with doctrinal change and has been described by its most forceful proponents in the US Navy as the 'overarching theory of war in the information age', requiring the development of new doctrine and concepts of networks and systems in order to facilitate the more efficient deployment of force and take full advantage of the strategic opportunity presented by the RMA (Dahl, 2002: 5; Meiter, 2006).

NCW is composed of four related pillars: information and knowledge superiority; assured access; forward sea-based forces and Effects Based Operations (EBO) (Dahl, 2002: 5). It is this fourth pillar of NCW – EBO – that has taken centre stage and forms the third main feature of US transformation (Farrell, 2008: 779). EBO, as Ho (2005: 172–5) demonstrates, are characterised by three main dimensions. Firstly a tactical dimension – 'strategy to task links, the integration with other planning processes and the use of both military and non-military means to prosecute the adversary' – a dimension that was employed extensively in both Operation Desert Storm and Operation Iraqi Freedom (Ho, 2005: 172). Secondly, an operational dimension – the conduct of rapid decisive operations and 'shock and awe' involving the close coordination between operational commanders and other actors through the networking of resources in order to reduce the fog of war and battlefield uncertainty (Ho, 2005: 174).[28] Finally, a strategic dimension – the use of networked activities and 'the application of all sources of national power to political, economic, military and diplomatic to address all elements of adversary national power' in order to achieve first, second and third order strategic effects against peer or near-peer competitors (Farrell, 2008: 793; Ho, 2005: 174).[29]

Hence over the 1990s EBO took on greater substance than the initial concept that developed following the Gulf War and began to focus on how to shape the behaviour of the enemy, not only through the use of force, but also through non-military options: economic, diplomatic, informational and psychological.[30] In short, EBO is about moving away from 'force on force' linear military attrition to more closely tailoring the desired objectives of a military campaign with military means that encompass not only traditional military instruments, but the full spectrum of national power (Echevarria, 2002: 131; Ho, 2005: 170).

Consequently, as Reynolds (2006) notes, US capability procurement has focused around NCW and EBO, with investment concentrated around several main areas in order to put in place the basis for a System of Systems that will allow commanders to picture the political, military, economic, social, information and infrastructure (PMESII) dimensions of operations and attain 'dominant battlespace knowledge (DBK)'[31] (Farrell, 2008: 797; Jordan et al, 2008: 110; Kagan, 2006: 212–19; Reynolds, 2006: 454; Ho, 2005: 175–81). The first key area of investment has been in information dominance and knowledge management and creation, necessitating the development of space-based, high-resolution intelligence and sensing systems (Reynolds, 2006: 454; Ho, 2005). Secondly, investment has cohered around precision guided munitions, in order to improve accuracy and economy in the application of force. Investment has also focused on increasing force mobility and the speed of force deployment and application, not only by investing in more mobile weapons systems, but also improving command and control (C2) and intelligence systems to 'achieve synergism in time, space, purpose and effect' (Reynolds, 2006: 454). Finally, capability procurement has centred around air and naval power in order to enhance the speed and scope of US power projection and the precision of force application by marrying advances in space and ground intelligence system with aircraft weapons systems, in order to endow the military with a 'stand off' advantage (Reynolds, 2006: 454).

The legacy of 'second order' change: Forces designed for the 'wrong kind of war'?

In spite of the 'capabilities-based' approach of the 2001 QDR and 2003 TPG, that was designed to ensure flexibility in the face of changing exigencies, civilian intervention by Rumsfeld championed a transformation centred upon a traditional notion of 'what future war will look like'. This picture of future conflict scenarios was drawn from the apparent successes of Air Power and Naval Support in executing Operation Desert Storm, Operation Iraqi Freedom, Operational Enduring Freedom and Operation Allied Force (Reynolds, 2006: 442) rather than theatres of 'irregular' conflict such as Somalia and the former Yugoslavia. Despite the post-invasion experiences of the US in Iraq and Afghanistan, and amendments, beginning with the 2005 National Defence Strategy,[32] designed to enhance the capacity of the military to undertake counterinsurgency (COIN) operations,[33] the transformation agenda has until very recently been predominantly focused upon rapid, decisive, effects-based operations against state-based opponents, network-centric capabilities and economisation on ground forces (Ho, 2005: 181–2).

As this section will highlight, important amendments to the Army/Marines approach to COIN have taken place, which represent the beginning of a second stage of US transformation that recognises the limitations of the 'transformative' effects of technology on the nature of warfare. Broader post-2005 changes to US defence policy objectives which place greater emphasis on the low-medium intensity aspects of 'Three Block Warfare', signal a series of important steps towards 'third order' change. Nevertheless, these changes form only the inception of the reforms which will be necessary to develop a 'balanced' force capable of waging both conventional Major Combat Operation (MCO) and 'irregular' war.

At the heart of the 'transformation' agenda lies the triumph of assumption that emerged within the Navy during the 1990s and gained broader currency within the military and civilian leadership during the late 1990s and 21st century that the 'information revolution' has fundamentally changed the nature of war and operational art[34] (Dahl, 2002: 1–24). The US military now enjoys a substantial advantage over its peers in the capabilities needed to engage in 'force on force warfare', destroy state-based adversaries and undertake regime change (Boot, 2006: 430–1; Reynolds, 2006: 435). This supremacy will become increasingly accentuated over the period until 2020, as the weapons systems and intelligence, command, control and communications capabilities that are associated with the 'transformation' process become available for use (Reynolds, 2006: 442).[35] Nevertheless, the transformative power of technology is questionable, both in conventional and 'irregular' conflict (Gray, 2006: 38–9).

As Press (2001) demonstrates, the utility of air power in force-on-force combat is disputed. In spite of the success of the US in targeting Serbian infrastructure and economy, the contested authority of US air power was illustrated by the Kosovo conflict of 1999, that highlighted how: 'a well-operated if obsolescent integrated air defence system can defend a ground force skilled at camouflage and deception' (Jordan et al, 2008: 112–13; Posen, 2003: 28; Stigler, 2002–3: 129–30; Walt, 2005a: 116; Williams, 2001: 48).[36] Likewise, US sensors and high precision munitions also encountered difficulties in detecting and destroying Taliban/Al-Quaeda positions in Afghanistan (Reynolds, 2006: 459; Stone, 2004: 420). Furthermore, the improvement of maritime and air defence systems of the near-peer competitors of the US may begin to undermine the 'stand-off' advantage enjoyed by the US by increasing the vulnerability of its Navy, Aircraft and overseas bases to attack (Boot, 2006: 341).

A second challenge for the US in conventional force-on-force combat is that of refining the operational dimension involved in exploiting the use of Precision Guided Munitions (PGM) and Information Operations (IOs) as part of EBO. This includes collecting the appropriate information about the enemy (his economy, industry, diplomatic relations, military forces and intentions) and the international system, allowing the correct application of military force and manipulation of the enemy (Frank, 2004: 72).[37] NCW has also been criticised for deficiencies in its 'theoretical' dimension, in particular the paucity of doctrinal development in areas such as the balance between the use of Mission Command[38] and commander engagement in operations; the reduction in the vertical command structure of units and the development of a 'common language' of NCW between all services (Farrell, 2008: 789; Meiter, 2006: 189–90).

Moreover, of perhaps greater significance is that faith in the RMA has led to a dangerous obsession with the ability of technology to deliver a sustained military advantage for the US in the post-Cold War era and has left it vulnerable in asymmetric conflict. The recent experiences of Afghanistan and Iraq highlight that although it would be exaggerated to claim that the US is structured to fight 'wrong kind of war' (for the capability to undertake conventional military operations remains a critical attribute of contemporary military forces), the US military lacks sufficient balance between high-intensity warfighting capabilities and those suited to stabilisation and COIN.[39] The US has been shown to be highly deficient in tackling irregular conflict and risks suffering defeat in the pursuit of its strategic interests at the hands of adversaries skilled in asymmetric conflict, who have been able to exploit the weaknesses in US force structure, capabilities and military doctrine that derive from the focus on NCW and EBO (Reynolds, 2006: 435; Sapolsky et al, 2009: 108). In short, the US has been found wanting in tackling 'small wars'[40] or what General Rupert Smith (NATO Deputy Supreme Allied Commander in Europe, 1998–2001) terms, 'wars amongst the people', which have become one of the defining features of the post-Cold War security environment (Betz, 2007; Gray, 2006: 46; Hoffman, 2005; Smith, 2006: 270).

The failure of the 'Afghan model' has illuminated the vulnerability of the US to light-infantry insurgencies when forced to deploy large numbers of troops in a 'clear, hold and build' approach[41] (Biddle, 2005–06; Byman, 2003; Malkasian, 2008: 81; O'Hanlon, 2002: 54–7; Posen, 2003: 30–6; Ricks, 2006).[42] As Betz (2007: 235) demonstrates, the limited reliance of guerrilla forces on logistical support, low concentration of insurgent forces, and difficulty of targeting due to the problem of distinguishing insurgents from the local population, combine to restrict the utility of air power, networking and in particular, EBO, in 'wars amongst the people'. Far from allowing the US to 'shape the behaviour of adversaries', EBO have provided an opportunity for poorly equipped, but highly motivated and organised forces in Iraq and Afghanistan to shape the character of warfare and behaviour of US troops, and exploit the weaknesses of the US military by drawing it into COIN operations (Boot, 2006: 388–9; McNerny, 2005: 210).

Although well-suited to conventional warfare and particularly to locations such as the air, oceans and deserts, the RMA and its associated concepts of NCW and EBO have failed to lift the 'fog of war' in land warfare (Betz, 2007: 235; Krepinevic, 2004: 108; Reynolds, 2006: 452; Stone, 2004: 422). These ideas have been based upon a miscalculation of the potential of technology to transform the nature of warfare, the result of the triumph of 'technological determinism' within the military deriving from erroneous lessons drawn from the initial post-Cold War security environment, beginning with the 1991 Gulf War.[43] The ease of the ground invasion of Kuwait and Iraq appeared to demonstrate the potential of the neutralising role of high-precision airpower and that conflict, as in the Cold War, would continue to be characterised mainly by conventional war against peer or near-peer competitors. Illustrative of the faith in the 'revolutionary discontinuity' brought about by technological change and the ability of the RMA to deliver 'decisive victory' for the US across the conflict spectrum, was the proposal in the mid-1990s by senior DoD officials to terminate the US Army history programme as part of officer training (Corum, 2007: 130).

Yet, as Hoffman (2005: 993) highlights, whilst exhibiting some new characteristics, contemporary 'small wars' are also typified by a great deal of continuity. Despite the valuable lessons learned by the US during the Vietnam War, from the post-Vietnam era to the 21st century, small wars have become the 'orphaned child of strategy' and of doctrinal development in the US (Smith, 2003: 29; Stulberg, 2005: 498). Vietnam left an enduring legacy with the military and civilian establishments during the 1970s and 1980s: that the US should avoid becoming embroiled in counterinsurgency operations at all costs and seek the rapid and decisive defeat of its adversaries. These 'lessons' helped to create a military, and civilian leadership that was highly receptive to the RMA (Smith, 2003: 29).[44] Hence the advancement of tactical, operational and strategic thinking on COIN operations has, until recently been confined to 'pockets of expertise' within US Special Forces (Corum, 2007: 128–31). Consequently, the US has faced significant difficulties in securing the peace following the application of rapid, decisive and overwhelming force, and is currently under equipped and poorly-resourced in undertaking effective manpower-intensive and infantry-led counterinsurgency and post-conflict reconstruction missions. This has led to overstretch in missions such as Afghanistan.[45]

Attaining 'balance'? The decline of EBO and the inception of third-order change

Hence a second 'transformational' challenge now exists for the US military – and in particular, for the Army and Marines. This is the challenge of creating not only a larger, but a better trained light infantry, skilled in tackling irregular warfare and counterinsurgency; one that is not just capable of supporting the rapid application of force against conventional forces, but also of putting 'boots on the ground' and endowed with the skills necessary to undertake Stabilisation and COIN operations (Betz, 2007: 222; Gray, 2006: 38).[46]

The emphasis on airpower and fixation on a technology-led 'transformation' and EBO has led to a relative lack of investment in infantry forces, further compounding the Army's ability to respond flexibly to changing exigencies by investing in new capabilities which are more suited to COIN operations. The 1997 QDR had, however, streamlined the Army and Marines, setting a baseline of 482,000 active troops for the Army (a reduction of 15,000 troops) and 175,000 active troops for the Marines (a reduction of 1,800 active personnel) (Conetta, 2007: 6). Although thrust to the forefront of the 'war on terror' in Afghanistan and Iraq, the Army and Marines received only 23.4 per cent of the defence budget in 2006, whereas the Navy and Airforce received 29.8 per cent and 30.3 per cent respectively (Reynolds, 2006: 460).

Furthermore, the dissemination of NCW throughout the armed forces has also encouraged doctrinal stagnation in the Army and Marines. Instead of preparing for a wide range of future eventualities, doctrinal evolution has followed the lead of the Air Force and Navy in the form of FCS that is applicable to only a small range of possible conflict scenarios. (Press, 2001: 5–7; Renner, 2004: 109; Reynolds, 2006: 459).

These deficits are captured pertinently by Betz (2007: 238): 'The problem, however, is winning "wars amongst the people", and for that the battlefield must be repopulated by soldiers whose training and mindset is inherently opposite to the "never put a man where you can put a bullet" logic of the RMA.' EBO also further undermines US COIN operations by eroding the capacity of forces to deviate from increasingly centralised planning (Frank, 2004: 78).[47] Such a highly-scientific 'system of systems' requires a significant level of centralisation and a 'long-screwdriver' approach to military operations that reduces the scope for intuition, flexibility and adaptability on the ground (Farrell, 2008: 31).

This approach acts very much to the advantage of adversaries in small wars, for as Stephen Biddle (2004: ix) demonstrates, one of the key advantages enjoyed by weaker forces in asymmetric combat is the ability to learn more quickly and translate lessons into doctrinal and tactical change. The problems faced by US command structures during the Iraqi insurgency were pertinently captured by General Peter Schoomaker, the US Army Chief of Staff (2001–7): 'We are a hierarchy trying to fight a network' (Boot, 2006: 413). Whilst future challenges for the US may involve conflict with near-peer competitors requiring the development of net-centric capabilities and EBO, they also dictate a focus on small wars and COIN – as outlined in General Charles Kulak's vision of 'three block war' and his emphasis upon the importance of the 'strategic corporal'[48] (Betz, 2007; Ho, 2005: 182–3). Hence the challenge of the second stage of transformation is one, not of reversing the RMA, but of ensuring the correct balance between high-intensity warfighting and peacekeeping/post-conflict reconstruction/COIN and a recalibration of military doctrine away from hierarchy and the long screwdriver approach in favour of the flexibility offered by Mission Command (Howard, 2006/07: 12). This is particularly important for the Marines and Army, who, in small wars, will be at the forefront of conflict that can vary across the conflict spectrum within a short time-frame.

As Terriff (2007: 151) highlights, within the Marines a set of institutional distractions, relating to the internal politics of capability procurement and institutional impediments led to a lack of consensus around General Krulak's vision of 'three block warfare' and an embedding of need to focus upon the 'ability to fight in large units as a component in a conventional style of warfare'. This view of future conflict scenarios was reinforced by the nature of the Marine Expeditionary Unit's combat experience in Operation Allied Force in 2001 and by the Marine's role in Operation Iraqi Freedom in 2003 (Boot, 2006: 391–401; Terriff, 2007: 151). Hence, Krulak's warning that victory would not be a result of technological dominance and that the transformation should focus on preparing for 'the war of tomorrow' – that was likely to be asymmetrical and complex and the 'stepchild of Somalia and Chechnya' – was not heeded. Instead, reform in the early 21st century has centred on preparing for conflict that more closely resembles the 'son of Desert Storm' (Terriff, 2007: 145–50).

Since 2004, the debacle in Iraq and Afghanistan and the threat of defeat has spurred the Combined Arms Centre and the Marine Corps Combat Development Command to build upon the agenda first outlined by General Krulak in the mid-late 1990s. This process has also been driven by the appointment of proponents of the need to prepare for 'irregular' warfare to senior positions across the military. Notable appointments included the promotion of General Peter Schoomaker to the position of Army Chief of Staff in 2003, the selection of Army General David Petraeus as Head of the Combined Arms Centre at Fort Leavenworth,[49] to lead up Army doctrine and leadership development and the appointment of Marine General James Mattis as Head of the US Marine Corps Forces Central Command (2006–7) (Betz, 2007: 225).

Rethinking the approach of the US military towards counterinsurgency took written form in the 'FM 3-24 Joint Army/Marines Counter-Insurgency Doctrine Field Manual' (led by General Petraeus) released in December 2006. FM 3-24 represents an important development. Since 1966, the Counter-Insurgency Doctrine Field Manual had been updated on only one occasion, in 2004 (FM3-07.22). TFM3-07.22 was an interim report that outlined a tactical-technical-organisational approach to COIN to allow the army to cope with tactical problems in Iraq and Afghanistan in the run-up to the release of FM 3-24.[50]

In contrast to its 2004 predecessor, FM 3-24 places cultural/anthropological approaches centre-stage and emphasises the operational and strategic aspects of conflict (Corum, 2007: 132; Hauser, 2007: 169). In doing so, the manual resurrects a number of the traditional operational features of US COIN operations, drawn from a thorough analysis of the history of COIN. FM 3-24 underscores, in particular, the importance of a close understanding of the local population. Hence the manual emphasises the centrality of an analysis of the 'broader context within which they [insurgents] are operating', including 'social structure', 'roles and statuses', 'social norms', 'culture', 'identity', 'beliefs', 'values', 'attitudes and perceptions', 'belief systems', and 'cultural forms';[51] the need to learn lessons quickly and the imperative of empowering even the lowest levels to adapt flexibly due to the 'decentralised nature of operations'.[52] FM 3-24 also places institution-building centre-stage in COIN operations and focuses upon the importance of training of host-nation forces to facilitate 'security under the rule of law', necessitating a 'long-term commitment' in 'helping friendly forces reestablish political order and legitimacy where these conditions no longer exist' (Corum, 2007: 133).[53]

In addition, FM3-24 recognises aspects of change in contemporary insurgencies – notably that they are characterised by 'loose organisations,' with 'different motivations' and lack a 'central controlling body'.[54] Consequently the manual emphasises the limitations of NCW in COIN operations by highlighting how: 'the more successful the counterinsurgency is, the less force can be used' and noting that 'sometimes the more force is used, the less effective it is'.[55] FM 3-24 also argues that 'some of the best weapons for counterinsurgents do not shoot'[56] (Corum, 2007: 133; Hauser, 2007: 169). Only one paragraph of the manual is devoted to an analysis of the utility of high-technology assets in COIN operations: information operations emerge as more significant tools.[57] This document contrasts markedly to the 'transformation' agenda outlined by Donald Rumsfeld and the assertions of George W. Bush and leading figures within the Bush administration, such as Condoleezza Rice, that US forces should not be employed in support of post-conflict reconstruction and peace-keeping, but instead restricted only to warfighting.[58]

At the strategic level, FM 3-24 outlines a shift away from a largely military-led EBO, towards greater coordination between government departments in the economic, political and informational aspects of COIN and inter-agency cooperation that is no longer dominated by the military (Corum, 2007: 137): 'wherever possible civilian agencies or individuals with the greatest applicable expertise should perform a task'.[59] This includes, for example, an enhanced role for the US State and Justice Department training of host-nation police forces. The manual also calls for greater input from agencies of other national governments, NGOs, Intergovernmental Organisations, multinational corporations, contractors and host nation civil authorities.[60]

Within the Marines, operational change has taken the form of the concept of 'Distributed Operations' that encompasses maneuverable ground units, decentralised leadership and a shift away from technology as a panacea for all problems (Terriff, 2007: 148–50). The development of 'strategic corporals' has also been accelerated through the instigation of advanced language and cultural training, creating regional specialists (Terriff, 2007: 155). In addition, in his 23 January 2007 State of the Nation Address, President Bush outlined plans to increase the Marine Corps by 21,000 troops (from 181,000–202,000) and the Army by 40,000 (from 507,000–547,000) by 2012, in order to raise the number of ground forces available for deployment (Conetta, 2007: 3).[61]

FM 3-24 has been followed by the development by the US Army Training and Doctrine Command (TRADOC) of the 'Human Terrain System' (HTS) that permits brigade and regimental combat forces to 'gather, consolidate, visualise, store and share socio-cultural information' and allows deployed units to access the expertise of social scientists (HTS, 2009a). The HTS is composed of Human Terrain Teams consisting of linguists, area studies specialists and civilian social scientists located within deployed brigades or regimental staff and Human Terrain Support Teams, which provide similar support at the divisional level. These teams are supported by a Research Reachback Centre (supplemented by a Subject Matter Expert Network) that provides analytical and research support to deployed HTTs and also archives this information in a Human Terrain Database. The work of the HTT is underpinned by the hard/software of the Map-HT Toolkit that allows socio-cultural information to be analysed, shared and archived (HTS, 2009b).

Another important cultural initiative includes an increase in the number of Foreign Area Officers (FAO) within the Marines and Army. During three years of training FAOs focus on developing regional expertise (on one of nine regional areas), cultural and political-military awareness and language competencies. Furthermore, senior officers within the Army and Marine Corps are now compelled to study the language, culture and religion of at least one country.[62]

The 'revolutionary' changes of FM 3-24 must, however, be contextualised within the broader direction to transformation provided by the last QDR of 2006. On the one hand, the QDR pointed to the need for a shift in emphasis in order to deal with the maturing and emerging challenges outlined in the 2005 National Defence Strategy.[63] Yet the 2006 QDR was illustrative of an overall process of military change that continues to be led by faith in the transformative power of technology suitable predominately for war against state-based adversaries. For example, until the advent of the administration of President Barack Obama (2009) the Army continued to devote significant attention to putting in place the structural and doctrinal reforms that will be necessary to implement the FCS system into combat formations rather than creating a balance in force structure and capabilities between the requirements of warfighting and stabilisation/COIN (Betz, 2007: 225).

The 2010 QDR promises, however, to deliver radical change. The first Defence Budget of the Obama administration (6 April 2009) signaled the beginning of a new focus on the capabilities and forces suited to theatres of irregular conflict by outlining cuts in a number of the key RMA programmes (NYT, 2009). These cuts include a restructuring of the FCS in order to accelerate the initial weapons, sensors and communications network, whilst canceling the development of the eight-man vehicles and undertaking a review of the overall FCS strategy (NYT, 2009). The Defence Budget also outlined cuts in the development of the Transformational (communications) Satellite system and capped the number of F-22 Fighter Jets at an upper ceiling of 187. The budget also cancelled the $13 billion development programme for a new VH-71 Presidential helicopter. Furthermore, the budget scrapped the Multiple-Kill Vehicle Missile Defence Programme and in September 2009, the Obama administration also cancelled National Missile Defence in favour of systems stationed on US Warships. The budget was designed to free up funds for an increase in the size of the Army, Marine Corps and Special Forces and for investment in ISR capabilities, including Predator and Reaper UAVs (an increase in daily flights of 127 per cent by 2011), as well as helicopter forces (NYT, 2009).

The changes outlined in the 2009 US Defence Budget form an important step towards the development of a balanced force capable of MCO as well as stabilisation/COIN. However, given the $11 billion costs associated with increases in the Army and Marines and the costs associated with capabilities, forces and training needed to conduct irregular warfare, further cuts will be necessary. Furthermore, although the budget seeks to increase the number of ships suitable for Littoral Waters by 55 by outlining a reduction in the number of aircraft carrier battle groups from 11 to ten, this reduction will not take place until 2040 (NYT, 2009). The budget also outlines plans to increase the speed of the testing of F-35 fighter and retains the ambition to purchase 2,443 of the planes (NYT, 2009).

Significant doctrinal and conceptual changes have also recently been initiated within the US military, particularly since the appointment of General James Mattis as Commander of US Joint Forces Command (JFCOM) on 28 September 2007. Following the lead of the US Army, who in 2007 noted that the concept of EBO was invalid within Army doctrine, Mattis formally removed EBO from US Joint Doctrine in August 2008. Mattis identified EBO as inappropriate within an operational environment requiring 'balanced' forces capable of both conventional and irregular warfare. Mattis also identified EBO as unable to respond to the dynamic and chaotic nature of conflicts like Iraq and Afghanistan (Mattis, 2008). Rather than the long decision cycles of EBO, such 'irregular' conflict requires the flexibility of 'mission-type orders' permitting and an integration of the 'human dimensions' of conflict, including imagination and unpredictability (Mattis, 2008). Mattis' decision was also strongly influenced by the failure of EBO and precision air-strikes by the Israeli Defence Force in the Second Lebanon War of 2006 (Kober, 2008: 32–3). As Mattis stated on 14 August 2008: 'EBO has been misapplied and overextended to the point that it actually hinders rather than helps joint operations' (Mattis, 2008: 105).

Effects based thinking is not, however, completely defunct and retains relevance for targeting and actions against an opponent's infrastructure, where effects can be planned and measured with greater accuracy (Mattis, 2008: 107). Furthermore, the changes codified by Mattis represents the convergence of US thinking around the European take on EBAO that places emphasis on the capacity of technology, not to change the nature of warfare, but to assist in the integrated delivery of kinetic and non-kinetic effects at the operational and tactical levels.

EBO has given way to a focus on Systemic Operational Design (SOD). SOD attempts to move away from the linear and mechanistic approach of EBO by applying systems theory to complex 'open systems' in order to enhance the capacity of commanders to use creativity and initiative in campaign planning in 'conflicts amongst the people' (Vego, 2009: 69–75).[64] This approach is outlined in greater detail in the US Army Training and Doctrine Command's 'Commander's Appreciation and Campaign Design' (CACD) of January 2008 that notes how: 'CACD describes a process to create a systemic and shared understanding of a complex operational problem and to design a broad approach for its solution'.[65]

In short, recognition of the disadvantages associated with the neglect of historical continuity in warfare and of the limited ability of technology to temper escalation has taken place within the US military. This is perhaps most pertinently highlighted by the invocation of the words of President John F. Kennedy in FM 3-24: 'You military professionals must know something about strategy and tactics and logistics...but also economics and politics and diplomacy and history. You must also know everything you can know about military power, and you must also understand the limits of military power. You must understand that few of the problems of our time have...been solved by military power alone'.[66] Following the experiences of COIN operations in Iraq and Afghanistan and observation of Israeli experiences with EBO in the 2006 conflict with Lebanon, the existence of a 'revolution' in military affairs has been drawn into question (Mattis, 2008). However, despite the changes outlined in the 2009 Defence Budget, the costs of high-technology weapons projects remain set to increase between 2010 and 2020 as many of the capabilities associated with the RMA-inspired transformation that reached its zenith in the 2003 TPG begin to come to fruition.[67]

The 2010 QDR will be the litmus test for the resolve of the civilian establishment and military to create the 'balance' in force structures and capabilities necessary to prevail in Afghanistan and cement the second stage of transformation. The 2010 QDR will have to promote investment in the capabilities and force structures necessary to conduct 'Three Block Warfare' without significantly undermining US conventional warfare capabilities, all within tight budgetary constraints. As Imlay and Toft (2006: 258) pertinently note: 'The US has invested almost all its resources in building and maintaining a military capable of countering threats from other states...the trick now will be to build a military capable of engaging shadowy foes in distant lands without simultaneously dissipating US capital invested in conventional warfighting and planning capabilities.' This process is underway, but it is far from complete.

Reforms to the instruments and objectives of European great powers' defence policies: A partial and selective emulation of the RMA

UK defence reform: 'Third-order' change

Britain's initial responses to the post-Cold War security environment, the 1990 'Options for Change' and 1994 'Frontline First: The Defence Costs Study', were piecemeal and evolutionary (Dorman, 2006: 152; Kaldor, 1995: 48–9). Both outlined only 'first order' changes to the 'settings' of the objectives and instruments of policy, retaining largely the same force balance, whilst reducing troop numbers (Dorman, 2006: 152; Kaldor, 1995: 48–9; McInnes, 1999: 75).[68] It was not until the 1997 Labour Government that 'third-order' reform was initiated by the 1998 Strategic Defence Review (SDR). In contrast to the military's Cold War role (the forward defence of NATO through high-intensity conflict with Soviet troops on the German plain), the Review outlined a wide scope of defence missions, emphasising peace-support and humanitarian operations and the prevention and diffusion of crises within and outside NATO's geographical scope. Hence SDR called not only for shifts in emphasis in existing defence missions, but also created a new role for the British military: 'defence diplomacy'.[69] As Rod Thornton (2003: 39) highlights: 'The changes introduced, were so fundamental as to question the role of the British Army: did it exist to protect the power of the state, or did British soldiers now have the primary role of humanitarian diplomats in uniform?' In short, the SDR placed a redefined strategy of forward defence at the centre of British defence policy objectives: that it is 'better to meet a crisis than to wait for it to come to you' (Dorman, 2006: 154).

In the light of these changing objectives the SDR also proposed significant structural reform. Between 1990 and 1997 the Conservatives had downsized the armed forces from 306,000 to 226,000; hence the Review did not involve large-scale reductions (other than a reduction in the Territorial Army from 56,000 to 40,000 troops). Instead the SDR reorganised the military to permit two small-scale deployments or one full-scale deployment. Crucially, the SDR institutionalised the Joint Rapid Deployment Force and Joint Force Headquarters which had been set up by the Conservatives in 1996.[70] The Review created the Joint Rapid Reaction Force, structured around Navy, Air and Infantry assets, permitting the swift expeditionary deployment of low-high intensity British military power, providing a focal point for investment in capabilities (King, 2005b: 325) and mirroring developments in US command structures (King, 2005b: 325; Shepherd, 2000: 21–2). The SDR also established the position of 'Chief of Defence Logistics' as head of the Defence Logistics Organisation, to take overall control of the three separate logistics organisations of the Army, Navy and Air Force.[71]

The 1999 Kosovo War demonstrated deficits in strategic lift capabilities, precision bombing and tactical communications, whilst operations in

Afghanistan and Sierra Leone also highlighted the requirement for lighter, more deployable and flexible forces with an explicit focus on tackling the threats posed by 'failed states', international terrorism and the proliferation of WMD. The refugee crisis and stabilisation operations during and following the Kosovo Conflict also highlighted the need for greater coordination of Other Governmental Departments (OGDs), Non-Governmental Organisations (NGOs) above the tactical level. This experience gave further urgency to thinking on the 'Comprehensive Approach' that had been initiated by the British experience of the negative impact of the 'bewildering' array of uncoordinated actors they had encountered in their deployment to Bosnia during the early 1990s (see Chapter 6 for further details).[72]

Following September 11 the 2002 'New Chapter' (a 'mini-review' of the armed forces) and December 2003/July 2004 Defence White Papers, 'Delivering Security in a Changing World' outlined additional changes to 'settings' of the policy instrument, in order to provide expeditionary forces capable of sustaining three small and medium-scale European-led operations or one large-scale operation, conducted with the US. The 2002 Defence White Paper also signaled an important change in the focus of the strategy of forward defence laid out in the SDR, from North Africa and the Middle East to global power projection (Dorman, 2006: 154–5). Changes were also introduced enhancing the coordination of civilian-military cooperation at the operational level through the initiation of OGD representation within the Defence Crisis-Management Organisation (DCMO) and at the Permanent Joint Headquarters (PJHQ).[73]

In short, the 'New Chapter' and in particular, the 2003/04 Defence White Papers, spelt out the implications of 'third order change' more clearly in terms of capabilities and military structures and also paved the way for new doctrinal development. These changes would involve an explicit – though selective – emulation of post-Cold War US military 'transformation'. Accordingly, the 2002 New Chapter and 2003/04 Defence White Papers instigated force transformation along three main axes: a shift from 'platform-centric planning to networked enabled capability' (NEC);[74] an effects-based *approach* to operations (EBAO) and the development of the military's expeditionary capacity by placing modularity at the centre of force planning (Benbow, 2009: 24).

Although NCW had received attention in the 2002 New Chapter, emulation of US transformation was particularly evident in the 2003/04 Defence White Papers which outlined NEC as the British approach to the networking of forces (Jordan et al, 2008: 111).[75] British NEC forms a more moderate emulation of US 'transformation' that seeks to exploit the tactical and operational advantages that technology can deliver, but is more circumspect about the potential of networking to transform the nature of warfare and deliver strategic effects (Farrell, 2008: 786–7). As Dorman (2006: 156) notes: 'NEC is not just a linguistic difference from US NCW, rather it reflects a difference in vision. NCW puts the centre at the system, in the British View this is incorrect. The system is just a means to an end and not an end in itself...'. NEC is progressing in an 'evolutionary' manner, following three stages: an 'initial stage' involving the improvement of interconnections between existing equipment in 2007; an intermediary or 'transitional' stage by 2015, by which time the development of new capabilities and equipment will permit greater integration and finally, a 'mature' state by 2020–30 characterised by synchronisation between joint military forces (Farrell, 2008: 787–8; Mandille, 2003: 50–1).[76]

Spurred by the experience of operations alongside the US in Kosovo, Afghanistan and Iraq, the British approach to EBO was initiated in 2003, led by the Joint Doctrine and Concepts Centre (renamed Development Concepts and Doctrine Centre in 2006) that had been established by the SDR to promote greater jointness in doctrine and conceptual development. At this initial stage, British thinking closely converged with the US concept of EBO and adopted a scientific approach to forecasting the effects consequent upon particular courses of military action (Boyce, 2003: 30–7; Farrell, 2008: 790–3).[77] However, in 2005 the term EBO was formally replaced by the Effects Based Approach to Operations (EBAO), reflecting the recognition that it was not military operations themselves that had changed in character, but the approach to operations (Farrell, 2008: 793). This mirrored the lessons that were being learned by the US Marines and Army in Iraq and Afghanistan, DoD Directive 3000.05, and the growing realisation within the US military that civilian agencies were often best suited to taking the lead in certain aspects of COIN operations, as elucidated in FM3-24.

The concept of EBAO has therefore been located within a multiagency approach to operations, emphasising the importance of non-kinetic effects and ensuring that, where appropriate, civilian agencies take the lead in operations that can vary quickly in intensity. This has come to be termed the 'Comprehensive Approach'[78] that seeks to fully integrate the diplomatic, military, economic and informational dimensions of military operations at the tactical, operational and strategic levels (Benbow, 2009: 29; Dorman, 2007a: 312; Farrell, 2008: 793).[79] Likewise, the development of doctrine associated with EBAO has shifted from a focus on operational end-states that envisage the 'defeat of the enemy', to include the creation of prosperity, security and 'reliable infrastructure and governance' (Farrell, 2008: 794). In short, EBAO differs markedly to EBO in that it integrates the lessons of Afghanistan and Iraq by recognising that the RMA has not transformed the nature of war. In contrast to EBO that focuses more on enabling rapid and decisive operations against conventional opponents, EBAO is conceived of as an approach that, embedded with the Comprehensive Approach, can facilitate the integration of all agencies of government in support, not only of war-fighting, but also the delivery of non-kinetic effects in longer-term

stabilisation and COIN operations: 'a cross-government effort on crisis prevention and management'.[80] As outlined in the updated UK Defence Doctrine
of 2008: 'the UK needs to maintain the ability to respond swiftly and deci-
sively across the full range of intervention scenarios, not just to prevent or
mediate violent conflicts, but also to stabilise situations in or emerging from
violent conflicts and to support recovery and reconstruction'.[81] Furthermore,
EBAO is focused on the tactical and operational, rather than the strategic
dimensions of military action (Farrell, 2008: 792–3).

The effects based approach also integrates the lessons learned from
the problems associated with the 'long screwdriver approach' to military
command in the US (the development of highly-centralised command
structures), both in conducting rapid and decisive EBO and in impeding
flexibility in COIN operations (Storr, 2003: 123). Instead of centralisation,
the British system of Mission Command remains in place. Rooted in the
concept of the 'corps d'Armee' of the Napoleonic Wars and Prussian military thought, the practice of Mission Command was formally adopted by
the British Army in 1987, its utility strengthened by operational experiences in Kosovo, Sierra Leone, Iraq and Afghanistan (see Chapter 6) (Dorman,
2006: 155; Storr, 2003: 119–21). Mission Command involves ensuring that
the military commander is clear on the political goals of the operation and
that these goals are communicated effectively to lower levels of command.[82]
This permits a balance between 'direction and delegation',[83] that allows for
'agility in execution', enhances the role of the 'strategic corporal' in operations whose intensity can vary rapidly and facilitates a higher tempo of
operations (Farrell, 2008: 788; Milton, 2001: 41–4; Storr, 2003: 123).[84] Mission
Command forms a key pillar of the British 'Manoueverist Approach'[85] to
operations. The Manoeuvrist Approach is, according to British Defence Doctrine, characterised by: 'momentum, tempo and agility, which, in combination aim to achieve shock and surprise' thereby 'shattering the enemy's
overall cohesion and will to fight, rather than his material' and delivering
the capability to attain effects disproportionately higher to the level of force
applied.[86]

NEC is therefore viewed as a means with which to strengthen the Manouevrist Approach and several of the core principles of war outlined in the
British Defence Doctrine, notably 'Offensive Action', 'Surprise', 'Concentration of Force', 'Economy of Effort', 'Flexibility', 'Cooperation' and Sustainability':[87] 'Control should then be reduced to a minimum, with the
commander exerting on a light touch on the tiller. Tempo will be increased as
subordinates are empowered to grasp the fleeting opportunities without reference to higher command, but secure in the knowledge that higher command
is aware of what is happening.'[88] The new ways of operating permitted by
NEC are useful not only to MCO, but COIN, creating, as Benbow (2009: 29)
notes: 'more mobile, flexible forces, able to draw on a far deeper and broader
range of information resources than before, more dispersed, yet more

effectively linked to other units and to fire and logistical support, able to respond far more rapidly and with greater agility'.

The 2002 New Chapter and 2003/04 Defence White Papers also involved further structural reform of the armed forces in order to enhance jointness and modularity. The Air Force was able to adapt to the requirements of expeditionary operations by placing a stronger emphasis on developing the ground attack capabilities of the multi-role Eurofighter Typhoon and through the acquisition of the Joint Combat Aircraft (Farrell, 2008: 799).[89] The Navy has undergone both a doctrinal shift from sea control and anti-submarine warfare to maritime force projection operations. Capability procurement has augmented the expeditionary capacity of the Navy. Major projects include the ordering of two aircraft carriers (Future Carriers, CVF) capable of deploying 40 aircraft (in comparison to the 22 aircraft of the existing carriers) which will be ready for service in 2016 and 2018; the deployment of six anti-air warfare Type-45 destroyers by 2009 and four Astute Class Submarines, the first of which entered into service at the end of 2009 (Farrell, 2008: 799).[90]

However, the Army has endured the most radical reform in order to facilitate speed and flexibility; change that has mirrored the 'transformation' of the US Army. The 1998 SDR had institutionalised the Joint Rapid Reaction Force and heralded a shift away from the heavy armoured divisions that had characterised the Army during the Cold War. The 2004 White Paper built upon these changes by outlining a more focused reform of the Army, involving the development of increasingly deployable brigades and setting out the future structure of the Army: two heavy armoured brigades, three medium weight brigades, one light brigade and the air assault and Royal Marine commando brigades (Farrell, 2008: 800).[91]

The Army's new force structure has been supported by the development of the Future Rapid Effects System (FRES), whose evolution began in 2001. FRES is a more modest and limited enterprise than the FCS of the US Army, embodying an 'extended family of network enabled platforms' in contrast to the highly-complex 'system of systems' of the FCS (Farrell, 2008: 803).[92] Nevertheless, FRES been developed in close coordination with the US FCS programme, particularly since 2004[93] (Farrell, 2008: 803). Likely to be operational by 2017, FRES involves 16 different forms of vehicle based around a single platform, capable of delivering 'medium-weight battlefield functions including protected mobility, light armour command and control, combat support and combat engineering' (Farrell, 2008: 800).[94] These developments have been complemented by the Joint Medium Weight Capability (JtMWCap) analytical concept for military operations. JtMWCap outlines a 'task-based, configurable and scalable medium weight land formation, optimised for intervention and decisive maneuver' to provide 'strategic reach', 'operational and tactical agility', 'sustainability' and 'endurance' (Farrell, 2008: 801). The 2008 Land Operational Concept outlines the goal of creating a 'balanced' Army that, by 2018, will be fully capable of participating in conflict that can vary in intensity at short notice across the 'continuum of conflict'; in short, of both MCO and the 'Three Block Warfare' situations encountered in stabilisation/COIN operations.[95] As Sir Richard Dannatt, Chief of the General Staff of the UK Army argues: 'We can no longer be prescriptive about taking part in either Major Combat Operations or Stabilisation Operations; the boundary between them has become increasingly blurred' (Dannatt, 2008: 58).

The UK has also made important strides in the area of capability procurement in support of C4ISR. Focused upon improving flexibility, agility and speed of response, C4ISR capability procurement has centred not only upon the development of precision guided munitions, but upon five systems in support of sensing, target identification and a communication network able to transfer information to commanders to initiate a timely response. These systems include the Skynet 4 and 5 satellite communication systems, Defence Information Infrastructure (DII) to 'provide the capability to exchange and share electronic information across Defence from foxhole to stores depot and from sensor to shooter'; the Bowman secure land tactical radio communication system to facilitate voice and data communication; the Falcon secure communication system at the operational level that replaces the Ptarmigan system; and Cormorant system linking command headquarters and expeditionary forces on deployment (Adams and Ben-Ari, 2006: 42; Dorman, 2006: 156; Farrell, 2008: 785; Mandille, 2003: 50; Posen, 2006: 180).[96]

Other notable capability investments in the area of ISR include the DABINETT programme, as part of the UK's Network Centric Collaborative Targeting System. Initiated in 2006, DABINETT will allow the military to process and collect information and enhances the UK's ISTAR (Intelligence, Surveillance, Target Acquisition and Reconnaissance) capabilities and bolsters interoperability with NATO and EU Allies.[97] The UK has also invested in stand-off sensors, such as the Reaper MQ-9, Soothsayer and Watchkeeper UAVs.[98] The Watchkeeper will be operational from 2010 and is fitted with the Advanced Joint Communications Node (AJCN) that endows it with a reprogrammable electronic warfare and communications capability. Britain has also acquired short-range UAV systems such as the Desert Hawk and Buster systems, in addition to the Merlin underwater UAV (Adams and Ben-Ari, 2006: 44–5).[99]

Manned aerial reconnaissance capabilities include 'Project Helix' that is upgrading Nimrod Maritime aircraft with Signal Intelligence (SIGNIT) capabilities (capable of undertaking both land and maritime missions) and the fitting of reconnaissance pods to the RAF's Tornado and Jaguar aircraft (Adams and Ben-Ari, 2006: 46).[100] The ASTOR airborne surveillance system, that became fully operational in 2008, will provide all weather long-range surveillance and target acquisition and is interoperable with the US JSTAR system.[101] The UK is also developing technologies which will allow constant surveillance of the battlefield, such as the Tactical Optical Satellite

(TOPSAT) (Flournoy and Smith, 2005: 91). Maritime Surveillance is provided by the Maritime Airborne Surveillance and Control (MACS) programme that is currently in the assessment phase and will endow the UK's two future aircraft carriers (CVF) with air and surface surveillance capability, in addition to battle-management of air-defence fighters.[102] The UK has also invested in human intelligence (HUMINT) teams to bolster its capacity to gather intelligence in asymmetrical conflict.[103] The overall analysis of intelligence and data takes place though the UKINTELWEB system and the Lychgate system of the RAF, which whilst not fully interoperable with other nations' intelligence systems, can be integrated with those of Australia, Canada and the US through the Integrated Broadcast Network and with French and German systems via the Griffin Wide Area Network (Adams and Ben-Ari, 2006: 46–7).[104]

Hence British armed forces reform has been strongly informed by changes that have taken place as part of the US 'transformation' process.[105] There are, however, important differences. Crucially, NEC and EBAO are much more limited in ambition than their US counterparts, EBO and NCW. The 2003/2004 Defence White Papers seek to achieve a higher degree of 'balance' and 'flexibility' than US reforms by permitting the simultaneous conduct of peacekeeping, post-conflict reconstruction and higher-intensity warfighting missions. Whilst the British military retains the capability to undertake major theatre conventional force-on-force warfare (albeit as part of a broader coalition), it is focused to a much greater extent than US armed forces on the challenges of irregular, 'small' wars and conflict of rapidly varying intensity.[106] NEC and EBAO also shun the 'long screwdriver' approach to command and control adopted by the US in favour of the flexibility offered by Mission Command and the concepts have been firmly embedded within the principle of Manoeuvre Warfare and the Comprehensive Approach.[107] As a consequence EBAO places a stronger emphasis on the role of non-kinetic effects than EBO.[108] The 'human element' is therefore central to NEC.[109]

As a consequence, rather than leading to a sudden and dramatic dissipation of EBAO the decline of EBO in the US has reinforced a number of the key British observations of the weaknesses of US EBO. As highlighted by the Director General of the DCDC in a letter on the implications of Mattis Commander's Guidance: 'The shift in the US position should cause us little difficulty. Far from causing a Stalinist purge of effects language from our doctrine, it has prompted us to refresh, and in some cases to restate more clearly, some well-established tenets of our doctrine whilst keeping the best of effects thinking from the past few years'.[110] The concept of effects-based thinking prevails, that shuns the more 'deterministic' aspects of EBAO and reflects the utility of effects-based approach in the targeting of closed systems and networks and the ability of the language of effects to describe 'how it is intended to bring about change' during campaign design and to 'encourage users think about the effect they, and their partners in a comprehensive approach to campaigning wish to achieve'.[111] These principles are reflected in JDP 3-40 'Security and Stabilisation: The Military Contribution' that forms the joint operational-level doctrine on the way the military should approach the stabilisation of failed or failing states and sets out in greater detail the role of the military within a comprehensive approach. JDP 3-40 notes that: 'Analysis, planning, execution and assessment then become a function of two questions: *What effect do we want to achieve* and *What actions will best achieve that effect?* This is not a reprise of a mechanistic form of Effects Based Approach to Operations, which simply does not work for complex and variable human systems'.[112]

As Dorman (2006: 155) demonstrates, even at the higher end of the force spectrum, reform has focused not only upon tackling state-based opponents, but: 'the way we want to use our forces against a determined, mobile, often disparate and elusive enemy'. The attempt to ensure balance across the conflict spectrum is reflected in the core operational outcomes of the 2003 DWP which are defined in terms of eight effects, varying from low-high intensity: Prevent, Stabilise, Contain, Deter, Coerce, Disrupt, Defeat and Destroy.[113] Whilst boosting the capacity to contribute to US-led high-intensity combat operations against state-based opponents, British military reform has also built upon the existing skill sets required to undertake stabilisation operations, COIN and irregular warfare. A number of skills of relevance to the operational environment were already strongly embedded within the military, having been honed during the colonial era and in Northern Ireland during the 1980s and 1990s and reinforced by the conduct of peacekeeping operations in the former Yugoslavia and Africa (see Chapter 6 for further detail).

The UK military – and in particular, the Army – is, therefore, attempting to strike a balance between the 'warrior ethos' and the broad range of skills necessary to undertake the lower-end spectrum tasks of 'Three Block Warfare' (Kiszely, 2006: 19). As Sir John Kiszely, former Head of the UK Defence Academy (2005–8) argues, the unpredictability, uncertainty, complexity and ambiguity of COIN necessitates 'minds that are agile, flexible, imaginative, enquiring, imaginative, capable of rigorous analysis and objective thinking, that can conceptualise and innovate' (Kiszely, 2006: 20).

The importance of cultural awareness to contemporary military operations was highlighted in the updated British Defence Doctrine of August 2008, that stated: 'the cultural and historical features of a situation or operating area are perhaps most important'.[114] This focus on the cultural aspects of contemporary conflict has led to the distribution of predeployment training packs and cultural appreciation booklets for both Iraq and Afghanistan by the Human Factors Branch of the Defence Intelligence Staff. These measures have been supplemented by the work of the Human Geographical Intelligence Branch (GEOINT) of the Defence Intelligence Staff that maps the distribution of tribal, ethnic, linguistic and religious groups within operational environments. The need to further develop cultural skills is also recognised by the 'Future Land Operational Concept' released in October 2008 that emphasises the importance of training that delivers an 'adaptive foundation': 'The demands and complexity of recent stability and counterinsurgency operations, linked to the potential concurrent nature of combat and stabilisation tasks have necessitated the *ad hoc* adaptation of skills and capabilities that should, in the future, be included as core elements of adaptive foundation training.'[115]

The growing recognition of the importance of cultural awareness is, however, most clearly evidenced by the development of Joint Doctrine Note 1/09 of January 2009: 'The Significance of Culture to the Military'. The document outlines two key changes to cultural training. Firstly, in the context of contemporary 'Three Block Warfare', a shift away from a rank/command-determined level of cultural capability training[116] to a task-specific structure for determining levels of cultural-generic and cultural-specific education. Secondly, the development of a Cultural Institute under the UK Defence Academy's Advanced Research and Assessment Group that will act as a mechanism with which to facilitate academic input from the social sciences.

A further set of initiatives are also currently under consideration. These initiatives include the development of a permanent cadre of cultural advisors; simulated military conflict (redteaming) with the input of cultural experts and initiatives to improve the management of cultural information, including closer, more formalised, UK/US collaboration. Finally, the development of a 'pool of regional expertise' is under consideration that will allow senior NCOs to focus on a specific country or region throughout their career and creating a database of cultural expertise.[117] These changes represent an important development in UK Defence Doctrine, in which the 'war-fighting ethos' has traditionally taken centre stage (Milton, 2001: 41–4).

There have, however, been growing criticisms of the balanced forces approach that attempts to respond to the challenges of 'Three Block Warfare' whilst retaining the capacity to conduct MCO. These criticisms were forcefully expressed by the June 2009 report of the Institute for Public Policy Research ('Shared Responsibilities: A National Security Strategy for the UK) that pointed to the difficulties faced by Britain, as a secondary power, in adequately preparing for both MCO and Stabilisation/Three Block Warfare conflict scenarios. The Report criticised, in particular, the commitment to what it identified as 'Cold War' systems, including CVF, the Joint Combat Aircraft (Joint Strike Fighter), Type 45 Destroyer,[118] Eurofighter Typhoon and three Astute submarines.[119] The British attempt to strike a balance between the capacity to undertake Major Combat Operations and 'three block warfare' will, of course, only be possible with adequate investment in the armed forces (Cornish and Dorman, 2009). The extent to which the current economic crisis is allowed to impact on defence spending will be an important factor determining Britain's ability to develop forces capable of delivering simultaneous/sequential low-high intensity conflict and MCO as part of multinational coalitions.[120]

Furthermore, the independent 'Review of Acquisition for the Secretary of State for Defence' undertaken by Bernard Gray points to an 'overheated' capability acquisition process that is characterised by accelerating costs and timescales.[121] The Report demonstrates that the key determinant of Britain's capacity to adapt to the changing security environment will rest not so much in the allocation of extra financial resources, but in the structuring of military input to defence planning. The document points to the need for urgent reform to the capability acquisition process that will allow civilian actors to exert greater control over the individual Services' capability procurement plans and prioritise procurement plans in line with financial constraints. Hence although a model of military best practice has emerged during the post-Cold War era, the new SDR process that will take place following the 2010 General Election is urgently required in order to deliver explicit guidance on the balance that should be struck between the capabilities and force postures relevant for 'three block warfare/COIN' conflict scenarios and those capable of addressing other potential conflict scenarios over the medium-long term, which may more closely resemble MCO (see Chapter 6).[122]

Table 1.1   Strength of the UK Armed Forces by Service 1990–2008

Service	1990	1997	2002	2003	2004	2005	2006	2007	2008
Army	152,800	108,800	110,100	112,700	112,700	109,300	107,700	106,200	105,100
Navy	63,300	45,100	41,600	41,500	40,900	39,900	39,400	38,900	38,600
Air Force	89,700	56,900	53,300	53,200	53,400	51,900	48,700	45,400	43,400
FTRS	–	–	2,000	2,400	2,200	1,700	1,500	1,600	1,800
Gurkhas	–	–	3,800	3,800	3,700	3,700	3,700	3,700	3,900
Locally Engaged	–	–	400	400	400	400	400	400	400
Total	487,300	348,500	320,900	321,000	322,400	315,300	305,300	294,100	282,600

Source: UK Defence Statistics (2007, 2008).

French defence reform: 'Third-order' change

Until 1994 the objectives of French defence policy were characterised by stasis and the perpetuation of the doctrine of national strategic autonomy. However, Prime Minister Edouard Balladur instigated a 'revolutionary' reform of defence objectives in the 1994 Defence White Paper (McKenna, 1997). In the context of complex new security threats, the White Paper outlined a 'paradigm shift' from strategic autonomy, to cooperation as part of NATO and, in particular, through the emerging ESDP and emphasised the necessity to develop a military capable of 'preventing and managing crises of variable intensity' (Irondelle, 2003a,b; Bloch, 2000: 36; Sutton, 2007: 302–7).

It was not, however, until the election of President Jacques Chirac in May 1995 that third-order change was initiated. The reform of 1995–6 built upon the changes to the objectives of defence policy and institutional forums initiated by Balladur. Not only would the role of the armed forces be to impose French or international will through 'coercive force', but also through the 'mastery of violence'. The new military doctrine was designed to ensure that the armed forces could be used as a tool with which to prevent and control the escalation of conflict, employing a 'totality of political, diplomatic, humanitarian and media actions', representing close convergence with the UK's concept of 'defence diplomacy' (Bloch, 2000: 43; Tiersky, 1997). Instead of nuclear deterrence, intelligence capabilities and command and control technologies began to take priority in French capability investment (Bratton, 2002: 93).[123]

The experience of French participation in the 1991 Gulf War and of peacekeeping during the Wars of Secession in the former Yugoslavia forcefully demonstrated the inadequacies of a reliance on the deterrent power of the *Force de Frappe* and a conscript army in tackling contemporary global and regional security challenges (Menon, 1995; Bloch, 2000).[124] Hence Chirac proposed radical structural reform ('Model 2015'). Model 2015 was implemented by three *lois-programmes militaires* (programme laws, LPM): the first between 1997–2002; the second between 2002–8; the third between 2009–15 (Bratton, 2002: 93; Sutton, 2007: 305–6).

The first LPM outlined the abolition of conscription and streamlined the military from 577,360 to 434,000 between 1996 and 2002 (Rynning, 2000: 63; Gregory, 2000: 92). This increased the number of forces available for deployment in support of full-spectrum tasks from 14,000 to 30,000 (outside Europe) or 50,000 men (within Europe) for a period of up to one year, in addition to the capacity to contribute a further 5,000 troops to coalition operations (Shepherd, 2000: 23). Mirroring the structural reform of US forces, French forces were reconfigured according to the principle of 'modularity', allowing flexibility in the face of changing security exigencies (Bloch, 2000: 38). Structural reforms took the form of the reduction of the army's operational forces from 239,000 to 136,000 troops and the development of specialised Army units each of 15,000 troops, composed of a heavy armoured group; mechanical group; rapid armoured intervention group and infantry assault group (Gregory, 2000a: 93). These formations benefit from centralised support services that can be drawn together at short-notice by four *Etat Major des Forces* (EMF) Headquarters (King, 2005b: 326). The Navy was also restructured, undergoing a cut in operational forces from 63,800 to 45,500) and reorganisation into a five key components: a naval action force; a submarine action group; a mine warfare group; a naval air group and strategic nuclear submarines (Gregory, 2000a: 94). The Air Force, cut from 89,200 to 63,000 operational forces, was restructured around four key components: the strategic nuclear airforce; combat airforce; projection

Table 1.2   The Troop Reductions of LPM 1997–2002

Service	Troop Numbers 1997 (Operational Forces)	Troop Numbers 2002 (Operational Forces)
Army	239,000	136,000
Navy	63,800	45,500
Air Force	89,200	63,000
Total	392,000	244,500

airforce and intelligence, surveillance and communications functions (Gregory, 2000a: 94).

Strategic planning was also restructured in 2002, with the reorganisation of the Centre for Planning and Conduct of Operations (CPCO) and Joint Staff for Forces Training (EMFE.IA) into a single strategic command: an Operational Headquarters and a Joint Task Force Headquarters, with Operational Staffs also established within each service (Le Bail, 2003: 73; Rouby, 2004: 12–13; Rynning, 2008: 11). This restructuring was designed to ensure the capacity to rapidly change operational modes in the context of the 'reversibility' in conflict intensity (Bezacier, 2003: 7). Furthermore, the Joint Force and Training HQ is responsible for the planning and conduct of multinational joint forces and was restructured in 2003 in order to ensure compatibility with American, British and German Joint Forces HQs and NATO Combined Joint Task Force (CJTF) HQs (Rouby, 2004: 13). Expeditionary power projection was also facilitated by the Army's separation of combat and logistics into two commands in July 1998. These commands comprised eight joint and five specialised brigades focusing on training expeditionary forces and a logistical command consisting of two support brigades, specialising in the provision of logistical support for expeditionary operations (Rynning, 2008: 10).

The large reductions in personnel were also accompanied by cuts in military hardware, which focused on stripping the Army, Navy and Airforce of Cold War legacy systems. The LPM 1997–2002 therefore included a 55 per cent reduction in heavy tanks; 47 per cent reduction in combat helicopters; a decrease in combat aircraft by 26 per cent, a 46 per cent increase in refueling aircraft and reduction of airforce helicopters by 77 per cent. The LPM also involved a 20 per cent cut in major surface vessels and 33 per cent decrease in maritime patrol aircraft.

LPM 2003–8 built upon its predecessor by giving greater substance to the process of transformation – embedding the professionalisation and 'jointness' of the armed forces and putting in place the basis for fully digitised and networked forces by 2015. This process began in 1998–9, when the Army outlined the *Numerisation de l'espace de bataille* (NEB) and culminated in the June 2004 project 'Future Land Action' that formed an important landmark in the shift towards networked forces (Leclerc, 2003: 8–9). The armaments procurements agency (DGA) has played a strong role in the development of an increasingly network-enabled military (Rynning, 2008: 16). The DGA underwent restructuring in 2004 in order to enable a stronger coordinating role for the French Joint Chiefs of Staff and the Office of the Secretary General of the Defence Ministry and has promoted a 'capabilities based approach' that seeks to ensure the continuous adaptation of French forces (Adams and Ben-Ari, 2006: 2).

The DGA's agenda has been bolstered by the creation in 2005 of the *Centre Interarmees de Concepts, de Doctrines et D'Experimentation* (Joint Forces Centre for Concept Development, Doctrine and Experimentation, CICDE) to lead up the development of joint forces doctrine and concepts. Additional impetus has also been fostered by the May 2005 amendment to the 1982 decree outlining the role of the French Chief of Staff (chef de l'etat major des armies (CEMA)). This amendment instigated three main changes to the role of the CEMA (Rynning, 2008: 18). The CEMA is now empowered to ensure coherence between the capability proposals of the three services which are put forward to the Minister; he has command over the day-to-day running of the three services and finally, he enjoys full authority in relations to joint doctrines and institutions (Rynning, 2008: 18).

As in the UK, French thinking on NCW initially involved close emulation of the RMA and concepts such as 'information superiority' (Chevalier, 2003: 37–9), but this has given way to the development of 'network enabled capabilities' and the recognition that 'technology is not everything' (Rynning, 2008: 4). NEB has taken the form of the SIC21 system that is intended to integrate all forces into one single network and is also interoperable with the networks of France's major NATO Alliance Partners, having been coordinated through the NATO 5-Power Interoperability Group and MIP. Three spearhead forces are on line to be fully networked and deployable by 2009: the armoured 2nd brigade, the light armoured 6th brigade and the Franco-German brigade.

French thinking on force development also recognises the limitations of technology in future conflict scenarios which, over the short to medium-term, are likely to be characterised by three block warfare and outlines the creation of 'balanced' forces, capable of 'multiple roles'. Hence the 'constitutive concept' that followed the 2005 Capability Transformation of the Land Forces emphasises the requirement of 'adaptability' across the conflict spectrum, the limitations of technology and the importance of 'the pivotal role played by soldiers as opposed to weapon or communications systems' and the role of the 'strategic corporal' (Rynning, 2008).

During the Cold War, French expeditionary forces had been small in number and light, designed for limited-scale intervention in Africa hence the main challenge of the post-Cold War era was to create heavier forces as part of an overall force that would be able to undertake *multiroles* (Bratton, 2002: 92; Utley, 2002: 135–40). Consequently, the transformation of the

Army has centred upon the development of Scorpion and the Future Contact System (SCF) (the French version of the FCS). Instigated in late 2004, Scorpion details the nature of the capacities land forces will require when engaging in future conflict (Rynning, 2008: 9). Its roots lie in the 2003 development of the 'Air-Land Operational Bubble' (BOA) that forms an intranet linking air and land units in a theatre of conflict (Chevalier, 2003: 37). Scorpion is centred upon the light armoured vehicle as a hub for other capabilities such as UAVs, mirroring the development of ground maneuver brigades by the US military as part of the FCS (Chevalier, 2003: 37). Scorpion and BOA form the first stage of the SCF, however, this remains in the early stages of development, despite the greater impetus fostered by the creation of the LTO battle-lab at the DGA (Lecinq, 2007: 69–72; Rynning, 2008).

A further major feature of LPM 2003–8 has been the development of an Effects Based Approach to Operations, outlined in the third Constitutive Concept of Land Forces of May 2006.[125] EBAO are aimed at encouraging 'synergy of effects', building upon the French tradition of 'effect majeur' (major effect) (Rynning, 2008: 12). Synergy aims to attain global operational effect by the identification of a final *etat final recherche* (end state) and the delineation of the appropriate application of force. Together with the two other core drivers of French reforms, NCW and expeditionary warfare, EBAO has facilitated greater interoperability with US Theater EBO systems and is supported by investment in a range of capabilities that will help France to narrow the technology gap with the US. French EBAO builds upon conceptual development that was instigated by the 1994 Defence White Paper and the principle of the Mastery of Violence that, as Charbonneau (2008: 101) highlights, focuses upon: 'destroying, neutralising or reducing the determining centres (which are not necessarily the armed forces) of the belligerent so as to eliminate its will/ability to fight'. Consequently, military officers are required to master multiple dimensions of military operations: the more traditional aspects of force, space and armaments as well as 'human networks', including humanitarian assistance, information and post-conflict reconstruction (Charbonneau, 2008: 106).

LPM 2003–8 has included investment in C4ISR capabilities facilitating real time targeting, shooting and target surveillance; the dispersal of force and concentration of effect; command and control systems and all-weather precision guided munitions endowing the military with a stand-off capability (Adams and Ben-Ari, 2006: 24; Bratton, 2002: 93–4; Rynning, 2008: 13). France currently has operational digital C2 programmes in each of the four services (Adams and Ben-Ari, 2006: 26–7). A particularly critical investment is the MARTHA system: a mobile operational control centre that facilitates the real time coordination of all Army assets on operation that has been gradually rolled out since 2005 (Boue, 2008: 34). Whilst the individual C2 systems of the three services were only partially interoperable with each other and with France's Alliance partners until the early 21st century, they have been united by the Joint Information and Command System that will link the C2 capabilities of all three services and will be interoperable with British and German C2 systems. Communication and computer capabilities take the form of the Fourth Generation Radio Programme and Automatic Transmission Integrated Network (RITA 2000) that entered service in 2005 (Wasielewski, 2004: 19).[126] The RITA 2000 system facilitates tactical communication and is interoperable with the systems of France's NATO and EU allies. In addition, tactical communication radios have been upgraded to include both tactical internet and GPS capabilities. (Adams and Ben-Ari, 2006: 28). These systems are supported by the French Syracuse 2 and Syracuse 3 Military Satellite Systems which entered into service between 1991 and 2006, contributing to NATO's Satcom post-2000 initiative and have been augmented by the ARISTOTE system that facilitates communication between commanders and deployed forces (Adams and Ben-Ari, 2006: 28; Posen, 2006: 180).

French ISR Projects are at an advanced stage (Adams and Ben-Ari, 2006: 29–33; Flournoy and Smith, 2005: 91). They include the Helios 1 and 2 earth observation satellites, launched in collaboration with the Italy and Spanish in 1995 and 2004 respectively and civilian/military Pleiades Satellite launched in 2008 in collaboration with Austria, Belgium, Italy, Spain and Sweden (Lansford, 1999: 25; Posen, 2006: 180). Airborne Ground Surveillance capabilities have taken the form of the Site Radar and Investigation Observation Helicopter (HORIZON), Airborne Radar Pods, attached to the Mirage F1-CR Aircraft and Super-Entendard 4 Aircraft and the Rapsodie ground radar system (Flournoy and Smith, 2005: 89). In addition, since 1998 France has upgraded its four Boeing AWACS aircraft through the Radar System Improvement Programme and Electronic Support Measures System that has enhanced the sensitivity of the AWACS' target identification (Adams and Ben-Ari, 2006: 31).

These initiatives have been supported by the acquisition of surveillance and reconnaissance UAVs by the air force, army and artillery (including not only portable UAVs for close range reconnaissance, but also Hunter and Eagle 1 medium altitude and longer endurance (MALE) UAVs) (Flournoy and Smith, 2005: 92). France is also investing in unmanned combat aerial vehicles (UCAVs), such as the Spwerwer B and the Dassault Neuron; a collaborative project with the Greece, Spain, Sweden and Switzerland (see Chapter 2) (Adams and Ben-Ari, 2006: 31–2; Flournoy and Smith, 2005: 92). In addition, France has acquired capabilities to allow the military to manage and interpret data from these ISR sources, notably the Multi-Source Interpretation Assistance System (SAIM) permitting the digital coordination of satellite, sea, air and ground radar, airborne, naval, terrestrial and space-based SIGNIT and electronic warfare capabilities (Adams and Ben-Ari, 2006: 33).

The June 2008 Defence White Paper has acted to reinforce the shift of force posture towards expeditionary power projection and the acquisition of C4ISR capabilities, outlining five strategic functions for the military:

knowledge and anticipation;[127] deterrence; protection;[128] prevention and intervention.[129] The DWP places a particular emphasis upon the importance of four key geographical areas for French security: the 'arc of crisis between the Atlantic and Indian Ocean' where failed states, weapons proliferation and threats to energy supplies threaten French security; the stabilisation of the Balkan region and the rise of a resurgent Russia. The White Paper also outlines a new area of increasing importance to French and European security: South East Asia, where growing strategic rivalries raise the threat of major conflict.[130]

In the context of these threats, the widening of French strategic interests to South East Asia and consequent requirement of broader power projection 'from the Atlantic Ocean to the Sea of Oman and the Indian Ocean', the DWP sets out changes to the operational goals of the armed forces, accompanied by a reduction of 54,000 employees (75 per cent of the reduction consisting of civilian positions) in LPM 2009–14.[131] For the Army the core goal is the capability to field 30,000 soldiers in support of expeditionary crisis-management operations within six months. This is part of an overall operational ground force of 88,000 troops, with 5,000 troops on standby and 10,000 troops designated to assisting civil authorities in the context of national crisis. The Navy's contribution to national security is structured around an aircraft carrier group that includes combat, surveillance and rescue aircraft and helicopters, 18 frigates and six nuclear submarines. These forces will endow the French with the capacity to deploy two naval groups to protect sea lines or to undertake amphibious operations. Finally, the Air Force is tasked with the capacity to permanently deploy five squadrons of aircraft on national territory and 70 aircraft on expeditionary operations. This will be attained through the creation of a joint fleet of 300 combat aircraft through the merger of the Rafale and Mirage D-2000 aircraft of the Air Force and Navy. The new joint fleet will be placed under the command of the Armies Chief of Staff and the single management of the Air Force.[132]

The White Paper also outlines capability procurement and organisational changes across the five main strategic functions of the armed forces. Notable changes in the area of knowledge and anticipation include the creation of a National Intelligence Council, chaired by the President and accompanied by a National Intelligence Coordinator; increasing the efficiency of information sharing within the diplomatic network; coordinating horizon-scanning activities; the recruitment of engineering, computer, imaging and language specialists and a doubling of budget for the development of space-based applications. The DWP also emphasises the special importance of UAVs in delivering airborne imaging and eavesdropping capabilities.

In addition to the 10,000 troops devoted to domestic crisis-response, the protection of national territory and population will be facilitated though a focus on sea, land, air and space-based capabilities to permit 'in-depth surveillance' of the French state. The DWP also outlines improvements in the analysis, response and detection of CBRN (Chemical, Biological, Radiological and Nuclear) threats, the creation of a political crisis-management centre to facilitate speedy response, the development of a Cyber-Defence Agency to guard against the protection of critical networks and the acquisition of 'over the horizon' and space-based radars. In the area of prevention, the DWP builds upon the notion of the 'mastery of violence' by emphasising the importance of a 'comprehensive approach' to domestic and international defence and security cooperation, including a wide range of tools: diplomatic, economic, military, legal and cultural. This 'comprehensive approach' involving an increased role for civilian assets is also central to the ability of the French military to undertake intervention of varying intensity (from 'civilian operations' to 'military operations proper').[133] Consequently the DWP outlines the planned development of a 'civilian force generation' concept and high-level political crisis-management centre to facilitate enhanced civilian/military coordination in crisis-management operations.[134]

Table 1.3   The Troop Reductions of LPM 2009–14

Service	2008 (civilian and military)	2014 (civilian and military)
Army	157,947	131,000
Navy	52,866	44,000
Air Force	64,990	50,000
Total	275,803	225,000

Source: 'Loi de Programme Militaire 2009–14', NOR : DEFX0821148L/Bleue-1. French Defence Ministry, 2009.

Hence the focus of capability procurement is on ensuring operational superiority in the context of missions that will require interoperability with coalition partners and the versatility to deal with conflict of varying intensity conducted 'amongst the people', necessitating high-levels of training and education for soldiers.[135] The Crisis-Management Concept of 2007 exemplifies this approach by recognising that the 'use of force alone cannot provide the definitive solution to a crisis'. Consequently, the French military will need to be capable not only of 'initial entry': 'the capability to lead a multinational operation and to participate, at the tactical level, alongside our strategic partners'; but also of fully participating in the implementation of a crisis-resolution strategy: of guaranteeing the effective use of all means at the nation's disposal, necessitating improved diplomatic, cultural and social links through interministerial partnerships.[136]

The need to develop the core attributes necessary for asymmetrical conflict of quickly varying intensity 'amongst the people' ('three block warfare') is also elucidated in detail in the French Army Doctrine publications, 'Doctrinal Manual for the Employment of Land Forces in Urban Environments of 2005' (TTA 980); 'Doctrine for the Employment of Land Forces in Stablisation Missions' of 2006, and the most recent doctrinal manual: 'Winning the Battle, Building Peace: Land Forces in Present and Future Conflicts' of January 2007. 'Winning the Battle' builds upon the principle of the Mastery of Violence, TTA 980 and 'The Doctrine for the Employment of Land Forces in Stablisation Missions' by outlining how military force can only 'establish the minimal conditions of strategic success'; the need to 'control violence' and to be prepared to shift operational modes and synchronise the application of kinetic and non-kinetic effects in conflict of rapidly varying intensity.[137] In short, whilst noting that preparation for MCO remains important, 'Winning the Battle' has a strong focus on the conduct of complex crisis-management operations.

The document outlines three key stages to contemporary land operations.[138] Firstly, intervention ('tactical knockout'), involving the application of high-intensity force, allowing the initial deployment of forces. Secondly, stablisation (the 'decisive phase'), in which the foundations are laid for reconstruction, necessitating a comprehensive approach that integrates the military, economic, legal, humanitarian and diplomatic contributions of state and non-state actors. Finally, 'normalisation' ('strategic success'), whereby an 'enduring political, judicial and social system accepted by the protagonists' is established, permitting the withdrawal of French forces (Bezacier, 2004b: 8–9; Coste, 2007: 9–12).[139]

The document highlights a strong level of convergence with developments in British COIN doctrine, emphasising several key steps in the successful conduct of the 'stablisation phase' of asymmetrical warfare: winning over the population by isolating the opponent, the application of minimal force (relying on the dissuasive power of force), improving security and facilitating the improvement of living conditions.[140] It also points to the importance of being prepared to undertake the disarmament of combatants, train local defence and security forces and play a catalytic role in setting in place the basis for broader nation-building, whilst ensuring that the military successfully delegates activities to civil actors at the appropriate time.[141] Furthermore, the Manual reinforces the centrality of jointness and combined operations, right down to the lowest tactical level throughout each stage of conflict.[142]

'Winning the Battle' is premised on a strong scepticism of the utility of technology to transform the nature of conflict and seeks to balance the gains that can be accrued by technology with 'human factors', which are central in harnessing the utility of technology in the context of expeditionary missions conducted amongst the people. In line with British Defence Doctrine, technology is viewed as a means with which to maximise manoeuvre and enhance force protection.[143] Yet technology only offers a means with which to 'know'

– human factors are critical in translating this into understanding. Accordingly 'Winning the Battle' emphasises the necessity for soldiers to develop a thorough understanding of the political and cultural dynamics of their operating environment, adapt to the opponent and to operate with civilian actors as part of a comprehensive approach. At the same time, soldiers are expected to retain the core of the 'warrior ethic' that is critical in endowing soldiers with the capacity not only to undertake the higher-intensity aspects of asymmetrical conflict, but also to endure in long-term deployments in which the intensity of conflict can change at short-notice.[144] Furthermore, the document recognises that whilst technology delivers a precision strike capability and the ability to gather information at distance, the 'control of violence' necessitates an appropriate balance between force protection and contact with the local population,[145] the development of crowd control techniques as well as reduced lethality weapons.

Consequently key areas of capability procurement in the 2008 Defence White Paper include the means of information, communication and space-based assets;[146] force protection (including against CBRN); a long-range precision-strike capacity; capabilities and training that will allow the military to operate in close contact with the population, often in urban environments; naval superiority particularly in littoral (coastal) waters and air superiority/mobility.[147] Intelligence capabilities also emerge as central, in order to develop a 'holistic knowledge of the theatre of operations', facilitate interministerial coordination and the synchronisation of both kinetic and non-kinetic effects.

Although not fully convergent with the principle of 'Mission Command', the French approach to military command also appears to be increasingly convergent with doctrinal developments in the UK and Germany. The French approach to peacekeeping in the initial post-Cold War era was characterised by a strong degree of hierarchy (Dalgaard-Nielsen, 2006: 107). However, the 'Doctrinal Manual for the Use of Force in Urban Environments' and 'Winning the Battle' point to the imperative for more decentralised forms of command and control: 'initiative' and 'decision-making' are required at all levels.[148] Training emerges as central in order to ensure subordinates have the necessary information to act according to the intent of the commander in situations requiring initiative. Training at the command level is focused on ensuring flexibility and adaptability in command headquarters which should be capable of shifting between operational modes.[149] Similarly the 'Crisis-Management Concept' developed by the CICDE in 2007 highlights the centrality of adaptable structures of command and although not explicitly referring to 'Mission Command', it notes the importance of developing 'more dynamic and decentralised' command and control structures.[150]

In summary, since 1994 France has shifted from a focus on territorial defence, deterrence and national strategic autonomy towards the capacity to undertake expeditionary crisis-management operations of varying intensity in support of a new form of 'forward defence': meeting threats to international instability at source, at an increasingly global level (Gregory, 2000b: 340). This shift, first outlined in the 1994 DWP, has been reinforced by the 2008 DWP that adds greater flesh – both conceptual/doctrinal and capability – to the bones of 'third order' change outlined 14 years previously. The new White Paper sets out the vision of a balanced, network-enabled military, endowed with C4ISR capabilities that attempts to adapt the RMA to the operational requirements of 'three block warfare', to the defence of national territory from the threat of WMD proliferation and terrorist attacks. At the same time the White Paper outlines the intention to retain the capacity to undertake MCO, albeit as part of multinational coalitions (Desportes, 2008a: 6–9).

Reforms to French policy instruments – military structures and capabilities – have emulated those of the US, in the form of the creation of joint command structures and capability investment structured around NEC and EBAO. However, the reforms undertaken as part of the LPM 1997–2002, LPM 2003–8 and those outlined in the 2008 DWP highlight the selective nature of this emulation. Like the British, the French have sought to attain 'balance' by creating force structures and capabilities which are appropriate not only to high-intensity warfighting against state-based opponents (as part of multilateral coalitions), but scenarios such as 'three block war'.[151] Consequently the adoption of the EBAO has been firmly situated within the 2008 White Paper's 'comprehensive approach' and focuses on achieving tactical and operational effects. Implicit in French thinking is recognition of the limited strategic impact of technological advances: the RMA is not viewed as a fundamental change in the nature of warfare and as an opportunity to control the process of 'escalation', but as a development in operational art. France has shied away from the 'system of systems' approach by the US. As stated in the 2008 Defence White Paper: 'Superior technology does not *per se*, guarantee operational superiority. The human factor [training and education of soldiers] will remain prevalent in complex operations where all instruments of national power and influence are brought to bear.'[152]

German defence reform: 'Second-order' change

Over the 1990s German policy-makers have promoted an increasingly active regional and global role for the *Bundeswehr* (Maull, 2000). Chancellor Helmut Kohl and Defence Minister Volker Rühe (1992–8) used the 1991 Gulf War and 1994 Srebrenica Massacre to legitimate widening the remit of German military action. This process culminated in the 12 July 1994 Constitutional Court Ruling, permitting German troops to operate outside NATO's geographical boundaries. Yet the CDU/CSU 1994 'Conceptual Guidelines for the Further Development of the *Bundeswehr*', developed by Rühe proposed minimal restructuring, downsizing the military from 370,000 including 170,000

Table 1.4   The Cornerstones of a Fundamental Renewal, June 2000

Personnel Category	Army	Air Force	Navy	Total
Professionals	112,000	47,000	19,000	178,000
Short Service Volunteers	21,000	3,200	2,800	27,000
Basic Conscripts	39,000	9,800	1,200	50,000
Total SSVs/Conscripts	60,000	13,000	4,000	77,000
Standing Forces	172,000	60,000	23,000	255,000

Source: 'Die *Bundeswehr* Sicher ins 21 Jahrhundert: Eckpfeiler fuer eine Erneuerung von Grund auf' (A Secure *Bundeswehr* in the 21st Century: Cornerstones of a Fundamental Renewal), German Federal Ministry of Defence, 2000.

conscripts to 340,000 with 140,000 conscripts and retained territorial defence as the core task of the *Bundeswehr* (Dyson, 2007: 63). The June 2000 'Cornerstones of a Fundamental Renewal' reform of SPD Defence Minister Rudolf Scharping (1998–2002) also outlined only first-order change to the 'settings' of policy, reducing the military to 277,000, including 77,000 conscripts.

This reticence to undertake bold reform was surprising, particularly given the suggestions of an independent Commission ('Common Security and the Future of the *Bundeswehr'*), known as the 'Weizsäcker Commission', set up by the SPD/Green Government to review the tasks and structure of the *Bundeswehr*. The Commission's Report (May 2000) codified the lessons of the Kosovo conflict, recommending radical structural and doctrinal reform: crisis-management as the *Bundeswehr's* core objective and a force of 240,000 with 30,000 conscripts, in order to ensure that Germany would be able to effectively contribute rapid reaction forces to the December 1999 Helsinki Headline Goals (HHG) and the pooling of European military capabilities (Dyson, 2007: 89–94).

Only in the *Verteidigungspolitische Richtlinien* (Defence Policy Guidelines) (VPR) of 21 May 2003 did SPD Defence Minister Peter Struck (2002–5) abandon territorial defence in favour of expeditionary crisis-management and prevention as part of the 'worldwide fight against international terrorism': Germany would be 'defended on the Hindukush' (Dyson, 2007: 122–3). Struck now explicitly referred to the *Bundeswehr* as an '*Interventionsarmee'* (Intervention Force)[153] that would be designed in order to facilitate deploy-

Table 1.5   The Recommendations of the Weizsaecker Commission, May 2000

Personnel Category	2000	2006
Professional and Regular Soldiers	203,000	210,000
Short-Service Volunteers	23,000	5,000
Basic Conscripts	112,000	25,000
Total number of soldiers	338,000	240,000

Table 1.6   Strength of the *Bundeswehr* by Service, June 2009

Service	Number of Personnel
Army	100,767
Navy	18,437
Air Force	45,697
Support Services	55,397
Medical Services	19,125
Professional Soldiers	187,500
Extended Service Conscripts	25,346
Basic Conscripts	34,534
Total	247,380

Source: Bundeswehr (2009a).

ment 'anywhere in the world'.[154] The reform therefore began the process of restructuring the military into a 35,000-strong 'rapid reaction force' designed for higher-intensity expeditionary warfare operations; 70,000 stabilising troops for low- to medium-intensity post-conflict reconstruction/peacekeeping missions and 147,500 support/logistical forces (Dyson, 2005: 380). The development of the 'rapid reaction force', commanded by a single *Generalinspekteur* (Chief of Staff) and a Joint Command Headquarters,[155] combined with Struck's strengthening of the Special Operations Division (KSK) (first established under Rühe in 1995), as the 'spearhead force of the new *Bundeswehr*', represents an important step towards convergence with the British Joint Reaction Force and French EMF model (King, 2005b: 327; Shepherd, 2000: 23).

The 2003 VPR also pointed to a growing convergence with US reforms, by outlining, for the first time, the need to focus on networked capabilities (and on enhancing interoperability with Alliance partners) in order to contribute to international crisis-management operations across the globe.[156] In line with the growing convergence of European states around the capacity to conduct 'Three Block Warfare' the VPR recognised that there are 'no clear cut dividing lines between the various types of operations'[157] and that the *Bundeswehr* will have to be capable of participating in missions 'across the entire mission spectrum down to high-intensity operations'[158] (Breuer, 2006: 213–14). Whilst shying away from explicit references to EBO and NCW, the VPR charted a 'capability focused'[159] approach to procurement and equipment planning centred around six core capability categories: command and control; intelligence collection and reconnaissance; mobility; effective engagement; support and sustainability and survivability and protection. The VPR outlined the necessity to focus in particular on three subcapabilities: 'strategic deployment; global reconnaissance and efficient, interoperable command and control systems and means'.[160]

The shift to full-spectrum tasks in the support of crisis-management and prevention, the fight against international terrorism and the proliferation of WMD was reinforced by the 2006 White Paper (DWP) on German Security Policy and the Future of the *Bundeswehr* that represents an important landmark in post-Cold War German military reform. It outlines in bold terms how the reformed *Bundeswehr* would allow Germany to 'actively shape its environment' and 'take preventative action against risks and threats to German security'.[161] The 2006 DWP builds upon the VPR's reference to a capability-based approach by heralding the 'transformation'[162] and permanent adaptation of the armed forces to the changing security environment. The *Bundeswehr* Analyses and Studies Centre in Waldbröl was reborn in July 2004 as the *Bundeswehr* Transformation Centre in Strausberg. The BTC acts as the 'think tank' of the *Bundeswehr* in support the process of 'Concept Development and Experimentation' (CD&E).[163] The BTC supports the national reform process and provides institutional protection for the principle of jointness and interoperability.[164] The institution plays an important (though not lead) role in coordinating conceptual and doctrinal development on Networking and in meeting the goal of reaching an initial capability for network-enabled operations by 2012. The BTC also improves the broader ability of the Defence Ministry to influence NATO CD&E and the defence planning processes of the European Defence Agency that is identified by the DWP as a central framework for future procurement planning.[165]

The 2006 DWP envisages a future *Bundeswehr* linked by an 'all embracing and interoperable information and communications network' permitting 'information, command and control superiority' as a means with which to facilitate the interoperability and jointness of the response and stabilisation forces in operations across the mission spectrum.[166] The White Paper identifies Networked Capabilities as critical in enabling the *Bundeswehr* to conduct EBO that is defined in the DWP as: 'the uniform planning and interaction of military capabilities in concert with other instruments, states and alliances'.[167]

German thinking on NEC since the 2003 VPR has taken the form of the Networked Operational Command Doctrine (*Vernetzten Operationsführung* (NetOpFü)). NetOpFü was initially closely associated with US ideas on NCW. Official documentation adopted the discourse of NCW: envisaging the developed of subnetworks within an overarching global network and citing US post-Cold War experiences as examples of the effectiveness and urgency of NCW (Streitkraeftebasis, 2009a, 2009b). Yet German conceptual development on networking is much closer to NEC than NCW. Like NEC, it seeks to harness the power of networking to facilitate the distribution of information and enhance adaptability, mobility and speed of reaction, and deliver maximum effects from military action, not only in high-intensity warfighting but across the conflict spectrum. This understanding of the potential contribution of network-enabled capabilities resonates with the British 'manouevrist approach'[168] that lies at the heart of NEC and emphasises the virtues of speed, flexibility, momentum, tempo and agility in the delivery of effects disproportionately higher to the action applied.[169]

Embedded within NetOpFü is a strong scepticism of the transformative power of technology. 'Faktor Mensch'[170] – the human factor – plays the 'decisive role'. Like NEC, NetOpFü is conceived of as enabling troops to overcome the impediments of military hierarchy and act with greater speed, flexibility and adaptability in combat situations.[171] Consequently training (particularly the ability of soldiers at low-levels of command to undertake quick and independent decision-making) is viewed as a critical area of improvement if the full potential of NetOpFü is to be harnessed.[172] Hence German doctrinal development dovetails closely with the British concept of 'Mission Command'. Indeed, the concept is explicitly invoked in the DWP as central to NetOpFü.[173]

NetOpFü is also situated firmly within the German take on the 'Comprehensive Approach', termed 'Networked Security'[174] that aims to bring all elements of national and international power – both kinetic and non-kinetic effects – to bear on crisis-situations. At the national level, this has involved the development of structures to facilitate interministerial cooperation, including a stronger role for the Federal Intelligence Service in central situation analysis, the development of a 'Crisis Response Centre' within the Foreign Office, a 'National Air Security Centre' and 'Joint Counter Terrorism Centre', supplemented by regular staff rotation and interministerial coordination training at the Federal College for Security Studies.[175]

German conceptual and doctrinal development on EBAO is, however, at an earlier stage, having taken strongest root within the *Luftwaffe* who sought to lead-up conceptual development on EBAO (see Chapter 5).[176] This is reflected in the 2006 DWP that provides a 'thin' definition of EBO (see above) and offers little in detail and substance, referring to 'effects based operations' only three times.

The White Paper also adds some flesh to the bones of the six capability investment categories elucidated in the 2003 VPR. However, whilst the DWP explicitly structures capability procurement around the development of NetOpFü, in order to facilitate the deployment of force across the mission spectrum and EBAO, it is less concrete on specific capability investment.[177] This reflects the relatively early stage of German conceptual and doctrinal development on NetOpFü and in particular, EBAO as well as the funding uncertainties of the German defence budget (Bauer, 2006). Force protection, stand-off and precision strike capabilities emerge as key areas of investment in order to furnish the Response Forces with the capabilities necessary for high-intensity power projection as part of multilateral coalitions. However, capability investment also focuses on areas of NetOpFü of relevance to the low-medium intensity missions, notably survivability and command and control, in addition to networking in order to ensure adequate interoperability with response forces.[178]

Although Germany lags behind the UK and France in capability investment on C4ISR, a set of major capability investment programmes in the area of C4ISR have been instigated since 2003, which have put in place the foundations for a network-enabled *Bundeswehr*. These programmes include the development of joint, networkable radio equipment in order to boost C2 capabilities and interoperability with EU and NATO partners. The tactical communications capabilities of the *Bundeswehr* have recently been upgraded through the Armed Forces Mobile Communications System (MobKommSysBw) that, since 2007, has permitted the networking of all radio communications systems on deployment with communication centres in Germany (Adams and Ben-Ari, 2006: 55). Communication capabilities and the interoperability of the German military with its Alliance partners have also been augmented through the acquisition of new Tactical Mobile Radio Networks in the German Navy (Link 22); the Air Force's Automatic Command Communications Network (AutoFue); fitting of the Multifunctional Information Distribution System (MIDS) to the Tornados and NH-90 helicopters of the Luftwaffe and Class 123 Frigates of the Navy as well as through the acquisition of Software Defined Radio Systems (Adams and Ben-Ari, 2006: 55).

The Army Command System (FueInfoSys H) is currently under development. 'FueInfoSys H' will integrate the Tactical Command Provision system (FAUST) that operates at battalion level and below and the Army Command and Control System for Digitally Supported Command of Operations in Staffs (HERO) that delivers C2 at the corps, division and brigade levels (Adams and Ben-Ari, 2006: 53–4; Billy, 2003: 56). The lack of interoperability between the C2 services of the *Bundeswehr* is also being addressed through the development of the 'C2 system of the Armed Forces' (FueInfoSys S). Communication within and between Command Posts has been enhanced through the acquisition of the BIGSTAF voice and data communication network that entered into service in three stages between 1998 and 2006 (Billy, 2003: 58). Finally, the SATCOMBw satellite communications system (fully operational from 2013) will facilitate the flexible deployment of expeditionary crisis-management forces (Adams and Ben-Ari, 2006: 56).[179]

The second major investment is a joint intelligence, surveillance and reconnaissance network (ISR). Germany already has substantial capabilities in the area of UAVs, reflecting its advanced technological base in UAV, and has deployed several UAV systems since the mid-1990s. These include the army's CL-289 MALE UAV as well as the LUNA, KZO and ALADIN devices, which are capable of shorter-range reconnaissance missions (Matzken, 2007: 73–4). Germany is also developing long-endurance UCAVs to replace its manned airborne ISR systems (Adams and Ben-Ari, 2006: 56–7). The *Bundeswehr* is building upon these systems by pushing ahead with the acquisition of 5 EUROHAWK MALE UAVs which will be interoperable with the US Global Hawk and will be put to the service of the NATO Allied Ground Surveillance Initiative. Germany will, in 2010, lease three Heron I medium altitude long-range endurance UAVs from Israel Aerospace Industries as an interim solution to meet operational requirements in Afghanistan. The *Bundeswehr's* ISR capabilities have also been improved through the SAR LUPE space-based reconnaissance system that was launched in 2006 as well as the purchasing of high-performance radar equipment (Flournoy and Smith, 2005: 91–3).[180] These advances in C4ISR capabilities have been accompanied by the development of the GAST (Common Intelligence Analysis and Evaluation System) that will provide a single database collating intelligence (Adams and Ben-Ari, 2006: 58). The ISR functions of the Luftwaffe have also been enhanced by the acquisition of 'Reccelight' Pods which entered into service in September 2009. By providing a tactical reconnaissance function, the Recce-light pods and groundwork stations supplement the 'wet film' reconnaissance pods that have been in operation since the 1990s.

Mobility and long-range airlift are being enhanced through 60 Airbus A400-M transport aircraft, the delivery of which will begin in 2012. Tactical mobility has also been strengthened by the acquisition of 243 NH-90 transport helicopters and the modernisation of 40 CH-53 Medium Transport helicopters in order to enhance their networking capability and ensure interoperability with the Tiger and NH-90 helicopters. Effective engagement is being addressed by the purchase of 80 TIGER multirole and near all-weather capable combat support helicopters; 410 PUMA air transportable infantry fighting vehicles which will replace the Marder tanks between 2010–20; a new ground-based air defence system to boost the missile defence capability of the air force and five Type K-130 Corvettes to augment the response and stabilisation forces of the Navy (Matzken, 2007: 74). Germany is also currently rolling-out an 'Infantryman of the Future' system that is equipping front-line infantry units with state-of-the-art clothing, personal equipment, electronics, optronics and weapons designed to improve lethality, survivability, mobility, sustainability and command and control capability.

The 2006 DWP also outlined the implications of 'transformation' for the structure of the Army, Navy and Airforce in a more extensive manner, building upon the modularisation of forces that had been first outlined in the 2003 VPR. The DWP heralded significant changes for the Army in particular and the development of several new structures: the Response Forces Division that is formed of two armoured brigades, capable of conducting joint high-intensity land force operations; the Specialised Operations Division, comprising the Special Forces Command and two airborne brigades; the Airmobile Division consisting of an Air Maneuver Brigade, three Army Aviation Regiments and the Army Troops Command, permitting the rapid and long-distance deployment of troops and capable of contributing to both response force and stabilisation force missions. For the Navy, restructuring has led to the combination of two boat flotillas into a single Flotilla (Flotilla 1) in order to streamline command structures, supported by a NATO Centre for

Excellence in Confined and Shallow Waters (CSW COE),[181] the reorganisation of the Destroyer Flotilla into Flotilla 2 and the development of rapidly available operational headquarters.[182]

Modularity has been underpinned by the creation of the Joint Support Service (JSS) to provide joint support services for all services in the *Bundeswehr*, under whose administrative control the *Bundeswehr* Operations Command and Special Forces Operation Command operate. The core support functions of the JSS include the provision of command and control organisation for operations abroad; the provision of disaster relief within the Federal Republic; logistical support; military intelligence and strategic reconnaissance.[183]

German defence reform therefore embodies a selective emulation of the RMA. NetOpFü is much more modest than its US counterpart, NCW, and is a case of only partial and delayed emulation that has much in common with the British take on networking, NEC. Rather than the high-centralisation of US command structures, the DWP emphasises the importance of Mission Command. Whilst boosting the ability of Germany to contribute to high-intensity warfighting operations and operations of varying intensity, the DWP is premised on the notion that the most likely missions that the *Bundeswehr* will face are those of low-medium intensity – notably civilian crisis prevention, conflict resolution and post-conflict peacebuilding.[184]

The 2006 DWP explicitly outlines the development of a 'balanced' expeditionary force structure and capability investments which, in preparing the *Bundeswehr* for full-spectrum operations, are increasingly convergent with British and French reforms. The White Paper sets out a vision of a military that will be capable not only of low-medium intensity, but also higher-intensity tasks as part of multinational coalitions under the UN, NATO and ESDP. The 35,000 troops of the 'response forces' have been allocated the specific role of 'combined and joint, high-intensity, network-enabled operations' – of undertaking rapid and decisive operations against state-based opponents and of 'meeting Germany's international responsibilities by participating in complex, high-intensity combat operations'. Combined with the 70,000 strong stabilisation force, this is intended to create a military capable of 'escalation dominance across the entire spectrum' and of participating conflict that can vary in intensity at short notice.[185]

Accordingly, the 2006 DWP shies away from the technological determinism of US 'transformation'. The DWP highlights how the networking of forces will be crucial to allow effective interoperability with ESDP and NATO alliance partners and how high-technology capability investment will augment the capacity of the *Eingreifskraefte* to undertake high-tempo, high-intensity crisis-management operations. Networked capabilities, particularly C2, also emerge as crucial for the stabilisation forces in delivering operation effects (not least in achieving jointness in 'three block war'). Yet transformation also dictates a focus upon 'social, intercultural and foreign language skills' necessary for the conduct of 'wars amongst the people'.[186]

Although these assets have long been part of the training for German soldiers (both in general training and training on deployment) recent experiences in Afghanistan have led to the development of two formal structures with the competence to lead up cultural training and advice. The Central Coordination Group for Intercultural Competence was established in 2009 at the Centre for *Innere Fuehrung* in Koblenz to enhance the overall focus on culture in military training and doctrine and train individual soldiers. The Centre for Intercultural Mission Advice was also set-up in 2009 and provides advisors who work closely with Commanders in mission planning and execution.

At the same time, there is an increasing recognition within the military of the need to be prepared to combine non-kinetic and kinetic effects. Many of the qualities associated with *innere Fuehrung* (critical reflection, intelligence, tolerance and intercultural competence) have been reinforced by the operational experience of low-medium intensity crisis-management operations in the Balkans during the 1990s and early 21st century. However, the demands of operations like ISAF also create the need for a 'warrior ethos', not only amongst the *Eingreifskraefte*, but also within Stabilisation Forces, who must be capable of dealing with the full spectrum of conflict intensity.[187] Although Germany has not developed a specific doctrine on COIN, the lessons drawn by the Army from Afghanistan are for a need to focus on 'Three Block Operations'. Whilst this does not imply a full shift towards convergence with the British approach to COIN, it does point to a growing recognition of the need to prepare for Stabilisation Operations which involve action that can vary rapidly in intensity (see Chapter 5).

Yet despite the development of a more professionalised 'rapid reaction force', Germany is not a case of 'third-order' change; its reform is only partial and represents 'second order change'. Although the restructuring of the military was designed to save 26 billion Euros between 2003 and 2015, the retention of 34,534 basic service conscripts remains not only a practical impediment to the development of a higher-intensity expeditionary capacity,[188] but also a financial burden at a time when funds are required for new capabilities to permit force projection and networked operations. This limits Germany's ability to contribute to medium-high intensity operations (Breuer, 2006: 216; Dyson, 2007: 111; Lungu, 2004a: 261–72; Sperling, 2004). These shortfalls in investment have been compounded by the comparatively late temporal location of Germany's shift from territorial defence to 'crisis-management' (that has led to investment in inappropriate equipment and capabilities during the late 1990s and early 21st century) and tight post-unification restrictions on defence spending, impacting on investment in new capabilities in support of NetOpFü (Breuer, 2006; Longhurst and Miskimmon, 2007: 91; Noetzel and Schreer, 2009: 19). As Chapter 5 will demonstrate, the flexibility of German defence procurement has also been undermined by the impact of organisational politics between the Single

Services. This has impeded a shift in investment away form platform systems to capabilities enhancing C4ISR and strategic mobility.

Furthermore, having been wedded to territorial defence until the early 21st century, Germany now faces a difficult process of doctrinal and conceptual 'catching up' with its European and NATO partners. British and French doctrinal evolution in expeditionary operations began at a much earlier stage in the post-Cold War era, leaving Germany lagging, not only in the area of EBAO, but also in the development of a more detailed COIN doctrine (Noetzel and Schreer, 2008; 2009: 19). Hence deficits in both capabilities and doctrine/training – whilst in the process of being remedied – have undermined the capacity of the *Bundeswehr* to contribute to operations at the higher-intensity spectrum of 'Three Block Warfare', such as ISAF (see Chapter 5).

Table 1.7 Defence Spending in Britain, France and Germany 1985–2008

State	1985	1990	1995	2000	2004	2005	2006	2007	2008 (estimated)
France	20,780	42,689	47,768	33,815	53,007	52,909	55,673	61,784	66,180
Germany	19,922	42,319	41,160	28,150	38,007	38,054	38,092	42,552	46,241
UK	23,485	39,590	33,836	35,608	49,061	55,894	59,076	68,903	60,499
US	258,165	306,170	278,865	301,697	464,676	503,353	527,660	556,961	579,940

Source: 'Financial and Economic Data relating to NATO Defence' Press Release, Public Diplomacy Division, NATO, February 2009, Communique PR/CP 2009 (09).
Based on exchange rates of 19 February 2009.

Table 1.8   Defence Expenditure as Percentage of GDP 1985–2008

State	Average 1985–1989	Average 1990–1994	Average 1994–1999	Average 2000–2004	2004	2005	2006	2007	2008 (estimated)
France	3.7	3.3	2.9	2.5	2.6	2.5	2.5	2.4	2.3
Germany	2.9	2.1	1.6	1.4	1.4	1.4	1.3	1.3	1.3
UK	4.4	3.7	2.7	2.3	2.2	2.5	2.4	2.5	2.2
US	6.0	4.6	3.3	3.4	4.0	4.1	4.0	4.0	4.0
NATO Total	4.5	3.5	2.7	2.7	2.8	2.8	2.8	2.7	2.6

Source: 'Financial and Economic Data relating to NATO Defence' Press Release, Public Diplomacy Division, NATO, February 2009, Communique PR/CP 2009 (09).
Based on exchange rates of 19 February 2009.

Table 1.9 Percentage of Defence Spending Allocated to Investment in Equipment 1985–2008

State	Average 1985–99	Average 1990–95	Average 1995–2000	Average 2000–2004	2003	2004	2005	2006	2007	2008 (estimated)
France	–	–	21.3	19.7	20.5	20.9	21.3	23.2	22.4	21.7
Germany	19.6	13.5	11.8	14.0	13.8	14.8	14.2	15.0	15.3	18.1
UK	24.8	21.0	24.8	23.8	22.6	22.8	23.1	21.2	24.2	23.0
US	25.6	25.1	26.2	24.8	24.5	24.6	24.5	25.1	26.5	27.3

Source: 'Financial and Economic Data relating to NATO Defence' Press Release, Public Diplomacy Division, NATO, February 2009, Communique PR/CP 2009 (09).

Based on exchange rates of 19 February 2009.

2
Convergence and Divergence in the Institutional Forums of Defence Policy: Functional Complementarity; Spatial and Temporal Differentiation

The dimensions of differentiation in European defence cooperation: Function, space and time

This chapter outlines the development of differentiated and complementary cooperation in post-Cold War European defence policy across three core dimensions: space (the territoriality of defence cooperation), function (the functions performed by the core institutions of European defence) and time (the temporality of cooperation).[1] Post-Cold War European cooperation in the area of security and defence displays a significant level of spatial differentiation. On the one hand, the borders of cooperation in matters of 'hard' security are defined by Russian power and influence in the East,[2] yet on the other hand a diverse set of intergovernmental arrangements have arisen within these territorial boundaries since the mid-1990s. Such arrangements include joint capability procurement programmes (e.g. OCCAR; FSAF; A-400 M; Tiger; Boxer; COBRA; FREMM; Eurofighter; Meteor and nEUROn, see Table 2.4) and the cross-national generation of crisis-management forces (e.g. EUROFORCES; EUROCORPS; NORDACPS, Movement Centre Europe; the Multinational Interoperability Council, Multinational Interoperability Panel and Baltic Defence Cooperation, see Table 2.5). These variously 'a la carte', 'variable geometry' and 'multiple speed' initiatives illustrate spatial fragmentation in the architecture of European security.[3]

However, the main institutions of European security – the European Security and Defence Policy (ESDP) and NATO – display a stronger degree of complementarity in membership.[4] Apart from Austria, Cyprus, Finland, Ireland, Malta and Sweden, all member states of the European Union are also participants in the Atlantic Alliance.[5] Of the 24 European NATO members, only Denmark,[6] Turkey and Norway are not full participants in the institutional structures of ESDP (see Table 2.1).[7] In short, within West and East-Central Europe the formal membership of ESDP and NATO illustrates a relatively low level of differentiation; it is in meeting the burdens of cooperation in terms of the provision of troop contributions and military capabilities where the greatest divergence exists – in the 'provision' or 'consumption' of security.

Nevertheless, amongst the European states which are formally integrated into both ESDP and NATO, there appears to be continued differentiation in the preference to route defence and security cooperation through one or the other structure. The potential for differentiation is magnified by the flexibility of these intergovernmental arrangements (Whitney, 2008: 23). Whilst British armed forces reform is a case of 'third-order' change – to the objectives and instruments of defence policy – this has not been accompanied by a shift of institutional forum. Despite playing an important role in the development of intergovernmental initiatives such as the 1998 Saint Malo Accord, 1999 Helsinki Headline Goals and 2003 European Security Strategy (ESS) and an incremental shift towards the embedding of British defence policy within ESDP, UK defence and security policy remains firmly anchored within NATO (Dorman, 2001; Dover, 2005; Dunne, 2004; Miskimmon, 2004). Although the 2004 UK Defence White Paper contains five references to ESDP, it only once refers to ESDP without 'ring fencing' this through reference to NATO or the US (Edwards, 2006: 12). Indeed, the DWP highlights explicitly how the most demanding expeditionary operations, particularly against state-based opponents, are only feasible with the involvement of the US.[8] Ensuring interoperability with the US – in command and control, operational tempo and capability procurement – emerges as a key theme. Hence the DWP places NATO's Allied Command for Transformation (ACT), (set up following the 2002 Prague Summit to encourage complementarity in capability procurement and structural reform amongst NATO members) centre stage, whilst the European Defence Agency, agreed at the Thessaloniki European Council in June 2003, takes secondary importance.[9] In short, Britain remains firmly committed to the trans-Atlantic relationship through NATO and the development of capabilities which will ensure continued interoperability with the US.[10]

The institutional forums of French defence policy have undergone significant change – from the 'semi-detached' defence policy of the Cold War to multilateral cooperation through the embedding of French Defence Policy within the European Security and Defence Policy. Contemporary French defence policy prioritises ESDP and capability development that will secure an autonomous European capacity for military action, although it is increasingly Atlanticised, symbolised by its return to NATO's integrated military command structures at the Baden-Baden/Strasbourg NATO Summit of 3–4 April 2009.[11]

The institutional forums of German defence policy continue to cohere around the traditional German 'bridge' role – between British/US and French preferences (Dyson, 2005: 376; Hyde-Price, 2000: 205–7). Indeed, it is possible to identify a 'bi-furcation' within the Federal Executive, between a highly-Europeanist and active Foreign Ministry in 'uploading' German preferences to ESDP and an 'Atlanticised' Defence Ministry, more reactive and resistant to the anchoring of defence policy within ESDP (Bulmer et al, 2000: 25; Dyson, 2007: 158; Goetz, 2003). Until recently, Germany has been a relative laggard in the development of interoperable crisis-management capabilities for both ESDP and NATO.[12] Similar differentiation is evident amongst Europe's smaller states: whilst Finland and Sweden prefer to route defence cooperation through ESDP, Denmark, Norway, Baltic, CEE and Balkan states are more Atlanticist in their orientation, focusing upon the provision of military forces and capabilities within the framework of NATO (Aguis, 2006: 188–98; Jones, 2007: 238; Kapiszewski and Davis, 2005: 191–219; Tashev, 2005: 127–51).

Such differentiation in the 'Atlanticisation' and 'Europeanisation' of the defence policies of European states would appear to signal strong divergence in European security cooperation. This begs the more fundamental question of what broader function these initiatives serve: are European states moving towards common or divergent policy objectives through ESDP, NATO, and instances of 'a la carte', multiple speed and variable geometry cooperation? Determining the level of complementarity and competition between these institutional arrangements, not least NATO and ESDP, is a central task in establishing the level and significance of differentiated cooperation in European security and defence.

This chapter will highlight how NATO and ESDP are converging around increasingly similar functions: a new form of 'forward defence' that involves tackling threats to international instability at source (Ben-Ari, 2005; Kaitera and Ben-Ari, 2008; Farrell, 2008: 798–9). Crucially, this growing duplication in function has been accompanied by spatial differentiation: the focus of ESDP on security threats emerging from within Europe's geopolitical neighbourhood and NATO's growing emphasis on global instability. Consequently NATO is increasingly acting as an institutional forum in which to develop capabilities that will be of benefit to ESDP; likewise the newly established European Defence Agency (EDA) and Headline Goals 2010 are fostering capability and doctrinal developments that are also of use to missions within the Atlantic Alliance and other coalition operations.

Functional, spatial and temporal complementarity and differentiation in the institutional architecture of European security

The case for differentiation: Duplication in function?

At first glance, the longer-term development of the EU as an increasingly militarised regional and actor since the launch of EDSP at the Helsinki European Council of December 1999 seems to herald the development of a rival security organisation to NATO (Art, 2004; Cimbalo, 2004; Pape, 2005; Posen, 2004, 2006). Whilst NATO, unlike ESDP, is an institution of collective defence, both

Table 2.1   Membership of the Core Institutions of European Security

State	ESDP	EDA	ESA	ESC*	WEU	OSCE	NATO
Austria	X	X	X	X	3	X	
Belgium	X	X	X	X	X	X	X
Bulgaria	X	X		X	4	X	X
Cyprus	X	X		X		X	
Canada			1			X	X
Czech Republic	X	X	1	X	2	X	X
Denmark			X	X	3	X	X
Estonia	X	X		X	4	X	X
Finland	X	X	X	X	3	X	
France	X	X	X	X	X	X	X
Germany	X	X	X	X	X	X	X
Greece	X	X	X	X	X	X	X
Hungary	X	X	1	X	2	X	X
Iceland					2	X	X
Ireland	x	X	X	X	3	X	
Italy	X	X	X	X	X	X	X
Latvia	X	X		X	4	X	X
Lithuania	X	X		X	4	X	X
Luxembourg	X	X	X	X	X	X	X
Malta	X	X		X		X	
Netherlands	X	X	X	X	X	X	X
Norway		1	X		2	X	X
Poland	X	X	1	X	2	X	X
Portugal	X	X	X	X	X	X	X
Romania	X	X	1	X	4	X	X
Slovakia	X	X		X	4	X	X
Slovenia	X	X		X	4	X	X
Spain	X	X	X	X	X	X	X
Sweden	X	X	X	X	2	X	
Switzerland			X			X	
Turkey					2	X	X
UK	X	X		X	X	X	X
US						X	X

Key
1 = Cooperation Agreement
2 = Associate Members
3 = Observer Members
4 = Associate Partners
* Iceland, Norway and Turkey and EU accession states are entitled to participation

institutions have emerged as institutional forums for coordinating similar defence policy objectives: a new form of 'forward defence' that tackles threats to international instability at source, through low, medium or high-intensity expeditionary crisis-management operations.

The 1999 Helsinki Headline Goals created a European Rapid Reaction Force (ERRF) consisting of 60,000 troops deployable at 60 days notice, sustainable for up to one year in the field, capable not only of fulfilling the low-end Petersburg Tasks,[13] but also of sustaining one medium- to high-intensity operation (Cornish and Edwards, 2005: 804–5). The Helsinki European Council of 10–11 December 1999 also established three main institutions to support ESDP, which reflect NATO's intergovernmental political-military structures: the Political and Security Committee[14] resembling NATO's North Atlantic Council; the EU Military Committee echoes the NATO Military Committee, whilst the EU Military Staff mirrors NATO's International Military Staff.

The civilian dimension of ESDP was launched at the June 2000 European Council in Feira, Portugal, and outlined four areas of priority: police, the rule of law, civilian administration and civil protection. At the Civilian Capabilities Commitment Conference of December 2004 the EU declared its capacity to undertake the potential deployment of up to 5,761 police officers to act in lieu of indigenous forces and to undertake advisory, assistance and training missions; the deployment of up to 631 prosecutors/judges/ prison officers in support of strengthening the rule of law missions; a pool of 565 civilian administration experts as well as 579 experts and 445 staff forming assessment/intervention/other specialised teams in the area of civil protection. The Conference also identified a further dimension of civilian crisis-management: monitoring, to which 505 personnel have been committed by EU member states.[15] This announcement followed a series of Civilian Capabilities Commitment Conferences and the development of the Action Plan for the Civilian Aspects of ESDP at the 17–18 June 2004 Brussels European Council.

Whilst the EU has bolstered the civilian aspects of its crisis-management capabilities, there has been a clear shift to establish structures facilitating robust, higher-intensity tasks in support of peace enforcement, exemplified by the Headline Goal 2010 and Battlegroup Initiative, approved by the March 2004 Brussels European Council (Ulriksen, 2004: 469–70). The Battlegroup Initiative created up to 15 Battlegroups, each consisting of 1,500 troops, deployable within 15 days, enhancing the EU's capacity to launch simultaneous low-high-intensity rapid-response operations, attaining operational capability in 2007 (Howorth, 2007: 107; Cornish and Edwards, 2005: 804).[16] This initiative has been accompanied by steps to ensure a 'comprehensive approach' to the planning and conduct of military operations that integrates civilian and military instruments through the establishment of a Civilian-Military Planning Cell within the EUMS in 2005.[17]

These efforts to institutionalise an autonomous European military capacity appear to present a nascent challenge to NATO's status as the preeminent institution of European security. NATO's development as a focal point for joint expeditionary operations began in earnest at the April 1999 Washington

Summit that resulted in an updated Strategic Concept. In addition to security, consultation, deterrence, defence and partnership, the Strategic Concept also outlined the non-chapter five mission of crisis-management as a core security function of the Alliance. This was given more concrete form by the NATO Response Force (NRF), developed at the November 2002 Prague Summit: a high-readiness, technically advanced, joint air, naval and infantry force of 21,000 troops, deployable within five to 30 days for up to three months and designed not only to undertake high-intensity warfighting tasks, but also disaster relief and peacekeeping. The NRF's troops and capabilities are drawn predominantly from the European NATO members (King, 2005a: 331).[18]

The 28–29 November 2006 Riga Summit endorsed the Comprehensive Political Guidance (CPG) that builds upon the 1999 Strategic Concept by identifying the core threats to NATO as international terrorism, the proliferation of Weapons of Mass Destruction (WMD), failed or failing states, regional crises, misuse of technologies and disruption of resource flows.[19] The Declaration is of significance as it highlights how this changing emphasis requires a shift in operational requirements and capabilities amongst NATO members in order to ensure the balance in force structure and capabilities to permit the simultaneous conduct of combat, stabilisation, reconstruction, reconciliation and humanitarian missions (CPG, 2006: pt. 6). CPG underscores the importance of strengthening NATO's crisis-management instruments and cooperation with the UN, NGOs and local actors in the conduct and planning of military operations.[20] The Bucharest Summit of 3 April 2008 began the process of adding greater substance to the 'Comprehensive Approach' by putting in place an 'Action Plan', focusing on the planning and conduct of operations, training and education and augmenting cooperation with external actors.[21] Nevertheless, the Comprehensive Approach remains at an early stage of development with coordination taking place largely on an *ad-hoc* basis (Binnendijk and Petersen, 2008).

Hence the EU is gradually developing the institutional mechanisms and policy instruments to facilitate the conduct of more robust missions at the higher end of the conflict spectrum. This appears to represent a growing competitor to NATO that is at the inception of developing its peace-support capabilities.[22] Functional duplication also appears to be evident in the 12 December 2003 European Security Strategy (ESS) that outlines a similar set of challenges to CPG, by heralding the EU's responsibility to contribute to global security by tackling the key threats of terrorism, the proliferation of WMD, regional conflicts, state failure and organised crime.[23]

Such a picture of competition is, however, misleading. Instead, it is more accurate to point to an increasing degree of complementarity and cooperation in terms of military capacity, command facilities and force planning[24] and a growing strategic coherence between NATO, the EU and subregional defence and security arrangements (Mowle and Sacko, 2007: 597–618; Rynning, 2005: 155, 172; Ulriksen, 2004: 468). This complementarity has been evidenced by the March 17 2003 Berlin-Plus Agreement that facilitated the inclusion of EU outsiders (Norway and Turkey) into ESDP structures. Berlin Plus also provides the EU with access to NATO operational planning, capabilities and assets for EU crisis-management operations and places the NATO Supreme Allied Commander in Europe (DSACEUR) in command of EU operations (under the authority and guidance of the EU's PSC).

In addition, Berlin Plus included arrangements to facilitate mutually reinforcing capability acquisition by establishing the EU-NATO Capability Group in May 2003 to foster complementarity in procurement initiatives (Cornish and Edwards, 2005: 814–18; Howorth, 2007: 170; Rynning, 2005: 175; Whitman, 2004: 430). This is a process that has been bolstered by attempting to ensure that the same country takes the lead role in developing matching capabilities within each institution (for example Germany's role as lead nation on strategic airlift capabilities within both NATO and ESDP). The work of the EU-NATO Capability Group is supplemented by regular meetings between EU and NATO officials (Matlary, 2009: 60–1).[25] Moreover, on 3 October 2005 a permanent NATO liaison within the EU Military Staff and a permanent EU planning cell at SHAPE were established (Cornish and Edwards, 2005: 812).

Whilst the EU is developing the capacity to undertake higher-intensity tasks (robust peace enforcement operations), for the time being the NRF remains heavier, more rapidly deployable and more focused on full-spectrum (particularly higher-intensity operations) than the EU Battlegroups. (Kaitera and Ben-Ari, 2008; Howorth, 2007: 14–15; Rynning, 2005: 157).[26] This is reflected in the nature of ESDP missions which have largely been at the lower end of the conflict spectrum (rule of law, policing/police advisory missions, security sector reform and border assistance missions), operational experience that is reinforcing the EU's expertise and credibility in civilian crisis-management and prevention.[27] Of the 20 missions so far conducted under ESDP, only four Operations (EU-FOR Althea, EU-FOR Tchad/RCA, EU-FOR Concordia and EU-FOR RD Congo) have involved the deployment of peace-support forces capable of conflict at the higher intensity of the conflict spectrum. In contrast, three of NATO's five current military operations (ISAF, KFOR (Kosovo Force) and Operation Active Endeavour) involve the deployment of troops prepared for operations at higher end of the conflict spectrum.[28]

In addition, NATO and the EU are emerging as organisations characterised by spatial differentiation in function. Although the strategic radius of EU operations has expanded significantly since 1999, ESDP missions are predominantly focused on ensuring stability within the geostrategic neighbourhood of the EU: the Western Balkans, Middle East, Sub-Saharan Africa and Caucuses (Jones, 2007: 216). The military deployments of the Atlantic Alliance have taken on a global character since September 11, as illustrated by its most prominent contemporary operation, ISAF in Central Asia.

European capability initiatives: Reflecting convergence around a partial and selective emulation of the US-led RMA

As the last chapter highlighted, it is possible to distinguish an increasingly distinct model of military convergence amongst Europe's Great Powers:[29] the development of joint, flexible military forces, capable of expeditionary missions at the full range of the conflict spectrum. This necessitates investment in C4ISR and capabilities appropriate not only to high-intensity conflict, but also to three block warfare situations. This convergence is being reflected in capability cooperation within ESDP and NATO and through subregional capability procurement and force generation initiatives. A focus on the substance of capability investment programmes under ESDP, NATO and subregional procurement initiatives also highlights growing complementarity, rather than differentiation in function. These initiatives cohere around augmenting Europe's military capacity to make a stronger contribution to the NATO Alliance through the NRF; in many cases capabilities which can also be deployed in support of autonomous European military action. As Adams and Ben-Ari (2006: 84) note: 'A number of capabilities developed in the NATO context remain important tools for coalition interoperability, even when the Alliance is not formally involved.'

ESDP capability procurement initiatives: From civilian crisis-management to facilitating full spectrum peace enforcement operations through C4ISR

The convergence of European states around a partial emulation of the US-led RMA is increasingly reflected in initiatives under the auspices of ESDP. The Battlegroup Initiative was supplemented by the development of the European Defence Agency (EDA),[30] approved at the Thessaloniki European Council of June 2003 and established by a Council Joint Action on 12 July 2004. The EDA was promoted in particular by the British in the context of the failure of NATO's Defence Capabilities Initiative (DCI) of April 1999,[31] and the Helsinki Forces Catalogue (agreed at the Capabilities Commitment Conference of 20 November 2000) to spur the pace of complementarity in European capabilities that would be of use to both ESDP and NATO (Posen, 2006: 169).[32]

Whilst strictly intergovernmental, non-binding and deficient in enforcement mechanisms, the EDA is nevertheless an important step towards European capability cooperation and cross-European acquisition, with the potential to act as a focal point for efforts to steer capability complementarity between EU and NATO member states in areas such as C2 and C4ISR (Posen, 2006: 181; Reynolds, 2007: 375).[33] It is the first EU-level agency charged with the task of identifying European capabilities needs, promoting European armaments cooperation, coordination in research on defence technology and strengthening the European defence industry. The

EDA works with national governments to review the 15 project groups of the European Capabilities Action Plan (ECAP) and to utilise the Capabilities Development Mechanism to address capabilities shortfalls.[34] The EDA has also taken responsibility for leading up the Headline Goals 2010 which outlined interoperability, sustainability and deployability as the core capabilities that would be necessary to achieve the capacity to conduct several simultaneous Battlegroup operations.[35] (Cornish and Edwards, 2005: 804; Howorth, 2007: 109).

Of particular note is the publication of the 'Long-term Vision for European Defence Capability and Capacity Needs (LTV)', endorsed by the EDA's Steering Board in 2006, that outlines the future C4ISR capabilities which will be required to undertake ESDP missions and charts six major capability development areas: command; inform; engage; protect; deploy and sustain.[36] The LTV forms the basis for a more comprehensive and detailed Capabilities Development Plan that is currently under negotiation, led by the Capabilities Directorate of the EDA. Furthermore, the EDA's 'Comprehensive Capabilities Development Process (CCDP)' process, involving all participating member states, has highlighted several areas of activity in which interoperability and joint procurement requires strengthening in order to facilitate Battlegroup Missions, in addition to augmenting the Europe's ability to contribute to the NRF.[37]

These areas include the improvement of software defined radio systems (interoperable with US forces), led by Finland, France, Italy, Spain and Sweden and the development of NEC technology, doctrine and concepts though a draft study conducted by General Rainer Schuwirth, the former SHAPE Chief of Staff. The EDA has also prepared a draft concept on NEC following an NEC Pre-Study to establish a joint vision between European states outlining the NEC required to conduct joint and coalition operations involving both civilian and military actors. In addition, the EDA has established project teams to assess capability requirements in the area of CBRN, including CBRN ordnance disposal and detection, identification and monitoring. Maritime Surveillance is another key area, where initiatives include the investigation of a Maritime Surveillance Network, air, surface and underwater unmanned vehicle systems and target identification.[38] The EDA has also provided a forum for the development of interoperable '21st century Soldier Systems' by states which lag behind the British and French in this area: Spain, Austria, Finland, Germany, Italy, Portugal and Sweden. Finally, the EDA has outlined the intention to build upon the A-400M acquisition programme by creating a pooled European Air Transport Fleet (EDA, 2008a).[39]

In addition, the EDA has instigated a set of collaborative projects in the area of Research and Technology, including a Joint Investment Programme on Force Protection (JIP-FP) that began in January 2007, covering five main capability areas: collective survivability; individual protection; data analysis; secured tactical wireless communications systems in urban environments and mission planning and training for asymmetric conflict.[40] This has resulted in eight JIP-FP projects, all of which will foster the technological development necessary to facilitate European C4ISR and the capacity to conduct full-spectrum crisis-management operations.[41] On 26 May 2008 a second, two-year JIP was launched by 11 EDA members to investigate Innovative Concepts and Emerging Technologies in defence (JIP-ICET) (see Table 2.2).[42] A further collaborative R&T project under the EDA is the 'Miracle' project on microsatellite cluster technology that began under the auspices of the West European Armaments Group in May 2004, but was transferred in June 2007 to the EDA. Miracle investigated the potential system architecture and technologies necessary for the use of clusters of SAR (Synthetic Aperture Radar) and ELINT satellites in the conduct of military operations and forms an important basis for the development of European ISR capabilities.[43]

Another important development under the EDA is the Code of Conduct on Defence Procurement (CoC) that establishes a European Defence Equipment Market. The CoC came into force on 1 July 2006 and forms an agreement by all participating EDA states (apart from Romania) to Europe-wide tenders for defence equipment contracts (see Table 2.2). Whilst voluntary, the CoC is an important step towards the development of a more internationally competitive European armaments market and builds upon the substantial progress made during the 1990s in consolidating the highly-fragmented European defence-industrial base. In 1990 the European defence industry was characterised by a plethora of small and medium-sized national firms; it is now possible to identify three major defence firms: BAE systems (UK) that has consolidated smaller UK companies (notably Marconi Electronic and the General Electric Company in November 1999); Thales (France; formerly Thompson-CSF) and EADS (a product of the 10 July 2000 merger of Germany's Daimler Chrysler, Aerospatiale-Matra of France and Construcciones Aeronauticas of Spain). However, when compared to the US, whose industry is dominated by two giant players (Lockheed Martin and Boeing), Europe's defence industry remains relatively fragmented.[44]

Furthermore, in November 2003 the European Space Agency (ESA), formerly an independent intergovernmental organisation, entered into a Framework Agreement with the European Commission's DG Transportation that provides a legal basis for cooperation between the ESA and EU. The Framework Agreement emphasises collaboration in areas such as launchers, earth observation, navigation and communication satellites (Adams and Ben-Ari, 2006: 127). An important initiative within this framework is the Galileo global navigation system that by 2013 will provide a European alternative to the US Global Positioning System (GPS). Although Galileo is designed as a civilian system, it has the potential to enhance NEC in both Battlegroup and NRF operations. Whilst French led, Galileo has proceeded in close cooperation with the US in order to ensure complementarity with GPS (supported by a 2004 cooperation agreement with the US). Cooperation in space policy is 'multiple speed', as membership of the ESA is dependent upon a state's space industry capacity in addition to its willingness to make financial contributions to the activities of the agency.[45]

A second European venture under the auspices of the ESA/European Commission Framework Agreement – the Global Monitoring for Environment and Security Programme (GMES) – was originally planned as a civilian venture, but will also act to develop Europe's global earth observation capability and contribute to NEC.[46] The Framework Agreement has been accompanied by the European Commission's November 2003 White Paper on European Space Policy, that highlights the requirement to develop space systems in support of ESDP.[47]

Europe's capacity to use space technology to enhance its ability to deploy force has been supported by the incorporation of the European Satellite Centre (ESC) into the EU in January 2002, as part of the transfer of functions from the WEU to the EU. The European Union Satellite Centre (EUSC) involves the participation of all 27 EU member states and also cooperates with third states, including Iceland, Norway, Turkey and EU accession states. The organisation has been used extensively in the support of EU and also UN-led military operations and collaborates closely with the EDA Intelligence Project Working Team in order to enhance the EU's Intelligence, Surveillance, Targeting and Reconnaissance (ISTAR) functions.[48]

Finally, the December 2004 European Council also established the Civilian Headline Goal (CHG) 2008 that built upon the existing commitments and capabilities of the EU in civilian crisis-management by developing rapid response capabilities. These capabilities include Civilian Response Teams (CRT) and more rapidly deployable police teams, including Integrated Police Teams (IPT) and Formed Police Units (FPU).[49] In the context of the rapidly expanding role of the EU in civilian crisis-management (into new areas such as security sector reform) and the increasingly urgent requirements for new structures and capabilities,[50] CHG 2008 was relaunched as CHG 2010 at the November 2007 Capabilities Improvement Conference. Consequently, CHG 2010 outlined several new priority areas for strengthening the EU's crisis-management capabilities: improving the quality of civilian capabilities; enhancing the availability of civilian personnel; developing instruments[51] and achieving synergies with the military aspects of ESDP, third pillar actors, non-EU states, other international organisations and actors from civil society. In short, capability investment programmes under the auspices of the EU have not only bolstered the civilian dimension, but have also begun to foster interoperability in C4ISR and put in place the foundations to equip the Battlegroups with the capabilities necessary to undertake 'robust' crisis-management operations.

Table 2.2 Major 'Multiple Speed' Capability Initiatives within the EDA

State	Software Defined Radio	21st Century Soldier Systems	JIP-FP	JIP-IECT	MIRACLE	Code of Conduct on Defence Procurement
Austria		X	X		X	X
Belgium			X		X	X
Bulgaria						X
Cyprus			X	X		X
Czech Republic			X		X	X
Estonia			X			X
Finland	X	X	X		X	X
France	X		X	X	X	X
Germany		X	X	X	X	X
Greece			X	X	X	X
Hungary			X	X	X	X
Iceland						
Ireland		X			X	
Italy	X	X	X	X	X	X
Latvia						X
Lithuania						X
Luxembourg					X	X
Malta						X
Netherlands			X		X	X
Norway			X	X	X	
Poland	X		X	X	X	X
Portugal		X	X		X	X
Romania						
Slovakia			X	X		X
Slovenia			X	X		X
Spain	X		X	X	X	X
Sweden	X	X	X		X	X
Turkey					X	
UK					X	X

NATO capability procurement initiatives: Augmenting C4ISR capabilities and interoperability

Recent developments within NATO, whilst tied into US policy and more influenced by US force transformation, are nevertheless increasingly centred on improving Europe's capacity to undertake full-spectrum operations by strengthening modularity, flexibility, jointness, EBAO and NEC (see Table 2.3). Although NATO does not yet enjoy a common C2 (command and control) capability, the Alliance instigated several important programmes during the 1990s which put in place the building blocks for the development of an NEC and are beginning to come to fruition.

Firstly, the Allied Command Europe Automated Command and Control Information System (ACCIS) that will underpin a future bi-Strategic Command automated information system by facilitating a common operational picture (Adams and Ben-Ari, 2006: 87). This process has been supported by the 'open system' December 2000 NATO C3 (Command, Control and Communications) NATO Technical Architecture Initiative (NC3TA) that outlines the main short-term technical requirements to enhance the interoperability of NATO's C2 systems. Secondly, the Air Command and Control System (ACCS), initiated in 1999 following the deficiencies in C2 demonstrated by the Kosovo conflict that will be integrated into national militaries in 2008 (ACCS, 2008). Thirdly, a NATO General Purpose Communications System (NGCS): a static network that will permit the communication of all data and voice information and will come online after 2010. Finally, the Multifunctional Information Distribution System (MIDS), a 'multiple speed' initiative, that was initiated in 1991 by the US and France (as programme leaders), supported by Germany, Italy and Spain and permits greater cross-platform telecommunications interoperability.

NATO also took strides to develop ISR (Intelligence, Surveillance and Reconnaissance) capabilities in the late 1990s. Since 1 July 1996, the coordination of NATO's C4ISR initiatives has been facilitated by the NATO Consultation, Command and Control Agency (NC3A) (formed by the merger of the SHAPE Technical Centre and NATO Communications and Information Systems Agency). The NC3A is tasked with coordinating interoperability between NATO partners in the area of C4ISR and suppport common-funded acquisition programmes in the area of C4ISR and collaborates closely with the EUMS and EDA (Flournoy and Smith, 2005: 65–6).[52] One particularly notable project under the auspices of the NATO C3 Agency is the Coalition Aerial Surveillance and Reconnaissance (CAESAR) programme that was launched in 2000 and is funded by the US (but conducted by NATO as a whole). CAESAR tests national and NATO air and space based C4ISR systems with the aim of creating a single interoperable system (Adams and Ben-Ari, 2006: 91).

National development of interoperable C4ISR technology and its application in crisis-management operations has also been facilitated by the establishment in 1998 of the Paris-based NATO Research and Technology Organisation (RTO) that was initiated as a result of the merger of the Advisory Groups for Aerospace Research and Development and Defence Research Groups.[53] The RTO has provided an important forum for the exchange of technical information and increased cooperation between NATO members in the development and operationalisation of defence technologies. The work of the organisation is structured through six technical panels: Applied Vehicle Technology, Human Factors and Medicine, Information Systems Technology, System Analysis and Studies, Systems Concepts and Integration and Sensors and Electronics Technology, in addition to the NATO Modeling and Simulation Group.[54] These subdivisions operate under the supervision of the RTO's Research and Technology Board (RTB) that consists of up to three science and technology representatives from each NATO member. The RTB answers to the North Atlantic Council through the Conference of National Armaments

Directors (CNAD) and Military Committee (MC).[55] In the ten years since the creation of the RTO its technical panels have organised over 700 task groups, lecture series and symposia (each led by different constellations of NATO member states) on a wide range of C4ISR capability issues and on the role of technology in the conduct of low, medium and high-intensity crisis-management operations.[56]

The November 2002 Prague Summit, however, formed a landmark in the development of the NEC capacity of European NATO members. The ability of European states to furnish the NRF with strategic lift, logistical and C4ISR capabilities emerged as critical for the viability of the initiative. The Prague Summit streamlined NATO command structures by creating two strategic commands: one operational; one functional, in order to facilitate crisis-management operations and the procurement of capabilities for such missions.[57] The Strategic Command for Operations based in Belgium is supported by two Joint Force Commands able to establish a land-based Combined Joint Task Force Headquarters (CJTF) in addition to Standing Joint Headquarters and a sea-based CJTF. The Prague Summit also established a strategic command for transformation (the Allied Transformation Center, ACT) based in the US, tasked with improving training, capabilities and testing doctrine and concepts in EBAO and NEC. Subordinate structures are distributed across Europe: a Joint Warfare Centre in Norway to support the ACT in the development of new technologies, modeling and simulation; the Joint Training Centre in Poland and the Joint Analysis and Lessons Learned Centre in Portugal. These Centres have been augmented by a further set of national and multinationally funded Centres of Excellence (CoE) dispersed across NATO's European member states. Of particular importance is the C2 Centre for Excellence based in the Netherlands that assists member states with developing interoperable C2 capabilities and doctrine (and also works closely with the European Defence Agency and EU Battlegroups).[58]

The core function of the Strategic Command for Transformation is to lead-up the Prague Capabilities Commitment (PCC) that built upon the April 1999 DCI[59] by outlining a set of specific capability commitments and timetables which would support the acquisition of capabilities necessary to deploy the NRF.[60] The main projects which have emerged from the PCC are Strategic Air and Sea-Lift Capabilities, Alliance Ground Surveillance (AGS), and Theater Missile Defence.[61] Improvements in airlift have taken the form of two initiatives following agreement upon specific responsibilities at the June 2004 Istanbul Summit. Firstly, the Strategic Airlift Interim Solution (SALIS), involving the chartering of Antonov An-124-100 transport aircraft by 16 countries, led by Germany. Secondly, 13 NATO countries, plus partner countries of Finland and Sweden finalised contract negotiations in June 2007 on the acquisition of three Boeing C-17 transport aircraft to develop NATO's Strategic Airlift Capability (SAC), the first of which will be delivered in Spring

2009, the final two entered into operation in mid-2009. Sea-lift capabilities are being developed by a sea-lift consortium led by Norway that is funding the chartering of up to ten 'roll on roll off' ships to permit the deployment of forces and equipment by sea.

These improvements in airlift build upon developments during the 1990s such as the NH-90 Naval (designed for anti-submarine and anti-surface warfare) and particularly, the NH-90 Tactical (Transport) Helicopters, which entered production on 8 June 2000, following studies completed by the NATO Industrial Advisory Group SG14. The project is being conducted through NHI Industries, a company established on 1 September 1992 by four partner countries (France (95), Germany (152), Italy (117) and the Netherlands (20)). Orders have also been placed by Portugal (ten) on 21 June 2001; Sweden (25), Finland (20) and Norway (24) in 2001, Greece (34) on 29 August 2003, Spain (45) on 28 December 2006 and Belgium (ten) on June 20, 2007.

The core NATO programme in the area of ISR is Allied Ground Surveillance (AGS) that involves the development of both manned (based on the Airbus A321 airliner which will carry the Trans-Atlantic Cooperative Radar (TCAR)) and unmanned radar platforms (based on the Global Hawk high altitude long endurance UAV), which are being led by the Transatlantic Industrial Partnership for Surveillance (TIPS) consortium (Flournoy and Smith, 2005: 33).[62] The AGS is designed to grant the NRF with a stand-off capability, in place of the Joint Surveillance and Target Attack Radar System (JSTAR) of the US Air Force that is currently used in support of the NRF.[63] The system entered the design and development phase in 2007, with completion scheduled for 2009, the cost shared by all NATO nations apart from the UK, that is proceeding with the Airborne Standoff Radar (ASTOR) system (Flournoy and Smith, 2005: 90).[64]

The updating of NATO's ISR capabilities through AGS has been supplemented by the Multi-Sensor Aerospace-Ground Joint ISR Interoperability Programme (MAJIIC), a five year technology demonstrator.[65] The project, launched in April 2005, is attempting to develop interoperable ISR systems through a common military website and will last until March 2009. MAJIIC is led by the US and also includes Canada, France, Germany, Italy, the Netherlands, Norway, Spain and the UK as partner nations. The current NATO AWACS fleet (Airborne Warning and Control System) that is comprised of 17 aircraft, provided by Britain, France and the US, is also being updated as part of AGS. By 2008 the AWACS will be capable of tracking more targets, receiving mission orders via satellite and will be interoperable with a broader array of weapon platforms (Adams and Ben-Ari, 2006: 91).

The PCC also included a commitment to examining the feasibility of the development of a Missile Defence system for NATO territory, in addition to a Theatre Missile Defence System (TMD) with a range of 3,000 km that will link with ACCIS to protect NATO troops on out of area deployments and augment the Alliance's C2 capabilities.[66] TMD has taken the form of the

Active Layered Theatre Ballistic Defence System (ALTBMD); a 'system of systems' including battle management command and control, early warning radar and sensors, approved by the North Atlantic Council in 2005. In September 2006 an international consortium,[67] was selected to develop a test-bed for TMD that is expected to attain initial operational capability by 2010. Finally, Britain, France and Italy are also leading improvements to the Alliance's Satellite Communications Capabilities through the 'Satcom Post-2000 Programme' that began in May 2004 and was operable from January 2005. The system will replace the NATO IV communication satellites by granting NATO access to the French Syracuse, Italian SICRAL and British Skynet satellite communications systems (SATCOM, 2008).

ACT has also provided a forum for the NATO NEC Project (NMEC), led by nine NATO nations (Canada, France, Germany, Italy, the Netherlands, Norway, Spain, the UK and US), that was launched in November 2003 and completed in 2005. The study examined the potential ways in which NEC would be utilised in the NRF and the implications for future NATO procurement programmes. NMEC has resulted in a 'roadmap' for the creation of NEC for all member nations that has been adopted by ACT as the basis for future capability development requirements (from which NEC initiatives such as MAJIIC – that plays a critical role in helping to develop common standards in areas such as the storage, processing and archiving of imaging – have derived) (MAJIIC, 2008). Following operations in Afghanistan, where the NATO Mission Secret (MS) Network (a wide-area network used to pass information between Alliance partners in theatre) has been highly successful, such standardisation initiatives hold the promise for significant strides in C4ISR interoperability between NATO partners. Hence, for the UK, for example, carrying the success of NATO STANAGS (Standardisation Agreements for Procedures and Systems and Equipment Components) into the area of IT, Network Systems and ISTAR systems forms a much more attractive focus of energy and resources than cross-national procurement projects, which have difficulty achieving economies of scale.[68]

In summary, European NATO members have made important strides to enhance capabilities and interoperability both with the US and each other in C4ISR, notably following the 2002 Prague Summit. This process has been led by the US in tandem with a group of core European NATO nations (France, Germany, Italy, the Netherlands, Norway, Spain and the UK), which have assumed the responsibility to push ahead with the development of military capabilities to be put at the service of the Alliance as a whole (Adams and Ben-Ari, 2006: 105).

Defence procurement initiatives outside NATO and EU frameworks: A la carte, multiple speed and variable geometry cooperation

Initiatives within NATO and ESDP build upon the achievements of a range of subregional 'a la carte' post-Cold War capability procurement programmes.

Table 2.3 Major Post-Cold War Capability Initiatives within NATO

State	ACCIS	ACCS	NGCS	MIDS	CAESAR	CoE	SALIS	SAC	Sea lift	NH 90	AGS	MAJIIC	ALT BMD	Satcom	NM EC	RTO
Austria	X	X				X				X	X					
Belgium	X	X	X								X		X			X
Bulgaria			X					X					X			X
Cyprus																
Canada	X	X	X			X	X	X	X		X	X	X		X	X
Czech Republic	X	X	X				X				X		X			X
Denmark	X	X	X				X		X		X		X			X
Estonia	X	X				X		X								
Finland						X		X		X						
France	X	X	X	X		X(3)	X			X	X	X	X	X	X	X
Germany	X	X	X	X			X			X	X	X	X		X	X
Greece	X	X	X							X	X		X			X
Hungary	X	X	X			X	X	X	X		X		X			
Iceland	X	X									X		X			
Ireland	X	X							X							
Italy	X	X	X	X				X	X	X	X	X	X	X	X	X
Latvia	X	X	X					X			X		X			X
Lithuania	X	X	X					X			X		X			X
Luxembourg	X	X	X				X				X		X			
Malta	X	X	X			X(2)					X		X			
Netherlands	X	X	X			X	X	X	X	X	X	X	X		X	X
Norway	X	X	X				X	X	X	X	X	X	X		X	X
Poland	X	X	X				X	X	X	X	X		X			X
Portugal	X	X	X			X	X	X			X		X			X
Romania	X	X	X			X	X				X		X			X
Slovakia	X	X	X			X	X				X		X			X
Slovenia	X	X	X	X		X	X	X		X	X	X	X			X
Spain	X	X	X						X	X					X	
Sweden							X				X					
Switzerland																
Turkey	X	X	X			X					X	X	X	X	X	X
UK	X	X	X			X	X		X		X	X	X		X	X
US	X	X	X		X			X			X		X			X

These initiatives have developed military hardware improving the capacity of the West European Great Powers to undertake joint high-intensity expeditionary warfare. Of particular note are the Eurofighter, nEUROn and PzH 2000 projects, in addition to the Organisation for Joint Armament Cooperation (OCCAR) and its associated projects (see Table 2.3).

The Eurofighter Typhoon, a project whose roots lie in the Cold War (the 1979 Anglo-German European Collaborative Fighter Project), involves the development (contract signed on 30 January 1998) of an Air to Surface, multi-role combat aircraft, capable not only of air combat but also air-ground support, by Austria (15 aircraft) Britain (232), Germany (180), Italy (121), and Spain (80).[69] Eurofighters will be delivered between 2003 and 2012, through an industrial consortium including BAE systems, Alenia Aeronautica, EADS Deutschland and EADS CASA. The Eurofighter's NEC and EBAO capabilities have been enhanced through the development of the Meteor radar-guided air-to-air Missile (contract signed in December 2002; production complete by 2010) by the MBDA group on behalf of Britain, France, Germany, Italy, Spain and Sweden.[70] The ground attack capability of the Eurofighter has also been boosted through Phase 1 and Phase 2 enhancements, which include the addition of automated laser-guided weaponry.

The PzH 2000 Armoured Howitzer, produced by Krauss-Maffei Wegmann has been under development since the early 1990s and has resulted in the delivery of 185 Howitzers to Germany; 70 to Italy; 57 to the Netherlands and 24 to Greece in 1998. The tactical mobility of the PzH 2000 makes it suitable for deployment in high-intensity expeditionary crisis-management operations, illustrated by its deployment by the Dutch in support of NATO's ISAF mission. However, the Howitzer's weight has created problems of strategic mobility, reflecting its original role as a weapon designed for territorial defence of the German plain.[71]

Finally, the 'nEUROn' UCAV is a demonstrator project designed to ensure the maintenance and development of the skills and knowledge in strategic technologies, strengthening European NEC. Originally launched as an autonomous project by France in 1999, since 2005, the project has involved the delegation of 50 per cent of work to other European partners. These include Alenia (Italy); Saab (Sweden), Hellenic Aerospace Industry (Greece); EADS CASA (Spain) and UAG (Switzerland).

OCCAR was established on 12 November 1996 to manage collaborative armaments programmes by France, Germany, Italy and the UK (joined by Belgium in 2003 and Spain in 2005). The organisation attained legal identity in September 1998 and has provided an important framework permitting the cross-national coordination of procurement, thereby helping to overcome the relative fragmentation of Europe's defence-industrial base. Membership is open to other European NATO/EU member states, which also have the option of participating in a procurement programme under a cooperative agreement (as is the case with the Netherlands, Luxembourg and Turkey). OCCAR has coordinated cooperation for several joint European ventures: FSAF; A-400 M; Tiger; Boxer; COBRA and FREMM.[72] Whilst a number of these ventures are Cold War legacy systems and are not focused specifically on C4ISR capabilities, several OCCAR-managed programmes nevertheless augment the capacity of European states to undertake crisis-management operations within NATO/ESDP frameworks.[73]

The FSAF (Future Surface-to-Air Anti-Missile Family), launched on 26 October 1998 has resulted in the development by France and Italy of common surface-to-air ground and naval-based anti-missile systems. The project has been procured under the Anglo-Franco-Italian Eurosam (ES) venture, established by Aerospatiale, Alenia and Thompson CSF in June 1989. Eurosam is also the focal point for the Principle Anti-Air Missile System (PAAMS), a joint British, French and Italian procurement programme that began in August 1999, developed in conjunction with UKAMS, a subsidiary of MDBA. The A-400 military transport aircraft, of critical importance to the development of European strategic lift capability is a joint procurement venture through Airbus, involving Belgium (seven), Britain (25), France (50), Germany (60), Luxembourg (one), Spain (27) and Turkey (ten). The Boxer, a multirole armoured utility vehicle, is also managed by OCCAR and produced by Germany's ARTEC consortium and the Netherlands Stork PWV. It will result, by 2009, in the delivery of 272 vehicles to Germany and 200 to the Netherlands, which will be compatible with the A-400 M, boosting the capacity of these nations to undertake crisis-management missions of varying intensity.

The merger of Aerospatiale-Matra (France) and Daimler-Chrysler Aerospace (Germany) in 1992 led to the development of Eurocopter that in 2000 became a subsidiary of EADS. Eurocopter has produced the OCCAR-managed Tiger multirole attack helicopter that began production in March 2003 and will be capable of providing air-ground combat support. This Franco-German venture involves the production of 80 helicopters each for the two lead nations, but has also attracted an order of 24 Helicopters from Spain.[74] A further project under the auspices of OCCAR, COBRA (Counter Battery Radar), involves a collaborative long-range, high-mobility battle-field radar system procured by Britain (seven), France (ten) and Germany (12), that was delivered in 2005. Produced by a consortium of EADS, Thales and Lockheed Martin (Euro-Art), COBRA will enhance the NEC capabilities of these three states in high-intensity crisis-management operations, in addition to military operations against peer-competitors. The final project routed through OCCAR is the Franco-Italian FREMM multirole frigate, which by 2010 will lead to the delivery of 27 anti-submarine warfare and land-attack general purpose ships (France, ten; Italy, 17).[75]

The development of OCCAR has been supplemented by the signature of a letter of intent (LOI) in 1998 by the UK, France, Germany, Sweden, Italy and Spain (Europe's main arms producing nations) 'on measures to facilitate the restructuring of the European defence industry', aimed at developing a more integrated European defence market. This 'variable geometry' initiative was followed by a 2001 Framework Agreement between the LOI nations aimed at developing compatibility in defence supply, export control, security of information, military research and technology, technical information, military R&D, technical information and military requirements (Adams and Ben-Ari, 2006: 114).

Franco-German cooperation in armaments procurement has been underpinned by the work of the Franco-German Research Institute (ISL) that was established on 22 June 1959 and employs around 230 French and German scientists and engineers (Krotz, 2007: 399). In recent years the Institute has focused on a range of research projects that will develop the C4ISR capacities of both nations. Core research areas include perforation, protection and detonics; aeromechanics and acoustics; optronics, lasers and sensors; launchers and pulse power and modeling and systems analysis. These main research groups also work on a set of multidisciplinary research projects which are developing demonstrators in the fields of medium-calibre weapons; guided supersonic projectiles; nanomaterials and protection against thermobaric (enhanced blast) effects.[76]

French leadership has also been evident in the development of Europe's space-based assets outside the framework of the EU and NATO. These comprise three main 'a la carte' initiatives:[77] the SAR-Lupe and Pleiades initiatives, and the 'Common Operational Requirements'. The Pleiades Programme is a civilian and military Optical and Radar Federated Earth Observation Satellite (ORFEO) system that was initiated on 29 January 2001 by France and Italy (Flournoy and Smith, 2005: 91). Pleiades led to the launch of radar satellites in 2005 and high-resolution optical satellites in 2007 which have a global imaging capability and will operate jointly with the French Helios 2 optical reconnaissance satellite and Italian COSMO-Skymed satellite system. In 2005, Austria, Belgium, Spain and Sweden also joined the initiative by signing cooperation agreements with France and Italy.[78] The SAR Lupe is a German reconnaissance satellite project, launched in 2000 and operational from 2008, that has involved the development of five satellites and one ground segment that will provide worldwide, all weather information.[79] However, following a cooperation Treaty of July 2002, SAR Lupe will operate jointly with the French Helios 2 system, Italian COSMO-Skymed and Pleiades satellites (Flournoy and Smith, 2005: 91). The progress made by these two initiatives in the pooling of space assets is being built upon through the French-led Common Operational Requirements that is developing a group of data-providers and users responsible for gathering and disseminating satellite imaging (France, Germany, Italy, Spain, Belgium and Greece) (Adams and Ben-Ari, 2006: 129). Together, these multinational arrangements form significant steps towards developing the space technology necessary to conduct networked operations.

Table 2.4 Major Bi-Pluri-lateral Capability Procurement Initiatives Outside EU/NATO Frameworks

State	Eurofighter	nEUROn	PzH 2000	OCCAR	FSAF	A-400 M	Tiger	Boxer	COBRA	FREMM	LOI	Galileo	Pleiades
Austria	X											X	X
Belgium				X		X						X	X
Bulgaria													
Cyprus													
Canada												X	
Czech Republic												X	
Denmark												X	
Estonia												X	
Finland												X	
France		X		X	X	X	X		X	X	X	X	X
Germany	X	X	X	X		X	X	X			X	X	
Greece			X									X	
Hungary												X	
Iceland													
Ireland													
Italy	X	X	X	X	X	X			X	X	X	X	X
Latvia													
Lithuania													
Luxembourg				1		X						X	
Malta													
Netherlands			X	1				X				X	
Norway												X	
Poland												X	
Portugal												X	
Romania												X	
Slovakia													
Slovenia													
Spain	X	X		X		X	X				X	X	X
Sweden		X									X	X	X
Switzerland		X											
Turkey				1		X			X				
UK	X				2	X						X	
US												X	

Key
1 = Participation under cooperative agreement
2 = The UK is participating in the Principle Anti-Air Missile System (PAMMS).

'A la carte' force generation initiatives outside NATO/EU frameworks

A number of predominantly French-led, subregional 'a la carte' multinational initiatives have also arisen during the 1990s aimed at developing high-readiness joint forces capable of participation in both NATO and ESDP missions, providing a cost-effective means to facilitate troop contributions by pooling capabilities (see Table 2.5).[80] These include the Franco-German Brigade – a Franco-German Army Corps, established in 1987, that was renamed EUROCORPS in 1992, reflecting its nature as 'a la carte' cooperation – open to all European NATO members and EU states. EUROCORPS was subsequently joined by Belgium in June 1993, Spain in July 1994 and Luxembourg in May 1996 and forms both a NRF and a contributor to an EU Battlegroup.[81]

The EUROFORCES were established in 1995 in order to facilitate troop contributions to the Petersburg tasks, but have since been brought under the auspices of ESDP. They are composed of two components: EURO-MARFOR, a European naval force of French, Spanish, Italian and Portuguese ships, established in 1995 and EUROFOR (European Operational Rapid Force), a multinational force comprising French, Spanish, Italian and Portuguese troops, capable of deploying up to a Light Division in support of Battlegroup operations. The same nations have also created the European Gendarmerie Force (EGF) in September 2004, capable of robust policing missions under military command (the deployment of up to 800 police within 30 days). The EGF has not only bolstered the EU's Civilian Crisis-Management functions, but has also contributed to NATO operations in the former Yugoslavia. The German-Netherlands Corps, based at Münster, was initiated in 1993 and activated on 30 August 1995. Since 2004 the Corps has acted as a NATO Response Force Headquarters,[82] capable of leading a NATO operation within 30 days and is equipped with advanced C4ISR capabilities including the German HEROS C2 system, Dutch TITAAN communications infrastructure, as well as UAVs (Adams and Ben-Ari, 2006: 53).

The European Amphibious Initiative (EAI) was established on 5 December 2000 by France, the Netherlands, Italy, Spain and the UK (but is also open to participation by other European NATO members and EU states).[83] The initiative is aimed at enhancing the interoperability of forces under both NRF and Battlegroup missions, whilst the European Air Group, launched on 27 June 1996 serves a similar function: the enhancement of interoperability between participating EU/NATO airforces. Initially established as the Franco-British European Air Group in November 1994, its membership has expanded to include Belgium, Denmark, Germany, Italy, Spain and the Netherlands between 1997 and 2006.[84]

The Sealift Coordination Centre (SCC) was initiated in June 2001 by nations working in NATO's High Level Steering Group's Working Group on Strategic Sealift (Belgium, Denmark, Germany, the Netherlands, Norway and the UK).[85] The SCC has formed a framework for the provision of strategic sea-lift assets (roll on/roll off ships) to NATO, by the UK, Denmark and Norway, but also the coordination of the chartering of private/military ships to the EU,[86] UN or ad hoc coalitions of NATO/EU states.[87] The European Airlift Centre (EAC) was a Franco-German initiative of 2001 (originally named the European Air Coordination Cell), designed to coordinate the military airlift of European members states and create a common European air fleet. It has since expanded to include both NATO and EU member states, including Belgium, Spain, Italy, the Netherlands, Norway and the UK.[88] The work of the SCC and EAC were brought under one roof on 1 July 2007 with the creation of the 'a la carte'[89] Movement Coordination Centre Europe (MCCE) that provides support to EU and NATO operations. The membership of the organisation has now expanded to include Canada, Estonia, Finland, Hungary, Latvia, Luxembourg, Slovenia, Spain, Sweden and Turkey.[90]

The Multinational Interoperability Council (MIC) is an example of 'multiple speed'[91] European cooperation. Formed by Australia, Canada, France, Germany, the UK and US in 1996 (joined by Italy in 2005), the MIC provides a mechanism with which to deal with the main issues that impact upon interoperability between these nations: doctrine, operational planning and NEC, with a particular emphasis on the development of interoperable C4ISR capabilities (Adams and Ben-Ari, 2006: 100).[92] The organisation acts as an important forum in which the European Great Powers and the other 'vanguard' European NATO members, most capable of contributing to coalition operations, can boost their interoperability with the US and non-NATO states. The MIC has established working groups on key C4ISR areas and also conducts of 'Multinational Experiments', including the annual 'Combined Endeavour' exercises. Since 1995 these exercises have tested the C4 interoperability, not only of MIC members, but also of other NATO, PfP and non-aligned nations, as well as multinational organisations. The May 2008 exercise included 40 partner nations, in addition to NATO and the South Eastern Europe Brigade.[93]

The 'multiple speed'[94] Multilateral Interoperability Programme (MIP), was established in April 1998 by Canada, France, Germany, Italy, the UK and the US, to deal with interoperability issue relating to C2IS (command and control information systems) across the full spectrum of expeditionary operations (MIP, 2008). The MIP was broadened in November 2003 to 18 further states (the Netherlands, Norway, Spain, Turkey as full members; Australia, Austria, Belgium, Bulgaria, the Czech Republic, Finland, Greece, Hungary, Lithuania, Poland, Romania, Slovenia and Sweden as observer members) who are developing technical interoperability solutions permitting data sharing. The Command and Control Information Exchange Data Model (C2IEDM), developed through MIP has become the standard model adopted by NATO.

It is also possible to identify three institutions of 'variable geometry' on the subregional level: NORDCAPS (Nordic Coordinated Arrangement for Military Peace Support), Baltic Defence Cooperation and the South Eastern

Europe Brigade. NORDCAPS was established in 1997 by Denmark, Finland, Norway and Sweden and joined by Iceland in 2003.[95] It forms a mechanism for enhanced cooperation between Nordic nations in the planning and conduct of crisis-management missions. Baltic Defence Cooperation (BDC) between Estonia, Latvia and Lithuania, is composed of four core projects: BALTBAT (a Baltic Battalion, established 1994); BALTRON (Baltic Naval Squadron, established 1997); Baltic Air Surveillance Network (BALTNET, established 1996) and BALTDEFCOL (Baltic Defence College, established 1998).[96] These arrangements are primarily designed to enhance the ability of the three Baltic states to contribute to NATO-led military operations by developing the C2 capabilities, military training and capacity necessary to generate joint, flexible and interoperable expeditionary crisis-management forces. Finally, the Multinational Peace Force South Eastern Europe (MPFSEE) or South Eastern Europe Brigade was initiated on 31 August 1999, including both non-EU and Partnership for Peace nations: Albania, Bulgaria, Greece, Italy, Macedonia, Romania and Turkey (Bourantonis and Tsakonas, 2003: 75–81). Although initially established as a force designed for deploy-ment within the Balkans under the auspices of NATO, the EU, OSCE or UN, MPFSEE has more recently (February–August 2006) contributed to NATO's ISAF mission.

Summary: A selective and delayed emulation of the revolution in military affairs

Britain, France and Germany have transformed the core objectives of defence policy from territorial and alliance defence to a new form of forward defence that meets threats of international security at source through expeditionary crisis-management operations. The West European Great Powers have undertaken convergence around the US model of joint, expeditionary power projection. Both Britain and France have successfully enacted reforms to their policy instruments, notably through reforms to their command structures and the creation of 'Joint Reaction Forces', structured according to the principle of modularity, permitting enhanced jointness between the three main services. This has been accompanied by the development of flexible and mobile medium-weight infantry forces. Such changes mirror the US integration of naval, air and land power, allowing the global projection of force (as part of multinational coalitions), making these two states cases of 'third-order change' (Boot, 2003: 43; Edmunds, 2006: 1068; King, 2005a).

Capability investment evidences partial convergence with the US-led Revolution in Military Affairs (Lungu, 2004a; Sperling, 2004: 453–9). As Sperling (2004: 457) highlights: 'French and British [military capability] concerns complement rather than compete with one another, despite their different levels of trust and preference for autonomy *vis-à-vis* the US'. Britain, France and Germany have undertaken emulation of the concepts of NCW and EBO, in the form of NEC and EBAO permitting continued interoperability with the

Table 2.5 Major 'Variable Geometry' and 'A La Carte Force' Generation Initiatives Outside EU/NATO Frameworks

State	Battlegroup Initiative	Eurocorps	Euroforces	EGF	EAI	MMCE	MIC	MIP	BDC	NORDCAPS
Austria	X	X						1		
Belgium	X	X			X	X		1		
Bulgaria	X							1		
Cyprus	X									
Canada						X	X	1		
Czech Republic	X							1		
Denmark		X			X					X
Estonia	X					X			X	
Finland	X					X		1		X
France	X	X	X	X	X	X	X	X		
Germany	X	X				X	X	X		
Greece	X	X						1		
Hungary	X					X				
Iceland										X
Ireland	X									
Italy	X	X	X	X	X	X		X		
Latvia	X					X			X	
Lithuania	X								X	
Luxembourg	X	X				X		X		
Malta										
Netherlands	X				X	X		X		
Norway	X	X				X		X		X
Poland	X	X						1		X

Table 2.5 Major 'Variable Geometry' and 'A La Carte Force' Generation Initiatives Outside EU/NATO Frameworks
– continued

State	Battlegroup Initiative	Eurocorps	Euroforces	EGF	EAI	MMCE	MIC	MIP	BDC	NORDCAPS
Portugal	X		X	X						
Romania	X							1		
Slovakia	X									
Slovenia	X							1		
Spain	X	X	X	X	X	X		X		
Sweden	X					X		1		
Switzerland										X
Turkey	X	X				X		X		
UK	X	X			X	X	X	X		
US	X						X	X		

Key
1 = Observer Status

US and the capacity to undertake autonomous operations with Europe's geostrategic neighbourhood. European reforms have, however, involved a stronger focus on the development of doctrine and capabilities permitting low-medium intensity peacekeeping and post-conflict reconstruction operations. This is part of the development by Britain, France and to a lesser extent, Germany, of 'balanced'[97] militaries, capable not only of participation in conventional major combat operations,[98] but also the demands of COIN/stabilisation, involving three-block warfare conducted 'amongst the people', where the intensity of conflict can vary quickly (Edmunds, 2006: 1070; Forster, 2006: 50; Sperling, 2004: 457–8).[99]

West European reforms have been predicated upon the limitations of technology to control the process of 'escalation' and 'transform' the nature of conflict. Elements of the RMA have been adopted with the potential to supplement the capacity of the major European powers to deliver not only high-intensity operational effects, but also non-kinetic effects at the lower end of the conflict spectrum. There has also been a stronger focus upon the ability to put 'boots on the ground' and on ensuring the development or sharpening of the cultural skills necessary to conduct effective COIN and stabilisation operations. Furthermore, the British, French and German take on networking is characterised by an emphasis on the importance of training and human factors in realising the benefits of technology. The West European Great Powers have broadly shunned the highly-centralised 'long-screwdriver' systems of systems approach that has been a hallmark of US networking and command structures. Instead, the RMA is viewed as a means with which to enhance the advantages of flexibility, speed and surprise than can be delivered through 'mission command' and the 'manoeuvrist approach'.

Hence the concept of EBAO that has underpinned European reform is focused on achieving tactical and operational effects and is more circumspect about the strategic advantage that can be delivered by the application by technology.[100] Like US EBO, EBAO involves a redefinition of the operational objectives of military action from tangible targets to part of a broader process of delivering a particular operational end state (Farrell, 2008). However, in contrast to US EBO that is focused on the synergising national power to deliver of largely kinetic, strategic effects against peer or near-peer competitors, British, French and German EBAO have been firmly framed within a 'Comprehensive Approach'. Hence European EBAO seeks to integrate all instruments of national power – kinetic and non-kinetic – to the planning and conduct of crisis-management operations which are conducted 'amongst the people' and can vary in intensity at short-notice across the conflict spectrum. Such 'three block warfare' operations involve asymmetrical conflict against mobile and disparate enemies and require the achievement, not only of traditional military operational outcomes like coercion and destruction, but also prevention, stabilisation and containment (Dorman, 2006; Farrell, 2008: 793; Rynning, 2008).

Yet despite the development of a Joint Reaction Force and a focus on NEC and EBAO since 2003, Germany remains something of an outlier. German reforms have proposed only successive alterations to the 'settings' of the policy instrument. Third-order change is hindered by the retention of conscription and the extent to which Germany lags behind Britain and France in the development of concepts and doctrine on EBAO and COIN and in investment in high-technology weapons systems in support of NetOpFü (Sperling, 2004: 457; Longhurst, 2003; Lungu, 2004b; Noetzel and Schreer, 2008, 2009). Nevertheless, Germany has since 2003 made important strides in the area of C4ISR and has begun to invest in the capabilities and doctrine which form important steps towards the capacity to undertake networked expeditionary crisis-management operations of varying intensity.

Although the decline of EBO in the US during the last two years is likely to impact upon the centrality of EBAO as a key organising concept of defence reform, this does not spell the end for effects-based thinking. Whilst it is a little early to make firm conclusions about the survivability of EBAO, as Chapter 1 has demonstrated, European EBAO already avoids many of the problems associated with EBO, including the reliance of EBO on an unattainable level of knowledge and predictability, the centralisation of command and control, rigidity and over-complex terminology (Mattis, 2008: 106). Recent changes in the US have reinforced many of the long-drawn conclusions within European military establishments about the utility of EBO following their post-Cold War operational experiences of crisis-management operations of varying intensity. Driven by a scepticism of the capacity of technology to change the nature of warfare, the European approach to EBAO has been embedded within a 'comprehensive approach' that emphasises the centrality of cooperation with civilian actors in the planning and conduct of military operations and the importance of knowledge of the history and culture of the operating environment. European EBAO has also been developed with sensitivity to the principle of 'mission command' and the 'manoeuvrist approach'. These principles and 'effects-based thinking' that eschews the many pitfalls of EBO but allows military and civilian actors to cooperate in working towards particular end-states remain highly relevant to the contemporary operational environment (see Chapters 4–6). Therefore, as Mattis (2008: 106) notes, the implications of the decline of EBO are more muted for the European Great Powers.

Whilst a great deal of national duplication continues to exist in armaments procurement, European defence and security cooperation through NATO, ESDP and other bi-pluri-lateral initiatives increasingly serves a common function: the generation of network-enabled expeditionary crisis-management forces capable of operating alongside both the US and other European nations in operations across the conflict spectrum (Dunn, 2001: 153; Howorth, 2007: 44–5; Lisbonne-de Vergeron, 2008: 32; Sperling, 2004: 458; Ulriksen,

Table 2.6 Patterns of Convergence and Divergence in Post-Cold War British, French and German Military Reforms

	Objectives	Instruments	Institutional Forums	Temporality
Britain	From Cold War role of territorial and alliance defence to global low-high intensity expeditionary crisis-management operations, as part of multinational coalitions.	Professional Force (from 1962). Reduction from Cold War Force of 370,000 (1990) to 226,000 troops. Creation of 'Joint Reaction Force' and more flexible planning and command capabilities in 1996/97. Capability procurement focused C4ISR on requirements of NEC and EBAO. Initial networked capability in place in 2007.	Continuity in prioritisation of NATO; though incremental shift towards embedding within ESDP following Anglo-French October 1998 Saint Malo Accord. Leadership role in 'bottom-up' promotion of European capabilities coordination through EDA and DCI/ACT.	Temporal Location: May 1997–July 1998, incremental shift towards embedding within ESDP in October 1998. Pace: 14 months. Sequencing: Objectives, Military Structures, Institutional Forums, Capabilities.
France	From Cold War role of territorial defence to global low-high intensity expeditionary crisis-management operations, as part of multinational coalitions.	Conscript Force (1905–1996); Professional Force (from 1996). Reduction from Cold War force of 400,000 to 250,000 troops in 1996. Creation of 'Joint Reaction Force', more flexible planning and command capabilities in 1996. Emphasis upon development of autonomous technology for ESDP and C4ISR in support of NEC and EBAO. Initial networked capability attained in 2006.	From 'semi-detached' defence policy during Cold War, between NATO and national strategic autonomy to post-Cold War prioritisation of ESDP, and increasingly active role in strengthening NATO. Leadership role in bottom-up promotion of European capabilities coordination through EDA and ACT.	Temporal Location: February 1994–October 1996. Pace: 32 months. Sequencing: Institutional Forums, Objectives, Military Structures, Capabilities.

Table 2.6 Patterns of Convergence and Divergence in Post-Cold War British, French and German Military Reforms
– continued

	Objectives	Instruments	Institutional Forums	Temporality
Germany	From Cold War role of territorial and alliance defence to global low-high intensity expeditionary crisis-management operations, as part of multinational coalitions.	Conscript Force (from 1956). Reduction from 370,000 troops with 170,000 conscripts (set by the 1990 Two Plus Four Treaty), to 252,500 troops with 50,000 conscripts by 2003. 'Creation of Joint Reaction Force', joint planning and command capabilities in and initiation of NetOpFü and EBAO in 2003; lower investment in C4ISR. Initial networked capability in place 2013.	Continuity in 'bridge role' between ESDP/ NATO and in 'bifurcated' Federal Executive in form of 'Europeanised' Foreign Ministry and 'Atlanticised' Defence Ministry. Strong 'bottom-up' role in promotion of capabilities through DCI/ACT and EDA; relative laggard and reactive in 'top down' implementation of their prescriptions.	Temporal Location: May 2003 – October 2003 (reform of objectives). Pace: 6 months (reform of objectives). Sequencing: Objectives; Capabilities (changes only to the 'settings' of Military Structures and continuity in institutional forums).

2004: 469–71). The establishment of the EDA, ACT and CoEs, combined with enhanced NATO/EU cooperation, are particularly important developments in this process; though the work of these organisations is not yet formally harmonised with that of OCCAR and the LOI process (Adams and Ben-Ari, 2006: 115–16). This functional complementarity is being reinforced by ESDP and NATO's growing spatial distinctiveness in function: the emergence of ESDP as a mechanism for Europe to engage with threats emanating from its geopolitical neighbourhood and of NATO as a global actor in the field of crisis-management (Lisbonne-de Vergeron, 2008: 26).

Post-Cold War European cooperation in the sphere of defence and security has taken a distinct territorial form: its geographical scope shaped by Russian power to the East and characterised by the emergence of vanguard states within these territorial boundaries. During the mid-late 1990s and early mid-21st century a 'core' group European nations (Britain, France and Germany) have materialised, whose leadership has increased the pace and extent of cooperation. These states have pushed ahead with the development of common military capabilities through intergovernmental, non-binding institutional arrangements under the auspices of ESDP/NATO, accompanied by *a la carte*, multiple speed and variable geometry subregional initiatives. A group of smaller, predominantly Western European and Scandinavian nations, particularly Denmark, Finland, Italy, the Netherlands, Norway, Spain and Sweden, have coalesced around the ability to make 'niche contributions' to Battlegroup and NRF forces through 'a la carte'/'variable geometry' joint procurement projects and force generation initiatives. CEE states, particularly those at Europe's Eastern frontier, emerge as net security consumers, rather than providers. The militaries of these states retain a higher proportion of forces committed to territorial defence and are predominantly focused on the provision of military capabilities under the auspices of NATO (Flournoy and Smith, 2005: 9; Howorth, 2007: 149; Valasek, 2005: 217–28; Williams and Gilroy, 2006: 110–11). Nevertheless, staunchly Atlanticist East European states, notably the Czech Republic, Hungary and Poland, are gradually proving more willing to route defence and security cooperation through ESDP (see Table 2.2).

Divergence in temporality: The temporal location, sequencing and pace of reform

The emergence of a 'core' Europe in security and defence cooperation has been a process characterised by differentiation in temporal sequencing. France has, since 1994, most single-mindedly pursued the 'Europeanisation' of its security and defence policies. It has led the way in attempting to enhance Europe's C4ISR capabilities in order to produce both an autonomous European capacity for military action and improve interoperability with US forces (Howorth, 2007: 45; Irondelle, 2003a; Rynning, 2000: 62–5; Sperling, 2004: 457). Although it is only possible to identify incremental change to the settings of British policy on institutional venues (in the form of the gradual embedding of British defence policy within ESDP following the October 1998 Saint Malo agreement), this followed a very different sequence to France, as the Saint Malo Initiative (October 1998) took place three months after the Strategic Defence Review ended (Dover, 2007: 5).

French and British 'third order' reforms also display divergence in temporal location, taking place in 1997–8 (UK) and 1994–6 (France) and the reforms differ in pace. The SDR was 14 months in duration, from May 1997 to July 1998. Reforms to French defence policy objectives began in February 1994 under Prime Minister Edouard Balladur, however, reform to the policy instrument was finalised in October 1996; a period of 32 months. Nevertheless, although British and French reform processes followed a similar temporal sequence in respect to the order of reforms to the objectives and instruments of policy, the 'paradigm shift' in French institutional forums to embeddedness within ESDP took place in conjunction with changes to the objectives of French defence policy in February 1994, well before changes to the instruments of policy, in October 1996.

Britain and France both set in place the key pillars of 'third order' change in the mid-late 1990s and invested in core capabilities that would begin to endow their militaries with strategic mobility and enhance their capacity to undertake joint expeditionary crisis-management operations. However, the precise form of their partial emulation of the RMA (NEC and EBAO) emerged only in the early 21st century. The British focus on NEC in support of EBAO emerged in the 2002 and 2003/04 Defence White Papers; whilst in France investment in NEC and the digitisation of the battlefield was placed firmly at the heart of defence policy by the LPM 2002–8 and strengthened by the 2008 Defence White Paper.

Since 2003, these two nations have been joined by a further emergent regional leader – Germany – Europe's third great power. Although the Federal Republic has displayed strong continuity in respect to institutional forums, in the form of the persistence of the 'bridge role' and 'bi-furcated' Federal Executive and is now developing a military that will allow it to adopt a stronger leadership role in European security, through the 1990s and early 21st century Germany played a more reactive role in European security cooperation (Adams and Ben-Ari, 2006: 124; Dyson, 2007, 2008; King, 2005a: 327; Lungu, 2004a). Germany's laggard role has been particularly evident in her more limited acquisition of C4ISR technology during this period and the temporal lag in the development of the rapid reaction forces necessary to contribute to European and Atlantic capabilities in low-high intensity crisis-management operations (Adams and Ben-Ari, 2006: 47–58; Dyson, 2005, 2007, 2008; Lungu, 2004a: 261–72; Shepherd, 2000: 26; Sperling, 2004: 456).

Indeed, German military reform is a case of significant divergence in all three aspects of temporality: in temporal location – with a shift to crisis-management and 'full-spectrum' operations taking place in 2003 – and in sequencing, as reforms to the objectives of policy have only been accompanied by change to the 'settings' of policy instruments. This has also led to divergence in conceptual and doctrinal evolution, illustrated by the advent of the *Bundeswehr* Transformation Centre in 2004 and the delayed process of Concept Development and Experimentation in support of joint, networked operations. By comparison, the British counterpart of the BTC, the DCDC, had been established in 1998, following the SDR, whilst the French DGA has sought to promote jointness since the 1996 reforms and has recently been bolstered by the creation of the CICDE in 2005 (Rynning, 2008: 5). Consequently, despite the ambitions outlined in the 2006 DWP, German capability procurement related to NetOpFü deviates from Britain and France, both of whom have progressed much further in the development of systems such as FCS. German doctrinal and conceptual development around EBO and COIN also lags behind that of the British and French. On the dimension of pace, whilst the *Bundeswehr* has undergone three main reforms during the post-Cold War era, in 1994; 2000 and 2006, each enacting incremental reform to the structure of the armed forces. When significant reform to the objectives of German policy took place, it did so over a comparatively rapid six month period: from May to October 2003.

The following chapter will examine the contributions made by realist and cultural approaches to understanding the patterns of convergence and divergence which have been outlined in this chapter. The theoretical approach neoclassical realism outlined in Chapter 3 will then be tested against its cultural competitors in Chapters 4 to 6 which undertake a closer examination of the processes of military reform in each of the three states and the development of national positions on ESDP, NATO and bi-pluri-lateral defence initiatives.

Section II

Theorising Defence Policy Convergence

3
Competing Theoretical Frameworks: Realist and Cultural Approaches

Neorealism and convergence: Anarchy, uncertainty and the 'push and shove' of international structure

Realism is a diverse and highly-contested school of thought, divided by debates about the analytical leverage that can be attained by focusing on the role of material and non-material factors and characterised by divergence about the level of analysis that should take precedence in understanding the behaviour of states in the international system. The roots of the theory lie in the work of Thomas Hobbes, who argued that human preferences are inherently in conflict due to the scarcity of material resources which can be employed to satisfy them, leading to an underlying incentive to employ or to threaten force and coercion. Without a 'Leviathan' (the modern state), endowed with a monopoly on legitimate violence allowing the imposition of order, justice, equity and the rule of law, a 'state of nature exists' (Kolodziej, 2005: 53–8). In this 'war of all against all' life is 'solitary, poore, nasty, brutish and short', as equal human beings rely on their own self-help efforts to compel others to comply with their interests (Kolodziej, 2005: 53–8).

Whilst the advent of the modern state allowed societies to escape the state of nature, it transposed the 'war of all against all' to the international level (Jervis, 1978: 167–8). States, as sovereign, independent units endowed with a monopoly of legitimate violence are resolved to remain autonomous and are unwilling to subject themselves to a higher power with the capacity to regulate international affairs. Hence Carl von Clausewitz posited that states exist in a condition of constant conflict and 'pure' or 'total' war – akin to the Hobbesian state of nature – in which all resources of the state will be mobilised in the effort to dominate the opponent through his decisive defeat (Howard, 1983: 70). Any moderation plays into hand of one's enemies; only the strongest survive. Hence the central premise of realist thought: that international outcomes are consequent upon the material, and in particular, military power that states are able to wield. As Thucydides (1951: 331) famously declared: 'The strong do what they can and the weak suffer what they must.'

However, although pure war was the logical outcome of relations between states that are primarily characterised by force, Clausewitz identified a set of factors which act to temper and dilute intensity of interstate conflict. The first factor is the material and moral limitations on resources that can be extracted from society and the extent to which these limitations on national resource can be translated into military power (Kolodziej, 2005: 60; Stone, 2004: 409–10). The second factor is the political context within which the war is fought – the more extensive the political goals that underpin the conflict, the more likely they will require the annihilation of the adversary (Stone, 2004: 410). Finally, friction – the uncertain environment within which military operations are undertaken – also acts to temper the process of escalation (Howard, 1983: 25–6).

In the interwar years and shortly after the Second World War, a body of realist thought, led by Hans Morgenthau underscored the role of domestic-level factors in determining state behaviour. Morgenthau's arguments built upon the work of Reinhold Niebuhr (1932), who argued that the conflict-ual interests of individuals create an inherent immorality in international politics, and the assertions of Thucydides and Machiavelli that power politics is motivated not only by fear and profit, but also non-material factors like glory (Skinner, 1981: 4). Morgenthau's 'biological' realism emphasised the centrality of 'the will to power' (*animus dominandi*) deeply embedded within the 'essence of human existence' (Morgenthau, 1946: 192). According to Morgenthau, the underlying nature of mankind creates an international system characterised by states struggling for supremacy, dictating that states focus on the reduction of relative power gaps through 'intelligent adaptation' – the demystification of other state's foreign policies; bluffing other opponents about one's own strengths and intentions and the evaluation of other states' power bases (Hobson, 2000: 48).

Yet Morgenthau argued that conflict is not simply a product of the systemic effects generated by the 'will to power', but that the intensity of the security dilemma[1] is dependent upon the internal properties of states, which impact upon structure of the international system (Hobson, 2000: 50–2). Hence the balance of power under the 'aristocratic international' differed greatly to that during the period of 'nationalistic universalism' due to the impact that democratic and nationalist revolutions of the 19th century had upon international morality, creating a more unstable and conflictual international system (Hobson, 2000: 50–3; Little, 2006; Morgenthau, 1966: 244–59). However, according to Morgenthau, a state's success in the international realm is determined by the extent to which states are able to adapt to the balance of power and anarchic international system (Hobson, 2000: 48). This requires the capacity to 'bluff' other states and domestic public opinion and decipher the attempts by other states to exaggerate or underplay their strength and intentions (Morgenthau, 1966: 145–53). This duality within the work of Morgenthau has led to the notion of 'two Morgenthaus', one emphasising the importance of the balance of power, the other prioritising unit-level variables (Little, 2006: 2–3).

In *Nationalism and After* E.H. Carr placed a high level of causal weight on the role of unit-level factors, by distinguishing between four periods of international history, whose characteristics were determined not by the impact of systemic anarchy, but by the specific features of states, which impacted upon international norms and the nature of the balance of power (Hobson, 2000: 56–9). Indeed, whilst emphasising the inherently conflictual interests of states and commonly categorised as a realist, Carr also explicitly challenged the notion that conflict was inevitable, by arguing that a 'post-sovereign' global society could be achieved based on global moral norms and a 'universal citizenship' (Carr, 1945: 37; Hobson, 2000: 59–61). Hence some, such as Linklater (1997: 321–38) argue that this places Carr closer to critical theory than realism (Hobson, 2000: 60–1).

Kenneth Waltz's neorealism builds upon a number of the core premises of 'classical' realist theories – that states are subject to the imperative of power; must oppose potential threats to their security and interests; are sensitive to relative gains and that states have inherently conflictual interests. However, in contrast to Carr and Morgenthau, Waltz (1959: 159–65) strictly separates levels of analysis by distinguishing between three 'images' of international relations. In the first image the conduct of states is governed by the actions of individuals; in the second image by the internal organisation of states, whereby differentiation in government and society incentivise action; in the third image the behaviour of states is governed by their relative power position in the anarchic international system (Waltz, 1959). In *Man the State and War* Waltz (1959: 225) argues that 'no single image is ever adequate'. However, Waltz adopts a more rigid position in *Theory of International Politics* (1979) by arguing that first- and second-image theories lack parsimony and analytical leverage, because, despite changes in the units – economic, social, technological, ideological and political – the nature of international politics remains constant. Instead, the third image – international structure – is the decisive independent variable that explains the external policies of states.

The central feature of Waltzian neorealism is the anarchic nature of the international system, analogous to the Hobbesian 'state of nature', that exerts powerful effects upon the behaviour of its units (states) (Sterling-Folker, 1997: 4–6; Waltz, 1979: 88–93). States are the central actors in the international system and functionally alike: sovereign, enjoying a monopoly of legitimate violence and centralised political systems. As there is no higher authority than the state, no state can be certain of the intentions of another, meaning that states cannot rely on each other for their security. Hence the system of states is characterised by insecurity and self-help, cooperation is short-lived and international organisations act as a vehicle for the pursuit of the great powers' interests.[2] The international system is therefore highly-competitive and one in which states, as rational and unitary actors, assess the costs and benefits of different strategies in maximising their security.[3]

These assumptions are, however, subject to a high level of contestation within realist theory. In particular, Waltz was ambiguous about the precise impact of anarchy on the behaviour of units in the international system: 'states at a minimum seek their own preservation, and at a maximum drive for universal domination' (Waltz, 1979: 118).[4] This illustrates divergence within realist thought over the extent to which the systemic level exerts 'push and shove' effects on states, and takes the form of a split within realist thought between 'defensive' and 'offensive' realists.

Defensive Realists argue that the ultimate goal of states is not relative power maximisation, but security.[5] Hence Joseph Grieco (1990: 40) characterises states as 'Defensive Positionalists', concerned primarily with protecting against losses in relative gains: '[realism's] fundamental insight is that states are defensively positional and compare performance levels out of fear that others may gain a higher performance level'. Defensive realists posit that systemic imperatives alone do not create a competitive international realm, as the security dilemma lacks the intensity attributed to it by Offensive Realists (Snyder, 1991: 10–13). As Zakaria (1991: 190) highlights, defensive realism emphasises how 'the international system provides incentives only for moderate, reasonable behaviour'.

Eric Labs (1997: 10) points to two factors which incentivise defensive postures and the maintenance of the *status quo*. Firstly, the ease of defence and the relative inexpense of focusing capability investment on the defence of existing territory rather than the acquisition of new territory. Secondly, the balancing behaviour that characterises the international system acts to disincentivise offensive strategies, as a state striving for universal domination will inevitably be confronted with an alliance of states that will attempt to thwart its expansion. Because states are rational actors, they will learn from the operation of the international system and the 'balancing' behaviour that is an inevitable consequence of offensive strategies. Consequently, the international system should not have such pervasive effects on the behaviour of its units, for states will strive for self-preservation rather than hegemony, thereby ameliorating the intensity of the security dilemma (Posen, 1984: 68–9).

These claims rest upon defensive realists' interpretation of Waltz's concept of 'socialisation': the idea that states become socialised into the 'norms' of the international system and more alike and that they therefore learn lessons from history. On this basis Posen (1984: 68–9) classifies himself as a 'historical realist', in contrast to Waltz's ahistorical realism in which 'the substance and style of international politics remains surprisingly constant' (Waltz, 1979: 110). Hence Defensive Realists posit that we must look not to the systemic, but the domestic level for the sources of state behaviour, not least when explaining the 'pathalogical' actions of the great powers, whose 'offensive' postures over history appear to contradict the systemic imperative of 'cautious behaviour', that dictates a moderate foreign policy and small, streamlined and defensive armies (Glaser, 1994–5; Snyder, 1991: 1–31; Taliaferro, 2000–1: 126–61; Zakaria, 1991: 191–3).

Offensive Realists[6] argue that due to the scarcity of security, states will be orientated towards offensive strategies, the accretion of power and capabilities and will inevitably strive for hegemony. States are 'offensive positionalists' that must 'think offensively toward other states even if their ultimate motive is to survive' (Labs, 1997: 11–12; Mearsheimer, 2001: 21). The focus of states on relative gains makes international cooperation inherently short-lived (Kolodziej, 2005: 130–1). Hence security can only be guaranteed by the pursuit of self-help strategies and the development of some form of offensive military capability, which exacerbates the security dilemma: 'What maters more are not the aims and intentions of states, but the effects of their self-help efforts...states...cannot know or predict with certainty the sources, timing, nature or actual probability of threats to their security' (Resende-Santos, 2007: 57). Whether specific threats exist or not states will constantly strive to maximise their power and influence: 'Every state would like to be the most formidable military power in the world because this is the best way to guarantee survival in a world that can be extremely dangerous' (Mearsheimer, 1994–5: 12).[7]

International politics is therefore characterised by power and fear and as Hyde-Price (2007: 9), Labs (1997), Mearsheimer (2001) and Resende-Santos (2007: 55–7) demonstrate, it is the first premise – the anarchic nature of the international system – that is the dominant feature of neorealism.[8] Anarchy and uncertainty are mutually reinforcing and create a pervasive and often highly-intense security dilemma in which a paucity of information about each others' intentions fosters an environment of suspicion and mistrust. This systemic context of inescapable insecurity overrides any learning/socialisation processes concerning the efficacy of offensive strategies.[9]

Yet the international system is not characterised by a constant state of 'pure war' and a security dilemma of such 'extraordinary intensity' (Posen, 1984: 68). History provides good deal of evidence that states do not always attempt to expand, sometimes preferring to act as 'defensive positionalists' or *status quo* powers and maintain their position within the international system. This can, however, be explained without recourse to unit-level factors or 'historical realism'. Instead, as rational actors, states act opportunistically and strategically to maximise their power under anarchy (Hyde-Price, 2007: 33; Kydd, 1997: 120). Variation in the tendency of states to adopt offensive strategies is dependent upon the costs and benefits associated with each opportunity to expand; upon the opportunities and constraints dictated by international structure.

Indeed, the following section will demonstrate that variation is contingent, not only upon the incentives offered by the balance of power, but also the 'balance of threat' (Walt, 1987).[10] States do not always seek to balance[11] aggregate capabilities and fear all states equally, but balance against the state(s) that is the most threatening (Donnelly, 2000: 60). Whilst the inherent uncertainty of international politics incentivises offensive strategies, the intensity of the security dilemma varies by region, due to the differentiated exposure of states and regions to the power and strategic interests of the dominant state. In the post-Cold War era this has induced some states, as rational short-term power maximisers, to undertake balancing behaviour against the US, whilst motivating others – including the European Great Powers – to bandwagon US power, in order to tackle more immediate and threatening foes. This dynamic leads to clustered convergence around regionally-specific patterns of defence cooperation.

Neorealism and the formation and maintenance of alliances: Explaining functional complementarity in institutional forums

According to Waltz, the propensity for conflict and cooperation within the international system is dependent upon the balance of capabilities (the 'balance of power') (Little, 2007: 191–5; Waltz, 1979: 170–1). It is possible to outline four main distributions of power that can exist: uni-polarity; bi-polarity;[12] balanced multipolarity and unbalanced multipolarity (Hyde-Price, 2007: 41–4; Mearsheimer, 2001: 44–5).[13]

Under uni-polarity, one state enjoys an overriding dominance in economic and military capabilities.[14] However, defensive and offensive realism diverge over the implications of uni-polarity for the behaviour of the dominant power. Defensive realism envisages that, with its security guaranteed, a superpower is likely to become a *'status quo'* power and withdraw to a grand strategy 'between isolationism and selective engagement' (Hyde-Price, 2007: 81). This necessitates a downsizing of military capacity and a streamlined military, capable of intervention, but only as a matter of last resort, leading to increased security competition in other regions as great powers seek to take advantage of the withdrawal of the dominant power. Offensive realism predicts that the dominant power in a uni-polar system will attempt to grasp the opportunity to maximise its security by expanding its influence in areas of strategic importance, amplifying its military and economic advantage over other states and that it will eschew international cooperation to achieve its ends. This necessitates an offensive military, capable of power projection and preventative strikes against potential competitors (Hyde-Price, 2007: 82; Labs, 1997: 11).

Multipolarity is a power configuration in which three or more great powers exist. It can take two forms: balanced (where these states enjoy relatively similar material power capabilities) or unbalanced (characteristic of systems in which one state enjoys a notable advantage in material capabilities, with the potential to strive for regional hegemony). As rational actors opportunistically assessing the advantages and disadvantages of particular strategies in maximising their power, influence and security, states under balanced multipolarity will eschew offensive strategies for regional hegemony in favour of cooperation. Conversely, unbalanced multipolarity acts to intensify the security dilemma, leading to an acute concern with other states' gains in relative power and a higher likelihood of conflict.

Post-cold war Europe: Balanced multipolarity under the offshore balancer

As Hyde-Price (2007: 83–6) and Mearsheimer (2001) demonstrate, the actions of the US over the post-Cold War era, particularly during the administrations of Presidents Bill Clinton (1993–2001) and George W. Bush (2001–9), presents evidence of power maximisation and offensive uni-polarity. US foreign and security policy has been characterised by an increased willingness to employ preemptive military force on a uni-lateral basis in a bid to reinforce US primacy in the international system, as forcefully elucidated by the 2002 and 2006 US National Security Strategies (Posen and Ross, 1996–7; Posen, 2003: 5–6). This policy has been accompanied by the development of a military increasingly capable of deploying full-spectrum force at a global level. As stated by US Defence Secretary, Donald Rumsfeld in 'Transformation Planning Guidance', 2003: 'Some argue the US should not change what are demonstrably the world's best military forces. History and current trends suggest that merely attempting to hold on to existing advantages is a shortsighted approach and may prove disastrous...if the US fails to transform we will see the rapid emergence of regional competitors and a world prone to conflict.'[15]

Rather than a global hegemon (Posen, 2003: 44; Wohlforth, 1999), however, it is more accurate to characterise the US as the world's only regional hegemon, enjoying dominance over the Western Hemisphere (Mearsheimer, 2001; Hyde-Price, 2007: 83). The US certainly enjoys substantial military primacy over potential competitors, notably in weapons systems technology, consequent upon its scientific and technical output and investment in R&D (Altmann, 2004; Paarlberg, 2004). Even in the context of the 'internationalisation of science', this lead remains highly resilient to challengers (Altmann, 2004: 65–6; Paarlberg, 2004: 142).[16] Yet despite the arguments of Posen (2003) and Wohlforth (1999: 17) who posit that US technological superiority places it in 'command of the commons',[17] it is more accurate to characterise the US as enjoying 'contested authority' over the commons. Command of the commons requires an overwhelming command of sea, land, air and space; yet deficiencies in US air (Posen, 2003: 24–30) and land power create 'contested zones' of US military power (Stigler, 2002–3).

As demonstrated in Chapter 1, in spite of the success of the US in targeting Serbian infrastructure and economy, the contested authority of US air power was demonstrated by the Kosovo conflict of 1999, that illustrated how: 'a well-operated if obsolescent integrated air defence system can defend a ground force skilled at camouflage and deception' (Posen, 2003: 28; Stigler, 2002–3: 129–30; Walt, 2005a: 116; Williams, 2001: 48).[18] The failure of the 'Afghan model', (an 'indirect' approach to counterinsurgency, applied both in Afghanistan and Iraq, in which indigenous forces were backed up by US advisors, Special Operations Forces and supported by precision air-strikes in the hope of minimising cost and risk to the US) also illuminated the vulnerability of US forces to light-infantry insurgencies when forced to deploy large numbers of troops in a 'clear, hold and build' approach (Anders et al, 2005–6; Biddle, 2005–6; Byman, 2003; Lebovic, 2008: 11–21; Malkasian, 2008: 81; O'Hanlon, 2002: 54–7; Posen, 2003: 30–6; Ricks, 2006). These weaknesses in US power derive, to a great extent, from the erroneous lessons drawn from the 1991 Persian Gulf War by US policy-makers – namely that the ease of the ground invasion of Kuwait and Iraq was achieved largely through the neutralising role of high-precision airpower, leading to relative lack of investment in, and tactical neglect of, infantry forces (Press, 2001: 5–7; Renner, 2004: 109)

Hence US authority in Eastern Europe, Eurasia, the Caucuses and in particular, North East Asia, is more contested than its authority over Western Europe and North, Central and South America (Hyde-Price, 2007: 44; Layne, 2006: 16; Mearsheimer, 2001: 40). Outside the Western Hemisphere the US acts as an 'offshore balancer', intervening only to prevent the rise of states that may challenge its preeminent position and to protect its vital economic and strategic interests (Hyde-Price, 2007: 45; Layne, 1997; Mearsheimer, 2001; Schwarz and Layne, 2002: 36–42; Walt, 2005b: 18–19).

Situated within the systemic context of offensive uni-polarity in which the US acts as Europe's 'offshore balancer', West and East-Central Europe are also subject to a dynamic of 'balanced multipolarity', in which a regional balance of power exists between Europe's major economic and military powers (Britain, France and Germany) (Hyde-Price, 2007: 67–74).[19] At the same time, defence and security cooperation in Europe is also subject to the constraints imposed by the contestation to US regional authority by Russian power and influence to the East. As the following section will demonstrate, this structural context creates a powerful incentive for the development of security cooperation in Europe that is increasingly complementary with NATO, yet subject to spatial and temporal differentiation.

European security and defence cooperation as 'reformed bandwagoning'

Neorealism suggests four possible responses to uni-polarity: balancing, buck-passing,[20] bandwagoning[21] and aggression.[22] Of these, the concepts of balancing and bandwagoning are most relevant and plausible for the analysis of European security. Balancing takes two forms: internal (the maximisation of domestic resources to attempt to recalibrate the balance of power, a process limited by the resource-technological basis of a state[23] and external (the formation of alliances with other, weaker, states) (Posen, 1984: 61). Balance of power theory predicts that when confronted with external threat, balancing will be more prevalent than bandwagoning (Waltz 1979: 126–7). The uncertainty of the international realm and concern with relative power dictates that states follow the strategy of least risk, allying only with weaker states whose gains in power will not pose a threat following the dissipation of an Alliance's utility, and amongst whom greater influence can be brought to bear (Walt, 1985: 5; 1988: 279).

Art (2004: 4), Layne (2006: 34–6), Paul (2004: 46–71), Pape (2005: 7–45) Posen (2004, 2006) and Walt (2002, 2005b: 129) argue that Europe is engaging in a form of 'soft balancing'[24] against the US. This concept refers to the use of non-military tools to frustrate uni-lateral action, forming the first stage of attempts by European states to contain a potential opponent, and the cultivation of future partners for a potential 'hard balancing' military alliance, explicitly directed against the US. The economic, military and technological superiority of the US negates the viability of internal balancing strategies, for all but those states most threatened by US strategic interests.

Balancing strategies are, however, inherently risky, demanding the allocation of substantial financial resources and run the gauntlet of provoking preemptive military action by the dominant power to stem the rise of the balancing coalition. Furthermore, despite arguing that ESDP represents a form of 'soft balancing', Pape (2005: 14) also highlights the crucial importance of aggressive intentions in spurring the construction of balancing coalitions. Whilst European states have a security interest in ensuring that uni-lateral action by the US in areas which both Europe and the US define as strategically important (such as Central Asia and the Middle East) does not prejudice their security, the US does not display aggressive intentions towards the EU.[25] As Lieber and Alexander argue: 'The US is plausibly threatening to only a limited number of states and terrorist groups. Most other major powers share the US interest in countering these regimes and groups... other major powers lack an underlying motivation to compete strategically with the US' (Art et al, 2005–06: 192).

The debate concerning whether states bandwagon with, or balance against, the strongest power in the international system forms a major fault line within neorealism. Whilst Waltz (1979: 126) argued that states will balance on the basis of aggregate capabilities, this view was famously challenged by Stephen Walt (1985, 1987),[26] who posited that states balance not only against capabilities, but against threat. Walt persuasively demonstrates how a less powerful state that is more proximate, endowed with offensive capabilities that permit rapid conquest and highly offensive in its intent[27] poses a greater threat than the dominant power in the international system (Walt, 1985: 8–12).[28] In short, the intensity of the security dilemma varies by region, not least for secondary states, which are often particularly sensitive to threats stemming from their geostrategic neighbourhood. Despite the arguments of Vasquez (1997: 904–5) and Legro and Moravcsik (1999: 36–8) who chide Walt for succumbing to degenerative[29] tendencies, Walt's overall argument is consistent with the core premises of neorealism.[30]

Variation in threat and the security dilemma is closely linked to the limitations of US hegemony outlined in the previous section: issues of geography and material capabilities, in addition to differentiated aggressive intentions that derive from US strategic interests. Only in the case of a truly global hegemon, capable of projecting power worldwide with equal ease, should we expect isomorphic responses from all states in the international system (Hyde-Price, 2007: 80; Mearsheimer, 2004: 185). Differentiation in the ability of the US to deploy power at the global level and territorial disparities in the strategic interests of the US means that despite being the dominant power in the international system, the US exercises its power in a manner that helps to reinforce the regionally-variegated intensity of the security dilemma (Hyde-Price, 2007: 80–1). This leads to clustered convergence around regionally-specific patterns of defence policy cooperation.

The balance of power and capabilities creates differentiation in the exposure of regions to US power and a concern, not only with the US, but also regional power balances and threats that emanate from a region's geopolitical neighbourhood. For some states, such as Iran, the US represents a foe, whose offensive capabilities, strategic interests and consequent aggressive intentions induce attempts at internal and external balancing.[31] For other states in the international system, including European states, the 'offshore balancer' is a potential ally against more immanent local threats. The status of Britain, France and the US as nuclear powers also reduces the likelihood of 'hard' balancing. Hence the second perspective, of European defence and security cooperation as illustrative of 'reformed' bandwagoning[32] appears to carry greatest analytical weight, suggesting that rather than incentivising differentiation between ESDP and NATO in the form of 'soft balancing' against the US, systemic forces are pushing European states towards functional complementarity in defence and security arrangements.

At first glance, balance of power and balance of threat theories offer divergent definitions of bandwagoning (Schweller, 1994: 80). According to Waltz, balancing involves aligning with the weaker parties to a conflict; bandwagoning joining the stronger. Consistent with balance of threat theory, Walt defines bandwagoning as joining 'the source of danger'. Yet as Schweller (1994: 81–2) demonstrates, such a definition misleadingly portrays bandwagoning as a form of surrender or defensive appeasement in the face of overwhelming might; as an attempt to draw the attention of the most threatening state away from its bandwagoning allies to other states within the international system. Bandwagoning behaviour is also motivated by profit and reward.[33] Hence as Schweller (1997: 928) states: 'It [bandwagoning] is no longer the opposite of balancing (i.e. siding with the actor who poses the greatest threat or has the most power), but simply any attempt to side with the stronger, especially for opportunistic gain.'

Whilst European states, as rational actors in the context of systemic anarchy, constantly strive for power accretion, with the ultimate motive of maximising their security, they are also subject to a set of structural constraints and opportunities which place limitations on their ability to expand.[34] These constraints and opportunities are a product, not only of the balance of power, but the balance of threat, making European states sensitive, not so much to relative gains *vis-à-vis* the US, but to other more immanently threatening actors in their geopolitical neighbourhood.[35] Bandwagoning offers the opportunity to profit and share in the spoils of victory against immediate, common opponents, outweighing the risk of exacerbating the power of the dominant state.[36]

Hence in the case of Europe, to which the US does not present a proximate threat, 'reformed' bandwagoning for profit is underway, as European states ally with the offshore balancer[37] in order to maximise their own power, influence, and crucially, security (Schweller, 1998: 67; Walt, 1985: 8). 'Reformed' bandwagoning is a means with which to maintain and manage the Atlantic Alliance within the context of complex post-Cold War security threats and strategic interests which have a largely unifying, but sometimes differentiated impact on Europe and the US (Press-Barnathan, 2006: 307–8; Hyde-Price, 2007: 112; Rynning, 2005: 170–5; Krahmann, 2005; Wohlforth, 2002: 103–4). Such common threats include containing the rise of potentially threatening rising powers,[38] combating terrorist networks and international crime emanating from 'failed states' in Africa and Central Asia, and stemming the proliferation of WMD (Cottey, 2008: 73).

The fear of 'entrapment' into US policy in areas where strategic interests diverge, or 'abandonment' through the withdrawal of the US security guarantee has incentivised policy leadership by the West European Great Powers (Britain, France and Germany) on behalf of pooling European military resources (Press-Barnathan, 2006: 307–8). European security cooperation therefore represents a European attempt to develop a 'division of labor' strategy within the Atlantic Alliance, allowing greater leverage on how to tackle issues of common concern following the failure of Europe's pursuit of a 'binding' strategy[39] through NATO during the Iraq crisis of 2003 (Press-Barnathan, 2006; Brooks and Wohlforth, 2005). As Matlary (2009: 100) notes: 'Almost all political influence in this policy area is based upon the ability to contribute to international operations.'

This reading of European security cooperation confirms the arguments of Brooks and Wohlforth (2005: 80, 91–3) who demonstrate how ESDP forms both an instance of meeting regional security challenges in the context of partial US disengagement and of 'a long term policy bargaining enhancement strategy', as EU states seek to maximise their power and influence in Washington by being 'a better partner of the US, not a competitor'. This demonstrates the important distinction between opposing particular US policies on which there is disagreement over means and ends and more general opposition to US power (Brooks and Wohlforth, 2005: 80). Hence whilst Pape (2005: 14–15) notes: 'how the unipolar leader wages war on transnational terrorism can reduce or improve the security of other major powers giving them a powerful security interest in how such a war is waged', this is not a sufficient incentive for balancing behaviour.

Reformed bandwagoning has taken place through a diverse set of initiatives. Firstly, through the 'Europeanisation' of NATO and creation of the NRF, granting increased influence in Washington, access to US capabilities and a global high-intensity capability in major theatre conflict.[40] Secondly, through the simultaneous development of an increasingly militarised ESDP, composed of small, self-contained Battlegroups, that includes the participation of non-EU NATO states such as Turkey and Norway. This initiative permits autonomous European action and collective 'milieu shaping' in cases of US disinterest stemming from fear of its own entrapment in conflicts of marginal significance to its strategic interests (Giegerich and Wallace, 2004; Hyde-Price, 2007: 88–90; Jones, 2007: 219; King, 2005b: 331; Posen, 2004, 2006: 180; Reynolds, 2007: 361; Rynning, 2005: 151, 157; Salmon and Shepherd, 2003; Whitman, 2004). Finally, reformed bandwagoning is taking place through the development of a set of multinational variable geometry/ *a la carte* subregional initiatives, led by the European Great Powers, which are designed to enhance the capacity and capabilities of European troops to contribute to both NATO and EU-led expeditionary crisis-management operations of varying intensity.

Neorealism and the sources of military emulation and innovation: Clustered convergence in military structures and capabilities

A focus on the 'push' and 'shove' effects of the international system delivers substantial analytical leverage in understanding the increasing functional complementarity of European defence cooperation. Similarly, neorealism also provides strong purchase in identifying the broad contours shaping post-Cold War convergence in the military structures, capabilities and doctrines of the West European Great Powers.

Military emulation is a central feature of neorealist thought and provides a powerful explanation that captures much of the temporality of European capability initiatives. As in the market place, where the 'invisible hand' of market competition determines the behaviour of firms, so the 'invisible hand' of anarchy rewards those who conform to its logic with an increase in power and security – and punishes those who do not, with decline, defeat and even destruction.[41] Neorealist accounts of military reform suggest that the anarchic logic of the international system drives change at the domestic level, leading to the adoption of new military methods (Posen, 1984). The systemic distribution of capabilities and consequent new security challenges, coupled with the necessity of survival in an uncertain, 'self-help' world, leads to three possible outcomes (which can be combined to varying degrees).

Firstly, the continuation of existing practices (policy stasis), whereby states fail to adapt to systemic imperatives and retain existing military objectives and instruments. Such stagnation will inevitably lead to a loss of power and influence, due to the 'punishment effects' exerted by the international system.[42] The second outcome is emulation, which constitutes the adoption of 'best practice': 'The possibility that conflict will be conducted by force leads to competition in the arts and instruments of force...contending states imitate the military innovations contrived by the country of greatest capability and ingenuity...competition produces a tendency towards sameness of the competitors...and so weapons of major contenders and even their strategies begin to look much the same' (Waltz, 1979: 127).

However, whereas Waltz (1979: 127) prioritises the distribution of capabilities and the balance of power as the drivers of military emulation, Joao Resende-Santos (2007) highlights how emulation should be understood as a rational response to the powerful effects of structural uncertainty and the logic of competition. States seek to minimise the costs and risks consequent upon their self-help efforts by emulating proven effectiveness in conflict, rather than emulating on the basis of 'aggregate capabilities', as this forms the quickest and most effective strategy that involves least risk (Resende-Santos, 2007: 51, 58–61).

The final outcome is innovation: 'the discovery of new knowledge, invention of new practices or their recombination in new forms' (Resende-Santos, 2007: 72). Innovation offers the promise of significant, though short-term, advantage over other states, due to the propensity of other great powers to mimic successful innovation.[43] Innovation is, however, inherently risky due to the potentially catastrophic implications of poor strategic choices.

A state's propensity to innovation/emulation is determined by the interplay between three factors (Resende-Santos, 2007). The first factor is the resource-technological basis of a state. The greater the capabilities of a state, the lower the risk that is associated with failed innovation/emulation. The second factor is the intensity of competition – as the security dilemma becomes more intense, the 'safety margin' of risk decreases. All but the most innovation-capable primary states will prioritise emulation as states become more risk averse and prefer the more certain and cost-effective results that emulation affords: 'innovation is a product of the delicate balance between potential risks and gains' (Resende-Santos, 2007: 73–4). The final factor is the presence of alliance options, which can provide an incentive to bandwagon on the power and innovations of other states in the international system.

International structure therefore acts as a selection mechanism on the basis of 'competitive effectiveness':[44] the extent to which a state's defence policy will allow it to maximise its power and influence and ensure its survival, autonomy and prosperity.[45] This systemic pressure leads to defence policy convergence; but a convergence that is both dynamic (consequent upon the constant competition that characterises international relations), and clustered (due to the variegated intensity of competition between particular states and regional differentiation in the intensity of the security dilemma) (Resende-Santos, 2007: 78; Taliaferro, 2006: 478). The central criterion at the heart of this selection mechanism that determines what is perceived as 'best practice' and the attractiveness of emulation, is proven success in great power war. Only in the absence of great power conflict will states follow Waltz's prescription and imitate the state of greatest capability (Resende-Santos, 2007: 81–2).

The pace of 'clustered convergence': Resource constraints, strategic learning and alliance options

Neorealism points, therefore, to three core factors which have determined the pace of the emergence of a pattern of post-Cold War 'clustered convergence' in Europe that is characterised by only a partial emulation of the US-led model of high-intensity force projection and RMA. Firstly, in the context of the relative absence of great power war and the diverse nature of conflict and threats in the post-Cold War international system, it has been difficult for European states to define 'best practice'. The implications of shifts in national power are not always immediately clear, impacting upon the temporality of military reform over the short-term. This is consistent with neorealism and correlates with the argument of Hyde-Price (2007: 32) that states, as rational actors, are in a constant process of 'strategic learning'[46] about how best to respond to structural imperatives in order to ensure that they can maximise their power and influence (Rathburn, 2007: 534; 2008: 317). Aaron Friedberg (1998) and Brian Rathburn (2007: 534) demonstrate that following significant systemic power shifts a temporal lag with systemic imperatives is likely as statesmen require time to become more familiar with the radical changes in their strategic environment and the new constellation of friends and foes. Such far-reaching change creates particular informational uncertainty and flux, requiring the readjustment and fine-tuning of strategy to the new configuration of constraints and opportunities. As Rathburn (2008: 316) notes: 'learning does not proceed smoothly in response to a changing systemic environment, but rather in a manner of fits and starts...power calculation is a complicated business'. Hence temporal lag reflects the potential costs of 'system punishment' that can stem from strategic miscalculation, incentivising states to err on the side of caution and only make decisions based upon information that is as complete as possible (within the ongoing constraints of systemic uncertainty). This is an important factor determining the slow and gradual emergence of joint European capabilities procurement programmes in the area of C4ISR over the post-Cold War era.

As Imlay and Toft (2006: 1) note the task of military planning is complicated by the 'fog of peace': 'an uncertainty rooted in three basic problems: that of identifying friend or foe, that of understanding the nature of war and that of determining its timing'. In the immediate post-Cold War era European states faced uncertainty about the precise implications of uni-polarity for the security relationship between European states and the US and uncertainty about the implications of a growing number of security challenges emerging from the dissolution of bi-polarity. This was accompanied by ambiguity about the nature of warfare over the short to medium-term. On the one hand, the US-led 1991 Gulf War, 1999 Kosovo Conflict, 2001 attack on Afghanistan and 2003 attack on Iraq, highlighted the utility of technological prowess in the context of expeditionary high-intensity war-fighting, demonstrating the apparent success of the RMA and the importance of retaining the capacity to undertake MCO (Boot, 2003: 41–58; Lungu, 2004a: 265). Yet, on the other hand, the Iraq conflict post-2003, the NATO ISAF mission and US/European operational experience in the former Yugoslavia and Africa during the 1990s, have demonstrated the dangers inherent in a reliance on air power, stand-off precision-strike weapons systems in the context of peacekeeping, post-conflict reconstruction and policing tasks and counterinsurgency operations (Betz, 2006: 507; Biddle, 2005–6; Byman, 2003; Cohen, 2004: 402–3; Day and Freeman, 2003: 308–13; Farrell, 2008: 806; Malkasian, 2008: 81; O'Hanlon, 2002: 54–7; Posen, 2003: 30–6; Ricks, 2006).[47]

Secondly, the nature of European states as 'second' and 'third-rank' powers, that constrains their resource-technological capacity to copy the RMA and magnifies the risks associated with innovation or full-blown emulation of the US-led RMA (Horowitz, 2006: 8; Resende-Santos, 2007: 73). Consequently, the European 'second-rank' Great Powers emerge as the leaders of the process of reformed bandwagoning; the 'third rank', smaller states as net security consumers, by simple virtue of their relative differential in material capabilities.[48]

The final factor is the presence of alliance options. The speed of emulation may also be affected by the presence of 'external balancing' options – that provides security for states over the short-term, allowing them to pool resources through Alliances or free-ride, slowing down processes of emulation (Resende-Santos, 2007: 90). As the previous section has illustrated, the post-Cold War balance of power and threat creates common incentives for Britain, France and Germany to bandwagon on US power in order to maximise their security over the short-medium term. Bandwagoning allowed the European Great Powers the relative luxury of being able to 'err on the side of caution' and base their defence reforms upon the lessons of operational experience alongside the US and observation of the

RMA in practice. This luxury was, however, only short-lived, as in the late 1990s and early 21st century the US has become increasingly unwilling to shoulder the costs of underpinning European security. As the US conformed to the dictates of offensive uni-polarity, the immediacy of threats from Europe's geostrategic neighbourhood instability in the Balkans and Caucuses, failed states in Africa and related threats of international crime, terrorism, migration and WMD proliferation as well as the urgency of building the potential to undertake autonomous European action through ESDP, were thrown into sharper relief. As Resende-Santos (2007: 90) notes: 'The higher the level of threat a state faces, the more prompt, rapid and extensive will be its military emulation...the less vulnerable the state is to changes in its external security situation, the more slowly it will respond to such changes.' These imperatives have been accompanied by the growing requirement for NATO states to renew their importance to the US as Alliance partners by putting place defence reforms that would allow them to carry a heavier burden within the Atlantic Alliance.

These predictions appear to be borne out by the empirical evidence. Emulation of the RMA and US 'best practice' are most prevalent in areas of least risk and lower cost. Emulation was initially evident in the reorganisation of military structures that took the form of the creation of Joint Reaction Forces, organised according to the principle of modularity; a process that was initiated in the mid-late 1990s in Britain and France and in the early 21st century in Germany. The threat of abandonment by the US became particularly evident in the run-up to the Kosovo conflict of 1999 that demonstrated to policy-makers the necessity of some form of emulation of the core features of the RMA in order to retain interoperability with US forces. Operation Allied Force acted to clarify the post-Cold War systemic imperative of the pursuit of a policy of reformed bandwagoning, explaining the timing of the Anglo-French St. Malo initiative in October 1999. The St. Malo Accord accelerated European initiatives designed to develop the interoperable capabilities which would furnish Europe with the capacity to undertake autonomous action within its geopolitical neighbourhood.

It was, however, only in the early 21st century, following the strategic and operational learning processes of the 1990s that 'best practice' has been identified. This has taken the form of a partial and selective emulation of the RMA. European states began to converge around the development of capabilities and doctrine (NEC and EBAO) which as Chapter 1 demonstrates are essential to ensure continued operability with the US and an autonomous European capacity for military action in operations across the conflict spectrum (both 'three block war and MCOs). This has created a basis for the growing cross-national collaboration on interoperable C4ISR capabilities under the EDA and bi-pluri-lateral capability procurement/force generation initiatives (Ben-Ari, 2005; Cohen, 2004: 396–7; Forster, 2006: 46; Mey, 1998: 316; Sperling, 2004: 456–9).

The temporality of reform to the objectives and instruments of defence policy: Variance in external vulnerability

The puzzle still remains, however, of why Europe's three Great Powers have converged around the partial emulation of the RMA with such different-iation in sequencing. As Waltz (1979: 124) recognises, threat-based theories such as neorealism are somewhat opaque in their provision of rigid guide-lines for the temporality of isomorphism. Nevertheless, as John Deni (2004: 513) notes: 'If one wants to test a theory's predictions, one must place some sort of temporal boundaries on a theory's predictions.'

Neorealism posits that executive decision-makers enjoy a high level of auto-nomy in translating threats from the international security environment into changes to military doctrine and structure and in overcoming domestic opposition and organisational politics (Desch, 1999; Posen, 1984: 239–41; Rynning, 2001/2: 85). Posen (1984: 59) argues that the level of civilian inter-vention on military doctrine is dependent upon the intensity of the security dilemma: on whether 'statesmen and soldiers perceive the possibility of war as remote'.

When the international system is characterised by periods of 'relative calm', military organisations will be typified by a 'tendency towards offen-sive, stagnant military doctrines, poorly integrated with political elements of a state's grand strategy' (Posen, 1984: 59). The logic of organisational politics dictates that organisations develop 'standard operating procedures' to routinise everyday tasks, which develop into programmes and military doc-trine. Over time, doctrine and programmes become ossified and may persist beyond their utility, due to the vested interests and sunk costs dependent upon their perpetuation, fostering a desire to maximise their autonomy and independence from civilian control (Posen, 1984: 45).[49] Sunk costs lead mil-itaries to shun radical change and to distaste for operational uncertainty which act to disincentivise military innovation (Posen, 1984: 54–5). Accord-ingly, militaries will also have an inherent preference for offensive military doctrines due to the increase in organisational size and wealth – and auto-nomy from civilian leadership – with which such doctrines are associated (Posen, 1984: 47–51). The desire for autonomy, coupled with interservice rivalry also leads to the disintegration of military doctrine and political ends (Posen, 1984: 51–4). Organisational theory posits that civilian intervention only takes place when an organisation fails – in the case of military, man-ifested by defeat in war. Yet even this is fraught by difficulty due to the reliance on the expertise of the military which, dominated by hierarchy, can offer only a 'thin innovation menu' (Posen, 1984: 57).

However, neorealism predicts that as the level of threat to the state increases, so does the control that can be exerted by civilians over the organisational self-interest of the military and processes of innovation/ emulation, due to the 'simple fear of defeat'[50] (Posen, 1984: 77): 'Fear of disaster or defeat prompts statesmen to question long-standing beliefs, to challenge service preferences, to alter budget shares, and to find new sources of military advice and leadership. Civilians intervene to change details, including posture and doctrine, not merely general principles.'[51] Consequently, for neorealism, divergence in the isomorphism of British, French and German defence policies is strongly determined by the opportunities for, and constraints upon, the expansion of power, influence and security: variation in 'external vulnerability'.[52]

Hyde-Price (2007: 47–8) and Jeffrey Taliaferro (2006: 467) argue that we must pay attention to three aspects of a state's external vulnerability which impact upon the speed with which states converge around similar defence policies: territorial size and population, geographical position and productive capacity. Over history, variance in geographical position and the temporality of the development of industrial productive capacity of the European Great Powers have placed constraints upon – and provided opportunities for – the expansion of power and influence by creating differentiated external resource dependencies and strategic interests which remain critical to the generation of national power.

Britain's status as an island nation and the relative absence of threat to its territorial integrity led to a focus on sea power that, combined with its strong productive capacity relative to other European nations deriving from early industrialisation and resource endowments, allowed Britain to build a substantial empire in Africa and Asia from the 17th to the 19th century. During the initial stages of the Cold War the UK had an enhanced sensitivity to the instability in West and Central Africa in order to protect its trade and investment and ensure that former colonies did not fall under Soviet influence (Jackson, 2006: 358). However, as Cumming (2004: 108) notes, Africa declined in strategic importance to the British during the postcolonial era. By 1987 Africa received only 3.2 per cent of British exports and accounted for 1.9 per cent of UK imports (Cumming, 2004: 108).[53] Following the end of the Cold War British strategic interests in Africa have been associated with dealing with the implications of failed states for international crime/terrorism and migration (Jackson, 2006: 356–8). Rather than resource dependency on former colonies, Britain enjoyed a good measure of self-sufficiency in energy supplies in the initial post-Cold War era, after the discovery of large reserves of North Sea oil and gas in the 1970s.[54]

Africa remained, however, of particular strategic importance for the French in the post-Cold War era. Although France was principally concerned with the European balance of power (German power in particular) and suffered from an impaired relative productive capacity that derived from comparatively late industrialisation, she nevertheless enjoyed opportunities for colonial expansion in the 19th century in North and West Africa and East Asia (Horn, 2006). France's former colonies, particularly in Africa, have fostered external resource dependencies which are crucial to the generation of national power, requiring the maintenance and development of expeditionary forces capable of protecting vital strategic interests (Griffin, 2007; Martin, 1989: 625–40). As Guy Martin (1989: 625) highlights: 'France suffers from an almost excessive dependence upon African sources of cheap minerals essential to her economy and national defence.'

From the mid-1980s until the mid-1990s, France was dependent upon Niger and Gabon for 36 per cent of the uranium required to power its nuclear reactors, which during the 1990s provided over 75 per cent of French electricity production, comprising 40 per cent of France's total energy requirements.[55] This dependency created a high-degree of sensitivity to instability in Africa (Griffin, 2007: 23; Martin, 1989: 625–40). Hence between 1990–7 France intervened militarily in Rwanda (1990–3, 1994), Gabon (1990), Togo (1991), Benin (1991), Zaire (1991, 1993), Djibouti (1991–3) and Cameroon (1994) (Griffin, 2007: 35–7). Whilst not all the above military interventions were directly related to ensuring access to mineral resources, resource dependency nevertheless formed an important motivation for intervention in support of a continued French policy of 'offshore balancing' that was aimed at maintaining the regional power balance in Africa during the early mid-1990s (Griffin, 2007).

By the late 1990s, the complexity of Africa's post-Cold War security problems and high-profile failures in interventions in Rwanda (Operation Turquoise, June–August 1994) and in the Central African Republic and Democratic Republic of the Congo (1996–7) led to a reduction in French willingness to rely upon Africa for key mineral resources and to a diversification of uranium sourcing to the US and Canada (Pederson, 2000). These changing strategic interests fostered a shift from a uni-lateral to a multilateral French approach to Africa in the mid-late 1990s, whereby French African policy became increasingly routed through the UN and EU. Indeed, France's largest intervention in Africa since 1997, involving the deployment of 2,000 troops to the Ivory Coast (2002–9),[56] took place under the auspices of UN Security Council Resolution 1464 (2003) and was motivated primarily by the necessity to protect French citizens as well as to avoid the negative security implications (not last large-scale refugee flows) which would derive from subregional instability in West Africa (Griffin, 2007: 24–32).[57] In the early 1990s, however, before this diversification in mineral resource dependency took place, unilateral intervention on the continent was listed as one of the six possible scenarios for military action in the 1994 French Defence White Paper, necessitating a sustaining the capacity to deploy expeditionary forces in Africa and the maintenance of French military bases in the region (Utley, 2002: 135–40).

German grand strategy over the 19th and early 20th century was determined by her situation in the European *Mittellage* and by an acute awareness of the imminent threat presented by the Russian Empire to the East, Austro-Hungarian Empire to the South and French to the West. The development of a substantial industrial base in the mid-late 19th century led to the 1897 declaration by Wilhelm II of a shift from *Europapolitik* to *Weltpolitik* and to a rapid expansion of the German navy in an ill-fated attempt to rival UK maritime power. However, Germany's geographical position and vulnerability on three borders ensured that by the early mid-20th century she focused on maximising power and influence over *Mitteleuropa* (whose foodstuffs and raw materials would permit German self-sufficiency in the resources critical in order to generate national power), rather than on colonial conquest in Africa (Keylor, 2006: 48–9, 76). Thus Germany's geographical position has left the Federal Republic relatively free from dependency on former colonies.

Furthermore, in the decades following the Second World War, heavy dependency upon the resources of *Mitteleuropa* or Eurasia was precluded by the inception of the Cold War. Germany sourced the majority of its energy needs from domestic sources, West European neighbours and the Middle East.[58] As a result, in the immediate post-Cold War era, Germany was able to satisfy its major energy needs from domestic sources (for example, brown coal that accounted for around one quarter of its total energy needs a this time) and from its near neighbours (the UK, Netherlands and Norway, which supplied the majority of Germany's oil and natural gas requirements) (EMF, 2008). Hence variance in German external vulnerability deriving from geography and history did not generate a pressing requirement for expeditionary power projection to protect vital overseas strategic interests.

In the mid-late 1990s German attention has, however, turned once more to *Mitteleuropa* and Eurasia as she has been forced, in the context of a drop in domestic coal production and the depletion of North Sea oil and gas reserves, to look further afield for sources of oil and gas and coal; notably to Russia and the successor states of the former Soviet Union (in particular Azerbaijan, Kazakhstan, Poland and Turkmenistan).[59] Yet whereas France enjoyed a substantial measure of potential freedom for uni-lateral military action in Africa, in order to secure access to vital uranium supplies, many of the Soviet Union successor states fall directly under Russia's sphere of influence, whose economic and military power creates significant disincentives to the German pursuit of influence in these regions through the use of military power.

Hence a 'third image' account of the temporality of convergence emphasises divergences in the temporality of the development of productive capacity and in particular, differences in geographical position, which have left an important legacy of differentiation in strategic interests amongst Europe's three great powers. In the post-Cold War era, this continued contributed to subtle, though important, variation in 'external vulnerability' between France – that was highly dependent upon the resources of former colonies – and Britain and Germany, which in the early 1990s displayed a stronger level of energy self-sufficiency or dependency upon more stable supplies from close European neighbours (Jackson, 2006: 351–2). For the French, however, material dependency upon the mineral resources of former colonies, led to an immediate post-Cold War concern with maintaining the capacity for expeditionary power projection in Africa at levels of varying intensity that was more pressing than for Germany and Britain.[60] In short, neorealism draws our attention to the role played by the strategic imperatives generated by external resource dependencies, notably energy – vital to the generation of national economic and military power – which exposed France to the increasing post-Cold War instability in Africa and clarified the process of strategic learning for France in the initial post-Cold War era, leading to earlier civilian intervention in military policy on behalf of expeditionary power projection than in the UK and Germany.

A further compelling structural explanation for early civilian intervention lies in the poor expeditionary capacity of the French military in the immediate post-Cold War era, when compared to the British and Americans (Gregory, 2000a: 43–51; Utley, 2000: 185–7). Although France maintained a residual capacity for expeditionary operations during the Cold War, power projection in Africa had been facilitated through the maintenance of a network of military bases in the region and the deployment of the lightly-armed *Force d'Action Rapide* (FAR), in which investment has been restricted from the early 1980s in favour of the *Force de Frappe* (Utley, 2000: 207). Deficiencies in French expeditionary capabilities had been forcefully highlighted by the 1990–1 Gulf War in which France had only been able to mobilise 19,000 troops from a combat ready army of 280,000 (Gregory, 2000a: 44) (see Chapter 4 for further details). The British, in contrast, had mobilised over 30,000 troops from a combat ready force of only 160,000. The Gulf War – as well as participation alongside the US and British forces in Bosnia – raised the possibility of a potential decline in relative power *vis-à-vis* the British and Americans in a new security environment that by 1994 increasingly signaled the necessity to deploy expeditionary forces as part of shifting coalitions (Giegerich and Wallace, 2004: 166; Gregory, 2000: 43–57; McKenna, 1997: 134). The poor expeditionary capacity of the French was further demonstrated by Operation Turquiose in Rwanda in 1994 (Utley, 2000: 195–7).

There are, nevertheless, significant limitations to a neorealist emphasis on divergence in external vulnerability in explaining the temporality of military reform; not least that France was able to diversify its sourcing of uranium with relative ease from Africa, to Canada and the US in the mid-late 1990s. This suggests that French external resource dependencies in the African continent were not sufficiently acute to induce the radical 'third-order' reforms to defence policy objectives which took place between 1994 and 1996 (Pederson, 2000). Divergence in external vulnerability is also unable to provide a compelling explanation for why Britain undertook military reform at such an early temporal location when compared to Germany, as both states were subject to relatively similar external vulnerability in the post-Cold War era, that they began with a measure of energy self-sufficiency or dependence upon close neighbours. The 1997 Strategic Defence Review was not so much a response to protecting strategic interests in former colonies, but was instead designed to create a policy instrument that would allow Britain to tackle threats to international instability emanating from inter- and intra-state conflict and humanitarian emergencies at the regional and global level. These were, however, security concerns which were shared by Germany, that through NATO enlargement had ensured stability around her Eastern borders by the late 1999 and faced a mounting caseload of expeditionary crisis-management operations as the 1990s progressed. As the Weizsaecker Report noted, Germany was, by May 2000 'surrounded by stability'. Yet it was only in 2003 in the context of the threat of the 'super-Gau' (super-catastrophe), following 11 September 2001, and the increasingly acute fear of 'abandonment' or 'entrapment' by a uni-lateral US, that Germany placed crisis-management at the forefront of its defence policy and began to develop military structures and capabilities capable of participating in expeditionary operations of varying intensity (Press-Barnathan, 2006).

The temporality and territoriality of European defence cooperation: Variance in external vulnerability and the alliance security dilemma

A strong degree of divergence also exists in the temporal location and sequencing of the commitment of European states to the process of reformed bandwagoning. As Chapter 2 has demonstrated, amongst the European Great Powers, clearly identifiable regional leaders and laggards are evident in the development of ESDP and NATO initiatives (Adams and Ben-Ari, 2006: 21–58). The divergent temporality of isomorphism in reformed bandwagoning can be partly explained by paying attention to variation in the 'external vulnerability' of European states.

For example, in order to understand the comparatively early temporal location of the Europeanisation of French defence policy and the early emergence of French leadership in post-Cold War European defence cooperation a focus on specific features of French 'external vulnerability' is critical, notably her geographical position. The 'Europeanisation' agenda outlined by Prime Minister Edouard Balladur in the 1994 Defence White Paper on the one hand, a response to the increasing clarity of systemic imperatives in the post-Cold War security environment: a mechanism with which to endow France and Europe with the military forces and capabilities to take independent military action in the context of US disinterest, in addition to exerting greater influence within the US by strengthening NATO (Barnathan, 2006: 304; Brenner, 2003: 198–9; Jones, 2007: 214; Posen, 2006: 167).[61]

The 'Europeanisation' of French Defence Policy was, however, also a means with which to ensure French influence within its regional milieu. By early 1994 the doctrine of 'national sanctuary' left France increasingly isolated in a critical policy area in European cooperation that could provide a forum for France to stake out a pace-setting role. This reflects long-standing French concerns about relative power within the EU (with German power in particular), and attempts to exert leadership and influence in European Defence Cooperation (Brenner, 2003: 198; Menon, 1995: 22; Utley, 2002: 134).[62] As German power and influence within the EU increased during the 1990s though its agenda-setting in creating a 'monetary Europe' (EMU), so the French under Prime Minister Edouard Balladur and President Jacques Chirac sought to revive efforts (that can be traced back to the development of the Franco-German Defence Council established in January 1988) to balance increasing German influence within the EU by carving out a lead role in shaping 'Defence Europe', as forcefully outlined in the March 1994 Defence White Paper (Howorth, 1998: 130–51; Menon, 1995: 27; Sutton, 2007: 302).

These systemic and regional imperatives also help explain the nature of post-Cold War patterns of French high-technology capability investment: support for an autonomous French and European military capability, the routing of France's response to the US-led RMA through ESDP and the 'Europeanisation' of the French defence industrial sector during the 1990s (Lungu, 2004b: 58–62; Sloan, 2002: 71; Sperling, 2004: 457; Utley, 2000: 185). Variance in external vulnerability provides a powerful motivation for the emergence of French leadership in the development of subregional bi-pluri-lateral force generation initiatives beginning in the mid-1990s, notably EUROCORPS and EUROFORCES, as well as French efforts to improve the European defence industrial base (Sutton, 2007: 302–3). Nevertheless, in line with the predictions of neorealism, the threat of abandonment by the US has led to an increased willingness by France to ensure complementarity between ESDP and NATO initiatives, illustrated by France's 2009 return to NATO's integrated military command structures under President Nicolas Sarkozy.[63] By virtue of its geographical position, Britain was less acutely concerned with the regional power balance in the immediate post-Cold War era and emerged as a co-leader of 'reformed' bandwagoning after the October 1998 St. Malo initiative, only once the threat of 'abandonment' by the United States became acutely pressing. France faced incentives to push ahead with European security cooperation at an earlier stage as a consequence of its sensitivity to relative power *vis-à-vis* Germany.

Variance in external vulnerability also explains differentiation in the scope and temporality of defence policy convergence between ECE states and West European states. Located on the borders of Europe, Central, and particularly Eastern European states are at the sharp end of many of the common challenges that face the West European Great Powers. These include migration flows consequent upon instability in the Caucuses and sub-Saharan Africa and international crime networks, creating an incentive to actively contribute to the pooling of European assets under ESDP. However, by virtue of their geographical position, limited productive capacity and small size, these states are particularly concerned with Russian power and influence. Security cooperation is therefore focused on demonstrating solidarity with the US, making such states unwilling to champion security arrangements through ESDP which could be perceived by the US as threatening the role and function of the Atlantic Alliance (Dunn, 2001).

Consequently the development of regional initiatives, such as Baltic Security Cooperation, by states at Europe's Eastern borders, were initially a means with which to prove the worth and loyalty of these states – as partners within the Atlantic Alliance and pay the 'price of protection' in order to avoid abandonment by the US (Kupchan, 1988: 324; Ringmose, 2009: 2). However, over time, as ESDP and NATO have become increasingly complementary, these structures have also acted as a forum in which to augment the process of facilitating 'niche' contributions to ESDP Battlegroup missions (Howorth, 2007: 149; Whitney, 2008: 28–9). Understanding the constellation of European 'insiders' and 'outsiders' in the process of 'reformed bandwagoning' through NATO and the EU also requires a focus on the distribution of capabilities: namely sensitivity to Russian power. The borders of European security cooperation outside OSCE (primarily an arena for the exercise of 'soft power') are conditioned by the difficulties associated with EU and NATO expansion into Russia's near abroad (Hyde-Price, 2007: 156–61).

In summary, the immediate post-Cold War period was one of heightened flux and uncertainty, incentivising initial policy stasis in Europe and bandwagoning on US power through NATO. However, important nuances in French 'external vulnerability' led to an early pace-setting role on ESDP; what Irondelle (2003b) terms 'Europeanisation without the European Union'. By the time of the Kosovo Conflict in 1999, systemic imperatives became increasingly clear for the other European Great Powers – in the form of the threat of abandonment or entrapment by the US and the emergence of more clearly defined security threats within Europe's geopolitical neighbourhood, leading to the emergence of ESDP.

At the same time, the limited resource-technological bases of European states and a relative absence of great power conflict magnified the risks associated with emulation of the US-led RMA, impacting on national processes of military reform and the willingness of states to go beyond reforms to military structures and instigate reforms to augment their C4ISR capabilities. However, the specific form of military emulation that is of greatest utility in maximising 'competitive-effectiveness' over the short-medium term has become increasingly evident. Consequently, recent reforms to the British, French and German militaries have converged around modular, joint expeditionary forces capable of undertaking operations at the full range of the conflict spectrum (albeit only as part of multinational coalitions). The emergence of military isomorphism amongst Europe's great powers has produced centripetal effects upon the smaller European states, for whom the risk associated with emulation is highest. Consequently, they have followed the lead of the UK and France by contributing to NATO and ESDP initiatives in a manner broadly equivalent to their material capabilities. Hence in a Europe characterised by balanced multipolarity, isomorphism in defence policy objectives and instruments is beginning to be reflected in complementary convergence of the functions of ESDP/NATO and *a la carte*, multiple-speed and variable geometry capability procurement and force generation initiatives.

Yet, despite the increasing pace of cooperation, defence procurement initiatives and pooling of national capabilities remain limited in scope. There continues to be a high level of duplication in capability acquisition amongst European nations and as the Former Head of the EDA, Nick Whitney (2008: 7) highlights, on average 70 per cent of European land forces remain focused on territorial defence.[64] In addition, the relative fragmentation of the European defence industry acts a further barrier to the development of an economy of scale that could help foster greater efficiency in defence spending. This reticence to specialise and pool capabilities derives from the 'alliance security dilemma' within the EU and NATO that acts as an impediment to deeper integration and has encouraged the development of flexible *a la carte*, multiple-speed and variable geometry arrangements outside NATO/EU structures (Shepherd, 2000: 26; Siedschlag, 2006; Snyder, 1984). Whilst the post-Cold War distribution of material capabilities and the emergence of military isomorphism are creating stronger incentives to pool resources, the international system remains highly uncertain. The fear of 'system punishment' fosters duplication in capability procurement and the retention of a broad national defence-industrial base in order to guard against the risk of a loss of power, influence and security that would stem from others reneging on their commitments.[65] The problem is compounded for states at Europe's eastern borders. These states face the twin imperatives of developing networked, interoperable expeditionary capabilities to enhance their credibility as Alliance partners, whilst sustaining national defence capabilities to respond to the heightened threat to their territorial integrity posed by Russian power (Longhurst, 2002: 67–9; Mannik, 2004: 33; Michta, 2002: 47).[66]

Neorealism: An insufficient account of temporal divergence

The analysis presented above demonstrates that variance in external vulnerability provides a substantial – but not fully sufficient – measure of analytical leverage in understanding the temporality of post-Cold War European defence reform processes. Neorealism offers a compelling account of the systemic forces propelling European states towards convergence across three of the main axes of defence policy identified in Chapter 1 (objectives, instruments and institutional forums). It is, however, temporality that provides the most significant stumbling block to neorealism's explanatory capacity. Variance in external vulnerability provides a convincing explanation of the divergent temporality and territoriality of European defence cooperation, but neorealism fails to fully explain the differentiated temporal location of reforms to military structures and capabilities. Indeed, according to neorealism, the tendency for isomorphism generated by the commonalities shared by the West European Great Powers in the post-Cold War era (similar relative material and productive power and size, competent government, their common West European regional location and consequent exposure to regional balanced multipolarity, US 'offshore balancing' and incentives to bandwagon on the back of US power) outweighs the diversity deriving from nuanced variation in external resource dependencies (Hyde-Price, 2007: 105). This raises questions about neorealism's explanatory power, for it is unable to fully explain why the European Great powers, when faced with powerful common socialisation pressures emanating from the international system, are converging with such significant temporal divergence (Taliaferro, 2006: 479).[67] It opens neorealism to the accusation that it fails to appreciate the important role of unit-level factors in determining the pace, sequencing and temporal location of military reform due to the emphasis neorealism places upon the security dilemma and overriding imperative of self-help in encouraging civilian leaders to prioritise the 'national interest' rather than domestic political interests (Farrell and Terriff, 2002: 274; Hyde-Price, 2007: 166–8).

Neoclassical realism and variable state power: The domestic sources of temporal divergence

The following section will highlight how neoclassical realism provides a mechanism with which to account for the important intervening role played by unit-level variables in delaying convergence with systemic imperatives (Hyde-Price, 2007: 167–8). In response to the prominent critics of neoclassical realism (Legro and Moravcsik, 1999; Vasquez, 1997) the section outlines an approach that retains a strong measure of the elegance and parsimony of neorealism. At the same time it delivers a more nuanced understanding the nature and impact of the 'transmission belt' that links changes in the international security environment to domestic policy change, explaining why states sometimes fail to follow the dictates of international structure in a timely manner (Rathburn, 2008).

Neoclassical realism combines neorealism's emphasis on the 'survival' motivation of states, with classical realism's focus on the dependence of political leaders on domestic society for material resources and support for foreign and defence policy goals. The theory argues that whilst over the long-run, states will seek to maximise their international influence, power and security according to their relative material power resources and the constraints and opportunities presented by the international system, 'state power' forms the central intervening unit-level variable explaining short-medium term temporal divergence from the dictates of international structure (Rose, 1998: 152; Taliaferro, 2006: 479–80).[68] This approach stands in contrast to neorealism, that posits that due to the intensity of the security dilemma, states face little constraint in maximising the resources that they can draw from society for foreign, defence and security policy goals (Waltz, 1979: 96).

However, whilst defensive realism can be thought of as 'reductionist' in its attempts to explain international politics though a focus on the behaviour of states and their internal attributes, neoclassical realism does not deny the status of international structure and states' focus on relative gains as the key independent variable determining international outcomes (Legro and Moravcsik, 1999: 28; Rose, 1998: 146; Taliaferro, 2000: 182, 2006: 480; Walt, 2002: 210; Waltz, 1979: 18–37). Neoclassical realism is, nevertheless, characterised by a great deal of contestation over the unit-level factors which are of significance in determining state behaviour over the short-medium term, with material and non-material variables incorporated on a somewhat 'ad hoc manner' (Rose, 1998: 165; Walt, 2002: 211).

Zakaria (1998: 38) integrates a wide set of variables which impact upon state power, including technological, ideological, racial, partisan and cultural practices – thereby developing a framework that is far removed from the theoretical parsimony of neorealism (Waltz, 1979: 19–20).[69] The focus of theorists such as Jack Snyder (1991), Randall Schweller (2006) and Stephen Van Evera (1999) on the independent role played by societal and cultural factors in determining foreign and defence policy also runs the risk of 'theoretical indeterminacy' and violates not only the parsimony and structural logic of realist thought, but also its material core, as forcefully argued by Legro and Moravcsik (1999: 29, 35–6).[70]

Randall Schweller (2004: 169) points to four core variables which affect state power and the ability of states to respond to external threat, leading to 'underbalancing':[71] elite consensus – the extent to which national elites share a common threat perception and are united on the appropriate mechanisms of response; government or regime vulnerability – the level of governmental vulnerability to sanction from powerful groups in society;[72] social cohesion – support for the institutions of the state[73] and social solidarity; finally, elite cohesion – the fragmentation of political elites by divides of ideology, culture, party faction, region, religion, ethnicity, class or bureaucratic interest.

Schweller's framework develops a sophisticated account of the variables which can impact upon state power. However, whilst recognising that the degree of elite consensus is partially dependent upon the ambiguity of the strategic environment, the process of threat identification is also a 'subjective one that is only partially determined by objective facts' (Schweller, 2004: 170). Furthermore, the inclusion of ideology and culture as unit-level variables which impact upon elite cohesion creates problems for neoclassical realism's claims to consistency with the core premises of realism, undermining the theory's materialist logic by conflating 'mind and matter' (Desch, 1998: 155–6; Mearsheimer, 1995: 91; Rynning, 2001–2: 90). As Morgenthau (1966: 103) reminds us, within realist thought ideas and ideology act as 'false fronts behind which the element of power, inherent in all politics, can be concealed'.

Although he develops a more streamlined and parsimonious account than Schweller, a similar problem also arises in the work of Jeffrey Taliaferro (2006), who argues that state power is dependent upon three intervening unit-level variables: ideology, nationalism and state institutions. According to neo-realist thought, nationalism, ideology and culture are tools that can readily be employed by statesmen in mobilising the state behind the national interest. Taliaferro posits, however, that ideology can act as an intervening variable inhibiting the ability of policy leaders to extract resources from the state (Taliaferro, 2006: 493). In addition, whilst recognising that national-ism is 'state sponsored' and generally an instrument deployed by the core executive in the extraction of resources from society, nationalism emerges, nevertheless, as an intervening variable, impacting on the extraction of resources (Taliaferro, 2006: 491).[74] By including these factors as intervening variables, rather than tools in the hands of policy leaders, Taliaferro opens the door to cultural approaches to military change, threatening to depart from realism's materialist ontology (Brooks and Wohlforth, 2000/01; Guzzini, 2004: 536; Legro and Moravcsik, 1999: 36; Krasner, 2000: 131; Schweller, 1999: 149; Twomey, 2008: 349).

In his structural realist account of post-Cold War European security Hyde-Price (2007: 48) also flirts with neoclassical realism. He argues that the transmission belt linking changes in the distribution of power within the international security environment to change in state policy is far from linear and that 'in exceptional circumstances, unit-level variables can have an important – indeed, a vital – role in defining grand strategy and national role conceptions'. In doing so, Hyde-Price also challenges the materialist base of realist thought, for in addition to economic resources and productive capacity he argues that cultural and normative factors form important interven-ing variables determining divergence with systemic imperatives. Hyde-Price (2007: 47) points to how 'blowback' can occur, whereby statesmen become trapped by the previous use of nationalism and ideology, creating a 'path dependency' that constrains the autonomy of the core executive to respond to systemic power shifts: 'grand strategies and national role conceptions are thus coloured by cultural, normative and ideological factors, which provide a prism through which the world is apprehended and policy preferences defined'.[75]

Hyde-Price (2007: 46–7) draws upon Michael Oakshott's concept of 'charac-ter' in European politics – that material conditions which persist for a period of time create 'channels' in which political activity resides: 'These sediments can harden over time and endure even if the material and structural con-ditions which gave rise to them change.'[76] This creates a temporal divergence that prolongs the process of strategic learning and the process of 'structural selectivity'. In short, whilst the 'glass' though which policy-makers view the international system is already tinted by the 'twilight' of imperfect in-formation that arises following a significant systemic power shift, Hyde-Price posits that sunk costs, path dependency and even culturally-embedded norms darken the glass further and increase the temporal lag in policy response.[77]

The model of neoclassical realism adopted in this study attempts to over-come these problems of theoretical indeterminacy by arguing that rather than acting as variables that impact upon state power, 'culture', ideology and nationalism primarily form tools that can be employed by policy leaders to draw resources from domestic society and maximise state power. The invoc-ation of threat not only to values, beliefs and identity, but also to direct phys-ical attack forms an additional mechanism with which to generate state power for foreign and security policy goals.[78] As Becker (2009: 357) highlights: 'How well the public experience of vulnerability [to external threat] can be polit-icised and controlled by the elite is central in amending the national identity and consequently in mobilising support for armed conflict.'[79]

Consistent with neorealism, security forms an 'exceptional' realm, endow-ing statesmen with the capacity to use tools such as nationalism and ideology in the process of 'internal balancing' and in overcoming the 'path depen-dency' and 'sunk costs' associated with 'channels' of established political activity.[80] As Posen (1993: 81) reminds us: 'nationalism is purveyed by states for the express purpose of improving their military capabilities'.[81] An intrinsic part of nationalism is the promotion of a common 'culture' – a shared set of 'symbols, myths and memories' – as a means with which to encourage homo-geneity, establish loyalty to the state and mobilise populations on behalf of responding to systemic imperatives (Billig, 1995; Posen, 1993).

Indeed, the boundaries between culture, ideology and nationalism are blurred and there is a significant level of contestation over their definition. Posen (1993: 81) defines nationalism as: 'The propensity of individuals to identify their personal interest with that of a group that is too large to meet together; to identify that on the basis both of a "culture" that a group shares, and a purported history that the group purportedly shares; and to believe that this group must have a state structure of its own to survive.' This definition draws upon the work of Ernst Haas (1986: 709) and Karl Deutsch (1966: 86–105) and is also echoed in the definition offered by Taliaferro (2006: 491).

Whilst Taliaferro defines ideology as: 'a series of widely held beliefs, causal relationships and assertions about the proper relationship between the state and domestic society and the role of the state in the international system across a range of issues: political, economic, social and military', it is, in prac-tice, very difficult to make a sharp distinction between the concepts of ideo-logy and nationalism. This is recognised by Freeden (1998: 750–1), who outlines how nationalism oscillates between being a '"thin centered" ideo-logy [limited in ideological ambitions and scope] and a component of other, already existing, ideologies'.

Furthermore, the concept of culture also includes many of the core features ascribed to nationalism and ideology, as illustrated by the definition of Duffield (1998: 769): 'Whether culture is defined in terms of assumptions, attitudes, beliefs, concepts, conceptual models, feelings, ideas, images, know-ledge, meanings, mindsets, norms, orientations, sentiments, symbols, values, world-views, or some combination of these concepts, it refers to the patterns of mental activity, or the habits of thought, perception and feeling, that are common to members of a particular group.' Given the amorphous nature of and high level of contestation over the constituent features of ideology and nationalism, the empirical chapter focuses on the broader concept of 'culture' that incorporates elements of national identity, historical memory and ideology. Furthermore, a systematic examination of the roles of all aspects of British, French and German nationalism and ideology in the area of security and defence is beyond the scope of this book and would be a topic meriting a separate volume (see Chapter 7).

Whilst ideology and nationalism can be used to encourage mobilisation and human and material sacrifice by populations, they can also be reinterpreted, reconstructed and invoked by policy leaders through education, the military and the press, as a means with which to manage the temporality of convergence with systemic imperatives. Indeed, Smith (1995: 13) highlights how nationalism exhibits: 'a chameleon-like ability to transmute itself according to the perceptions and needs of different communities'. The core executive emerges as the critical 'identity entrepreneur' in this construction and reconstruction of national identity, particularly relating to defence and security policy (Beissinger, 1998: 176; Reicher and Hopkins, 2001: 49). As Becker (2009: 341) notes: 'Dominant elites are the carriers of the building blocks for the construction and reconstruction of national identities. They mobilise people and direct collective action through their ability to influence the definitions of national identities so they require the sought after mobilisation and action.'

Hence in contrast to Hyde-Price (2007: 46–8), Schweller (2004) and Taliaferro (2006), who point to the way in which nationalism, ideology and organisational culture constrain the range of options available to policy-makers, the perspective on neoclassical realism adopted in this book relegates such factors very much to the second tier of intervening variables. The approach argues that nationalism, ideology and culture form resources for policy-makers – though resources which can, at times, be difficult to master (Becker, 2009: 357). For example, the capacity of the core executive to employ 'culture' as a tool in the policy process can be more restricted in the run-up to national elections (see Chapter 6), or by a Federal system that is characterised by frequent elections at the state level which have important implications for the ability of the Federal government to push through its overall political agenda (see, in particular Chapter 5). The institutional structure of the state (Federal/Unitary) can therefore act to increase the sensitivity of the core executive to public opinion on defence policy.

Nevertheless, 'matter' trumps 'mind'. It is the combination of external vulnerability with domestic material power relations that determines whether culture, ideology and nationalism will be used as tools on behalf of the 'national' or the 'domestic' interest. The invocation of 'organisational', 'institutional' and 'strategic' culture or ideology as intervening or independent variables overlooks the way in which the 'sediments' identified by Oakshott can be deliberately exploited by policy-makers in response to a set of domestic incentives in order to manage the process of adherence to systemic imperatives. Instead of focusing upon nationalism and ideology as variables in and of themselves, attention should be paid to variability in the leadership traits and skills of policy leaders in deploying these tools effectively to maximise state power and manage the temporality of reform processes over the short-medium term.

A concern with the quality of leadership is the focus of Sten Rynning's neoclassical realist account of French military reform. Rynning (2001–2: 90) argues that although the international distribution of capabilities – relative material power – is the key driver of convergence, 'strategic leadership' by statesmen emerges as the crucial determinant of state power. He identifies three facets of strategic leadership: strategic innovation – the role of statesmen in linking strategic agendas to doctrinal and structural change; institutional protection – the ability of political leaders to anchor new ideas within political institutions, manage institutional venues and disadvantage alternative ideas, proponents of the *status quo* and vested organisational interests; finally, 'allied cooperation' – the framing of reform with common 'strategic readings' of a state's international partners, legitimating change (Rynning, 2001–2: 90–2). Convergence and divergence can therefore be explained by a focus upon the strength of the international power shift and the extent to which policy leaders are able to successfully manage these three aspects of policy change: 'Shifts in national power provoke policy change...only after central decision-makers have structured the reform process and articulated a new doctrinal blueprint capable of winning significant domestic support' (Rynning, 2001–2: 104–16).

However, whilst Rynning (2001–2: 114) emphasises the intervening role played by policy leadership in managing doctrinal change, neoclassical realism also draws our attention to the central role played by domestic power relationships and their impact on the extent of autonomy the core executive enjoys in defence and security policy implementation – in determining temporal divergence (Taliaferro, 2006: 487–90). As Rose (1998: 147) states: 'Power analysis must also examine the strength and structure of states relative to their societies, because these affect the proportion of national resources that can be allocated to foreign policy'. In short, although policy leadership is an important variable, it is not a sufficient account of temporal divergence. Indeed, whilst it would be erroneous to factor out the role of individual leaders (not least as the core executive and statesmen emerge as such important actors within realist theory), assessing the influence of 'first-image' variables on international politics and the precise impact of individuals and personality on the course of history is a process fraught with difficulty and intangibility and would require research beyond the scope of this study.[82]

Instead, the institutional structure of the state (the degree of centralisation), the formal constitutional powers of the core executive (Presidents/Prime Ministers/Defence Ministers) over defence policy and nested and interlinked policy subsystems (defence/budgetary/social policy) form the decisive variables in 'balancing domestic power' (Dyson, 2008). Domestic material power structures act to condition the ability and willingness of policy leaders to provide timely 'strategic leadership' on behalf of convergence with systemic power shifts (Taliaferro, 2006: 486). Hence, whilst policy leaders are endowed with particularly effective policy tools to effect change in the area of security defence, whether they will use ideology, nationalism and perpetuate bureaucratic interests in order to protect the *status quo* and policy stasis over the short-medium term, or to promote 'timely' military emulation/innovation, is dependent not only on systemic-level factors, but also the level of executive autonomy. Executive autonomy can play a crucial role in determining whether these tools are used over the short-medium term to manage the temporality of reform or to respond swiftly to systemic imperatives.[83]

As Chapter 6 will demonstrate, the continued impact of organisational politics between the Single Services on UK procurement policy and temporal management of reform during the last three years is much a consequence of the low executive autonomy enjoyed by the Labour Government in the second half of its term in office (2007–10). Organisational politics between the Single Services has also impacted upon German defence reform and derives from frequent local elections which reduce the capacity of the core executive to make rational prioritisations in defence capability procurement (see Chapter 5).

Hence the concept of 'executive autonomy', with its focus on domestic material power relationships – state structure, the linkages between policy subsystems and the formal competencies of the core executive in defence policy – develops a materialist dimension that runs through the diverse stands of neoclassical realism. It builds, in particular, upon the distinction made by Mastaduno, Lake and Ikenberry (1989: 467–8) between 'hard', unitary states which are centralised and more autonomous from society, capable of resisting pressures militating against resource extraction and 'soft' states, which are decentralised and constrained and therefore face greater opposition to 'internal balancing'. Aaron Friedberg (1987) also highlights the centrality of domestic governing arrangements and posits that states with concentrated power are best able to overcome domestic interests and maximise national power. A similar idea underpins Randall Schweller's concept of 'regime vulnerability' – that, amongst other factors, encompasses the idea that governments which are more vulnerable to regular sanction by the electorate (such as federal political systems) will display a greater tendency to underbalance (Schweller, 2004: 173).

Whilst integrating the insights of classical realism concerning the importance of 'second' order variables, in the form of domestic material power relations, 'executive autonomy' emerges only as an intervening variable, mediating the inevitable effects exerted by uncertainty, fear and power, which are inherent in international relations. Hence the analysis attempts to move beyond what is alleged by some to be neorealism's 'foolish parsimony' (Byman and Pollack, 2001: 146) whilst retaining the materialist coherence and distinctiveness of realist thought (Legro and Moravcsik, 1999: 2; Zakaria, 1991: 178–9).

Chapter 4 will demonstrate how the temporal location, sequencing and pace of post-Cold War British, French and German reforms is dependent upon the balance of power and threat, coupled with the autonomy afforded to the political executive in defence policy by domestic power relationships. The extent of executive autonomy conditions whether policy leaders, over the short-medium term, will undertake 'strategic innovation' or promote 'strategic stasis' and whether 'institutional protection' will be given to new ideas or to Cold War policies on the objectives and instruments of defence policy. Executive autonomy is also the key intervening variable in explaining the extent to which policy leaders will be preoccupied with the domestic political ramifications of the 'framing' of military reform within NATO/EU 'allied cooperation' or with the 'national interest' and systemic imperatives. The analysis has important implications for cultural approaches to military change (see following section) as within a context of low executive autonomy, 'culture' emerges not as an independent causal variable, but instead as a resource employed by policy leaders in the 'balancing of domestic power' (Rynning, 2001–2: 116; Klein, 1988) and in the temporal management of reform.

The competing theoretical approach: Culture and military reform

Strategic culture and path dependency

The cultural turn in strategic studies argues that realist approaches cannot provide a full explanation of the scope and temporality of military reform because they treat the preferences of actors as given; national preferences and international reality are instead socially constructed (Katzenstein, 1996; Longhurst, 2003, 2004: 10; Wendt, 1992: 391–425). Norms emerge as a cause of action and constitutive, expressing actor identities, shaping how actors define their interests and providing standards of appropriate behaviour (Farrell, 1998; Gray, 1999). Culturalists regard military policy as driven by ideas rather than material factors, representing a 'culturally bounded, institutionally-embedded pattern persisting over time' and a national security culture that: 'predispose(s) societies in general and political elites...toward certain actions and policies' (Berger, 1998; Duffield, 1998: 27; Farrell, 2005b: 2). As Fischer (2003: 28) states: 'It is not that institutions cause political action; rather it is their discursive practices that shape the behaviour of actors who do'.

Hence the objectives of British, French and German defence policy are not conditioned by the imperative of self-help in an anarchic international system, but are instead subjective and consequent upon their distinct 'cultures of national security'.[84] The persistence of territorial defence as the core objective of German defence policy until 2003 stems from the 'culture of anti-militarism' that is deeply rooted in the German political-military elite and society (Duffield, 1999).[85] This continues to predispose Germany to focus on low-medium intensity crisis-management operations (Breuer, 2006: 206–20; Dalgaard-Nielsen, 2006; Longhurst, 2004). Similarly, the more active post-Cold War roles of Britain and France lie in the long-established traditions of low-high intensity expeditionary power projection that characterised their defence policies during the colonial era (Miskimmon, 2004; Thornton, 2003; Smith, 2005; Wallace, 1992).

Longhurst (2003) and Irondelle (2003b) emphasise the role of 'path dependency' in social causation. This mirrors the insights of historical institutionalism that argues that institutions push historical development along particular paths, hence the effects of systemic forces are mediated by inheritance from the past (Hall and Taylor, 1996). Institutions embody tool-kits of action that provide actors with ways of defining problems and 'logics of appropriate behaviour' in a given situation – determining the persistence of conscription in France until 1997 and in Germany until the present day (Longhurst, 2003; Irondelle, 2003b). As Irondelle (2003b: 176) states: 'On the question of conscription vs. professional armed forces the [French] army found itself faced with a question not just of practicability, but of identity.'

In her work on British and French military doctrine Kier argues that in order to understand changes in military policy we must not only play close attention to the role played by ideas, in the form of the 'organisational culture', that limits what can be 'imagined as possible', but also to the changing domestic political context and civil-military relations (Johnston, 1995: 41–2; Kier, 1995, 1997). Hence for Kier, culture forms an intervening variable: 'Domestic politics set constraints; the military's culture interprets these constraints; the organisational culture is the intervening variable between civilian decisions and military doctrine' (Kier, 1995: 68, 1997: 31).

Explaining policy change: Critical junctures, policy learning and normative entrepreneurship

Culturalist accounts have drawn criticism for their inability to explain change, as they posit that policy displays a high level of inertia due to deeply-embedded nature of 'core' or 'central' beliefs (Dalgaard-Nielsen, 2006: 10–11). Change is gradual, with radical change only possible in the context of 'external perturbations' or 'critical junctures' – seismic and formative historical events that illustrate the failure of existing objectives and instruments of defence policy and empower new actors and policy ideas within institutions

(Berger, 1998: 20–1; Duffield, 1998: 261; Johnston, 1995: 34; Longhurst, 2004: 13: 17).

Farrell (2005a: 450) argues that military organisation is shaped not by material factors and the imperative of survival in a self-help world, but by global norms of conventional warfare 'which provide the basic template for military organisation – namely that of standing, standardised and technologically structured military forces', the roots of which lie in transnational organisational fields and are disseminated through professional networks. Farrell (2005a: 459–61) distinguishes between 'well-established' and 'poorly-established' norms (norms that are 'poorly defined, new or not widely accepted'). When faced with transnational norms that resonate with dominant domestic norms, norm transplantation/grafting will proceed uncontested (Farrell, 2002: 81). However, when faced with external challenge, the more established a norm is, the more likely it is that it will be 'bolstered' (the allocation of greater resources to the practices dictated by the norm at risk in order to prevent its failure) rather than 'stretched' (expanding the boundaries of what is deemed acceptable) (Farrell, 2005a: 459–61).

Yet, there is also room for agency in overcoming this rigidity. Farrell (2001) recognises the importance of external perturbations in creating an opportunity to challenge 'well-established' norms – not least due to the large-scale personnel changes that can occur in periods of crisis, echoing the observations of Rosen (1991) and Zisk (1993: 173–4). However, he also highlights two central intervening factors that determine the ability of cultural agents or 'norm entrepreneurs' to instigate radical normative change: their 'proximity to the decision-making apparatus within the target community' and 'their effectiveness in framing debate and achieving closure' (Farrell, 2001: 85).

Public policy theories elaborate on the structure/agency dynamic at the heart of policy change – notably the 'advocacy coalition framework (ACF)' and 'multiple streams framework' (Hay and Wincott, 1998; Kingdon, 1995: 110; Sabatier and Jenkins-Smith, 1999: 117–69; Zahariadis, 1999: 73–97). Irondelle posits a synthesis of these two approaches in explaining the professionalisation of the French armed forces in the context of 'path dependency' (Irondelle, 2003b: 170–1). Whilst exogenous shock is critical, the policy entrepreneur is decisive in spurring 'critical conjunctures' – coupling the three streams of the policy process – problems, policies and politics (Irondelle: 2003b; Kingdon, 1995: 110; Zahariadis, 1999).

The presence of competing advocacy coalitions are, however, also important (Irondelle, 2003b: 170–1). The ACF conceptualises policy as the result of competition between coalitions structured by policy beliefs and values. Change is not only the result of competition amongst interests, but also learning, within and between coalitions. Initiating or hindering policy-learning processes are vital tools in the hands of policy entrepreneurs in controlling the scope and direction of policy change (Sabatier and Jenkins-Smith, 1999: 145). Hence in France a 'professional armed forces advocacy coalition' provided the 'innovative options' on which Chirac was able to act as a policy entrepreneur (Irondelle, 2003b: 170).

Longhurst (2004: 22) and Dalgaard-Nielsen (2006) also emphasise the dynamic nature of strategic culture. Such accounts argue that policy change reflects the role played by policy leaders and 'political-military elite voices within the national strategic community' (Longhurst, 2004: 21) as 'political/ norm entrepreneurs' (Dalgaard-Nielsen, 2006: 11, 20) or 'strategic culture agents' (Longhurst, 2004: 22).[86] In accordance with Anthony Gidden's 'Theory of Structuration', change is dependent upon the ability of actors within the political executive and broader defence and security policy subsystem to 'create culture', altering 'peripheral' and 'operational' beliefs through the control of legitimate discourses on defence and security policy and in using such discursive tools to 'rise above the culture they are socialised into and actively attempt to manipulate it' (Dalgaard-Nielsen, 2006: 11–13).[87] This normative entrepreneurship by the 'gatekeepers' and 'agenda-setters' of a strategic culture (Longhurst, 2004: 22) redefines actors' perceptions of their interests by refashioning the institutional rules and cognitive paradigms that persist within society and the institutions involved in defence policy agenda-setting and implementation (Dalgaard-Nielsen, 2006: 12–13; Fischer, 2003: 30–1; Glenn et al, 2004: 233).

The concept of strategic culture overlaps with the work of the Copenhagen School (CS) on 'securitisation'. Whilst the CS starts with the realist understanding of security as an exceptional realm, changes to the objectives of defence policy emerge from normative processes (Buzan et al, 1998). The extent to which an issue is identified as a security threat depends upon the role of 'securitising actors'[88] in defining an issue that is already 'politicised'[89] as a threat to one or more 'referent objects'.[90] Hence the redefinition of security threats takes place through an act of 'securitisation',[91] drawing an issue into the realm of exceptionality. At the heart of this process lies the 'speech act' – the use of discourse to convincingly articulate a new issue in security terms as an existential threat to 'referent objects' to the public and the defence and security policy subsystem.

The CS has, however, been criticised for its 'internalist', Derridian position – the assumption that speech acts have productive power and the ability to cause, change and found new structures of significance in social relations (Balzacq, 2005; Stritzel, 2007). Stritzel (2007: 365) argues in favour of an 'externalist' position: that closer attention must be paid to the 'social sphere' within which the 'speech act' takes place. The success of a 'speech act' will be determined by three forces: the performative power of the articulated threat; its embeddedness within existing discourses and the positional power of the actors who influence the process of defining meaning (Stritzel, 2007: 370). As Stritzel (2007: 367) states: 'it is their embeddedness in social relations of meaning and power that constitutes both actors and speech acts', moving the securitisation literature towards a focus on the extent to which actors are able to work within the preexisting cultural context, to determine how international issues are perceived. Despite its more recent emphasis upon the role of agency and discourse in reshaping belief systems (Longhurst, 2004; Dalgaard-Nielsen, 2006), strategic culture offers a strongly 'externalist' account of 'securitisation'. It suggests that the social context within which 'securitising actors' operate is more restrictive than Buzan et al (1998) posit, offering less scope for the identification of new issues as security threats, playing a decisive role in shaping the objectives of defence policy, the appropriate policy instruments and military capabilities.

In her focus on organisational culture, Kier argues that in order to understand changes to military doctrine, closer attention must be paid to civil-military relations – change is dependent, not so much upon the level of dissonance between changes in the international security environment and a military's organisational culture, but upon the level of civilian consensus on the domestic role of the armed forces: 'the greater the civilian consensus about the position of the military in the state, the more likely it is that international threats and opportunities will shape their decisions' (Kier, 1997: 141).

Normative approaches lead us to believe that divergence in national preferences on institutional forums should be understood as the product of norms rooted in 'founding moments' – formative experiences or 'critical junctures' – and in long-term socialisation processes consequent upon participation in international institutions (Longhurst, 2004: 17). Culturalists who emphasise longer-term convergence in British, French and German preferences on institutional forums argue that this is not only a product of systemic incentives, but also reflects 'norm convergence' and the internalisation of common values (Jones, 2007: 218; Howorth, 2007: 188; Meyer, 2006: 11). Normative convergence is a product of policy-learning processes consequent upon interaction through joint military operations and 'elite socialisation' within EU and NATO institutional forums, leading to the gradual convergence of domestic norms concerning the objectives and instruments of defence policy and the development of a 'European strategic culture' (Cornish and Edwards, 2005; Howorth, 2007: 188; Jones, 2007: 218; Meyer, 2005: 536). The contradictory nature of the relationship between the EU and NATO – both complementary and overlapping – lies in the piecemeal, evolutionary and gradual nature of norm convergence (Howorth, 2007: 191). As Meyer (2006: 11) argues: 'Normative convergence in these areas does not mean that national beliefs have become fully compatible...only that differences have narrowed.'

Hence the cultural turn in strategic studies, whilst subject to internal contestation (Duffield, 1998: 774–7; Johnston, 1995: 36–43; Longhurst, 2004: 8–16), argues that temporal location, sequencing and pace of military reform is determined by norms which are institutionally and societally-embedded and emphasises the impact of historical experience and collective memory in determining policy choices (Longhurst, 2004: 22). These norms constitute the identities of actors and form 'tool kits of action', mediating systemic pressure and displaying a high-degree of inertia (Dalgaard-Nielsen, 2006: 12–13; Gray, 1999; Irondelle, 2003b: 176). In cases of 'misfit' between the changing international security environment and domestic norms, convergence is either rapid and 'fundamental' (in the case of a critical juncture), or incremental, taking the form of fine-tuning (Longhurst, 2004: 18). However, change to the 'cultural core' is not simply the product of structural factors or 'historical pressures' (Berger, 1998: 16–21), but depends upon the role of political leaders in the core executive and actors within the broader defence and security policy subsystem as political entrepreneurs/securitising actors on behalf of cognitive change (Dalgaard-Nielsen, 2006: 11–13, 20; Longhurst, 2004; 20–2; Stritzel, 2007), or upon 'civilian' consensus concerning the domestic role of the armed forces (Kier, 1997: 141).

The following chapter will, however, demonstrate that military policy and the temporality of reform processes cannot be fully explained through cultural approaches. A normative analysis is unable to provide a convincing explanation of the divergent temporal location of 'third-order' military reform in the UK (1997–8) and France (1994–6). The strong civilian consensus on the domestic role of the armed forces in the UK and institutionally and societally-embedded norms concerning the military's (low-high intensity) global role in crisis-management and prevention would lead one to expect reform at an earlier, or at least similar, 'temporal location' than France, where 'third-order' change was delayed by a 'path dependent' commitment to conscription (Irondelle, 2003b). It is also difficult to explain the slow pace of British reforms (14 months), given such an 'enabling' normative context. This is all the more perplexing when compared to the pace of the 2003 reform to policy objectives in Germany (six months). Cultural accounts imply that the German 'culture of anti-militarism' should have ensured a more incremental pace of reform than in the UK due to societal and institutional resistance to radical reform to policy objectives and changes to the 'settings' of the policy instrument.

As neorealism suggests, rather than constitutive and a cause of action, culture emerges as more of tool in the hand of policy leaders, preoccupied with the maximisation of state power and international power and influence. But it is also a tool that can, under certain conditions (low executive autonomy), be put to use to manage the temporality of convergence with systemic imperatives. Hence in order to understand patterns of post-Cold War military convergence, we must look to the causal role played by material power relationships at the international level and the intervening role of domestic power relationships – to international structure and executive autonomy.

Section III

Testing Cultural and Realist Approaches: Defence Policies Between International Structure and Executive Autonomy

4
France: Domestic Incentives and Timely Adaptation to Systemic Imperatives

In France, normative accounts emphasise the critical roles played by Edouard Balladur in redefining the objectives of defence policy in the 1994 Defence White Paper and by President Jacques Chirac and Prime Minister Alain Juppe in 'manufacturing culture', by using the 1991 Gulf War and French participation in UN peacekeeping operations in Bosnia to generate a perception of crisis concerning appropriate policy instruments, notably the 'citizen in uniform' (Bloch, 2000: 2). McKenna (1997) and Irondelle (2003b) argue that Chirac and Juppe, spearheaded an 'advocacy coalition' in favour of a professional military. This normative entrepreneurship initiated policy-learning to institutionally-embedded beliefs on conscription, leading to a new civilian consensus around the domestic role of the armed forces and the need for the creation of a professional armed force (McKenna, 1997: 135–6). 'Third-order' change could then be implemented despite the preferences of the military for a 'mixed force' of conscripts and professionals, an analysis that also appears to confirm the arguments of Kier (Bloch, 2000). For Irondelle (2003b) path-dependency forms the decisive variable explaining the pace of reform and the 32 months that elapsed between reform to the objectives and to the institutional forums of policy and the creation of a professional armed force. This account has much in common with the 'externalist' securitisation account of Stritzel (2007), who argues that closer attention to the social context of the 'speech act' is necessary – in this case the social context was highly-restrictive, slowing down policy change. However, neoclassical realism and a focus on 'executive autonomy' provides a more convincing explanation of patterns of convergence and divergence in the temporality of reform.

Cohabitation and the pace of third-order reform

The French President enjoys a high-level of autonomy in defence policy, incentivising strategic innovation on behalf of convergence with systemic imperatives (Gordon, 1992; McKenna, 1997; Rynning, 2000: 64–5; Rynning, 2001/2). This autonomy is a product of several factors: the unitary state;

nature of military policy as the *'domain reserve'* (reserved domain) of the President; low salience of regional and local elections compared to Germany; prolonged window of opportunity open to French Presidents to enact policy change due to the seven year term of office (until 2002 when it was reduced to five) and weak linkages between the social and defence policy subsystems (Gregory, 2000a: 22–32; Gordon, 1992; McKenna, 1997). As McKenna (1997: 138) notes: 'his [the French President] extraordinary powers with regard to national defence weaken the argument that he is obliged to consult with any persons concerned with defence matters'.

The formal powers of the President in defence policy are, however, not uncontested (Gregory, 2000: 23). During cohabitation the nature of defence and security policy as the *'domain reserve'* is particularly open to challenge (Gregory, 2000a: 27–8). This section will highlight how deficits in Presidential autonomy during cohabitation (1993–5) are a central factor in explaining the pace of 'third-order' reform. The empirical evidence undermines culturalist arguments that posit the importance of civilian unity over the domestic role of the armed forces in determining convergence with systemic imperatives (Kier, 1997). Neither can change be explained by analysing the role of Chirac as a 'securitising actor' or norm entrepreneur, spearheading an 'advocacy coalition' affecting 'peripheral, operational and central beliefs' of national strategic culture and building civilian consensus around change to the policy instrument (Dalgaard-Nielsen, 2006: 12–13; Irondelle, 2003a,b).

French operational experience during the 1990/91 Gulf War was an important factor driving the early reform of the French military. During the conflict the French had only been able to mobilise 19,000 lightly armoured ground troops (the *Dauget Division* that also included 2500 logistical and support forces) from a combat ready army of 280,000. The French contribution to Operation Desert Storm also included 2,400 naval personnel and 1,160 air-force staff manning 60 aircraft, three destroyers and five frigates (Gregory, 2000a: 44–5). The British, on the other hand, had mobilised 36,000 personnel (including 29,000 ground troops), 80 aircraft and 23 ships from a combat ready army of 160,000 (Gregory, 2000a: 45; McKenna, 1997: 134).

Operation Desert Storm therefore demonstrated significant inadequacies in the military's capacity to participate in joint, multinational operations. These weaknesses derived from France's poor logistical and power projection capabilities, inadequate force protection, poor command and control and precision-strike capabilities, insufficient supplies of ammunition, as well as the need to improve information warfare and generate strategic intelligence (Faupin, 2002: 46–7; Gregory, 2000: 50; Howorth, 2001: 162; Utley, 2000: 186–7). Utley (2000: 185) cites a French Army colonel who upon the arrival of French Forces in the Gulf Region, noted: '[the military had] no real anti-missile protection, it [was] difficult for [them] to see and hear, though a lack of electronic means, and [they] lack[ed] heavy weaponry in case of an Iraqi attack'. In short, the Gulf War raised the specter of a potential decline in relative power relative *vis-à-vis* the British and Americans (Giegerich and Wallace,

2004: 166). As Gregory (2000: 53) notes: 'After the Gulf War it became evident that to uphold its rang in a context of disparate and geographically varied threats to international or regional stability, France would find itself involved in conflicts in many different parts of the world and in different ad hoc coalitions.'

Operation Turquoise in Rwanda (June–July 1994) conducted on a uni-lateral basis (under a UN Security Council Resolution) also reinforced a number of the core lessons of the Gulf War, in particular, the deficiencies in French power projection. The operation had been possible only due to the presence of prepositioned French troops and demonstrated the poor power projection capabilities of the Air Force that had to charter 40 aircraft at some considerable difficulty (Utley, 2000: 195). As Utley (2000: 197) highlights, the Rwandan operation demonstrated: 'the discrepancies of France's global ambitions and her military means'.

In the aftermath of Desert Storm the French military moved to establish structures which would act as an important first step to remedying the deficiencies identified by the Gulf War: the Joint Military Intelligence Agency, Joint Special Operations Command and Joint Planning Staff (Faupin, 2002: 47). The lessons of the Gulf War also expressed themselves in the *Loi de Programme Militaire* 1992–4. Space intelligence and communications capabilities (3 per cent increase in investment), jointness, mobility and strategic reach (7.4 per cent) received a notable hike in investment at the expense of nuclear modernisation, in which investment fell by 6.6 per cent (Gregory, 2000a: 79). LPM 1992–4 included investment in the Syracuse II and III and Helios I and II satellites and Sarigue intelligence gathering aircraft and in AMX10RC light tanks, VBL armoured cars, combat helicopters, anti-tank and air-defence missiles. Other important features of the LPM included investment in the *Charles de Gaulle* aircraft carrier; the development of a second carrier from 1997 and the purchasing of NH-90 anti-submarine and tactical transport helicopters (Gregory, 2000a: 81). These investments were financed, in part, though a cut in the size of the army from 280,000 to 225,000 by 1997.

More comprehensive reform to the structure of the French armed forces was, however, associated with significant opposition, both within the military and French society. Although there was growing recognition of the need for more deployable forces and for investment in conventional forces following the difficulties encountered in the Gulf War, the imperatives of the post-Cold War security environment remained too opaque to make far-reaching decisions on force structures in the early 1990s. As Utley (2000: 187) notes: 'The uncertainties of the post-Cold War period weighed heavily on French political and military calculations in the early 1990s.'

There was little consensus in the early mid-1990s amongst the public in support of an all-volunteer force and only a 'nascent' advocacy coalition promoting the end of conscription (Irondelle, 2003b: 179–80; Sabatier and Jenkins-Smith, 1999: 135).[1] Whilst the political centre-right (Union for

French Democracy (UDF) and Rally for the Republic (RPR)) was broadly in favour of professional forces, the French left opposed the abolition of conscription (Rynning, 2001–2: 96, 106). This 'civilian disunity' was reflected in Assembly complaints that President Chirac had failed to consult MPs and the general public and public opinion, which was strongly against the abolition of conscription in 1995 (Irondelle, 2003b: 180; McKenna, 1997: 138). Indeed, even the Defence Minister, Charles Millon, was opposed to a fully-professionalised force (Bloch, 2000: 36). The all-volunteer force was also a surprise for the military that, in the context of Balladur's 1994 White Paper, had drawn up its own model of structural reform under the guidance of General Jean-Rene Bachelet ('The Army of the 21st Century') outlining a 'mixed model' of conscripts and professionals.

The empirical evidence attests not to path-dependency as the determinant of the pace of reform (32 months), but points instead to the intervening roles played by domestic power relationships during cohabitation from 1993–5 (Gregory, 2000a: 71). Under cohabitation President Francois Mitterrand lacked several key domestic material power resources in defence policy, explaining why as Howorth (2004: 216) puts it, Mitterrand 'progressively lost his touch and fought shy of essential structural reforms'. Prime Minister Edouard Balladur (RPR) claimed defence policy to be a 'shared domain', necessitating a greater level of compromise in the policy sector (Bloch, 2000: 35). Although the timing of the 1994 Defence White Paper can be partly explained by the desire of Balladur to stake out a 'Presidential' image, the radical changes to the objectives of French Defence policy outlined in the document were made possible by a post-Cold War strategic context whose imperatives were becoming increasingly clear following events in the former Yugoslavia (Gregory, 2000a: 82). As Chapter 3 has highlighted, the need for a pace setting role in European defence following Germany's lead role on EMU also played an important role in spurring the early 'Europeanisation of French exceptionalism'.

However, the forthcoming Presidential elections of April–May 1995 provided little incentive for Socialist or Centre-Right candidates to act as a 'strategic innovators' and open-up debate about the instruments of defence policy – not least on conscription – due to the uncertain electoral benefits of campaigning on behalf of professional armed forces. This helps to explain why Chirac 'carefully avoided talking about all-volunteer forces' and 'at no time suggested abandoning conscription' during the 1995 election campaign (Gregory, 2000a: 84; Irondelle, 2003b: 180). Likewise, whilst adapting the objectives of Defence Policy to the radical changes in France's strategic environment, Balladur's Defence White Paper also argued for a mixed army of both professionals and conscripts.

It was only upon the election of Chirac as President in May 1995 that the domestic window of opportunity opened for strategic leadership on reforms to the policy instrument (McKenna, 1997: 135). The experience of operations with the British in the Gulf and Bosnia had left Chirac convinced that the British military should be the 'model against which the French would measure themselves' (Laird and Mey, 1999: 55) and that professionalisation would be the only means with which to operate effectively in the context of the complex multinational crisis-management operations, which, by the time of Chirac's election, increasingly characterised French military deployments (Sloan, 2002: 68; Laird and Mey, 1999: 53).

Although Chirac's base closures elicited protest, particularly in North-East France, his seven-year term of office and the end of cohabitation allowed him to promote third-order policy change by pointing to the challenges and opportunities presented by the international security environment, the imperative of meeting the Maastricht Convergence Criteria and long-term savings associated with professional armed forces (Faupin, 2002: 56–7; Tiersky, 1997: 3). Military reform also presented an excellent opportunity for Chirac to gain early political credit and profile himself as a political innovator (Bloch, 2000: 36).

Chirac's autonomy was further enhanced by the nature of linkages between the social, finance and defence policy subsystems. In Germany the implications of third-order reform for social policy encouraged the Finance Ministry under both the Kohl and Schröder governments to oppose convergence with systemic imperatives in order to meet the Maastricht Convergence Criteria. Conversely, the French Finance Ministry enhanced Chirac's autonomy in defence policy: 'The reform of the armed forces in 1995–6 directly originated in budget cuts...the fundamental issue of the single currency enabled the Treasury to have unprecedented power under the 5th Republic over defence policy' (Irondelle, 2003a: 219–20).

Although the Finance Ministry supported Chirac's reform agenda, during cohabitation (1993–5) the same institution, led by Edmond Alphandery of the opposition UDF, had employed its 'unprecedented power' to militate against change, acting as a powerful veto-player. As Irondelle (2003b: 177–8) demonstrates: 'The Finance Ministry and its powerful Budget Committee favoured the continuation of conscription for financial reasons'. In addition, the constraints of cohabitation also increased the sensitivity of Mitterrand to opposition to professionalisation from the Interior Ministry, led by Charles Pasqua of the Gaullist RPR Party, that benefited from recruits serving in the police force and civil security (Irondelle, 2003b: 178).

In short, in 1995 Chirac enjoyed not only a clearer picture of systemic imperatives than Mitterrand, but also much greater 'executive autonomy' and incentives for action than the former President had experienced. Rather than the manifestation of path-dependency or a culturally-embedded commitment to conscription, the protracted pace of reform was an outcome of the domestic material power relationships under cohabitation which circumscribed an entrepreneurial leadership role on the abolition of conscription from 1993–5.

The process of 'third-order' reform reflected the material power resources at Chirac's disposal in French defence policy and formed a case of entrepreneurial policy leadership: 'Chirac used all the resources of his policy leadership to ensure the change to a professional army against the wishes of both the armed forces and the Defence Ministry' (Irondelle, 2003b: 182). This stands in marked contrast to Germany, where Defence Ministers emerge as key figures in the management of reform processes. The Presidential proposals for reform were drawn up within a select working group, the *Comite Stratégique* (Strategic Committee) that granted privileged influence to close political confidants of Chirac, such as former Minister of Defence Pierre Messmer as well as a number of key military figures (Bloch, 2000: 36; Gregory, 2000: 90; Rynning, 2000: 63). The *Comite Stratégique* did not, however, have formal power in the reform process, but was instead a policy forum that was tasked with the more limited role of generating ideas for the *Conseil de Defence*. The *Comite Stratégique* formed the first stage of 'institutional protection', allowing the President to engineer a *fait accompli* by endowing the reform process with gravitas. This gravitas helped to marginalise any potential opposition to strategic innovation not only within the military but also within the broader political system, particularly the Left (Faupin, 2002: 48).[2]

Chirac provided further 'institutional protection' to 'third-order' change through the empowerment of the Defence Ministry's Strategic Affairs Division (SAD) that had been strengthened under Balladur and Pierre Joxe (Defence Minister 1991–3) (Gregory, 2000a: 90). Joxe had recognised the necessity for an empowered Chief of Staff and a horizontal organisation of the military, rather than vertical, separate services, allowing greater military-political cooperation in the context of out-of-area and low-medium-intensity operations (Bloch, 2000: 36; Rynning, 2001/02: 110). The SAD was also closely aligned with the Foreign Ministry, a strong supporter of a professional force, acting as a 'broker' of change within the Defence Ministry (Irondelle, 2003a: 220). Hence Chirac was able to compel the Chiefs of Staff to professionalise the armed forces (Irondelle, 2003b: 183; Laird and Mey, 1999: 53).

The President's decisive 'strategic innovation', the cooption of key military figures into the *Comite Strategique*, the 'institutional protection' afforded by the SAD and reforms instigated to the 'lessons-learned' process (see below) allowed Chirac to delegate the technical details of force structure to the military (Bloch, 2000: 36–9).[3] 'Executive autonomy' ensured that Chirac could leave the detail of reform to the military, confident in appropriate change to the policy instrument and in his ability to implement the reform model (Bloch, 2000: 36). It is also important to note that Chirac's strategic innovation was seized upon by military planners as an opportunity to renew France's strategic importance (McKenna, 1997: 136). These factors combined to inform the military's development of an enhanced force projection capability and embrace new doctrine (the 'mastery of violence'), in addition to the more traditional 'coercion by the means of force', as its two key operational modes.

The emergence of 'best practice': Operational experience and the triumph of the French RMA school

As outlined in detail in Chapter 1, LPM 1997–2002 began the process of French investment around networked capabilities – notably in C2 and ISR – as well as capabilities to enhance strategic mobility (Bratton, 2002: 93; Gregory, 2000: 94).[4] Nevertheless, the period following the 1994–6 defence reforms was characterised by a strong degree of contestation over the precise extent to which capability investment and doctrinal evolution should emulate the weapons systems and concepts associated with the US-led RMA. As Bratton (2002: 96–101) highlights, it is possible to identify three main strands of thinking within the French military during the post-Cold War era concerning the validity of the RMA as the guiding concept for French transformation: the '*Jeune Ecole*'; the 'Sceptics' and proponents of the 'New Operational Art' (NOA) or 'French RMA School'.

The '*Jeune Ecole*' emerged during the early mid-1990s and cohered around officers based largely within the Navy and Air Force. They argued that technological advances permitting a system of systems – notably intelligence gathering, new command and control capabilities, satellite reconnaissance, UAVs and PGM – provided an opportunity to place France at the forefront of future Kosovo-style peacemaking operations and higher intensity conflict against near-peer competitors. The notion of a technological revolution in military affairs and its potential utility in peacemaking operations was also supported by prominent figures from the civilian establishment, such as former defence minister Charles Million (1995–7) (Bratton, 2002).

The 'Sceptics' identified the RMA as largely irrelevant to the challenges French armed forces were likely to face in the post-Cold War era. They argued that, in contrast to the US, France would be unlikely to undertake conflict against a peer or near-peer competitor, but that she faced instead the qualitatively different challenge of peacekeeping and post-conflict reconstruction operations. Whilst some of the intelligence, surveillance and reconnaissance capabilities associated with the RMA may prove useful in such a context, the capabilities required in low-intensity peacekeeping operations were not 'stand-off', but a willingness to put 'boots on the ground' and sustain casualties (Bratton, 2002: 98–9). Furthermore, the Sceptics argued that the RMA was not only unsuitable for France, but that it also represented a threat. A reform process focused around emulation of a US-led RMA would leave France filling a niche in a US dominated 'system of systems', locked into American policy and ever more subject to US hegemony (Bratton, 2002; Rynning, 2000: 72).

Finally, the 'French RMA School' identified the RMA as a case of the development of Operational Art, rather than a 'strategic rupture' (Bratton, 2002: 100; Gongora and von Riekhof, 2000: 3; Gere, 2000: 129–39). Consequently the challenge for the French military would be to adapt this NOA to the kinds of missions that French would be likely to face: namely peacekeeping and post-conflict reconstruction. It is the French RMA School that has triumphed. As demonstrated by Chapter 1, France, like the UK, has undertaken a partial, selective emulation of the RMA, in the form of NEC and EBAO. This emulation focused upon enhancing its capacity to assist in the delivery of operational effects across the conflict spectrum and undertake 'Three Block Warfare', whilst retaining the ability to conduct MCO as part of multinational coalitions. Implicit within the French approach is a strong degree of scepticism concerning the 'transformative' implications of technological advances for the nature of warfare.

The temporality of French capability investment around NEC is broadly comparable to that of the British (see Table 2.6) and reflects a similar structural dynamic: the partial lifting of the post-Cold War 'fog of peace' and emergence of a model of 'best' practice in defence capability acquisition and doctrinal reform (Imlay and Toft, 2006). As Faupin (2002: 53) highlights, decisions on capability investment following the reforms of 1995/96 have included: 'a period of prudent maturation to make sure that the changes that have occurred in the national and international environment are long-lasting'. The 'fog of peace' has been dissipated by two main dynamics. Firstly, French operational experiences and secondly, observation of the successes and failures of the US-led RMA in practice.

Operational experiences during the 1990s in Africa and the Balkans reinforced to policy-makers and the military the requirement of developing balanced forces capable of dealing with crisis-management operations of rapidly varying intensity (Giegerich and Wallace, 2004: 166–7; Tardy, 1999: 72–5). Deployments within the former Yugoslavia during the 1990s (notably, UNPROFOR, SFOR, IFOR and KFOR) had a particularly important impact on French doctrine on OOTW. Until the mid-1990s French doctrine on peace operations had focused upon traditional peacekeeping missions (operations taking place following a ceasefire and with the consent of the warring parties) or upon peace imposition (to oppose the threat of the use of force or the use of force by an aggressor) (Gregoire, 2002: 6). Such missions necessitated adherence to the principle of impartiality and the use of force only in self-defence.

However, the inability of international peacekeepers to protect civilians under UNPROFOR and experiences under IFOR and SFOR demonstrated the existence of a new form of peace operation: peace restoration that required the capacity to respond more robustly. This form of operation was first given written expression in the 1995 Directive of the French Chief of Staff, Admiral Jacques Lanxade (1991–5), who noted that contemporary peace operations were characterised by a lack of consent and a 'continuum of conflict' (Gregoire, 2002: 4). These conclusions mirrored the operational lessons that were being learned by the UK military, as outlined in 'Joint Warfare Publication 3-50' of 1997 (Rollins, 2006: 88).[5]

Operation Allied Force of March–June 1999 provided an emphatic lesson that humanitarian intervention would require high-intensity warfighting capabilities. In the 1991 Gulf War France provided less that 4 per cent of combat aircraft (which were unable to operate at night) and conducted only 1 per cent of all combat air sorties (Utley, 2000: 185, 207). However, in the Kosovo conflict France proved its worth as an Alliance partner by undertaking 12 per cent of combat air sorties (non-US NATO members undertook 47 per cent of combat air sorties) and utilising its ISR assets to make a limited contribution to intelligence gathering (Bratton, 2002: 93; Gregory, 2000: 45; Yost, 2003: 88). French Mirage 200D aircraft had also proved successful in delivering laser-guided bombs by both day and night.

Consequently, as in the UK, Kosovo reinforced position of proponents of the need to respond more fully to the challenge of battlefield digitisation (Yost, 2003: 88–90). The conflict spurred further investment in stand-off precision strike weapons systems and the enhancement of C4ISR capabilities, not least information systems and secure communications networks, whose poor interoperability with those of the US had hampered cooperation (Giegerich and Wallace, 2004: 166; Yost, 2003: 88–90). The dependence of France and its other NATO partners on the US for 95 per cent of its intelligence during the Kosovo conflict also underlined the lessons of the 1990/91 Gulf War about the requirement to push ahead with national and European-level investment in satellite and UAV systems (Yost, 2003: 89–91). In addition, reliance on US electronic attack capabilities reinforced the need to update the jamming capabilities of the Rafale and Eurofighter (Yost, 2003: 89–91).

The process of lesson-learning following the 1995–6 reforms was bolstered by strong civilian leadership, facilitated by the nature of defence and security policy as the *domain reserve* of the President that, outside periods of cohabitation, narrows the opportunity for dissent. Chirac's autonomy in defining the role of military force in French foreign policy was, however, further enhanced by events in Bosnia, notably the July 1995 Srebrenica Massacre. This event acted to endow French participation in NATO's Operation Allied Force with a strong level of legitimacy, despite the absence of a UN mandate. Chirac was, therefore, able to construct a broad political consensus across the centre-left/centre-right behind the Kosovo conflict (Rynning, 2000: 64–7). Whilst participation in Operation Allied Force was initially accompanied by dissent and public debate, it was confined to the right wing of the RPR and the left wing of the French Socialist Party. As Rynning (2000: 76) notes: 'Informed elite criticism floundered during Kosovo.' This lack of dissent contrasts markedly to the contestation that accompanied Mitterrand's deployment of peacekeeping troops under UNPROFOR in the former Yugoslavia in 1992 (Utley, 2000: 190–4). The growing consensus surrounding the role of the French military in 'humanitarian' intervention gave the operational lessons of the conflict greater resonance and gravitas. The Kosovo conflict therefore acted to confirm the validity of the 'third-order' reforms to the French military that had been enacted by LPM 1996–2002 and, as in the UK, formed an important stage in the identification of 'best practice' by pointing to the imperative of an emulation of key elements of the US-led RMA (Yost, 2003: 88–90; Rynning, 2000: 76).

Hence, by the mid-late 1990s, it was increasingly clear that French land forces would have to prepare to act with 'active impartiality': to use minimum force to defend civilians and the mandate of a mission and to undertake conflict that could vary from low-high intensity (Gregoire, 2002: 6). Although the experiences of operations in the Balkans demonstrated the need for precision-strike stand-off capabilities, they also highlighted the importance of developing the capabilities and doctrine necessary for the deployment of ground forces in complex crisis-management operations. This imperative was reinforced following the contribution of 2,650 troops to SFOR in 1996 and 4,600 soldiers to KFOR in 1999 as leader of Multinational Brigade North (Utley, 2006: 67). The potential for 'a brutal reversibility at short notice' in the intensity of missions was particularly evident in these operations, not least during the deployment of the 3rd Mechanised Brigade under KFOR (Michel, 2005: 6).[6] SFOR and KFOR therefore provided a powerful lesson that French forces would need to be endowed with the structures, doctrine and capabilities which would facilitate the concurrent conduct of deterrence, COIN and interposition and master the application of both kinetic and non-kinetic effects (Michel, 2005).

These experiences were of great importance in informing the 2001–2 cycle of the Future Land Action Study and its interim report of September 2002 that pointed to a scepticism about the transformative implications of battlefield digitisation and the need for both senior commanders and subordinates to prepare for greater subsidiarity in command and control (Leclerc, 2003: 8–9). Consequently, although the more ardent RMA Sceptics were marginalised by the late 1990s and the acquisition of C4ISR systems formed the backbone of LPM 2003–8, operations during the 1990s had also highlighted the importance of the 'human factor' in operations conducted 'amongst the people' (Bratton, 2002: 94; Charbonneau, 2008: 99–100).

These learning processes within the military were accompanied by civilian leadership around the development of networked capabilities. As Rynning (2000: 68–9) notes of French Defence Minister Alain Richard (1997–2002): 'Richard has taken a professional pride in the convergence between French and US capabilities...Richard argued that only France and the US were capable of undertaking the full variety of tasks demanded by NATO. It is interesting to note that a French Defence Minister so strongly argues that a US standard must measure French success'. This civilian leadership on behalf of emulation of the RMA derived from the imperative of retaining interoperability with NATO Alliance partners, not least the US that had been highlighted by the Kosovo conflict. The development of C4ISR capabilities were also viewed by French policy-makers as vital in precluding a loss of relative power on ESDP to the British following St. Malo by ensuring the capacity of the French to lead a medium-sized autonomous European operation.

The lessons of the Balkans have been further reinforced by the French experience of post-Cold War 'operations amongst the people' in Africa. These operations have demonstrated the imperative of military structures, doctrine and capabilities capable of delivering both kinetic and non-kinetic effects and which pointed to the limitations of technology in complex crisis-management operations. As the Commander of the Combined Arms Battalion under UNSOM II (May 1993–March 1995), Colonel Pierre De Saqui De Sans, noted: 'The combat operations in Mogadishu have clearly demonstrated that nowadays in matters of crisis-management it will not always be possible to...take advantage of our technological superiority, contrary to what happened in the Gulf War' (De Saqui De Sans, 2004: 55).

The importance of preparation for 'Three Block Warfare' was clearly evidenced by Operation Artemis, a humanitarian mission conducted under the auspices of ESDP in the Democratic Republic of Congo (June–September 2003), to which France contributed 1,785 of the 2,200 troops. Operation Licorne (September 2002) involved the deployment of 4,000 French troops to implement the Marcoussis Peace Agreements in Sierra Leone provided a particularly important set of operational lessons (Utley, 2006: 69). The operation highlighted the importance of the 'deterrent' power of the threat of force, the requirement for flexibility in doctrine and the need for command structures and Theater HQs to be capable of adaptation from the initial entry stage of an operation to the delivery of environmental planning capabilities[7] (LeCerf, 2008: 34). Operation Licorne also demonstrated the centrality of HUMINT, PSYOPS, task flexibility at lower levels of command, the centrality of jointness[8] and the importance of combat helicopters in facilitating land manoeuvre (Bohineust-Comalat, 2008: 8–11; Bore, 2006: 95–8). In addition, the operation highlighted some significant deficiencies in intelligence collection and processing: a shortage of specialised sensors, weak coordination between intelligence actors, a requirement for in-source treatment analysts, poor control of reporting, the lack of a structured database and problems in dealing with the increasing file size of electronic imagery (LeBot, 2006: 11).

The French also contributed 1,000 soldiers to EUFOR RDCongo (July–December 2006) whose mandate was to protect civilians and provide support to the UN Mission to the Democratic Republic of Congo during the electoral process. The experience of Operation Benga under EUFOR RDCongo highlighted, once more, the need to master the simultaneous application of effects across the conflict spectrum. Key lessons identified included the importance of cultural understanding and of jointness in the provision of intelligence, airlift and fire support, as well as the 'decisive advantage' that could be delivered by UAVs (Ternynck, 2008: 75–6). Furthermore, the operation demonstrated the need to ensure rigorous operational planning, whilst leaving room for flexibility in the conduct of operations, thereby reinforcing the importance of the principle of 'subsidiarity' and greater autonomy for subordinate levels of command (Pau, 2007: 81).

Indeed, post-Cold War operations have had important implications for the French approach to command and control. Whilst French command and control has traditionally been characterised by a stronger level of hierarchy than the UK and Germany, 'peace restoration' missions and have spawned a growing realisation of the utility of greater flexibility and the delegation of responsibility (Roussel, 2004: 18). For example, following the experience of commanding a brigade as part of the multinational joint forces operation in Kosovo in 2000, Major General Louis Sublet noted that whilst 'a certain degree of control has to be obtained', 'it was essential to delegate responsibility'.[9] As the Commander of the French Army Doctrine and Senior Military Training Command, Lieutenant-General Andre Soubirou, outlined in 2003: 'The break with the past is at the cultural level...and the development of subsidiarity within hierarchical relationships constitute the core of this'.[10]

French thinking on command and control in the context of networked operations of varying intensity has also been influenced by a second important factor: observation of the successes and failures of the US-led RMA. Whilst demonstrating a powerful lesson about the capacity of technology to attain rapid and decisive 'initial entry', French observation of the US experience of networked operations during Operation Iraqi Freedom highlighted the limitations of technology. These limitations were identified as the potential for dependence on vulnerable information processing systems and crucially, the centrality of 'human factors' to realising the potential of battlefield digitisation.[11] The conflict pointed to the inability of the 'human factor' to keep up with the pace of the 'decision-making loop' (as the US Army was 'overtaken by its own speed').[12] Operation Iraqi Freedom also highlighted the pitfalls of overcentralised leadership, which, it was noted by General Bernard Thorette (Chief of Staff of the French Army, 2002–6), created too great a distance from events on the ground.[13] Furthermore, the French perceived the US version of NCW as raising the potential for a dangerous level of political interference at the operational level of conflict.

Consequently, following the observation of others' and France's own operational experiences during the post-Cold War period the imperative of 'greater decentralisation and dynamism' in command and control arrangements was given formal expression in the 'Doctrinal Manual for the Employment of Land Forces in Urban Environments',[14] the 'Crisis-Management Concept' and 'Winning the Battle, Building the Peace'.[15] As Brigadier General Vincent Desportes, Commander of the French Forces Employment Doctrine Centre, notes: 'The only way leading from now on to success is indirect command: definition of the objective and of what should not be done much more than what should be done...the art of command is to know how to encourage individual initiative while knowing how to demand as and when needed formal discipline' (Desportes, 2008d: 52).

Post-Cold War crisis-management operations have also demonstrated the importance of the principles of manoeuvre at the higher-intensity end of the conflict spectrum (termed the 'lightning principle').[16] As in the UK, the focus of the application of NEC at the higher-end of the conflict spectrum has been upon the opportunity provided by RMA technologies to dictate the tempo of operations by enhancing speed and maneuverability (the principle of *'foudroydance'*),[17] rather than to mass firepower and attrition (Auriault, 2003: 12). Control of the tempo of operations has been identified as central, not only in attaining 'initial entry' to conflict zones, but also in limiting the need to use overwhelming firepower and avoiding the deterioration of peace restoration operations into asymmetrical conflict (Gombeaud, 2003: 34; Gregoire, 2002: 8).

The events of 11 September 2001 also formed an important juncture in French defence policy. The attacks signaled to policy-makers the importance of ensuring the capacity to deploy expeditionary forces at a global level as part of the war on terrorism, in addition to the need to secure French territory against terrorist attack (Bezacier, 2005: 4–8; Meyer, 2005: 10–11). French participation in Operation Enduring Freedom was initially limited to 500 troops, deployed in and around Kabul, as well as 200 special forces in the south of Afghanistan. The French also provided 100 personnel and two transport aircraft based in Tajikistan as well as 11 naval vessels under the aircraft carrier Charles de Gaulle (Task Force 150) deployed in the Indian Ocean/Gulf of Oman (Gregory, 2003: 139; Utley, 2006: 69). The French troop commitment in Afghanistan was expanded in 2006 by the provision of 1,100 extra soldiers to ISAF. French forces remained, however, deployed in Kabul and participated in largely low-medium intensity peacekeeping and training operations. The French ISAF contingent was further strengthened by President Nicolas Sarkozy in 2008 through the deployment of 700 extra troops in the East of Afghanistan, bringing the total number of French forces under ISAF to 3,070. French forces in Afghanistan have, during the last two years, been increasingly drawn into higher-intensity operations as the security situation around Kabul and in the East of Afghanistan has deteriorated.[18] These experiences, combined with the observation of doctrinal developments on COIN in the UK and US have reinforced the imperative of preparing for 'Three Block Warfare' (Perron de Revel, 2007: 85–8).

On the one hand, Afghanistan has reinforced the need to acquire RMA-style capabilities. The initial lessons of Operation Enduring Freedom demonstrated the need to further invest in air and sea lift capabilities to permit strategic mobility and in precision-guided munitions (Bratton, 2002: 96). Integrated manoeuvre (*'Aerocombat'*)[19] has also emerged as a critical aspect of the Afghan campaign in the delivery of effects across the conflict spectrum (Desportes, 2008c; Maecheler, 2008: 19–25).[20] ISAF has, therefore, thrown into sharper relief the need for the training of greater numbers of forward air controllers and reinforced investment in imagery intelligence (IMINT), notably UAVs, UCAVs, as well as helicopters and fixed-wing aircraft (Chereau, 2006: 28; Coppolani, 2006: 10; Kohn et al, 2008: 86–9). ISAF has also demonstrated the need to train dedicated Joint Terminal Air Controllers (JTAC) in order to synchronise air and land forces and ensure effective air-land maneuver, not least as a means with which to limit civilian casualties (Kohn et al, 2008: 86–9). Furthermore, the operation has highlighted the requirement to refine doctrinal development on joint operations in the 'third dimension' involving sea, land and air based assets that began development during the late 1990s. These experiences played an important role in informing the development of the 2004 Army Doctrinal Manual on digitised operations in the 'third dimension': *'Principes D'Emploi De La Fot Numerisee de Niveau 3'* (Previsani, 2008: 15–17; Zimmermann, 2008: 26–8).

At the same time, the limitations of technology to operations under ISAF have been clear. Afghanistan has provided an excellent opportunity to observe at first-hand the weaknesses associated with the technological fixation that has underpinned US military transformation. As Lieutenant Colonel Marie-Dominique Charlier of the Forces Employment Doctrine Centre noted in 2008, the key problem encountered by the Americans in Iraq and Afghanistan was that: 'war was carried out like a technical action isolated from its political environment...the lack of anticipation and social studies was typical of the intervention in Afghanistan (2001)' (Charlier, 2008: 13). The French lessons from observation of the RMA are perhaps most pertinently encapsulated by Lieutenant Colonel Marc Humbert, French Liaison Officer to JFCOM: 'Technology is great but that winning card is supposed to stay in human players' hands and serve them...As a matter of fact no weapon system would equal brainpower. Our American friends are cruelly learning from that, at their own expense, each day. Might such blindness show us a clearer way' (Humbert, 2008: 106).[21]

ISAF has, therefore, underlined the importance of 'human factors' in the conduct of 'three block warfare'. The operation has reinforced the lessons from previous crisis-management operations concerning the need to balance the gains in force protection that can be attained through technological advances (for example in combating improvised explosive devices) with the tactical advantages accrued by retaining close contact with the population and the application of minimum force (Cholley, 2006: 13–15; De Corbet, 2008: 98–100; De Lajudie, 2008: 114–17; Nicol, 2008: 13–14). Furthermore, whilst precision strike capabilities have emerged as vital in helping to minimise collateral damage, Afghanistan has demonstrated how their effective use can only be based upon intelligence gathered on the ground through HUMINT (Desportes, 2006: 3–4).[22] As a consequence, the experiences of Afghanistan have acted to impart the importance of the 'soldier as sensor'[23] and the deficiencies of a 'systems of systems' approach to networking in highly complex battlefields (Coppolani, 2004: 20; Desportes, 2006: 3–4).[24] ISAF has also underlined the deficiencies identified in intelligence acquisition and processing during Operation Licorne (LeBot, 2006: 111–14).

As a consequence of these experiences, changes have been instigated to the training of Army Intelligence Officers at the Army Intelligence Study and Training Centre (CEERAT) in order to ensure that officers have the capacity to process the complex information arising from asymmetrical conflict. There has also been a stronger a focus on intelligence in the collective training for staffs' functional cells organised by Land Forces Command (Bourin, 2006: 38; Coppolani, 2006: 11; Poucet, 2006: 74–7).

Furthermore, ISAF has reinforced the need to focus on the role of the French military in training local security forces and developing governance structures (Caplain, 2007: 16–17; de Villiers, 2008: 59–61). The 'lessons-learned' process following early operations in Afghanistan threw into sharp relief the requirement for a unified approach to the training of national security forces spanning the participants in complex multinational operations, the need to establish a centralised documentation database on the territories covered by Operational Training Detachments (OTDs) and for greater planning when considering the human and material means necessary for the OTDs (Gouriou, 2007: 93–6; Zbienen, 2004). Cultural training and HUMINT also emerged as vital in the delivery of effects across the conflict spectrum (Chereau, 2006: 28).

As a consequence of these experiences in Afghanistan and the increasing number of expeditionary operations conducted in urban areas during the 1990s, the Army National Training Centre established a Military Operations in Urban Terrain Training Centre (CENZUB) in September 2006 (Nicol, 2004: 29). In addition, a number of changes were instigated to the training of younger Army Officers at the St Cyr-Coetquidan Schools following deployments in the Balkans which focused on the skills necessary in complex crisis-management operations (Boene, Nogues and Haddad, 2004: 39). CENZUB has also reviewed existing training scenarios within the Force on Force Training Centre and Command Post Battle Command Training Centre in order to ensure adequate preparation for scenarios such as 'three block warfare'. These changes have resulted in the development of Staff Intelligence Adaptation Courses and of an Intelligence Officer Curriculum (Bourin, 2006: 40–2; Kergus, 2007: 47–9; de Lammerville, 2006; Moriniere et al, 2007: 50–2). In recognition of the need for greater decentralisation of command and control in Three Block Warfare, CENZUB places particular emphasis upon training company-level commanders in situational awareness in order to permit them to 'grasp opportunities' and to prepare junior NCOs to 'take the initiative' (Nicol, 2004: 24). Furthermore, CENZUB organises mission-specific preparation sessions for units about to be deployed (conditioning for projection (MCP)) (Kergus, 2007: 47–9).

The conflict in Afghanistan also illustrated the need to improve the institutional architecture underpinning the 'comprehensive approach', in particular, to shift from a centralised form of interministerial coordination to an 'inter-ministerial network' (Charlier, 2008: 11–20; Joana, 2008: 20–3).

The operation reinforced the importance of expanding the role of the Crisis-Management Coordination Cell within the Foreign Ministry to a more permanent and structured form of inter-agency coordination throughout the duration of a crisis and provided an important impetus for the development of the Political Crisis-Management Centre outlined in the 2008 White Paper (Gout, 2007: 13–15).

ISAF has, in addition, provided further signals of the efficacy of more decentralised forms of command and control in order to allow flexibility in the face of quickly changing exigencies (Charlier, 2008: 11–20). Indeed, the conflict has spurred the instigation of a study, commissioned in 2008 by the French Army Chief of Staff and carried out by the Forces Employment Doctrine Centre and Deputy Chief of Staff, to review how the Army can adapt its doctrine, training, equipment and organisation in a more rapid and effective manner (Michon, 2007: 45–6; Vouteau and De Solages, 2008: 101).

Hence the lessons imparted by post-Cold War crisis-management operations led the US definition of EBO to be sceptically received within French military circles (Desportes, 2007: 4–8). As in the UK, EBAO is the favoured approach and is viewed by the French as a means with which to enable coherence between the application of both kinetic and non-kinetic dimensions of modern conflict (Desportes, 2007: 4–8). Furthermore, post-Cold War operations in Africa, the former Yugoslavia, the French presence in support of UNFIL in Lebanon since September 2006 and the 1,000 strong contribution to the Multinational Interim Force in Haiti in 2004 also highlighted the centrality of the embedding EBAO within a 'Comprehensive Approach' (Chamas, 2007: 22–4; Charlier, 2008: 11–20; Joana, 2008: 20–3; Richier and Morel, 2007: 12). The integration of civilian and military capabilities that this approach permits is viewed as critical in permitting the military to 'face any type of situation' and 'manage a reversible continuum of low-high intensity actions' (Chamas, 2007: 22–4; Richier and Morel, 2007: 12).

The resonance of past doctrinal developments with contemporary challenges

Post-Cold War operational experiences, combined with close observation of the operation of the RMA and its associated concepts of NCW and EBO in Afghanistan, Iraq as well as observation of the experiences of the Israelis in the Second Lebanon War of 2006 have built upon many of the principles inherent in the concept of the 'Mastery of Violence' that underpinned the 1994–6 French Defence Reform (Bezacier, 2004b: 9).[25] The conceptual core of contemporary French defence reform – EBAO and the Comprehensive Approach – resonates strongly with the emphasis that Mastery of Violence placed upon mastering the multiple dimensions of military operations, not least the non-kinetic side of the conflict spectrum: humanitarian assistance, information and intelligence and post-conflict reconstruction (Bezacier, 2004a: 4–11; Desportes, 2008a: 8).

However, contemporary challenges have a much deeper resonance within French military doctrine, as the core features of the 'Mastery of Violence' and its focus on the delivery of a combination of both kinetic and non-kinetic effects can be traced back to doctrinal developments during France's operational experiences in former colonies: the First Indo-China War (1946–54)[26] and, in particular, the Algerian War of Independence (1954–62).[27] As Brigadier-General Vincent Desportes notes: 'We notice a large widening of the military job. It is only a come-back to the reality of yester-year; the reflection of the return of history' (Desportes, 2008a: 8).

Following four years of unsuccessful conflict against the Algerian *Front de Liberation Nationale* (FLN) General de Gaulle – elected with 78 per cent of the popular vote in 1958 and empowered by the constitutional changes of the 5th Republic which strengthened the autonomy of the core executive in matters of defence policy – was in a particularly strong position to develop and champion a new strategy. Under De Gaulle's strategic leadership, the French military began to critically examine the lessons of operations in Indo-China (Thompson, 2008: 14), leading to a number of important tactical and operational changes to French COIN.

The 'Centre for the Teaching of Pacification and Counter-Guerilla Warfare' that had been established in 1956 began to place an important emphasis on training officers on Algerian history, culture and Islamic beliefs. Furthermore, the military developed the *Sections Adminisratives Specialisees*: small groups of Army Officers who focused on governance, administration and development in Algeria (Thompson, 2008: 12–13). Central to French doctrinal development on COIN were non-kinetic effects, which also characterise contemporary doctrinal development: the importance of information, humanitarian aid and the role of the military in providing the foundations for reconstruction (the development of infrastructure, jobs, education, healthcare and administrative structures) (Thompson, 2008: 13).[28]

At the same time, important changes to the tactical dimensions of COIN operations were taking place under the leadership of the Commander in Chief of Forces in Algeria, General Maurice Challe. General Challe instigated concepts[29] which would resonate with post-Cold War conceptual development on expeditionary crisis-management: the principle of modularity, the importance of professional, specialist and highly-trained forces; jointness and mission command (Charbonneau, 2008: 98–9). Challe promoted decentralised command and control structures in order to increase mobility, manoeuvrability and speed of response by 'allowing one commander in his own area of operations to quickly put into action all logistical and operational forces to "bring the greatest effort to bear"' (Thompson, 2008: 19).

Challe also emphasised the importance of modularity and jointness between airpower and infantry/special forces as a means with which to enhance mobility, speed and surprise and utilised airpower for surveillance and reconnaissance, ground support, command and control and psychological operations (Desportes, 2008b: 3; Lasconjarias, 2008: 72–4; Thompson, 2008: 16–17). Elite, specialist forces were identified as central to successful COIN, as evidenced by the development of the *Commandos de Chasse* (lightly armed, mobile Commandos) and *Reserve Generale* (highly armed, yet nevertheless mobile, intervention forces) in 1958 (Thompson, 2008: 16).

In short, French operational experiences during the initial post-WW2 period acted to demonstrate some of the fundamental characteristics needed to undertake contemporary 'three-block warfare'. These attributes included the importance of balanced, joint forces, capable not only of exploiting the advantages of technological innovations in the delivery of kinetic and non-kinetic effects, but also of low-intensity psychological information operations, reconstruction efforts and the development of local administrative capacity, in addition to the importance of decentralisation in command and control, enabling the role of the 'strategic corporal'.

The attempt to hold onto the French Union in Indo-China and Algeria was a losing battle, given British decolonisation and US opposition to colonialism. Yet, as Cogan (2006: 245) highlights, the withdrawal from Algeria in 1962 was not accompanied by a sense of defeat. Although the lessons-learned in Algeria were marginalised by the Cold War imperatives of doctrinal evolution and capability investment around nuclear deterrence and territorial and alliance defence, the experiences of French COIN in Algeria had a 'carryover effect' (Cogan, 2006: 245) and formed a basis for doctrinal development around French expeditionary crisis-management in the early post-Cold War era (Gregory, 2000: 14). In these colonial experiences lay the roots of the principles of 'modularity' and the 'Mastery of Violence' that, in its focus on the role of non-kinetic factors in controlling the process of 'escalation' has formed an important stop in the evolution of French thinking on EBAO and the 'Comprehensive Approach'.

However, whilst past practices dovetailed with post-Cold War challenges and formed an important intellectual foundation for the development of doctrine on the conduct of complex crisis-management operations of quickly varying intensity, it is not the legacy of the past that has determined the precise trajectory of doctrinal and conceptual development. Instead, the emergence of 'best practice' has been based upon operational experience and the observation of the RMA in practice. As this section has demonstrated, experiences of 'wars amongst the people' in the Balkans and Africa during the 1990s provided a powerful lesson about the requirement for balanced military forces, capable of joint, multinational operations across the spectrum of conflict and about the relevance of past experience and doctrine to contemporary challenges. This context has necessitated a critical application of existing doctrine, combined with a partial and selective emulation of the RMA that has been tailored to meet the requirements of 'Three Block Warfare', as well as the capacity to undertake more conventional MCO (as part of multinational coalitions). These operational experiences have dovetailed with French observation of the strengths and limitations of US EBO and NCW, particularly following the Iraq conflict, Israeli attack on Lebanon in 2006[30] and joint operations with the US in Kosovo and Afghanistan, to facilitate the triumph of the French RMA School.[31]

The crucial determinant of the overall temporality of the reform process was not, however, the presence of culturally and institutionally-embedded norms concerning the role of the French armed forces or even the repository of knowledge provided by the experience of the dissolution of empire. We must, instead, look to the macro-political level and to the presence of strong strategic leadership by Chirac, who pushed through third-order reform to the armed forces in 1996 in the face of considerable opposition within the military and amongst the general public. Driven by the imperative of retaining interoperability with US and acquiring the capacity to lead autonomous operations of varying intensity under ESDP, Chirac used his formal power resources to ensure institutional protection (through the SAD in the 1997/98 reform and later through the restructuring of the DGA, CICDE and CEMA) for a focus on joint expeditionary power projection. Although Chirac's decisive strategic leadership was incentivised by systemic pressures, it was facilitated by a high level of executive autonomy that allowed Chirac – in stark contrast to German policy leaders – to overcome domestic veto players and deliver a timely response to the dictates of international structure.

With third-order reform institutionalised, the precise detail of doctrinal and capability development could be left to a military whose input into defence planning had been structured to ensure objectivity (see below). The broad focus on NEC, EBAO embedded within the Comprehensive Approach that emerged as a result of this 'bottom-up' process was then formally codified by the June 2008 Defence White Paper. The DWP also acted to provide clear and unambiguous 'top-down' civilian guidance on the precise implications of post-Cold War operational experiences for force structures and capabilities.

Managing military input into defence planning: Ensuring adaptability at the tactical and operational levels

Lesson learning within the Army has been facilitated by a rigorous approach to ascertaining the implications of operational experiences for doctrine and capabilities at three key levels: in the field, at the staff level and in military training (La Maisonneuve, 2004: 36). Following deployment under KFOR that demonstrated the advantages associated with the UK and US approach to identifying and implementing 'lessons-learned', the Joint Staff and Operations Division adopted the Anglo-Saxon 'Experience Feedback' (RETEX) mechanism between May 2000 and 2003. Whilst the adoption of RETX was an attempt to strengthen the objectivity of the lessons-learned process it was, in particular, an attempt to improve the implementation of the lessons of operational experience (Le Bail, 2003: 73; Serveille, 2004: 47–8).

The RETEX process is coordinated by the Army Exercises and Operations Feedback and Assessment Centre (CEREX) and follows four key phases: data collection, data analysis, verification and follow-up. An Officer is appointed within a Mission HQ focusing specifically on Experience Feedback. This Officer is at the heart of a network of RETEX Officers who are distributed across different brigades and who input information on the key areas of successes and failure during operations/exercises to a HQ-level database. The information collected in this database is then analysed by CEREX. The collection and analysis phases benefits from the organisation of 'actor symposiums': intensive interactive exercises undertaken by between eight and 12 high-level personnel returning from the operation/exercise (Fruchard, 2001: 13). These symposiums, organised by the external agency, RGA SYSTEMES, allow the key actors in an operation/exercise to explore the myriad of factors which contributed to operational success or failure including equipment, doctrine, training and procedures and also provide the opportunity for participants to suggest potential solutions. (Fruchard, 2001: 13; Voute, 2001: 7). This process of data collection and analysis is supplemented by individual testimony sessions (Voute, 2001: 7).

Once the final mission report has been concluded and proposals for potential solutions drafted, the validation process takes place. Problems which are in urgent need of rectification are dealt by the commands of the three main services under the 'short loop validation process' (Voute, 2001: 7). Other issues with longer-term implications for conceptual development, or whose implications remain unclear, enter the 'long-loop verification process' and are dealt with by the Joint Armed Forces Staff. The information gained through the lessons-learned process is disseminated within the military through the Optimised Electronic Management System (GEODE) (Le Bail, 2003: 73; Serveille, 2004: 47–8; Voute, 2001: 7). The final step of the RETEX process involves following-up the measures implemented after key deficiencies have been disseminated (Voute, 2001: 5–7).

The roll-out of RETEX since the year 2000 has not been without its difficulties. The major problems involved inadequate manpower in RETEX teams and the persistence of poor administrative procedures which have hampered the final 'follow up' stage of RETEX on the transmission of lessons-learned to decisions on capabilities and training (Le Bail, 2003: 73; Voute, 2001: 7). These difficulties led to the development of a network of RETEX experts at the level of the Joint Staff and within each of the three Services. The RETEX network is tasked with determining the make-up of teams gathering information at the operational level; with acting as a joint assessment committee for the validation process and with forming a standing assessment group to oversee the follow-up of actions needed to remedy the deficiencies identified (Le Bail, 2003: 74).

A further set of actors from the Staff Level are also involved in Army RETEX and doctrinal development. The Documentation and Research Centre conducts studies on future scenarios and provides access to historical documentation, whilst the Army Doctrine Centre (CREDAT) coordinates the drafting of Army doctrine. Finally, the Historical Study Centres focus on implications of past operational experiences and doctrine. Since 2005 the work of CEREX and these other Staff-Level organisations has been coordinated by the CICDE that oversees all doctrinal development within the three main services (Bezacier, 2004c: 3).

Doctrine is not, however, the sole responsibility of the Staffs and CICDE. The French military places a strong focus on the synergy between doctrinal development and education/training. Training is viewed not only as a means with which to disseminate key doctrinal principles, but also as a way to refine and further develop doctrine (Bezacier, 2004c: 3). French Army Officer training also places great emphasis on critical thought. As Bezacier notes: '[Doctrine's] purpose is not to freeze military thought...On the contrary it calls for permanent critical thinking' (Bezacier, 2004c: 3).

The War College (ESG)/Higher Military Education Higher Staff Course (CSEM), prepares senior officers to exercise conception and decision responsibilities within national and international operational Army staffs. Central to the Higher Staff Course is the training of commanders to think critically about doctrine: to view doctrine as an 'evolving framework' and encourage 'independence of action, freedom of speech, creativity and imagination' (Amelineau, 2004: 9–12). Although training is conducted by CREDAT Officers, it also includes speakers from Allied Forces and from other branches of the French Armed Forces (Amelineau, 2004: 9–12). As Major General La Maisonneuve notes, training attempts to ensure: 'Permanent intellectual provocation and an incitement to creativity in order to provide the students with a taste for freedom of action and efficiency' (La Maisonneuve, 2004: 36–8).

In Branch Schools officer students not only study doctrine, but are also encouraged to contribute to its development as part of the course, as many of the students have a significant level of operational experience (Martigny and Cabon, 2004: 16). Those responsible for operational training (DGF) within the branch schools are also intimately involved in the development of doctrine within the Prospective and Studies Directorate (DGF) and are the 'first to check quality and clarity of doctrine' (Martigny and Cabon, 2004: 16). Trainers from other branches are also included in the drafting of branch-school doctrine in order to ensure that it is consistent with 'jointness' and combined arms operations (Martigny and Cabon, 2004: 16).

The development of doctrine and capabilities is also informed by individual RETEX studies which focus on specific challenges and draw upon the lessons of numerous operational experiences. An excellent example of such a study is the Study on the Capacities Necessary for a Combined Arms Task

Force to be Deployed Within Urban Areas (CAPAZUB) that was conducted by CEREX between July 2003 and January 2004.

CAPAZUB formed an important cornerstone of the 2005 'Doctrinal Manual for the Employment of Land Forces in Urban Environments' and the work of CAPAZUB was purposefully structured in the attempt to achieve objectivity. CAPAZUB was overseen by a steering group composed of Land Forces Command, the DGA, CREDAT and the Army Planning and Organisation Department, who collectively identified respondents and the wording of questionnaires (Zbienen, 2004: 56–7).[32] Furthermore, the methodology used to collate expertise within the French military was developed in partnership with the external agency RGA SYSTEMES (Zbienen, 2004: 56–7). Finally, CAPAZUB also integrated studies, conducted by CEREX, of foreign lessons-learned from recent British, Israeli and US land operations in urban environments.

The study led to the identification of 42 key threats/hazards which impact on the conduct of joint operations in built up areas; of 177 capacities needed for combined arms task force deployments in urban areas, in addition to a number of courses of action to be mastered and task organisational changes to be effected (Zbienen, 2004: 57–8). Implicit within the study's conclusions is the necessity to adapt the RMA to the challenges posed by 'wars amongst the people'. Crucially, CAPAZUB highlights a willingness to question the *status quo* and think critically about the implications of contemporary operations for doctrine and capabilities.

Such flexibility and openness to criticism is the product of civilian leadership that has played a vital role in ensuring that French doctrinal development and capability acquisition has been based upon the lessons operational experience and observation of 'best practice' rather than the logic of institutional politics, by carefully structuring military input into defence planning. Following 'third-order' reform in 1995/96 the coordinating role of the French Joint Chiefs of Staff and DGA on questions of doctrine and capabilities have gradually been strengthened as French expeditionary operations have increased in their number and complexity.

However, the pace and scope of the US military transformation process heralded by Transformation Planning Guidance in April 2003 provided a particularly important impetus to the restructuring of French military input into Defence Planning. TPG and the threat of abandonment by the US following the 2003 attack on Iraq signaled the urgency of acceleration of French acquisition of key RMA systems in LPM 2003–8, in order to retain interoperability with the US and ensure French influence by retaining a 'first-in capability' and the capacity to act as a 'lead-nation' in NATO or ESDP missions (Bezacier, 2003: 5).

Hence, for the civilian administration, the restructuring of military input to defence planning served three main purposes. Firstly, given the increasing clarity of the nature of conflict in the early 21st century and the role of

French military forces in a uni-polar world, to provide institutional protection for an accelerating transformation of the French armed forces based around a selective emulation of the US-led RMA that would be tailored around the capacity to undertake networked, joint, combined arms operations capable of delivering a wide range of operational effects (Bezacier, 2003: 5–7). Secondly, by improving the RETEX process, to ensure that within these broad parameters, military input to capability acquisition and doctrine around NEC and EBAO during and beyond LPM 2002–8 reflected, as closely as possible, the lessons of operational experiences. Reforms to RETEX would ensure that the French military would be able to identify 'best practice' and implement the key lessons as quickly as possible with an increasingly complex and shifting operational environment. Finally, to strengthen French input into NATO CD&E following the development of ACT at the 2002 NATO Prague Summit.

Consequently, the DGA was restructured in 2004 to allow a stronger coordinating role for the French Joint Chiefs of Staff and the Office of the Secretary General of the Defence Minister. In addition, the French Chief of Staff has, since 2005, been allotted a more prominent role in ensuring jointness in the doctrine of the three services and coherence in defence capability acquisition. The CICDE, created in 2005 has also acted as a focal point for the dissemination of jointness and enjoys overall responsibility for the coordination of doctrine. Furthermore, the *Centre de Doctrine d'Emploi des Forces* (Forces Employment Doctrine Centre, CDEF) that was established in 2004 (placed directly under the authority of the Army Chief of Staff) has helped to foster a critical attitude towards doctrinal development by providing an atmosphere of experimentation and inducing critical analysis of existing assumptions and ideas. This critical approach is illustrated by the CDEF's quarterly publication 'Doctrine' that, from 2003, has acted as a forum for lively debate and opinion pieces (written by experts from across the French Armed Services and those of other militaries) on the development of French Army doctrine and capabilities, as well as the lessons of French, American, British and German operational experiences.[33]

These institutional structures have helped to ensure that, as far as possible – within the ongoing constraints of uncertainty about the evolving nature of war – the major lessons concerning military 'best practice' at the tactical and operational levels have been ascertained, not only from French operational experiences, but also from the observation of the experiences of the US and others. France's nature as a secondary power and its ambitious attempt to maximise its power and influence through its military instrument does, of course, place budgetary restrictions on the extent to which France is able to translate the lessons identified by the military into capability investment (Le Bail, 2003: 74). Whilst the 'short-loop' RETEX process allows for urgent operational requirements to be met, the lengthy timeframes associated with the development of major new weapons systems can also lead to shortages in equipment as operations change in character. Nevertheless, when compared to the UK, major French equipment programmes are subject to much lower delays: an average delay of 1.5 months per year (compared to the UK's average of six months per year), and are also subject to lower cost over-runs.[34]

High executive autonomy and strong civilian control over capability acquisition

The structuring of military input into major capability procurement programmes has facilitated a stronger level of civilian control than in the UK and Germany and has allowed France to avoid an 'overheating' of its equipment programme that is as severe as that encountered by the UK. French capability planning follows a highly-streamlined and centralised structure. Three staff work under the direct authority of the French Defence Minister on issues of procurement: the Chief Executive of the DGA, that is responsible for research and development on equipment and defence industrial policy; the Chief of Defence Staff, responsible for decisions on the key requirements and deployments of capabilities and the General Secretary of the Administration, who is responsible for budgetary issues and legal affairs.[35] Although the support of equipment in service is delivered by single service organisations under the Chief of Defence Staff, the DGA has the authority to make key decisions on changes to a weapons system throughout its development and deployment and places staff within the single service organisations to help foster greater objectivity in procurement.[36]

Furthermore, unlike the UK's Defence Equipment and Support (DE&S), whose tasks and responsibilities were identified by the Gray Report as lacking clarity, the DGA is given three explicit tasks: to prepare for future requirements; deliver the key equipment for ongoing operations and promote French defence exports.[37] The structure of the Ministry reflects these tasks and is composed of three divisions: a division dealing with the delivery of weapons projects; a division responsible for weapons procurement strategy and a division for arms exports. In addition, whilst at DE&S, technical expertise is quickly lost due to high-levels of staff rotation and the UK services enjoy the capacity to make appointments within the organisation, the DGA employs over 5,500 technical experts on a permanent basis who assist in the running of key programmes.[38]

Furthermore, in contrast to the lax financial planning associated with the UK's Comprehensive Spending Review – that fails to set adequate budgetary limits over a sufficient time horizon and does not hold key actors to account for unbalanced budgets – the French LPM, passed by the French Parliament, sets out the military budget and major capability investment projects over six-year periods. The key decisions on major capability projects are also subject to greater civilian control than in the UK and the French Defence Minister takes full responsibility for decisions on priorities.[39] The lead organ in this process is the Ministerial Investment Board (MIB) that takes decisions on the progression of key projects, ensuring that major projects are approved four times by the MIB before their deployment.[40] Military input to decisions on capability investment is channeled through a subcommittee comprising members of the Armed Forces, whilst a further subcommittee of experts from the DGA provides advice on whether projects will be deliverable to budget and on time.[41] It is, however, the Minister who takes full responsibility for balancing the different perspectives provided by the experts of the DGA and armed forces and who takes the key decisions on which projects should receive priority within the strict budgetary constraints of the LPM.

The 2008 White Paper also set out key areas for improvement in the procurement process: budget planning; technical management and the coordination of procurement and support activities.[42] The core measures to tackle these areas have included strengthening the capacity of parliament to scrutinise the LPM, improving performance management to focus more strongly on financial and risk management; the development of a reporting cycle that enhances the oversight powers of senior management through monthly management accounts; reports to the Defence Minister every three months on the status of the cost, timing and performance of projects and finally, annual reports to Parliament.[43]

The 2008 Defence White Paper was also critical in setting clear guidelines on the future trajectory of transformation and in ensuring that the lessons of recent operational experiences were translated into the capability programme and force posture. Like the defence reforms of 1995/96, the 2008 DWP was preceded by a Commission tasked with examining the changing strategic context of French defence and security and the implications for the structure and capabilities of the armed forces. The broad membership of the Commission – which included not only representatives of the armed services, but also representatives of a variety of government ministries, as well as parliamentarians, academics, representatives of think tanks and industry – acted to invest its conclusions with gravitas. It is, however, critical to note the importance of the high-level of autonomy of the core executive in Defence policy, deriving from the formal competencies of the French President and the long window of opportunity following Presidential elections to make substantial cuts in military personnel, change force postures and to make changes to capability acquisition projects with implications for job losses. This has delivered a strong capacity for the core executive to exert control over the capability acquisition process and questions of force posture and dampen the impact of organisational politics between the single Services.

France, ESDP and NATO: The selective use of Gaullism to frame reformed bandwagoning

According to cultural explanations of policy change, the post-Cold War shift from 'national sanctuary' to the 'Europeanisation' of French defence policy is a product of 'socialisation processes' to which the French elite were subject at the European level (Irondelle, 2003a; Riecker, 2006: 525). Such accounts also draw attention to the central roles of President Jacques Chirac and Prime Minister Alain Juppe as 'norm entrepreneurs' in developing a sense of crisis consciousness and promoting policy-learning concerning the failure of 'splendid isolation' and, in its place, championing an advocacy coalition that promoted a Europeanised military policy. This resulted in 'paradigm change' to the cognitive and normative elements of French defence policy-making (Irondelle, 2003a: 222). Culturalists posit that the sequencing and temporal location of French changes to the institutional forums of defence policy (1994), that preceded reform to the objectives of policy, reflect the identification and resonance of ESDP with deeply-embedded Gaullist norms concerning the role of France as a 'Third Force' in international politics and the 'Europeanisation' of French exceptionalism.

In order to understand why French changes to institutional forums took place at such a comparatively early temporal location (1994), a focus on specific features of French 'external vulnerability' is critical, as demonstrated in Chapter 3. Although the 'Europeanisation' agenda and the Saint Malo Initiative allowed Chirac to bind the French left-wing to 'third-order' reform (Rynning, 2001/02: 113) 'executive autonomy' ensured policy leaders could focus, not on the domestic political ramifications of 'allied cooperation' (a more pronounced feature of policy leadership by German Defence Ministers), but on the 'national interest' and convergence with regional and systemic imperatives.

The central pillars of French national strategic 'culture' which had become embedded within 5th Republic France and formed the core of Gaullist ideology – national strategic independence and grandeur – were a key tool in the mobilisation of public support behind ESDP (Gregory, 2000a: 11–22). Yet, as in the German case culture emerges as malleable and elastic. Rather than a constraint on action, culture, under the conditions of high executive autonomy, formed a resource in legitimisation of convergence with systemic imperatives. As Howorth (2001: 161–2) pertinently notes: 'Presidents sought to derive both personal and national advantage from blowing the Gaullist trumpet', despite the increasingly pressing uni-polar imperative of developing a closer relationship with Washington manifested by the gradual rapprochement with NATO that took place under Presidents Mitterrand and Chirac. The invocation of Gaullist ideology has been a hallmark of Chirac's discourse on ESDP. The Gaullist norm of national strategic autonomy and broader Republican ideology were refashioned to frame the embedding of French defence policy within ESDP and the Europeanisation of French industrial policy (Marcussen et al, 1999: 619–22). As Chirac stated of the ESS: '[The ESS Represents] A Europe which…places at the heart of everything it does respect for a number of principles…which constitute both a French Republican Codes of Ethics…and a shared code of ethics for Europe' (Edwards, 2006: 12).

However, the threat of abandonment or entrapment in a uni-polar world and French pursuit of a strategy of reformed bandwagoning necessitates not only the development of an autonomous European capacity for action, but also strengthening of the Atlantic Alliance and French influence within Washington (Press-Barnathan, 2006). This has induced an incremental Atlanticisation of French defence policy that gathered pace during the Presidencies of Mitterrand and Chirac and reached a critical juncture on 11 March 2009 with President Nicloas Sarkozy's announcement of French reintegration within NATO's integrated military command structure. Within the context of French deployment in Afghanistan as part of ISAF, the paucity of influence associated with providing 7 per cent of NATO troops, 12 per cent of the NATO budget, yet enjoying only 1 per cent of command positions, became untenable.[44] The reintegration of France into NATO military command structures was, of course, a process that had begun at a much earlier stage in the post-Cold War era. French participation in NATO operations in Bosnia during the early 1990s compelled France to establish new links with the three Major Subordinate Commands accountable to SACEUR and develop stronger cooperation with SHAPE (Gregory, 2000a: 72). This was followed by the decision in 1995 to attend the Defence Ministerial meetings of the Atlantic Alliance (Lisbonne-de Vergeron, 2008: 18).

Reintegration into NATO command structures did, however, form a highly-symbolic and formal break with a core pillar of Gaullism. The move engendered significant opposition amongst the French public and politicians of both the left and right, who stood against the move on the basis that France was 'joining the race with Britain to be America's pet' and aligning itself with the 'American war machine'.[45] The President of the UDF, Francois Bayrou (1998–Present) described the event as an 'amputation' for France.[46] Whilst President Sarkozy was empowered to take on his critics by the nature of defence policy as a domain reserve, he also sought to construct a policy narrative that would mobilise public opinion. Reintegration to NATO's Command Structures was framed firmly within Gaullist discourse by Sarkozy: as a 'break with method, not principles' and a means with which to ensure French 'independence'.[47] A full role in NATO's military command structures would, it was argued, facilitate deeper European integration in defence by reassuring France's alliance partners of her intention to ensure complementarity between NATO and ESDP. At the same time, reintegration would enhance French power by granting increased influence in Washington: 'a state alone, a solitary nation, is no nation with influence'.[48]

The French case highlights that neither 'culture' nor 'international structure' can fully explain policy convergence and divergence. 'Culture' – notably Gaullist ideology – emerged as a tool that was highly malleable and was used selectively to sell convergence with systemic imperatives. Whilst Gaullism emphasised national primacy, it was a rhetorical tool that proved relatively adept in framing the 'Europeanisation' of French defence policy. Gaullism was also successfully invoked in a highly 'hollowed out' and paradoxical form to justify the increasing 'Atlanticisation' of French defence policy that became more visible under Sarkozy (Gregory, 2000a: 20; Howorth, 2001: 162). It is crucial, however, to recognise the importance of the window of opportunity afforded by the unitary French state to remould Gaullism: in early 2009 Senate elections (21 September 2008) were behind him and National Assembly/ Presidential elections were far on the horizon in summer 2012. Outside of periods of cohabitation the long window of opportunity between elections combines with the formal powers of the French President in defence policy to offer the President a high-level of autonomy in defence policy.

In summary, neoclassical realism provides a compelling account of the content and timing of French Defence Reform. The high-levels of autonomy enjoyed by the core executive in the sphere of defence policy have formed an important determinant of the ability of the French to respond to the imperatives of international structure and the post-Cold War operational environment in a timely manner. There is, of course, a strong element of fortune in the timing of the French electoral cycle that, in 2007, delivered a window of opportunity to recalibrate French force posture and capabilities at a point when a model of military 'best practice' for likely conflict scenarios over the short-medium term became increasingly apparent. As Chapter 6 will illustrate, the UK electoral cycle has, in contrast, incentivised the postponement of an SDR process until the new Parliament in 2010. French Defence Policy has, however, also benefited from clear and streamlined structuring of military input to defence planning that prioritises civilian control in decision-making on key capabilities. The LPM process also permits strong civilian control over the defence budget and capability acquisition over long-term planning horizons.

5
Germany: Domestic Constraint and the Temporal Management of Reform

Cultural accounts of policy change dominate the literature on German defence reform. Longhurst (2003, 2004: 150) emphasises the role of 'path-dependency' and strategic culture in explaining German commitment to Cold War policy instruments (notably conscription), determining the sequencing of German reform (reform to the policy objectives followed by only partial reform to the policy instrument). Maull (2000) and Berger (1998) point to 'the German 'culture of anti-militarism' in informing the objectives of defence policy and temporal location of the shift towards expeditionary crisis-management (Dalgaard-Nielsen, 2006: 12; Katzenstein, 1996; Longhurst, 2003). For cultural accounts of German defence policy, as Howorth (2004: 219) states: 'The role of ideas, values and norms is paramount'. These ideas, it is argued, have formed a powerful normative structural constraint on the willingness and ability of political figures to enact policy change, disincentivising the 'securitisation' of new issues and the development of new defence policy objectives (Stritzel, 2007: 365). Entrepreneurial action by political leaders on behalf of a 'crisis consciousness' or 'norm entrepreneurship' on behalf of a more 'interventionist' role for the armed forces, force projection and a professional military, is associated with great political risk (Dalgaard-Nielsen, 2006: 144; Howorth, 2004: 219–20; Hyde-Price and Jeffrey, 2001: 704–7; Longhurst, 2004: 147).[1]

However, a focus on neoclassical realism and executive autonomy provides a more convincing account of the process and outcome of reform. The nature of Germany as a federal 'negotiation' democracy increases the sensitivity of the core executive to the politics of base closures (Armingeon, 2002: 90; Dyson, 2005: 365). Combined with the close linkages between financial, budgetary and social policy in the form of the large number of conscientious objectors providing cheap labour to an overstretched social system, this creates a powerful material constraint on the ability and willingness of figures within the core executive to undertake 'strategic leadership', promote new policy ideas (crisis-management/prevention and a professional Bundeswehr) and respond to the changing international security environment (Dyson,

2007: 62–6).[2] This suggests that executive autonomy, rather than the normative constraints of strategic culture and the 'social sphere' in which a 'speech act' is embedded (Stritzel, 2007: 362), forms the key determinant of the success of a securitising act, by incentivising policy leaders to champion 'securitisation' processes in the first place.

These interlinked policy subsystems led to an interest by the powerful German Finance Ministry under Theo Waigel (1989–98) and Hans Eichel (1999–2005) in the promotion of policy stasis on the instruments of defence policy (conscription) due to the negative repercussions of 'third-order' change for German adherence to EMU's Stability and Growth Pact and budget consolidation (Breuer, 2006: 212; Dyson, 2007: 106, 167). 'Executive autonomy' is further compromised by the diffusion of competencies on defence policy within the core executive anchored in the Basic Law. Whilst the Chancellor plays a central role in formulating general defence policy guidelines (the Kanzlerprinzip), the Defence Minister emerges as crucial in the implementation of policy and in controlling the scope and temporality of policy change (the Ressortprinzip) (Mayntz, 1980: 142–3).[3]

Executive autonomy in German defence policy also appears to be further circumscribed by the constitutionally-mandated oversight powers enjoyed by the Bundestag over expeditionary troop deployments. As Born and Hänggi (2008: 206) highlight, the Bundestag enjoys extensive powers: a simple parliamentary majority is required for the prior approval of overseas troops deployment and the Bundestag can also stipulate the mandate of a mission, make decisions on operational issues (rules of engagement (RoE), command and control, risk assessment and budget), determine the length of a mission and the right to visit troops on deployment. In contrast, the oversight powers of the UK Parliament extend only to the approval of a mission's mandate and the right to visit troops on deployment, whilst the French National Assembly has the right to vote on overseas troop deployments, but only four months following the initiation of a mission (Aust and Vashakmadze, 2008: 2225). As a consequence, culturalist approaches argue that the German core executive is particularly exposed to the anti-militaristic public opinion and security culture (Matlary, 2009: 151–3, 156).

Although such constraints can act as a difficult hurdle to troop deployments (not least during particularly sensitive periods such as federal elections) one must be careful not to overstate the impediments to executive autonomy. The constraints imposed by German law leave the core executive a good deal of freedom for maneuver, not least in sanctioning higher-intensity operations against immediate threats. The Parliamentary Participation Act stipulates that the Bundestag enjoys a much more limited role in 'urgent' situations of national, or collective, defence and can only sanction the deployment of troops after 'urgent' operations have commenced (Aust and Vashakmadze, 2008: 2234).[4] As Aust and Vashakmadze (2008: 2234) note: 'The role of parliament remains rather limited where a rapid military response to an existing external threat is required'. Furthermore, recent rulings of the Federal Constitutional

Court have endowed the executive with the power to determine what constitutes an 'urgent' situation (Aust and Vashakmadze, 2008: 2234). Indeed, seen from a realist perspective, stricter parliamentary oversight presents a more limited constraint on executive autonomy, given the malleability of culture and the ability of policy leaders to exploit 'public vulnerability' in the mobilisation of society behind conflict.

Yet, although culture displays a good deal of malleability it can under particular circumstances, be a difficult tool to wield. This is evident in the German case, where the systemic imperatives of the Cold War and post-war reintegration into the Western community of nations incentivised the development of an 'anti-militaristic' policy narrative that required significant remoulding to dovetail with the security challenges of the post-Cold War era. However, the key difficulty lies not in identity and culture itself, but in the impact of domestic material power relations on the capacity of the core executive to reshape 'culture'. In France and the UK, the unitary state provides a sustained window of opportunity between elections for policy leaders to deploy culture in the articulation of new policy narratives in support of significant changes to the objectives, instruments and institutional forums of defence policy. The German federal system places stronger constraints on the autonomy of the core executive to deploy culture as a tool. These restrictions derive form the regularity of state (Land) elections which have important implications for the capacity of the governing coalition to push through its broader political agenda. In the absence of a clear sense of public vulnerability deriving from a pressing crisis, these restrictions on executive autonomy can create a higher-level of sensitivity to public opinion and parliamentary opposition, incentivising an incremental 'salami-slicing' approach to changes to defence policy.

Hence the German case draws our attention to a key weakness of the literature on strategic culture: that culture is not a stand-alone variable, but instead can be a tool in the hands of political leaders within the core executive who are preoccupied with domestic politics: the ramifications of reform for the electoral success of their political party and personal political ambitions (Dyson, 2005: 362, 2007: 104). This implies the instrumental use of culture by political elites in the domestic political and temporal management of reform (Farrell and Terriff, 2002: 8; Johnston, 1995: 39–41; Klein, 1988: 136), opening cultural approaches to attack from neoclassical realism for 'conflating mind and matter' (Rynning, 2001–2: 90). Crucially, it points to the central role of 'executive autonomy' and domestic material power relationships in explaining the temporality of patterns of convergence around systemic imperatives.

The selective use of 'culture' by the core executive: Framing radical change to policy objectives and stasis to policy instruments

In the immediate post-Cold War era, German 'security culture/identity' was characterised by two core attributes which had become embedded during the Bonn Republic. Firstly, anti-militarism, that has manifested itself in a 'culture of restraint': the use of military force only as a very last resort (Berger, 1998: 317–56; Maull, 1990–1: 91–106). As Duffield (1999: 781) notes: 'It long ago became conventional wisdom that the function of the...*Bundeswehr*, should be limited almost exclusively to national self-defense and that Germany should never again develop significant power projection capacity'. German anti-militarism also embodies a strong domestic element: a distrust of military institutions that derives from the discrediting of Prussian militarism and statism that took place during the post-war period (Kvistad, 1999). This anti-militarism fostered a strong attachment to the principles of *'Innere Führung'*[5] and the 'citizen in uniform' (Duffield, 1999: 782; Kvistad, 1999: 235–42; Walz, 1987).

The second key principle of German security 'culture' is multilateralism: the anchoring German foreign and security policy within international institutions. This principle has been closely associated with the notion of *Berechenbarkeit*: the virtue of reliability to one's international partners. As Duffield (1999: 782) highlights, 'not to fulfill Germany's international obligations and responsibilities would undermine the country's credibility in the eyes of its partners'.[6]

Rather than expressions of German security 'culture', however, these principles could also be viewed as rational responses to the Cold War security environment and post-war restrictions on German sovereignty that placed strict limitations on German freedom of action, precluding the use of the military as a tool of foreign policy and the development of an expeditionary capacity. In the flux of the immediate post-Cold war period, established policy responses exhibited a strong measure of ossification: as systemic imperatives only slowly became apparent, German statesmen 'erred on the side of caution'. Consequently the Iraq War of 1990/91 was dealt with by 'cheque book diplomacy' and the policy tools of the Bonn Republic (Dyson, 2007: 57). As the 1990s progressed these two core principles of German security 'culture' would, however, be used selectively and refashioned in order to justify conformity not only to emerging systemic pressures and to negotiate parliamentary control over military deployment, but also to conform to the constraints of low executive autonomy in defence policy.

CDU Defence Minister Volker Rühe (1992–8) exhibited an activist leadership role in responding to the challenges of the international security environment and expanding the objectives of defence policy in the initial post-Cold War period (Dyson, 2007: 58–62). He hesitated, however, in translating this into reforms to the objectives and instruments of defence policy once his domestic strategic room for manoeuvre narrowed. Chancellor Helmut Kohl and Rühe identified electoral dangers in structural reforms to the *Bundeswehr* in 1993–4 when the prospects for the government in the October 1994 federal elections looked bleak (Dyson, 2007: 63).

Faced with a slow-down in the German economy and the threat of unrest within the CDU/CSU and electorate at the prospect of widespread base closures – as well as the fear that operational learning processes might overstep his carefully-constructed 'salami-tactic' – Rühe instituted a *'Denk-verbot'* (ban on thinking) within the Defence Ministry on issues of doctrinal or structural change, providing 'institutional protection' to territorial defence and conscription (Dyson, 2007: 66–8). He appointed conservative officials within the Ministry to act as 'gatekeepers' to the flow of policy ideas, blocking policy-learning processes about the inadequacies of a conscript force and territorial defence.[7] These processes were beginning to take root within the ministry in the context of the changing security environment and *Bundeswehr* missions in the Adriatic (1992–6), Cambodia (1992–3), Somalia (1993–4) and Bosnia (1993–5) (Dyson, 2007: 113). The narrowing of 'executive autonomy' in defence policy incentivised Rühe's promotion of 'stasis' rather than 'strategic innovation' in his 1994 reform (Dyson, 2007: 62–3; Lungu, 2004a: 264).

The widening of the *Bundeswehr's* remit, not least the discursive process that accompanied intervention as part of IFOR in Bosnia in December 1995, demonstrates the elasticity of cultural values and their instrumentality in the context of enhanced executive autonomy. IFOR was a particularly sensitive mission that involved the deployment of Tornado aircraft and raised the possibility of high-intensity role for the *Bundeswehr* and encountered a high-level of opposition amongst the German public and Parliament (Breuer, 2006: 209; Dyson, 2007: 59–61). With Federal elections far on the horizon (September 1998) and empowered by the increasing gravity of the instability in Germany's backyard, Rühe developed an activist policy narrative that justified the expeditionary deployment of the *Bundeswehr* through the invocation of 'Germany's new international responsibility'[8] to contribute to and strengthen multilateral approaches to peacekeeping. Rühe's policy narrative focused, in the context of the Srebrenica massacre of July 1995, on the special responsibilities of the Federal Republic to protect human rights.[9] This persuasive policy narrative was successfully combined with lobbying of the more reticent 'pacifist' Green Party members of the *Bundestag's* Defence Committee (including the organisation of fact-finding missions to Bosnia) in order to overcome parliamentary hurdles to deployment. As Baumann and Hellmann (2001: 61–82) highlight: 'The rhetoric of responsibility, which in itself conveyed the impression of continuity, was utilised to pave the way for significant change'.

At the same time, Rühe was quick to stimulate public fears of the use of the *Bundeswehr* as an instrument of foreign policy in order to justify the retention of territorial defence and conscription as executive autonomy narrowed during the mid-1990s (Dyson, 2005). Rühe therefore employed discourse that associated military professionalism with worldwide intervention and by describing professional soldiers as 'Rambos', who would undermine the principle of *'Innere Fuehrung'*.[10]

Under SPD Defence Minister Rudolf Scharping (1998–2002) the political and temporal management of reform also took the form of actively mediating systemic imperatives for 'third-order' change to the objectives, instruments and institutional forums of German defence policy, particularly those presented by the April 1999 Kosovo War. The mobilisation of the public and of pacifist SPD and Green Party MPs behind military intervention as part of NATO's 'Operation Allied Force' without a direct UN mandate was framed within a highly-emotive public discourse by Scharping, Chancellor Gerhard Schroeder and other elite figures, such as Foreign Minister Joschka Fischer (1998–2005). Scharping linked participation in the Kosovo conflict to German post-war identity and 'security culture' by predicting an impending genocide and by claiming that there was serious evidence of the existence of concentration camps in Kosovo – a narrative that was facilitated by sensationalist reporting of Serbian atrocities in the tabloid press.[11] As Baumann and Hellmann (2001) note: 'In the light of Srebrenica it was now widely accepted in the German political elite that the legacy of German history should not only be to call for "no more wars" (*"Nie Wider Kreig!"*) but also for "no more Auschwitz" (*"Nie wieder Auschwitz!"*)'[12]

The dissemination of an activist policy narrative in advance of German participation in Operation Allied Force was facilitated by two key contextual, material factors which enhanced executive autonomy. Firstly, the nature of instability in Kosovo as an urgent crisis within Germany's geostrategic neighbourhood that contributed to a sense of 'public vulnerability'. Secondly, by the temporality of the conflict that began in April 1999, allowing the core executive to exploit the window of opportunity for action that had been delivered by the wide margin of the SPD/Green victory in the September 1998 Federal Elections.

The implications of the Kosovo conflict for reforms to the objectives and instruments of German defence policy were codified by the Weizsäcker Commission. The Commission's report of 5 May 2000 was, however, marginalised by Scharping, despite the consensus that the policy forum had generated amongst its participants about the need for a military orientated to crisis-management/prevention, a dramatic reduction of conscription and the development of an autonomous European military capability (Dalgaard-Nielsen, 2006: 123; Dyson, 2005: 364; Longhurst, 2004: 105). Scharping was successful in ensuring policy stasis and impeding policy learning and exerted a strong measure of control over the context of ideas within which reform took place. He did so by blocking change agents within the policy subsystem – not least within the Defence Ministry – through the appointment and empowerment of conservative figures and an authoritative leadership style that was described as a 'quiet style of terror' (Dyson, 2007: 103). At the macro-political level Scharping sought to restrict the capacity of critics of conscription to challenge his veto-role by bringing forward the Commission's report to May 2000 that had the effect of closing down the possibility for a societal debate about the function and structure of the *Bundeswehr* (Dyson, 2005: 369; Dyson, 2007: 104).

The selective use of German security 'culture' also formed a key tool in the control of policy learning. For example, as criticism of conscription grew within the SPD in early 2002 following the decision of 16 November 2001 to deploy German soldiers in Afghanistan,[13] Scharping, like his predecessor Rühe, sought to play on the fears of the German public by associating professionalisation with the image of an increasingly militarised German foreign and security policy and accused his colleagues of populism: 'with their unfounded comments they [SPD members] are playing in to the hands of those who want to turn our *Bundeswehr* into a professional and almost unchecked tool for deployment in pursuit of interventionist policies'.[14]

The promotion of policy stasis became increasingly difficult to reconcile with Germany's expanding international role during Peter Struck's (2002–5) tenure as Defence Minister due to the growing disjuncture between German policy and systemic imperatives. German participation in ISAF and the development of the NRF was accompanied by a complex and skilful leadership role from Struck in the 2003 reform. Struck combined 'strategic innovation' to the objectives of German defence policy with only partial change to the instruments of defence policy and prevented forces for change from shaping policy on conscription (Dyson, 2005: 377–80; Longhurst, 2004: 113–15). Strategic culture formed a key resource, used selectively by Struck to control the policy process. German history justified change to the *Bundeswehr*'s tasks and its new and explicit role as an '*Interventionsarmee*' ready for deployment in any part of the globe[15] as critical to renew Germany's long-standing commitment and responsibility to its UN, NATO and EU partners.

At the same time strategic 'culture' was used to impede change to the structure of the *Bundeswehr* by invoking the importance of conscription for civil-military relations and the principle of '*innere Führung*', as well as by emphasising the utility of conscripts in undertaking low-medium intensity peacekeeping operations (Dyson, 2005: 371).[16] In legitimising the new defence policy objectives it is also crucial to note the role of Peter Struck and other elite figures, such as former *Generalinspekteur* Wolfgang Schneiderhan (2002–9), in exploiting the sense of public vulnerability to external threat, notably to international terrorism and the possibility of Germany suffering a '*Super-Gau*' (super-catastrophe) on the scale of September 11 (Becker, 2009). In the short-medium term following September 11, the threat of the '*Super-Gau*' provided a compelling justification for the defence of Germany in distant theatres of conflict and facilitated the use of the term '*Interventionsarmee*' to describe the new *Bundeswehr* (Utley, 2006: 76–7).[17] The exploitation of a sense of 'public vulnerability' to attack as a mobilising tool behind the ISAF mission has, however, been hampered over the longer-term by the fact that Germany is yet to suffer a direct attack from Islamic terrorists.

The 2003 VPR and its claim that 'Germany would be defended on the Hindukush'[18] was accompanied by a particularly assertive and emotional policy narrative from Struck that firmly anchored the continued commitment to conscription within the legacy of German history and identity: 'Armed forces cannot be conceived in a vacuum that takes no account of the particular tradition and history of a country. The integration of the *Bundeswehr* into society and the close relationship between military service and civil society remains one of the greatest success stories of the Federal Republic... Conscription is the expression of readiness to serve society...They (conscripts) sense each day the satisfaction and pride of their parents in the difficult path they have chosen by serving their country'.[19]

Arguments in favour of continuing conscription were becoming increasingly tenuous. When – after claiming in a newspaper interview that conscription was 'critical to avoid a separation between society and the military' – Struck was further probed by the interviewer on the issue of civil-military relations, he conceded that the possibility of the development of 'state within a state' was no longer an issue.[20] Whilst under Scharping the development of an *Interventionsarmee* had been raised as a bogeyman to justify the retention of conscription and territorial defence, Struck was compelled to find another justification, now that crisis-management was the core objective of German defence policy. 'Those' who wish to turn 'our *Bundeswehr*' into an 'unchecked instrument for intervention' had remained ill-defined in Scharping's policy narrative.[21] Struck, however, raised a more disturbing rationale that subtly played on German historical memory. Conscription would now act to protect German society from itself – from making rash and hasty decisions about the deployment of its new '*Interventionsarmee*': 'my fear is much more that society could be inclined to send a professional army on deployment without consideration'.[22]

This argument carries little water, however, as German troops on expeditionary deployment (particularly combat troops) are already overwhelmingly composed of career soldiers or conscripts who have voluntarily extended their service (Breuer, 2006: 215). Indeed, as Breuer (2006: 215), Edmunds (2006: 1069) and Longhurst (2004: 124) demonstrate, professional and specialist forces are an imperative for both low-medium and higher-intensity expeditionary operations; a requirement that is reinforced by the tendency of contemporary expeditionary operations to vary in intensity at short notice. Accordingly, in the context of the ISAF mission and post-Cold War crisis-management operations undertaken by the *Bundeswehr*, opposition to conscription within the Defence Ministry began to mount, with several Generals calling for more 'highly-trained fighters' and expressing their bitterness about the role of *Zivildienst* in producing policy stalemate.[23]

The analysis presented above suggests that under circumstances of enhanced executive autonomy culture, national identity, ideology and historical memory in the area of defence policy offer a significant degree of room for maneuver for elite figures. Whilst the established channels of political activity associated with the foreign and security policy posture of the Bonn Republic were strongly ossified in the initial flux of the post-Cold War period, the German core executive had the capacity to selectively invoke and refashion the core features of national security culture. Rather than acting as constitutive and a cause of action, culture formed a resource for policy-makers that was much more malleable, elastic – and indeed, paradoxical in its content – than the literature on German strategic culture suggests. The core principles of German security culture were used on the one hand to generate a sense of continuity within which radical changes to defence policy objectives could be framed, yet on the other hand to legitimate stasis in reforms to policy instruments.

Nevertheless, as Rynning (2001–2) argues, policy leadership emerges as an important unit-level variable in shaping the temporal location, sequencing and pace of military reform. Although Chancellors set the strategic guidelines for policy change and their support was necessary for the development and implementation of reform, control over the scope and pace of policy change was consequent upon the 'day-to-day' management of the policy sector and ministerial policy leadership (the *Ressortprinzip*) (Dyson, 2005: 372–3). Policy change to the doctrine, and particularly structure, of the armed forces depended much on the ability of Rühe, Scharping, and Struck to open-up or block processes of policy learning and political debate, within the policy subsystem and macro-political level; to negotiate constitutional constraints on the role of the *Bundeswehr* and to obtain parliamentary approval for the *Bundeswehr*'s deployment.[24] This involved close attention to the use of strategic culture as a resource with which to justify their chosen leadership roles and frame policy proposals (Dyson, 2005, 2007: 173–4). This process was one that required significant leadership skills, given the need to negotiate parliamentary constraints and selectively invoke a 'security culture' that required significant reshaping to meet the challenges of global expeditionary deployment.

The difficulties faced by the Grand Coalition is selling the Afghan conflict have been magnified by the presence of Franz-Josef Jung at the helm of the Defence Ministry (2005–9). under the CDU/CSU/SPD Grand Coalition has demonstrated the importance of leadership traits and skills in the mobilisation of society behind conflict (Sueddeutsche, 2009a). Jung's information management skills, oratory skills and capacity to mobilise public opinion and opposition MPs behind the ISAF mission were so poorly perceived that his tenure at the helm of the Defence Ministry was described by his CDU colleague, and former Defence Minister, Volker Rühe as 'disastrous' (Die Zeit, 2009a; Sueddeutsche, 2009a).[25] *Der Spiegel* wrote of Jung in 2007: 'He gives the impression that he does not have the confidence to be Defence Minister. He is constantly fearful of making mistakes'.[26] In the year 2007 a poll highlighted that 39 per cent of the German public did not know who Jung was[27] and the Minister has only been saved from resignation by the weakness of the opposition under the Grand Coalition (Die Zeit, 2009a).

However, the critical variable impacting upon the capacity of the government to sell the conflict in Afghanistan as 'war' and expand the scope of

German participation under ISAF lies, however, in the impact of domestic material power relations. As neoclassical realism recognises, although culture, nationalism and ideology are primarily tools in the hands of policy-makers, they are tools that can, in certain circumstances, be very difficult to wield. Cultural approaches neglect the restrictions imposed on the German core executive's ability to articulate new policy narratives on behalf of strategic imperatives by a political system that is characterised by frequent elections at the state level.

In the absence of a sense of vulnerability to attack or a compelling crisis within Germany's geopolitical neighbourhood and with looming Federal elections, the imperatives of international structure are conveyed by a much slower transmission belt. Whilst Allied pressure for greater German burden-sharing increased during 2008 the capacity of the German government to press for an increase in the scope of German involvement in Afghanistan was restricted by the forthcoming Federal elections of September 2009, in which issues of defence and security were highly-sensitive (Times, 2009). This domestic context incentivised an attempt to push debate on the *Bundeswehr's* role in ISAF under the carpet (Matlary, 2009: 156). Furthermore, the lack of a direct attack on German territory by Islamic terrorists has also undermined the capacity for the core executive to exploit a sense of public vulnerability to attack (Becker, 2009).[28]

Allied pressure for greater German burden-sharing has also been exerted within an overall atmosphere of increasing uncertainty about the extent of the Obama administration's longer-term commitment to the ISAF mission since its election in November 2008 (Die Welt, 2009). On the one hand, General Stanley McChrystal has argued for a US troop surge of 40,000. At the same time, Vice-President Joe Biden has spoken out in favour of a more limited military presence and for targeted UCAV attacks on Taliban and Al-Qaeda militants in Afghanistan and Pakistan (France24, 2009a). The September 2009 Federal Elections delivered a clear mandate for the CDU/CSU/FDP and opened up a slim window of opportunity to 'sell' a stronger role in the Afghan campaign to the German public.[29] However, the German government is unlikely to commit further troops until the intentions of the Obama administration become clear and a longer-term strategy for Afghanistan and timetable for the handover of security and governance functions to indigenous forces is agreed at the international conference on Afghanistan on 28 January 2010. This uncertainty about the US commitment and the overall political and strategic direction of the campaign has created little incentive for German policy leaders to attempt to use culture, ideology and nationalism and to manipulate public vulnerability on behalf of an expansion the German troop commitment above its ceiling of 4,500 (4,245 are currently deployed). Furthermore, the narrowness of the window of opportunity provided by the Federal election acts as disincentive to greater burden-sharing under ISAF: the CDU faces an important election in May

2010 when it will attempt to retain control of Germany's most populous and economically-powerful State, North-Rhine Westphalia. Hence, whilst German public opinion points to a strong reticence to deploy troops in a higher-intensity capacity in Afghanistan, it is not a stand-alone causal variable explaining Germany's reticence to deploy extra troops (Matlary, 2009: 152).

The decisive causal factor in determining German temporal divergence in defence reform lies in the deficits in executive autonomy in defence policy to which the Chancellors and Defence Ministers were subject, which incentivised their choice of leadership role. Low 'executive autonomy' explains why the 1994 and 2000 reforms only outlined changes to the 'settings' of policy and the delayed temporal location of reform to the objectives of German defence policy (2003). Executive autonomy also determined the sequencing (reforms only to the settings of the policy instrument) and pace of reform (six months). Struck was keen to engineer a *fait accomplis* and close down the possibility for a macro-political debate on reform to the policy instrument in the face of increasing domestic opposition to conscription within the SPD/Green coalition and the development of a 'mature' advocacy coalition championing an end to conscription (Dalgaard-Nielsen, 2006: 126; Dyson, 2005: 377–85; Longhurst, 2004: 133). The pace of reform to the objectives of policy and its specific temporal location (at the beginning of the 2002–6 legislative period) also reflected the SPD's concern to implement the base closures consequent upon a 35,000 troop reduction well in advance of the next Federal elections (Dyson, 2007: 120–2).

There are, however, two further factors which undermine the capacity of the *Bundeswehr* to expand the intensity and scope of its contribution to ISAF. Firstly, the limitations imposed by the current capabilities, training and doctrine of the *Bundeswehr*. The German military has only recently begun a transformation process that will adapt it to the challenges of the contemporary expeditionary operational environment. This is a factor that is compounded by the *Bundeswehr's* lack of historical experience in COIN. Secondly, organisational politics between the Single Services – the impact of which has been magnified by low executive autonomy – has also played a role in reducing the dynamism of defence capability procurement (see following sections).

The development of NetOpFü and the struggle to prepare for irregular warfare

The temporal management of reform by the core executive not only applied the brakes to investment in C4ISR capabilities, but also hindered conceptual and doctrinal development, particularly in the area of EBAO and COIN. It is only comparatively recently that the German Defence Ministry has been liberated from the '*Denkverbot*' on conceptual development around expeditionary crisis-management that had been applied most forcefully under Rühe and Scharping. Indeed, as this chapter will demonstrate, the liberation from the *Denkverbot* is not fully complete and still applies to the abolition of conscription and key doctrinal issues. Political interference continues to stand in the way of the development of a comprehensive COIN doctrine that will allow the *Bundeswehr* to undertake higher-intensity 'stabilisation' tasks.

NetOpFü has, nevertheless, undergone considerable conceptual development and, like its French and British counterparts, is emerging as a selective emulation of NCW focused around enabling the delivery of a wide range of operational effects and an enhancement of the Manoeuvrist Approach and Mission Command. Although it is important to acknowledge that resource constraints limit the capacity of the Federal Republic to pursue a full-blown emulation of the RMA,[30] three additional factors emerge as critical in determining the trajectory of C4ISR procurement and doctrinal development. Firstly, the recognition of the strengths and limitations of the RMA consequent upon observation of the RMA in practice; secondly, observation of the 'third-order' reform processes of other EU and NATO 'secondary powers', particularly Britain and France, which preceded the German reforms of 2003 and 2006 and finally, German operational experiences during the post-Cold War era.

The partial and selective emulation of the RMA undertaken by France and the UK focused around the adaptation of the technologies associated with the RMA to deliver both kinetic and non-kinetic effects provided an indication of 'best practice' in NEC.[31] Yet it is only following more recent operations under ISAF that the *Bundeswehr* has begun to consider the implications of 'Three Block Warfare' for doctrine and capabilities. As the security situation has worsened in North of Afghanistan, ISAF has acted to demonstrate the importance of developing the capacity to simultaneously apply a range of kinetic and non-kinetic effects.[32]

In contrast to Afghanistan, the majority of operational experiences following the Constitutional Court ruling of July 1994 – including UNSOM II, IFOR, SFOR, KFOR, Operation Amber Fox, Operation Concordia and INTERFET in East Timor (1999–2000) – involved low-medium intensity tasks (Dalgaard-Nielsen, 2006: 108). The 4,000 troops committed to IFOR undertook principally medical and logistical tasks, although the contribution of 3,000 troops to SFOR included forces prepared for higher-intensity conflict (Utley, 2006: 73). Considering the post-war constraints on her expeditionary capacity, Germany made a significant contribution to NATO's 1995 Operation Deliberate Force, deploying 14 Tornado Aircraft in support of the suppression of air defences and undertaking 1.4 per cent of all air sorties flown (Utley, 2006: 73). Germany also played an active combat role in NATO air strikes against Serbia during Operation Allied Force, her 14 Tornados undertaking 1 per cent of combat sorties, as well as reconnaissance flights. This operation was followed by the commitment of over 5,000 troops to KFOR as part of the leadership of Multinational Brigade South and the deployment of 560 troops in NATO's Operation Amber Fox in Macedonia in 2001–2 (Utley, 2006: 73–4).

Whilst early post-Cold War operations focused largely on the lower-end of the conflict spectrum, they began to demonstrate that the *Bundeswehr* would have to be prepared to deploy 'minimum force' in complex crisis-management operations to protect civilians (not least following the 1995 Srebrenica Massacre) and enforce the mandate of missions.[33] Operations in the Balkans also provided the impetus behind reform to *Bundeswehr* command structures to promote greater jointness and interoperability with Alliance partners. Operation Allied Force acted as a particularly important spur to the development of what has become a broad consensus within the *Bundeswehr* about the need to respond to the process of battlefield digit-isation initiated by the US.[34] The Kosovo conflict instigated investment in C2 assets which were viewed as vital in order to enable interoperability with ESDP/NATO Alliance partners. The conflict also underlined the impor-tance of investment in air assets permitting strategic mobility.[35] Further-more, the reliance on the US for intelligence in Operation Allied Force – that came in a processed, analysed form, rather than raw data – acted as a wake-up call to invest in ISR assets and provided the impetus behind the acquisition of SAR LUPE satellites and German involvement in cross-national European satellite projects.[36]

However, exposure to peace support operations in the Balkans during the 1990s led to a particularly strong focus on the importance of 'human factors' in conflict. The emphasis on humanitarian and civilian tasks in post-Cold War operations highlighted at an early stage the importance of 'networked security', as German deployments proceeded in close coop-eration with NGOs and the German Foreign, Interior and Development Ministries (Dalgaard-Nielsen, 2006: 108). As a consequence Germany has made strong progress on the development of a comprehensive approach (Networked Security) to the planning and conduct of military operations.[37]

Post-Cold War operational experiences underlined, therefore, the necessity of developing the lower-intensity skill sets needed to conduct 'wars amongst the people': the requirement that soldiers be prepared for the 'political, humanitarian, economic and cultural aspects' of the operational environment and 'capable of cooperation with civilian and military actors at the national and international levels'.[38] German experience of low-medium intensity peace-support operations during the 1990s reinforced the utility of the prin-ciple of *Innere Führung* that, amongst other values, emphasises the centrality of culturally-aware and educated soldiers (Dyson, 2007: 20). The importance of such skills sets has been bolstered by observation of the RMA in practice, most notably the lessons that FM 3-24 draws from the experiences of the US Infantry and Marines in Afghanistan and Iraq.[39] The new focus of the US under General Stanley McChrystal (Commander of ISAF and US Forces in Afghanistan from June 2009) on 'winning hearts and minds' has been met with satisfaction by leading figures within the German military, who see this as a vindication of their emphasis upon the importance of non-kinetic factors in irregular conflict.[40]

These skill sets at the lower-end of the conflict spectrum have, however, been developed at the expense of preparation for participation in higher-intensity 'Three Block Warfare' situations. As Dalgaard-Nielsen (2006: 112) highlights: 'The cult of the warrior was weak or absent within the *Bundeswehr* and the focus on political and historical education and democratic values strong. To complement this apparently non-offensive style, deployed German units also engaged actively in humanitarian and civilian tasks...'.

The lack of a 'warrior ethos' amongst German troops is also reinforced by the analysis of Matlary (2009: 151) who notes that: 'German troops have an unflattering history of being reticent to fight in situations where it is needed, such as in Prizren in Kosovo in 2004 where they were accused of "hiding in the barracks like frightened rabbits" in a German police report'. Such a claim – that amounts to an accusation of cowardice – is highly-unfair and must be contextualised by the fact that, due to excessive civilian inter-ference in military planning, German military doctrine remains at odds with the challenges of missions such as ISAF. The military's non-offensive military doctrine had also been reinforced by the nature of the operational experiences faced by German soldiers in the initial post-Cold War era. Although pre-operational training during the 1990s prepared German units for the 'worst case scenario', the missions in the Balkans were in the word of one Defence Ministry insider 'only slightly more dangerous than staying in Germany'.[41]

The ISAF mission is, therefore, the first time that German troops have been exposed to intensive and sustained fighting. Although German troops trained for high-intensity conflict in more conventional conflict scenarios during the Cold War, soldiers did not expect conflict to arise. These experiences contrast markedly to those of the British and French militaries which were exposed to high-intensity (and often irregular) conflict in a variety of theatres during the Cold War. As a source within the German Defence Ministry noted: 'The *Bundeswehr* before the Afghan mission was like a football team training, but thinking that there would be no game at the weekend, consequently their mindset was not prepared for higher-intensity missions like ISAF'.[42]

The non-offensive approach of the *Bundeswehr* was outlined in the Army Doctrine, *Truppenfuehrungsgrundsaetze Herendienstvorschrift* 100/100 (HDV 100/100) that was updated in 2000 following experiences in Bosnia. In contrast to British and French Army doctrine that, by 1997, pointed to the need to prepare for missions characterised by a 'continuum of conflict', the document distinguished between high and low intensity conflict and focused on fight-ing, peace-support and humanitarian aid as separate conflict categories.[43] The lower-intensity operational experiences in the Balkans are also reflected in the structural reforms to the *Bundeswehr* outlined in the 2003 VPR: the creation of separate 'stabilisation' forces focused on training for post-conflict reconstruction and 'attack' forces capable of undertaking the higher-intensity 'initial entry' stage of operations. Although the stabilisation forces are capable of more robust tasks and are interoperable with the *Eingreifskraefte*, they lack the capacity to undertake the tasks associated with highest end of 'Three Block Warfare' and Stabilisation/COIN operations (i.e. the 'clear' and 'hold' stages of COIN).

Hence, as a result of low executive autonomy and the incentivises this provides for civilian interference in the development of military doctrine – as well as the impact of the largely low-medium intensity German operational experiences during the post-Cold War era – the *Bundeswehr* is presently struggling with the issue of how to integrate high- and low-intensity effects in 'conflict amongst the people'. Furthermore, due to the temporal delay in the development of *NetOpFü* the *Bundeswehr* also faces a more pressing challenge of determining the role of C2 and ISR assets in such conflict scenarios.[44]

There are, however, encouraging signs of adaptation to the contemporary operational environment. German experiences of operations in Afghanistan have begun to demonstrate the importance of preparing land forces for a rapid 'reversibility' in conflict intensity (Noetzel and Schreer, 2008a: 45–6).[45] Debate within the *Bundeswehr* has intensified over the competencies identified as critical to German land forces, with an increasing recognition of the need to tailor training to the challenges of fighting Three Block Warfare 'amongst the people' and for focus not only on 'intercultural competence', 'intelligence', 'strategic ability', the 'ability to organise under pressure' and 'the capacity to work as part of multinational forces', but also on 'resilience/ character' and 'warrior qualities'.[46]

US pressure for a more robust German involvement in ISAF led to Germany assuming command of Regional Command North on 20 June 2008 and to participation in higher-intensity operations such as Operation Harekate Yolo II of October 2007 that was conducted in the provinces of Faryab and Badghis (Miskimmon, 2009: 571; Noetzel and Schreer, 2008b: 220).[47] The operation involved offensive military action by the *Bundeswehr* and highlighted a number of deficiencies in undertaking COIN, most notably the inability of the *Bundeswehr* to effectively integrate military and civilian instruments in 'Three Block Warfare' situations. As former General Inspector of the *Bundeswehr* Harald Kujat (2000–2) notes, the lack of German experience in operations of varying intensity and inappropriate doctrine and training has led to 'operational miscalculations' and, in particular, difficulties for soldiers and commanders in judging when and how to apply higher-intensity force (Kujat, 2009).[48] Operation Harekate Yolo II demonstrated, therefore, the imperative ensuring preparation for exposure to higher-intensity conflict 'amongst the people' (Kujat, 2009; Noetzel and Schreer, 2008a: 45–6). These conclusions have been reinforced by Operation Eagle, that sought to provide security in Kunduz in the run-up to the Afghan elections on 20 August 2009 (Kujat, 2009) and German leadership, since mid-2007, of the ISAF Quick

Reaction Force (comprising a combat force of 250 troops) in the North of Afghanistan.[49]

The *Bundeswehr* has, however, a long road to travel in developing its capacity to undertake COIN, in particular in doctrine and training. As Working Group One on 'Personnel Development' at the 'Human in Transformation Workshop' organised by the *Bundeswehr* Transformation Centre on 20 June 2006 noted, the three core elements of 'three block warfare' – fighting, mediating and rebuilding – will characterise the likely tasks of the German soldier in the near future. However, Working Group One goes on to warn that 'The warriors in the army are a clear minority'.[50] The Working Group notes that in order to be able to undertake Three Block Warfare, the separation of competencies, between stabilisation and higher-intensity tasks may not be desirable and that the key identity of all soldiers should be that of the 'fighter'.[51] As a consequence of the long-term dominance of a non-offensive military doctrine that was reinforced by post-Cold War experiences in the Balkans, the German army is at a distinct disadvantage in tackling insurgency. COIN requires the ability not only to undertake offensive military action but crucially, to combine a wide-range of operational effects. These conclusions are also evident in the recommendations of Working Group Four on '*Innere Fuehrung*' that notes how non-offensive military doctrine is no longer valid in theatres such as Afghanistan.[52]

Germany is, therefore, taking slow steps to remedy deficiencies in its approach to irregular conflict as the pressure of recent operational experiences in Afghanistan has grown and political and military hierarchies[53] have begun to recognise the nature of conflict in Afghanistan, as 'Three Block Operations',[54] rather than a classic stabilisation mission (Noetzel and Schreer, 2009: 18).[55] The updated HDV 100/100 of 2007 forms an important move towards the development of a more nuanced German approach to irregular warfare by emphasising the potential for 'reversibility' in conflict situations and the need to develop the capacity to shift operational modes at short notice.[56] However, the document continues to place a stronger emphasis on the delivery of non-kinetic effects in irregular warfare than the British and French approaches to irregular warfare and it does not represent a detailed and explicit COIN doctrine (Noetzel and Schreer, 2009: 20). The document fails to deliver a coherent picture of how to engage in three block warfare: in particular, on how to apply higher-intensity actions in 'wars amongst the people'. As a high-ranking source within the German Defence Ministry stated: 'The main challenge for the commander and the soldier over the coming years will be to learn how to switch between operational modes'.[57]

Hence in the area of military doctrine the *Bundeswehr* continues to suffer from a '*Denkverbot*' applied by a core executive that, due to the constraints of the Federal system on executive autonomy, is highly-sensitive to the implications of radical change to the role of the *Bundeswehr*. The Army is being forced to tread a delicate line between ensuring it is putting in place the foundations for a higher-intensity role in Afghanistan without officially preparing COIN doctrine. It cannot be seen to overstep the parameters set by the 'salami-tactic' of its political masters, who have portrayed the ISAF mission as one of classic stabilisation. The Army is, therefore, attempting to interpret the concept of 'stabilisation' as broadly as possible to ensure that operational experiences are reflected in a doctrine that is of use to German soldiers. Doctrine writers are also quietly putting in place the intellectual foundations for a comprehensive and explicit COIN doctrine as a supplement to Army doctrine on stabilisation operations by undertaking a rigorous analysis of approaches to COIN in the UK, US and France (Noetzel and Schreer, 2009: 20).[58] Indeed, the development of an explicit COIN doctrine is one of the key themes currently under discussion within the Coordination and Decision Committee of the German lessons-learned process.[59]

This level of political interference in doctrine is, however, causing some problems for the military in fulfilling its mandate in Afghanistan. As the operational context in Kunduz increasingly moves towards one of COIN, in which small pockets of insurgents have to be isolated and fought, inappropriate doctrine puts German soldiers at risk. However, although official doctrine does not fully reflect the nature of current tasks under ISAF, training has, since 2007 been increasingly focused on a more 'aggressive approach', supported by increasingly robust RoE.[60] The 'stabilisation' forces now receive pre-mission training that will allow them to undertake more robust and offensive action and deliver effects across the conflict spectrum.[61] Experiences in Afghanistan also spurred the development of the *Einsatzfuehrungsstab* in June 2008 (a ministerial-level organisation responsible for operational planning, leadership and follow up) that will act to improve decision-making during the conduct of expeditionary operations by more effectively linking the MoD, Parliament and Cabinet (Noetzel and Schreer, 2009: 19).

As a consequence of the operational experiences in the Balkans and Afghanistan, the German approach to NEC emphasises the capacity of technologies associated with the RMA to facilitate the speedy, efficient and effective application of military action 'across the entire conflict spectrum'.[62] *NetOpFü* is to be put to the service not only to higher-intensity tasks but employed within a comprehensive approach to operations that 'effectively combines military and civilian instruments'.[63] Like British and French NEC, *NetOpFue* is also based upon scepticism of the ability of technology to transform the nature of conflict. *NetOpFue* emphasises the 'human factor' as the decisive element in the successful harnessing of technological advantage on the battlefield. NetOpFue is predicated on the assumption that training and the careful adaptation of command structures will be vital in ensuring that soldiers and leaders are supported and not overloaded by technology in missions across the conflict spectrum (Van der Giet and Schreiber, 2003: 21).

Operational experiences in complex crisis-management operations have also acted to reinforce the importance of *Auftragstaktik* (mission command), a principle that has been central to German military thinking since the development of the Prussian General Staff. As a high-ranking source within the German Army stated: 'The key leaders and decision-makers in contemporary operations are not Generals, but Sergeant Majors, Corporals and Lieutenants'.[64] Consequently, *NetOpFü* demonstrates convergence with the British concept of NEC in its emphasis on mission command and the vital role of training and human factors: 'Network enabled operations place high demands on decision-makers at all levels...the ability of deployed soldiers to act in accordance with the higher commander's intent – mission command, in other words – will be even more indispensable than before'.[65] Also inherent within German doctrinal development on *NetOpFü* is the recognition of its potential to endow the *Bundeswehr* with the ability to achieve effects disproportionate to the level of force applied through increased speed, flexibility momentum, tempo and agility (Laupert, 2008: 6–8; Van der Giet and Schreiber, 2003: 21). This mirrors the lessons learnt by the British about the continued centrality of the 'Manoeuvrist Approach' and the importance of 'old fashioned virtues' of speed and surprise, rather than a focus on the capacity of NEC to permit the massing of firepower and attrition.[66]

Two factors have emerged, however, which threaten to undermine the centrality of the principles of the Manoeuvrist Approach and the *Auftragstaktik* within NetOpFü. Firstly, the practical experience of digitisation in operations and exercises has led to the temptation for commanders to be drawn into the 'tactical weeds'.[67] It is, however, recognised by commanders that the balance will swing back from direction to delegation as commanders accrue greater experience with the use of C2 systems in military exercises and operations.[68]

Networking has also been accompanied by the problem of enhanced accountability. Whereas the 'fog of war' once made it difficult to discern whether correct procedure has been followed, digitisation leads to a 'data trail' that could end in the prosecution of commanders. Following the German role in the 4 September 2009 air strike in Kunduz that killed a number of civilians and the threat of prosecution for Colonel Georg Klein, who ordered the air strike, there has been a marked reticence for commanders in the field take the initiative. Decisions are now taken at an increasingly high level of command. Furthermore, after the Kunduz airstrike commanders are gathering inappropriate levels of information for operational needs and are being drawn down to the detailed tactical level, in order to protect themselves from accusation that they acted irresponsibly, should an action result in civilian casualties.[69]

German thinking on EBAO has gathered pace following the acceleration of EBAO's conceptual development within NATO after the November 2006 Riga Summit. The *Luftwaffe* has taken a lead role in the conceptual development of German EBAO. The *Luftwaffe* identified in EBAO an opportunity to expand their role in military operations that had been largely confined to reconnaissance and strategic lift during the post-Cold War era.[70] In May

2007 the *Luftwaffe* released *Die Konzeptionelle Grundvorstellung der Luftwaffe zum EBAO* 'The Conceptual Ground Rules of the *Luftwaffe* on The Effects-based Approach to Operations' (KGv Lw zu EBAO) that outlined the goal of developing a *Luftwaffe* that would be capable of acting as an 'interoperable "owner and facilitator" of effects, sensors and support services across the entire possible spectrum of EBAO'. 'KGv Lw zu EBAO' argues that technology has to be harnessed to achieve the simultaneous delivery of a range of operational effects – with an emphasis on the role of the *Luftwaffe* in control of the process of 'de-escalation'. The document explores in particular, the capacity of technology to improve the mobility, survivability, intelligence capabilities, command and control functions of the *Luftwaffe* and argues that investment in these technologies will significantly enhance the capacity of the Air Force to support civilian actors in stabilisation operations as part of '*Vernetzte Sicherheit*'.

Although KGv Lw zu EBAO was a reaction to the apparently growing importance of EBAO to interoperability with NATO Alliance partners, it had a clear political agenda. The paper's purpose was to stake out the *Luftwaffe's* centrality to EBAO in advance of a more general conceptual paper on EBAO that would encompass the entire *Bundeswehr*.[71] Indeed, the approach to EBAO outlined by the Luftwaffe encountered a strong-level of resistance within the Army. The Army has been receptive to 'effects-based thinking', seeing the approach as a vindication of its traditional approach to military planning: imagining the desired end-state and considering the variety of kinetic and non-kinetic means which will be required to achieve it. The capacity of effects-based thinking to provide a means with which to deliver a broad spectrum of effects by facilitating the integration of civilian actors in the planning and conduct of operations through 'networked security' has also been welcomed by the Army.[72]

The *Luftwaffe's* perspective on EBAO was, however, viewed by the Army as overly-formalistic and mechanistic due to its emphasis on quantitative 'measures of performance' and 'measures of effectiveness'. In this sense, the *Luftwaffe* definition of EBAO cohered much more closely with the US concept of EBO. This was a consequence not only of the early stage of thinking on EBAO within the German military and reactiveness of Germany to US thinking transmitted through NATO, but also of the attempt by the *Luftwaffe* to position itself as the key enabler of EBAO.[73] For the Army, this approach threatened to impose a level of rigidity and an assumption of knowledge of the operational environment that would not be achievable at the tactical level.[74] KGv Lw zu EBAO threatened to undermine the advantages delivered by the Manoueversit Approach and *Auftragstaktik*.[75] Hence whilst the 'KGv Lw zu EBAO' initially enjoyed some support outside the *Luftwaffe*, particularly within the BTC, the position of the Army has been strengthened by the recent shift of the US military away from EBO following experiences in Afghanistan and observation of the difficulties encountered by the Israeli Defence Force with EBO in the Second Lebanon War (Kober, 2008: 32–3).[76] These events have raised some questions within the *Bundeswehr* about the status of EBAO as a key organising concept of the transformation process, particularly within the Army.[77] However, although the Army prefers the looser concept of 'Effects-Based Thinking', the Air Force and Navy continue to promote a more traditional understanding of EBAO.[78] Much will depend upon the position adopted by NATO as a whole on the future of EBAO, illustrating the reactiveness of German doctrine and CD&E to NATO developments. As a senior figure within the Bundeswehr Transformation Centre noted: 'Rather than base our decision whether to persist with EBAO on the judgement of one US General (Mattis), we will await guidance from NATO. For now, the tasking of the International Military Staff remains valid and EABO is not under scrutiny'.

Germany is, however, a long way from being able to deliver a joint operational picture that will shorten reaction cycles and enable EBAO. Only in 2013 will Germany reach a basic (initial) network enabled capability, when a large demonstrator exercise is planned that will test equipment, training and deployability on operation.[79] The *Bundeswehr's* current focus is, therefore, on putting in place the foundations for EBAO by dealing with the implications of the roll-out of C2 capabilities for command structures and joint, multinational operations (the so-called 'Common Enhancement' process) through a series of joint military exercises (Kirchgaessner and Marahrens, 2008: 25). The *Bundeswehr* is presently struggling with the creation of a joint operational picture that integrates the needs of all arms of the military, in which the three main Services (and those of their international partners) and their different levels of command automatically receive relevant information.[80] Indeed, the *Bundeswehr's* ambitions in NEC are much more limited than those of the other European Great Powers. For example, the UK military retains the ambition to field a Division that will be interoperable with US forces (to avoid the problem evidenced by Basra where the US had to 'step down' in technology to work with the British). Within the German military the maximum that is hoped for within present financial constraints is the development of interoperability between small units of the *Bundeswehr* and US forces. These units will only be capable of fielding a more advanced network enabled capability that will achieve shorter reaction cycles by 2020/1 at the earliest.[81]

Managing military input into defence planning: Increasing adaptability at the tactical and operational levels

The institutional structures which will facilitate Germany's process of 'conceptual catching-up' with her European partners and the continual adaptation of capabilities, doctrine and training within a quickly changing operational environment have only been established for a short period of time. Germany has, nevertheless, taken some important steps since 2006 to improve the 'lessons-learned' process and to accelerate the *Bundeswehr's* transformation around the principle of jointness and interoperability with Alliance partners.

Before 2006 the German 'lessons-learned' process lacked overall coordination. Following the first major out of area operations in the early 1990s under IFOR, an officer was appointed to an operational headquarters with the specific responsibility for evaluating the key lessons for doctrine, capabilities, procedures, and command structures and training. This officer delivered daily reports to sections for *Einsatzaufwertung* (Operational Assessment) within the individual Planning Staffs, who analysed the information, checked whether other units had encountered similar problems, agreed on actions and undertook follow-up.[82] However, there has until recently been no formalised 'long-loop' process dealing with the implications of operations for jointness.[83] Decisions upon the implications of longer-term deficiencies for CD&E were instead left to the single Services of the *Bundeswehr* which were expected to identify problems and propose changes, following the submission of a written report from the Joint Commander on operation.[84] Hence although the lessons-learned process was able to identify some of the short-term implications of operational experiences, it lacked an impartial follow-up mechanism and was much weaker in assessing the broader implications for CD&E, capabilities, training and major doctrinal changes.[85]

The complexity of the operational environment and increasing number of operational experiences with broader implications for joint operations and interoperability have led to a number of important changes to the lessons-learned process since 2006. In 2004 the InfoSysEEBw database based at the *Einsatzfuehrungszentrum* (Bundeswehr Operations Command) in Potsdam was initiated. At this early stage InfoSysEEBw was simply a data collection tool where operational reports could be stored. The key step in the transformation of the lessons-learned process came in June 2008 with the establishment of the *Einsatzfuehrungsstab* and the creation of the section for *Einsatzauswertung* within the Joint Staff. The Army has also benefited from the increasing manpower allocated to the lessons-learned process, in particular from officers appointed at the *Heeresamt* and *HerresfuehrungsKommando* who are responsible for lessons-learned.[86]

The section for *Einsatzauswertung* is tasked with three core lessons-learned tasks which impact on overall 'Operational Quality': Operational Analysis/ Readiness (the relevance of current doctrine, organisation, training, leadership, personnel and capabilities); Operational Effectiveness (the extent to which operations have succeeded in delivering key effects) and Efficiency (cost-benefit relationships).[87] The process of Operational Analysis has undergone significant development since June 2008. The observations arising from field reports are now logged in to InfoSysEEBw. Once these reports enter the system the Bundeswehr Operations Command undertakes initial analysis and decides which service should take the lead role in further analysis and follow-up. The individual service must then respond with a plan of action within an agreed timetable. Any steps taken by the service and its discussions with other actors such as weapons manufacturers or the *Fuehreungsakademie der Bundeswehr* are entered into InfoSysEEBw. This process ensures that the Operations Command is able to follow-up the implementation of lessons-learned and the measures undertaken by contingents on the ground. Lessons-learned are also identified through workshops and seminars with commanders from an operation in order to assess the implications for military doctrine, training and capabilities. These workshops are conducted by the BTC's Institute of Social Sciences that also prepares three questionnaires for commanders which are completed before, during and following deployment.[88]

InfoSysEEBw has therefore proved effective as a 'staffing tool' in allocating responsibilities and checking follow-up and as a library/database for reports from Mission Contingents. Combined with the establishment of the *Einsatzfuehrungsstab* and section for *Einsatzauswertung*, InfoSysEEBw has improved the efficiency of the collection, analysis and follow-up stages of the 'short-loop' lessons-learned process, enhancing the focus of the lessons-learned process on improving key areas such as jointness and the use of C2 systems. These changes have also led to the refinement of predeployment training exercises which are now more closely focused on actual operational scenarios and to the acceleration of training in areas identified as suffering from manpower shortages, such as forward air controllers.[89] In addition, the lessons-learned process has been a key element in providing the evidence necessary to legitimate a shift towards increasingly offensive and robust RoE under ISAF which allow the German troops to engage suspected insurgents without waiting to come under fire.[90]

Furthermore, the *Einsatzsofortsbedarf* permits the three armed Services to acquire equipment urgently required for operations providing that the equipment costs under five million Euros, can be bought 'off the shelf' with no development costs attached and is acquired with a period of 12 months. Requests are adjudicated by the Integrated Working Group for Capability Analysis (IAGFA) that consists largely of military personnel, but also includes a representative of the Defence Ministry's Budget Director. For example, following the experience of the deployment from April 2007 of six Tornados of the AG51 'Immelmann' Squadron in reconnaissance operations in Afghanistan, the Air Force quickly identified the need for a reduced post-flight imagery processing time, for higher-quality imagery and for more flexible pod sensors. Consequently, the *Luftwaffe* was able to quickly acquire 'Reccelight' tactical reconnaissance pods and groundwork stations for its Tornados, the first two of which came into service in September 2009. The normal acquisition timeframe for the system would have been up to five years.[91]

The lack of coordination of the 'long-loop' lessons-learned process has also recently been improved. The Services and the Bundeswehr Operations Command work together in the identification of a 'top list' of the key topics which require immediate attention and cannot be met through the

Einsatzsofortsbedarf or through incremental changes to training or doctrine under the 'short-loop' process. This list is currently composed of 12 issues: the development of mobile command posts; C2 capabilities; the requirement of a helicopter for medical evacuation in Afghanistan; convoy operations; the development of COIN doctrine; mission preparation; repair and spare parts supply; the protection of field camps and facilities; means of airborne reconnaissance; intelligence reporting; counter IED doctrine and the reduction of technical mission difficulties (such as legal issues relating to health and safety regulations).[92]

The definition of the measures necessary for their potential solution are characterised by a high-level of competition between the Services and battles over which service will take the lead.[93] This competition has, for example, characterised the issue of the improvement of Airborne Reconnaissance. Whilst the Air Force was chosen by the Bundeswehr Operations Command to take the lead on the topic, the Army has a keen interest in these capabilities, and has raised a number of objections to developments suggested by the Air Force.[94] This has slowed down the identification of potential solutions. The Bundeswehr Operations Command is also examining mechanisms to further strengthen the objectivity of the identification of solutions to lessons-learned by facilitating greater input from the BTC and NATO CoEs.[95]

Furthermore, the 'top list' is agreed at the Coordination and Decision Committee that is composed of 40 members who examine the proposals suggested by the individual Services. Membership of the Committee includes representatives from the individual Services, the Coordination Group for Transformation, the *Abteilung Ruestung* (Capabilities Department of the MoD), BTC, and specialists in training and CD&E. The broad constituency represented by this committee also help to ensure that although the individual Services have a strong level of input in identifying problems, solutions are not endorsed which are broadly out of line with operational requirements. Furthermore, institutional protection for financial constraints is provided by the presence of representatives of the MoD Budgetary Section. The work of the Coordination and Decision Committee has been supplemented by the establishment in 2009 of two steering committees (one at the level of the *Einsatzfuehrung*; the other at Desk Officer level) which are responsible for coordinating the implementation of the long-loop lessons-learned process.

However, the ultimate decision-making authority on the prioritisation of major changes to capabilities, doctrine and training rests with the Military Advisory Board. This Board is dominated by military input, composed of the Director of the Joint Operational Staff, Chiefs of Staff of the Army, Navy, Air Force, Medical Services and Logistical Support as well as the *Generalinspekteur* and the Minister of Defence. The Board therefore forms an arena for organisational politics between the Services, impeding the flow of operational lessons into the capability and equipment programme.[96]

These changes to the lessons-learned process are, however, recent, hence *Einsatzauswaertung* is very much a 'work in progress'. A number of problems and difficulties have emerged. The first major problem since the roll-out of InfoSysEEBw is an overload of information and the inability of InfoSysEEBw to help with 'knowledge development'. Whilst training and mission hand-over allows commanders to learn from the experiences of others there is no search engine that is able to sort the relevant information for different levels of command and allow them to directly access the comments of their predecessors on deployment.[97]

In addition, although the lessons-learned process has been useful in iden-tifying non-urgent operational issues, such as equipment shortages, it has, so far, been less useful in quickly identifying and resolving issues at the tac-tical, doctrinal level. This problem derives from the emphasis on post-mission reports which fail to capture the rapidly-changing nature of operations and enemy tactics. When tactical issues are identified, their solution, once agreed, is integrated into the six-month training course that takes place in advance of operational deployment, but this process takes time and is not well-suited to COIN operations. A series of proposals are underway to try to draw infor-mation from the field in a more continuous manner. However, improvement is impeded by the shortage of German infantry forces under ISAF. The urgent need to maximise troop presence on the ground has left little space for the inclusion of extra officers focusing on the speedy delivery of reports.[98]

Furthermore, a persistent problem of doctrinal stagnation within the indi-vidual Services remains. This problem derives not only from the *Denkverbot*, but also from the comparatively rigid process of doctrinal development. Military doctrine is constructed in a highly-consensual manner between the Services. No one individual has the capacity to over-ride objections to changes to military doctrine, making even minor alterations to doctrine a highly-bureaucratic and drawn-out process.[99] This approach contrasts markedly to France and the UK where doctrine is developed in a more organic and evolutionary manner and benefit from the capacity of the 'service agnostic' CICDE and DCDC to take the initiative in leading-up doctrinal change.

The broad direction of transformation – the focus on joint, networked and interoperable expeditionary forces – has, however, been provided through strong top-down leadership from the civilian leadership channeled through former *Generalinspekteur*, Wolfgang Schneiderhahn who is viewed within the military as the 'father' of the transformation process.[100] The civilian leadership of the MoD has also taken steps to attempt to endow the transformation process – in particular the principles of jointness and interoperability – with a strong measure of institutional protection through the development of the Bundeswehr Operations Command and BTC.

Since its establishment in 2004, the BTC has played an increasingly impor-tant role in the development of doctrine and CD&E within the Services. The BTC acts as the intellectual and conceptual 'muscle' of the Joint Staff.

However, unlike the DCDC and CICDE, the BTC does not enjoy the power to lead up doctrinal and conceptual development. Instead, the BTC acts as a 'think-tank' and plays a coordinating role by organising working groups and workshops on CD&E and doctrine around NEC, EBAO, interoperability and jointness.[101] Despite its more limited competencies, the BTC has emerged as a key partner in the CD&E and doctrinal development of each service. The power of the BTC lies in its strong agenda-setting role in helping to develop visions of the key warfare scenarios which will guide the future trajectory of transformation. Lobbying of the BTC and its cooption at the early stages of conceptual development around doctrine and capabilities is, therefore, viewed as increasingly vital by the Single Services.[102] The BTC's competencies are also gradually expanding. The organisation has, for example, begun to work with the project managers of the Federal Office of Defence Technology and Procurement in order to facilitate greater harmonisation within the capability programme and is also seeking to expand its resources and role in coordinating doctrinal development across the *Bundeswehr*.[103]

Indeed, the urgency of adapting to the new agenda of jointness has led the Single Services to be receptive to reform to their structures in order to improve their methods of information gathering on military 'best practice' by working more closely with international partners in the development of joint, inter-operable doctrine and capabilities. Such changes are viewed as a critical means with which the Single Services can strengthen their influence over the trajectory of the transformation process. For example, the *Luftwaffe* (German Air Force) began a structural reorganisation on 30 January 2006. This reorganisation was designed to allow the *Luftwaffe* to respond more quickly to changes in the operational environment. The restructuring facilitated a closer relationship with NATO's Joint Air Power Competence Centre (JAPCC) CoE and has also enabled smoother cooperation with NATO by mirroring the command structures of the Atlantic Alliance. In this way, the Luftwaffe is more exposed to the lessons of 'best practice' consequent upon the experiences of her NATO partners and is able to hone its interoperability. These changes were perceived by key figures within the Luftwaffe as a means to secure greater influence within the Ministerial-level Coordination Group for Transformation and the BTC.[104]

Furthermore, the *Luftmachtzentrum* (Air Power Centre) that was created in 2006 brings together the conceptual and operational work of the Luftwaffe Command sections for planning, telecommunications and operating procedures. The *Luftmachtzentrum* acts as the main 'muscle' of the Luftwaffe for CD&E. The organisation provides the conceptual input for the Working Group on Luftwaffe Transformation that takes the main decisions on the *Luftwaffe's* position on NEC/EBAO and decides which capability proposals will be proposed to the Ministerial-level Coordination Croup for Transformation. The *Luftmachtzentrum* works closely with the BTC and JAPCC.[105] This international input into Luftwaffe CD&E adds extra weight and gravitas to the *Luftwaffe's* capability proposals within the Coordination Group for Transformation.[106]

Hence, as a consequence of the pressure to adapt to the logic of jointness and following the reforms adopted by the Services, the jointness agenda is being quickly disseminated throughout the *Bundeswehr* despite the delay in its inception. Jointness is progressing particularly well in the area of intelligence and in the logistical Services provided by the *Streitkraeftebasis*.[107] There is also increasing cross-service cooperation, for example in the development of approaches to the use of the sea as a basis for land and air deployments, on air-land integration (the German version of the 'Air-Land Bubble') and more generally on refining the interoperability of C2 systems under *NetOpFü*.[108] The traditional consensual approach to the development of military doctrine has had a positive effect on the development of joint doctrine, due to the high-level of collaboration between the Services whose views are solicited and integrated (Belde, 2004: 31).

Nevertheless, some institutional resistance has been present to the rapid changes wrought since 2003. A 'them and us' attitude toward the development of a culture of 'jointness' and to the role of the Joint Staff in leading up 'joint' projects still prevails in some areas of the Services.[109] This opposition is, however, being rapidly eliminated through the changes to the mechanisms of military input to defence planning. Important changes to training have also taken place, such as the Advanced Joint Staff Course that has been delivered by the *Fuehrungsakademie* since 2004 and is disseminating the principle of jointness throughout the leadership of the separate Planning Staffs.[110]

It is, therefore, increasingly recognised within the Planning Staff that for a service to thrive it must comply with the mantra of jointness and interoperability. It is also important to note that many sections of the Defence Ministry had privately become dissatisfied with the retention of territorial defence as the core objective of the *Bundeswehr* until 2003, particularly following the processes of operational learning which had take place during the post-Cold War era.[111] The focus on jointness that has accompanied the early stages of transformation therefore gained broad support as a means with which to renew the relevance of the *Bundeswehr* in multinational operations.

Such organisational changes have acted to enhance the capacity of the *Bundeswehr* to respond to the rapidly changing operational environment by fostering a stronger focus on the imperatives of jointness and interoperability. The process of *Einsatzauswertung* is also putting in place the institutional mechanisms to enhance the dynamism of *Bundeswehr* in identifying and following-up the implications of operations for doctrine and training. However, the translation of these lessons into changes to the capability programme and force posture is hampered by organisational politics between the Single Services, the effects of which are exacerbated by the tight constraints of low executive autonomy.

Low executive autonomy and the exacerbation of organisational politics in capability acquisition

The Single Service Chiefs enjoy a high-level of power to set the agenda on military equipment and capability procurement. The ability for the individual Services to secure the agreement of the *Generalinspekteur* and civilian leadership for investment in their central capability projects is dependent upon the support of the other two branches of the armed forces, in addition to the backing of the Joint Service Support Command (*Streitkraeftebasis*) and Central Medical Service (*Zentrale Sanitaetsdienst*). This consensual dynamic acts to the detriment of objective decision-making on capability procurement. It also allows organisational politics to emerge in debates at higher-levels of the MoD (such as the Coordination Group for Transformation) on the adoption of conceptual papers which have serious implications for capability acquisition.[112]

The major debates on capability procurement take place within the IAGFA that is composed of representative of the Bundeswehr Chiefs of Staff, Director General of Armaments, Chiefs of Staff of the Armed Services, Director of Defence Administration, IT Director and MoD Budget Director (who is present in an advisory role only). IAGFA translates the broader direction to defence policy provided by the 2006 Defence White Paper and Coordination Group for Transformation into key decisions on capability procurement. These decisions are expressed as 'System Capability Requirements' which detail the key requirements across different areas of activity and following protracted negotiations eventually result in a Final Functional Requirement that details the precise capability/equipment to be purchased.

Although the organisational structures charged with the implementation of capability projects – the BWB and Information Technology Department – are 'civil servant heavy', the agenda-setting process on military capabilities is dominated by military input, particularly from the Single Service Chiefs. The Coordination Group for Transformation and IAGFA were described by one interview partner as akin to a 'bazaar' and 'log-rolling' exercise, in which the Single Services trade-off support for each others' major 'glamour' projects.[113] This situation is compounded by the lack of subordination of the Single Service Chiefs to the *Generalinspekteur*, who acts as in an advisory role to the Defence Minister and whose only formal power over the Services lies in his ability to relieve the Service Chiefs of their Command.[114] As a consequence, although former *Generalinspekteur* Schneiderhan was able to promote a focus on networked, joint and interoperable forces (principles which were anyway clearly becoming imperative following the Services' experience of area operations), his capacity to translate these principles into more fundamental reforms to military capabilities has been more limited.[115]

Unlike France and the UK where windows of opportunity to make significant changes to force posture and capability projects emerge following Presidential/Parliamentary elections, German Defence Ministers face narrower executive autonomy due to the regularity of important regional elections. Hence, rather than causal, organisational politics is a reflection of the constraints of the German Federal system on the ability of Defence Ministers to take tough decisions on base closures and on the sensitivity of the core executive to the political-fall out of job losses in the defence sector.[116] As a high-level source within the German Defence Ministry noted: 'In Germany we have two (Land) elections per year. There is no possibility to push through radical reform to capability acquisition or force structure'.[117] This lack of political will to reform the capability acquisition process acts as a structural limitation on the ability of 'service agnostic' organisations like the BTC and Bundeswehr Operational Command to foster greater objectivity in conceptual development and capability procurement.[118]

There is, however, a stronger capacity for civilian intervention in ensuring that the equipment and capability programme coheres to budgetary constraints. Parliament enjoys the right to decide on the purchase of equipment and capabilities costing over 25 million Euros. This is, however, a rather blunt instrument. The content of capability and equipment projects are presented as a *fait accomplis* to Parliament. Oversight is restricted to either rejecting the project as a whole or reducing the size of an order. Furthermore, Parliamentary control over major projects acts as an extra disincentive to changes to the direction of capability investment. Once money has been approved by Parliament it cannot be redistributed without repeating the approval process and the long, drawn-out negotiations with the Parliament's Budgetary Committee.[119]

Parliament also approves the Bundeswehr's budget on a yearly basis following negotiations between the Defence and Finance Ministries. This has the important effect of setting tight financial constraints on capability procurement projects. However, when combined with ineffective civilian control over the content of capability procurement, tight financial constraints exacerbate the incapacity of the armed forces to shift the more serious UORs into the main equipment programme and to invest in C4ISR capabilities. As a consequence, the German Defence Ministry is investigating the advantages of the Spiral Development Model that introduces a capability at 80 per cent of its technological potential. This model will not deal with the root causes of the time delays and cost over-runs associated with the German acquisition process. It will, however, permit more realistic planning than the current model of capability development in which the implications of delivering a capability at less than 100 per cent of its potential are often not formally considered until much later on in the development stage.[120]

The German Federal Auditing Office is also mandated to investigate defence procurement projects, however its oversight capacity is restricted by the limited manpower it has available for the task.[121] Furthermore, the data acquired on time slippage and cost over-runs of major projects is not available in the public domain. As a senior figure in the Defence Ministry noted: 'This lack of transparency and accountability lies in a complex mesh of interests – the individual Services, BWB and Budgetary Departments of the Finance and Defence Ministries – who wish to cover-up their mistakes. These interests are allowed to prevail due to the lack of political will to reform the acquisition process that derives from the unwillingness of politicians to take on the German Defence Industry'.[122] Reforms to the German capability and equipment acquisition process which were designed to enhance the relationship between the *Bundeswehr* and the German Defence Industry and shorten development time – notably the May 2004 Customer Product Management scheme – have therefore had little overall impact on the efficiency of the German capability procurement process.[123]

The institutional forums of German defence policy: Between systemic and domestic incentives

The institutional forums of German defence policy continue to cohere around the traditional German 'bridge' role, between British/US and French preferences (Dyson, 2005: 376; Hyde-Price, 2000: 205–7; Hyde-Price and Jeffrey, 2001: 706). Indeed, it is possible to identify a 'bi-furcation' (Goetz, 2003) within the Federal Executive, between a highly-Europeanist and active Foreign Ministry in 'uploading' German preferences to ESDP and an 'Atlanticised' Defence Ministry, more reactive and resistant to the anchoring of defence policy within ESDP (Bulmer et al, 2000: 25; Dyson, 2007: 158).

Cultural approaches posit that the German 'bridge role' and 'bi-furcated Federal Executive', split between a 'Europeanised' Foreign Ministry and 'Atlanticised' Defence Ministry, is a result of the institutionally-embedded norms consequent upon the post-war experience of rehabilitation into the international community and the concomitant necessity to negotiate and broker French and US concerns through the EU and NATO respectively (Goetz, 2003; Hyde-Price, 2000: 205–9; Miskimmon and Paterson, 2003: 325–45; Miskimmon, 2007: 195). It also reflects the need to broker agreement between the two dominant advocacy coalitions competing over the institutional venues of defence policy: one characterised by Europeanist ideology, centred on the SPD/Greens; the other by an Atlanticist ideology, embedded within the CDU/CSU and FDP (Gutjahr, 1994: 135–46; Dyson, 2005: 374–5).

However, neoclassical realism provides a more convincing explanation of German preferences on institutional forums than neorealism or cultural accounts. Whilst 'allied cooperation' over the long-run reflects systemic imperatives, unit-level factors in the shape of domestic material power relationships form important intervening variables. This explains the active role of the German Foreign Ministry in developing ESDP and the Defence Ministry's reactive 'laggard' role in dealing with the implications of ESDP for the objectives and instruments of German defence policy (Dyson, 2007: 173–4; Hellmann et al, 2005: 160; Wagner, 2005).

Defence Ministers were critical in determining the extent and manner in which German defence policy was Atlanticised and Europeanised. The greater 'institutional credibility' of NATO within the Defence Ministry is more than just a product of 'elite socialisation' and 'institutionally-embedded norms'; it stems from the unwillingness of Rühe, Scharping and Struck to appoint or promote pro-Europeanist *Vordenker* (innovators) within the Defence Ministry for fear of domestic political implications (Dyson, 2007: 173–4). This was an attempt by Defence Ministers to avoid the potentially destabilising effects that framing reform within 'allied cooperation' as part of ESDP could have upon the political and temporal management of reform due to the pressure it would create within the Defence Ministry to abolish conscription. Such far-reaching structural reforms would have implied damaging repercussions for the social and financial policy subsystems and initiated politically-sensitive base closures (Dyson, 2005: 366–9). In short, the Defence Ministry has been locked into domestic institutional structures that gave little incentive to 'Europeanise' the *Bundeswehr* and instead promoted the active leadership of Defence Ministers in shaping and using the ideologies of 'Atlanticisation' and 'Europeanisation' in the interests of their own domestic political agendas (Dyson, 2007: 152).

Conversely, German Foreign Ministers have benefited from a greater level of autonomy in promoting 'allied cooperation' through the EU. This is a consequence, not only of the long-term role of the Foreign Ministry as the senior coordinating Ministry pursuing European integration, but also of Foreign Ministers' status as leaders of smaller coalition partners (until the SPD's Frank-Walter Steinmeier in 2005), reducing their sensitivity to the electoral fall-out of base closures and financial implications of the abolition of conscription. A focus on domestic power relationships helps to explain why both Klaus Kinkel (Liberal Party Foreign Minister 1992–8) and Joschka Fischer (Green Foreign Minister 1998–2005), concerned with the limitations of territorial defence objectives and a conscript-based policy instrument, sought out (ultimately unsuccessful) roles as 'strategic innovators' on behalf of a professional military, orientated towards crisis-intervention tasks (Dyson, 2007: 68–71, 95).

Whilst the domestic political implications of the embedding of policy within EU/NATO represent a significant intervening variable impacting on policy choices of institutional venue in the short-medium term, Germany, in line with the UK and France, has become increasingly willing to put its weight behind the development of the military capabilities that will facilitate European autonomy in security and defence in its geopolitical neighbourhood (Barnathan, 2006: 304; Brenner, 2003: 192). This strategic imperative became particularly pressing for Germany in the context of the 2002 US Security Strategy and in the run-up to the 2003 Iraq crisis that brought home to policymakers the urgency of far-reaching reform in order to avoid a loss of relative power (Dyson, 2007: 39–40; Rynning, 2005: 158–9). The intensified fear of 'entrapment' or 'abandonment' by the US (Barnathan, 2006: 307–8) led to changes to the objectives of German defence policy in an attempt to gain greater influence within the US and ensure a measure of European autonomy of action by contributing to the pooling of European military resources, routed through both NATO and ESDP.[124]

Hence in the 2003 Defence Policy Guidelines, Struck framed the changing objectives of German defence policy as a means with which to contribute to the development of an ESDP as the 'European Pillar' of the Atlantic Alliance (Dalgaard-Nielsen, 2006: 152; King, 2005a: 49). Struck also set in place C4ISR capability investment programmes in support of networked capabilities, as well as structural reforms to the army, navy and airforce, bolstering modularity and jointness, reforms that were reinforced by the Grand Coalition's Defence White Paper of 2006, thereby strengthening the *Bundeswehr's* capacity to provide troops for both the NRF and Battlegroups and UN Standby Arrangement System.[125] At the same time, although increased national investment in C4ISR capability programmes has formed a key pillar of German 'reformed bandwagoning', Germany also has become increasingly willing – within the constraints imposed by the alliance security dilemma – to put its weight behind joint procurement projects under the auspices of the EDA, ACT and bi-pluri-lateral initiatives. These initiatives form a crucial means by which Germany can close the technology gap with her EU and NATO partners, overcome particularly tight budgetary constraints and her inherent resource constraints as a 'secondary' power.[126]

This evidence provides a strong refutation of the argument put forward by Matlary (2009: 157) that 'domestic factors now completely trump international pressure' in German defence policy. Rather than a case of 'Europeanisation' and 'elite socialisation' (Miskimmon, 2007), Germany's increasing willingness to develop capabilities in support of the Battlegroups and NRF represents the growing adherence of the Federal Republic to the powerful socialisation effects of the material forces of international structure. The pessimistic conclusions drawn by those who emphasise the impact of the 'culture of anti-militarism' on the potential for German contributions to higher-intensity ESDP/NATO operations overlook the distance that has been traveled on the road to such operations. Colin Bennett (1991: 19) reminds us that policy convergence is a 'process of becoming, rather than being alike' and, as neoclassical realism expects, the pressure of international structure is inducing German convergence with 'best practice', despite the significant domestic constraints of low executive autonomy. This is clearly evidenced by the changes to the objectives of German Defence Policy in 2003 and steps currently being taken by Germany to develop the networked capabilities and troops necessary to conduct 'Three Block Operations', as well as the institutional reforms undertaken since 2006 to accelerate the transformation agenda and enhance the lessons-learned process.

Travelling the road to convergence: Continued deficiencies in capabilities and doctrine

This chapter has offered an alternative explanation for German reticence to pull its weight in the process of 'reformed bandwagoning' as manifested by its largely low-medium intensity role in the North of Afghanistan. Culturalists, such as Duffield (1999), Longhurst (2004) and Miskimmon (2007: 192–3) emphasise the constraints imposed on the state power of the Federal Republic by its 'special anti-militaristic political culture' (Matlary, 2009: 151). Such accounts of German defence policy neglect the deliberate management of the temporality of convergence with systemic imperatives under conditions of low executive autonomy. Rather than culture, it is low executive autonomy that continues to circumscribe the capacity of the core executive to pursue enhanced influence in Washington through greater contributions to ISAF's efforts in Afghanistan. Low executive autonomy induced the persistence territorial defence until 2003, of conscription until the present day and restricts the capacity of the core executive to deploy culture as a tool on behalf of a more offensive military role. Executive autonomy reduces the ability of the core executive to take a more pro-active role in tackling the impact of organisational politics on capability acquisition and foster greater adaptability in procurement.

Despite the recent advent of the BTC and more rigorous process of lesson-identification and follow-up, the legacy of the *Denkverbot* has left the Defence Ministry with an atmosphere that is not as receptive to critical thinking and open debate on the implications of operational experience for doctrine and force structures as is the case in the UK and France. This lack of transparency is most clearly evidenced by the classified nature of German military doctrine that limits the capacity for the *Bundeswehr* to engage with external actors, such as the academic community in the refinement of military doctrine. It also acts as an impediment to 'networked security' by distancing military doctrine from civilian actors. Finally, the classified nature of military doctrine also means that it is unavailable to reservists, who cannot update their knowledge when not on operation.[127]

The lack of doctrinal sophistication on COIN in HDV 100/100 (2007) is, therefore, unsurprising given the level of conceptual stagnation that existed within the Defence Ministry during the *Denkverbot*, and following the retention, until 2003, of territorial defence as the core task of the *Bundeswehr*. The difficulty of employing culture as a tool in support of a changing role for the *Bundeswehr* also creates an incentive for a higher-level of political interference in doctrinal development than is the case in Britain and France.[128] This problem is further compounded by the thin historical experience and 'institutional memory' of the *Bundeswehr* in tackling insurgency. Although doctrinal writers pay close attention to doctrinal developments on COIN and irregular warfare in France, the UK and the US (receiving, for example, early drafts of new doctrinal proposals from their liaison officers in these countries), Germany is learning how to undertake 'Three Block Warfare' from a single example: Northern Afghanistan.[129] Steps are being taken to remedy these doctrinal deficiencies, but the development of German doctrine and training around 'Three Block Operations', NetOpFü and EBAO is a process that will take some time.[130]

The process of military transformation and investment around C4ISR capabilities has also been impeded by the restrictions on executive autonomy which derive from the fiscal constraints associated with German reunification. As Chancellor Schroeder noted: 'No other member of the EU had a [fiscal] burden as heavy as the one carried by Germany following reunification. This made it much easier for other EU states to respond to changes and to deal with the challenges posed by the international economy from the 1990s to the present day' (Schroeder, 2007: 88). Such a restrictive fiscal context forms an important causal variable in explaining Germany's low level of defence spending in relation to its GDP when compared with Britain and France (see Table A.2).

Hence, although traveling the road of convergence, the *Bundeswehr* remains – for the time being – deficient in tackling the challenges posed by 'Three Block Warfare' and is incapable of participating in combat operations of the scale and intensity of those undertaken by the British and Americans in the South of Afghanistan (Kujat, 2009).[131] Upon returning from a six-month tour of duty in Afghanistan in August 2009, Brigade General Jorg Vollmer released an internal paper outlining 155 deficits in training and equipment with grave implications for the success of the German mission as the security situation in Kunduz worsened (SWR, 2009). Vollmer telling noted that the number of '*Eingreifskraefte*' deployed in theatre were far too low to secure the province of Kunduz and that training would have to focus more closely on '*Kampfeinsaetze*' (high-intensity fighting) (SWR, 2009). As Noetzel and Schreer (2008a: 217) also highlight: 'The ISAF mission demonstrates the *Bundeswehr* is critically short of specialized units which are in high demand during counterinsurgency operations...'.

Indeed, a confidential source within the German Defence Ministry stated of the *Bundeswehr's* current capacity to undertake the higher-intensity tasks associated with Three Block Warfare: 'The *Bundeswehr* is now growing up. Despite political constraints, it is heading steadily in the direction of the doctrine and capabilities needed to undertake "Three Block Warfare" operations and to convergence with the British and French. But you can't expect a five year-old to do the same tasks as an eighteen year-old'.[132] This observation is reinforced by the Noetzel and Schreer (2009: 19) who note: 'MoD Defence Planning for 2009 acknowledges that the capability for robust missions of the German stabilisation forces which are conceptually earmarked for conducting operations against irregular enemies, can only be markedly improved in a long-term perspective'.

The unwillingness of German policy leaders to commit substantial ground troops to the areas of most intense fighting, in the South of Afghanistan is therefore, understandable.[133] This reticence derives in part in a set of policy narratives which are difficult to master following the use of 'anti-militaristic' ideology and nationalism to frame Germany's rehabilitation into the international community during the Cold War. However, the key variable lies in the constraints imposed by the electoral cycles of the Federal political system on the capacity of the executive to reshape these narratives and the objectives and instruments of German Defence Policy.

Within such a context, as Aust and Vashakmadze (2008: 2235) highlight, the constraints of parliamentary approval for the deployment, mandate and RoE of expeditionary troops can form a useful resource for the core executive in the management of the temporality of convergence with systemic imperatives. These constraints form a means with which to deflect international criticism of the *Bundeswehr's* current weaknesses in undertaking operations which require the simultaneous application of both non-kinetic and kinetic effects.

6
The United Kingdom – From Strategic Innovation to Stasis

British strategic culture is identified by Miskimmon (2004: 89–92, 95) as embodying four core aspects. Firstly, a desire of the British to 'punch above their weight' in defence and security that stems from memories of the rapid loss of relative power that occurred following the post-war dissipation of the British Empire. Secondly, a sense of global responsibility for peacekeeping and humanitarian intervention that is also an outcome of the UK's colonial heritage and thirdly, a commitment to the development and maintenance of a nuclear deterrent. The final pillar of British strategic culture is an instinctive Atlanticism, whose embededdness derives from socialisation processes consequent upon Britain's strong post-war commitment to NATO.

Cultural approaches posit that what at first appears 'radical', 'third-order' change to the objectives and instruments of British armed forces in the SDR, actually resonated with deeply-embedded norms within the British military (Thornton, 2003). Convergence with systemic imperatives did not challenge the Defence Ministry's embedded 'logic of appropriateness' and UK 'national security culture', as the military's Cold War function had been grafted onto an understanding of the role of the armed forces that allowed smooth adaptation to the SDR's Baseline. The military's historical task in building and maintaining Empire developed a conception of the role of the army as fighting small wars outside Europe, the perception of 'war as jape' and a 'distaste for inactivity' – the military had therefore retained its 'colonial focus' throughout the 1970s and 1980s (Thornton, 2003: 42–6). These embedded norms help explain why, although reforms to force structures were dependent upon internal MoD expertise, they reflected the objectives set out in the SDR's baseline (McInnes, 1998: 832).

Miskimmon (2004: 95) emphasises not only the role of institutionally-embedded norms, but also those rooted in British society: 'The UK's colonial past, coupled with its institutional-embedding in the international community, has created a sense of responsibility and global outlook, in the minds of the British public and political elite regarding the UK's international responsibilities for peacekeeping and crisis-management'. Hence new security challenges and policy instruments were not objective, but were instead identified by their resonance with inheritance from the past: 'the army had old wine that flowed well into the new bottles' (Thornton, 2003: 57).[1] Such accounts overlaps with the arguments of 'externalist' securitisation theorists, who posit that successful speech acts must connect with this underlying social context, for the speech act is 'historically intertextual and translates past meaning structures into the present' (Stritzel, 2007: 375).

This chapter will, however, highlight how closer attention to systemic pressures and domestic material power relationships provides a stronger account of the process and outcome of reform. Furthermore, the chapter finds that although approaches to warfare at the tactical and operational levels developed during the colonial era resonate strongly with the challenges of contemporary COIN and 'Three Block Warfare', British Defence Doctrine does not reflect the persistence of culturally/institutionally embedded norms. It reflects, instead, the objective utility of many of the previous British experiences of COIN to the post-Cold War operational environment. The chapter will demonstrate how the lessons of past experience have been applied to contemporary challenges in a largely critical manner. Consequently, although the principles of maneuver warfare and mission command have been reinforced, post-Cold War operational experiences have attenuated the dominance of the 'warrior ethos' that has traditionally stood at the centre of British Defence Doctrine. This has led to changes to the doctrine and training of land forces that now seeks to deliver an 'adaptive foundation' and enhance the cultural skills necessary to undertake 'conflict amongst the people'.

The pressures of ongoing operations in Afghanistan and Iraq and the 'institutional protection' provided by the UKDA and DCDC have acted as important drivers of the identification of 'best practice' in doctrine and conceptual development. Organisational politics has, however, been prevalent in capability acquisition that has been subject to insufficient civilian control and crucially, has not been set rigid budgetary limitations, leading to overbidding and underestimations of the cost of major procurement projects.

The strategic defence review: Brokerage to facilitate strategic innovation

The unitary state and centralisation of power in the British core executive leads to a comparatively low salience of local elections, providing a sustained 'window of opportunity' between parliamentary elections to implement reform, minimising the political impact of base closures consequent upon military restructuring. In addition, the links between social and defence policy subsystems are relatively weak in the UK, as the abolition of conscription in 1962 ensured there was no system of 'community service' providing cheap labour for the British social system.

However, although these material power relationships grant the core executive a high level of autonomy in the implementation of reform, the formal powers of the core executive in defence policy are not as distinct as in France, where power is concentrated in the hands of the President. The lack of a written constitution makes it more difficult to identify the 'formal' competencies of the core executive in defence policy. At the same time the broad contours of post-war UK defence policy have largely been characterised by bi-partisan consensus, apart from the Labour Party's position on nuclear weapons during the 1980s (Dorman, 2007a: 320; Keohane, 1993).

The evolutionary approach that typified defence reform during early mid-1990s under the administration of Prime Minister John Major (1990–7) was a reflection of the 'murky' flux and uncertainty that characterised the initial post-Cold War security environment. Far reaching reform at an early stage would have been associated with a high level of risk and an increased possibility of making faulty strategic choices (Kaldor, 1995: 49). As McInnes (1998: 824) highlights: 'a defence review could be rapidly overtaken by events'.[2] Although post-Cold War strategic imperatives became increasingly clear in the mid-1990s following the 1991 Gulf War and conflict in the former Yugoslavia, this coincided with a reduction of 'executive autonomy' for the Conservatives in the context of internal party disunity over Europe that ruled out innovation on institutional venues and impending parliamentary elections in which defence was not a key issue.[3]

The 1997 Labour Government, buoyed by a large parliamentary majority, was well-placed to engage in strategic innovation and saw in the SDR an opportunity to stake out an image as a forward-thinking party in an area in which it traditionally lacked an image of competence.[4] However, Defence Secretary George Robertson played the role of 'policy broker'. In contrast to Chirac's marginalisation of opposition through the *Comité Stratégique*, strategic innovation in Britain was consensual, with several summer seminars and appointment of an expert group to summarise the conclusions.[5]

This 'brokerage' role in strategic innovation was a result of two factors. Firstly, following Labour's defection from the tradition of bi-partisan consensus on the issue of nuclear weapons in the 1980s (identified as an electoral mistake by 'New' Labour politicians) Prime Minister Tony Blair (1997–2007) and Defence Minister George Robertson (1999–2004) were keen to 'bind-in' the Conservative opposition and create an image of competence (Chalmers, 1999: 62; Cornish and Dorman, 2009: 251; McInnes, 1998: 827–8). Secondly, Labour wished to open up the decision-making process to input from the Foreign Office, in order to ensure that the SDR's baseline would reflect Labour's 'internationalist' Foreign Policy. Accordingly, Foreign Minister Robin Cook chaired the three summer seminars with Robertson. This was a strategy of 'brokerage to facilitate entrepreneurship' (Dyson, 2005: 374).

Unlike France, where 'executive autonomy' permitted a top-down leadership style by President Chirac, but necessitated 'institutional protection' in the form of the French Defence Ministry's SAD, such 'institutional protection' was not provided in the UK. Instead of establishing a separate review team, existing structures and in-house staff were used.[6] Institutional protection was unnecessary as the consensual bi-partisan approach to 'strategic innovation' acted to imbue the SDR's emphasis upon new security risks and strategic mobility with sufficient *gravitas* to leave the process of reforms to the policy instrument in the hands of the Defence Ministry (Cornish and Dorman, 2009: 248). Additionally, there was widespread support within the Ministry for radical doctrinal and structural change, which was viewed as an opportunity to strike an appropriate balance between the combat 'teeth' and support 'tail' of the military after Conservative reductions in logistical support (Dover, 2005: 515–16). Hence executive autonomy incentivised strategic leadership that facilitated the embrace of doctrinal and structural reform – the emphasis upon 'defence diplomacy' and the development of globally deployable forces, designed for low-high intensity tasks.

The overall pace of UK 'third order' reform (14 months), which cultural approaches have difficulty in explaining, reflects not only the logistical complexity of the review process, but also the configuration of domestic power relationships and linkages between budgetary and defence policy; namely the Treasury's wish that the SDR did not precede the Comprehensive Spending Review.[7]

Adding flesh to the bones of the SDR: The emergence of NEC, EBAO and the comprehensive approach

'Doctrine must be refined to meet the demands of the first day of the next conflict, drawing upon, but not constrained by, the experience of the last.'[8]

It was not until the 'New Chapter' of July 2002 and December 2003/July 2004 Defence White Papers that the implications of third-order change were more clearly spelt out in terms of capability acquisition and doctrinal/conceptual developments (see Chapter 1). As Dorman (2006: 152) notes of the SDR: 'The approach to the RMA and asymmetric warfare debates in the US was effectively to maintain a watching brief...most of the capabilities were still geared towards re-fighting the Gulf War.'[9] This initial emphasis upon changes to policy objectives and military command structures, followed by investment in procurement around NEC, reflects the insights of neorealism: in the absence of an immediate threat to the territorial integrity of a state, policy-makers in 'secondary' states will tend to err on the side of caution, follow the strategy of last risk and cost and commit themselves to significant defence procurement initiatives only when strategic imperatives and their associated 'best practice' in capability investment become clear and pressing (Freedman, 1998: 65). The risks associated with an early emulation of the RMA were pertinently highlighted by Vice Admiral Sir Jeremy Blackham, Deputy Chief of Defence Staff, Equipment Capability (1999–2002), in February 2000: 'What technology has done is create an electronic flank...If we use technology ineptly, fail to integrate

projects properly within an overall programme, pick the wrong technology, fail to spot the weakness which an opponent could exploit, or simply
do nothing, we leave ourselves at a potentially staggering disadvantage'
(Blackham, 2000a: 34).

Farrell (2008: 787) points to the role of 'realist' factors in determining the
selective emulation of the core concepts and capabilities that underpin
the RMA in the 2002 and 2004 White Papers: British resource constraints as
a 'secondary power', the complexity of the RMA, as well as operational
experience alongside the US in the 2003 Gulf War that demonstrated the
importance of 'old fashioned' virtues of speed, surprise and superior warfighting. However, Farrell also argues that cultural factors were prominent
causal variables in determining the precise trajectory of reform. Scepticism
of technology and the British system of Mission Command that is resistant
to networking are identified as core features of the organisational culture
of the British military (Cassidy, 2004: 67–9; Farrell, 2008: 788). One could,
however, also view these features as having been bolstered by the objective lessons derived from observation of the RMA in practice and British
operational experience, rather than rooted in the subjectivity of culture.

The origins of Mission Command lie in Prussian military thought (*Austrags-
taktik*) and the concept forms a key element of the British Manoeuvreist
Approach to warfare. As Danchev (1998: 33–5) and Kiszely (1998) demonstrate, the core features of the Manoeuvreist Approach can be traced back to
Sun Tzu, but also to the British theorist J.F.C. Fuller (1928), and the 'indirect
approach' of Basil Liddell Hart (1929). It was not, however, until the mid-
1970s that Manouver Theory was revised, following the release in 1976 of the
US 'Active Defence' operational doctrine that was criticised by US theorists
such as Stephen Canby (1979), William Lind (1979) and Edward Luttwak
(1979, 1980/81) for its overemphasis on attrition (Kiszely, 1999: 37). The principle of Manouver Warfare and its associated concept of Mission Command
was only formally adopted in place of Montgomery's 'set piece battle' by the
British military in 1987, as US/NATO debates on Manoeuvre Warfare, championed by proponents such as General Sir Nigel Bagnall (Chief of the General Staff, 1985–9), began to influence thinking within the British Army Staff
(Kiszely, 1999). This relatively recent adoption of the Manoeuvreist Approach
by the British military casts some doubt on the depth of the concept's
'cultural roots' (Melvin, 2002: 39; Newsome, 2007: 67; Storr, 2003: 119–21).[10]

Post-Cold War thinking on British military doctrine in Peace Support Operations began in 1993 with the establishment of the Army's 'Inspector General
of Doctrine and Training' and 'Headquarters of Doctrine and Training'. The
formation of these bodies at such an early stage reflected an increased openness within the British military hierarchy to new thinking on the development of operational art following debates on the utility of Manouever Warfare
in the mid-1980s (Frantzen, 2005: 93; Melvin, 2002). During the early mid-
1990s British military doctrine made a sharp distinction between war and

peacekeeping, peace-enforcement and COIN (collectively known as Operations Other than War, OOTW) (Frantzen, 2005: 106). 'Wider Peacekeeping' published in 1994 continued to emphasise the importance of impartiality and consent and drew a great deal of internal criticism within the Army for failing to take into account the lessons that Bosnia had imparted about the need for a more active military role in peace-enforcement. The document was quickly replaced by 'Joint Warfare Publication 3-50' that envisioned a much more 'robust' role for Land Forces in peacekeeping operations (Rollins, 2006: 88).

However, the British Defence Doctrine of 1998 formed an important watershed in British thinking on expeditionary crisis-management operations, reflecting the strategic and military lessons of operations in Bosnia during the 1990s (Cassidy, 2004: 185–99; Frantzen, 2005: 108; Kiszely, 1998: 39). The document pointed to the 'continuum of conflict' – the increasing tendency of military operations to vary quickly in intensity across the conflict spectrum – and consequently to the difficulty of making sharp distinctions between OOTW and high-intensity conflict (Frantzen, 2005: 108). Within this new operational context, the application of force would have to be tailored to specific points on this continuum. As Frantzen (2005: 108) highlights: 'Rather than achieving defeat through attrition and destruction alone...the document warns against the concept of unconditional surrender and destruction as an end in itself and reminds of the need for thinking beyond wining a war militarily'. Hence British conceptual development during the late 1990s, based upon the experiences of an increasing number of crisis-management operations, pointed to the need to invest in capabilities, training and doctrine that would enable the military to achieve a wide range of operational effects and coordinate its activities with those of other national and international agencies and actors.[11]

At the same time, the challenges of the post-Cold War security environment underscored the imperative of maintaining interoperability with US forces, necessitating some form of emulation of the RMA to allow the UK to 'plug and play' with US systems and the development of capabilities that would permit the capacity to undertake high-intensity MCO, in addition to 'three block warfare' (Blackham, 2002: 28–30). Kosovo and the implications of St. Malo also meant that the UK would need to develop the capacity to lead medium-sized European or coalition high-intensity operations in the absence of US involvement.[12]

Indeed, the Kosovo conflict played a central role in determining the course of UK capability procurement. Operation Allied Force reinforced the changes instituted to defence policy objectives and command structures by the SDR that had facilitated greater modularity and jointness. The conflict also highlighted several networking and battlefield digitisation capabilities in need of urgent acquisition in order to further enhance jointness, ensure the capacity to strike targets at speed and allow the UK to remain a credible Alliance partner to the US (Blackham, 2000a, 2000b, 2002; Dorman, 2006:

156).[13] C2 capabilities were singled out as an area in critical need of investment, having been proved lacking in the transfer of real-time information from ISR assets, which had also been identified as deficient. Furthermore, information operations and strategic airlift were distinguished as areas in urgent need of further development.[14] However, although Operation Allied Force did not include a ground campaign, a notable lesson of the conflict included that the armed forces would have to invest in capabilities and doctrine that would permit the conduct of warfare across the 'continuum of conflict' and develop peacekeeping skills. This was a lesson that was further reinforced by British operational experience under KFOR and Afghanistan.[15]

At the same time, the initial stages of the Afghanistan conflict also further underscored the imperative of emulating core features of the RMA in order to ensure that the interoperability gap between the UK and US, particularly in C2, did not widen, making investment in secure data links and the Link 16 Joint Tactical Distribution System a priority (Day, 2002: 38–43). In addition, the conflict highlighted the utility of UAVs; the need to invest in ISTAR and increases in bandwidth, in order to reduce 'sensor to shooter' time; to develop computer programmes that would ensure commanders are not overwhelmed by information and to continue investment in AWACS and air-to-air refueling capabilities (Day, 2002: 38–43).

Hence by 2002 the imperative of constructing a balanced and flexible force that would permit not only MCO, but the capacity to conduct 'three block war' had begun to gain wider currency within the military. As Brigadier Mungo Melvin, Director of Land Warfare at the UK MoD argued in June 2002: 'British Land Forces should be prepared to conduct conventional warfighting, counter-terrorism, and to win over the population simultaneously...Many of these are missions that human beings rather than technology are good at' (Melvin, 2002: 42).[16]

Consequently, even in the immediate aftermath of the 2003 invasion of Iraq, that appeared to reinforce to US policy-makers the validity of the RMA and its capacity to control the process of 'escalation' in war, British thinking on networking focused on the role that high-technology assets could play in enhancing the capacity to conduct 'three block warfare' (Burridge, 2003: 20). The lessons from the initial stages of the Iraq conflict highlighted the importance of the UK Phoenix UAV, the US Predator UCAV and Global Hawk UAV in delivering ISR and in facilitating the conduct of operations across the conflict spectrum.[17] These experiences played an important role in the acquisition of three Reaper UAVs which became operational in 2007 and have played an important role in delivering ISR in the Afghan conflict (BBC, 2008b). Yet the limitations of UAV technology were also clear to the British. As the Commander-in-Chief of Joint Strike Command, Air Chief Marshall Brian Burridge (2003: 23) noted in the immediate aftermath of the first stage of Operation Telic: 'We also need to consider how we might manage winning "hearts and minds" as we provide peacekeeping and humanitarian aid within geographical proximity of high-intensity warfare, if the high-intensity warfare is being fought without human risk and by "robots". We cannot afford...to win the war but then lose the peace.'

In short, the British experiences of operations across the conflict spectrum during the 1990s had taken firm root within the military by the time of the conflicts in Afghanistan and Iraq, evidenced by the embedding of the concept of Defence Diplomacy since the 1998 SDR and the notion of the 'continuum of conflict' that had been outlined in the 1998 edition of British Defence Doctrine. Consequently, whilst initial effects-based thinking within the UK JDCC dovetailed closely with conceptual development in the US (Farrell, 2008: 791–2), the operational experiences of the 1990s fostered a strong level of resistance to suggestions of a full-blown emulation of EBO and the 'system of systems' approach of NCW.[18] Operational experiences in Bosnia, Kosovo, Sierra Leone, Iraq and Afghanistan also served to impart the centrality of harmonising the collaboration of international organisations, the media, NGOs and OGDs at the tactical, operational and strategic levels, permitting delivery of non-kinetic and kinetic effects and utilisation of all elements of national power.[19] EBAO has, therefore, developed with a stronger focus on the delivery of non-kinetic effects than EBO and has been firmly rooted within the Comprehensive Approach (Farrell, 2008: 795). For these reasons the decline of EBO in the US and the UK transition to 'effects-based thinking' has not involved a great conceptual leap, as British EBAO had, by mid-2007, already recognised many of the pitfalls of US EBO.

The British 'lessons learned' process on military command and control has also been influenced by observation of post-Cold War US military operations which have provided a good deal of evidence that the 'long screwdriver' approach to military command is associated with significant drawbacks in operations across the conflict spectrum (McColl, 2004: 52). The Iraq conflict, in particular, raised concerns about the potential of a 'long screwdriver' approach to undermine the virtues of tempo and surprise, as well as its tendency to foster a focus on the delivery of purely kinetic effects. As Major General John McColl, Commandant of the Joint Services Command and Staff College (2003–4) observed (2004: 52–3): 'NEC if badly managed can compress the command structure, neutering operational and tactical level decision-making, drawing senior Commanders down into the tactical weeds where they do not belong...US and NATO forces have kinetic overkill against most potential adversaries and yet there is a danger of losing the non-kinetic post-conflict phases in Afghanistan and Iraq'.[20] This observation at close quarters of the increasingly ambivalent experiences of the US with the utility of technology in 'wars amongst the people' and of the negative implications of a lack of attention to 'human factors' in NCW and EBO was, of course, confirmed by FM 3-24 in December 2006. As Farrell (2008: 797) pertinently notes, operational pressures have led to the US employing greater flexibility in command

and control: 'The pressure of operations in the field has led the best US field commands to ignore their own doctrine...and to treat warfare as an art rather than a science.'

This observation of the RMA in action has been supplemented by British military operations, both preceding and in the immediate aftermath of the SDR, which delivered valuable lessons about the utility of the Manouverist Approach and Mission Command. Operations in Bosnia, demonstrated the applicability of the Manouverist Approach to OOTW at both the operational and tactical levels (Kiszely, 1998: 39). Kosovo (1999) and Sierra Leone (Operation Palliser, 2000) also acted to underscore the importance of the balance 'between direction and delegation' provided by Mission Command (Dorman, 2006: 156–7, 2007b: 192; Storr, 2003: 123). As Brigadier Mungo Melvin, former Director of Land Warfare at the UK MoD, noted in 2002: 'The *real* challenge of Command and Battlespace Management is how to design our C4I systems to conduct Mission Command better' (Melvin, 2002: 40).[21] The close collaboration between the MoD, Foreign and Commonwealth Office (FCO) and Department for International Development (DfID) during Operation Palliser further underscored the importance of a 'comprehensive approach' to military operations and areas for improvement by highlighting several deficiencies in common understanding and collaborative working between government Departments, particularly between the MoD and DfID (Dorman, 2007b: 196).

The operational experiences of the 2003 attack on Iraq also demonstrated to the British the utility of decentralised leadership. The 'Lessons Learned' report of the Iraq conflict outlines how: 'despite the continuing need for refinement, UK warfighting doctrine, broadly based on the tenets of mission command, manoeuvre warfare and decisive effect is sound'.[22] Indeed, the conflict illustrated how Mission Command, in combination with C2 capabilities, could enhance Britain's capacity to contribute to coalition warfare: '[mission command will] allow us to exploit better the relationships between command and control that are relevant to good decision-making in an information rich environment. It will also allow us to adapt more intelligently to the *ad hoc* command and control arrangement that necessarily characterise coalitions of the willing.'[23] As a consequence of these operational experiences, NEC and EBAO have been firmly embedded within the Manoeuverist Approach and its associated concept of Mission Command. As Major General J.B.A. Bailey (2004: 50) notes: 'On the modern battlefield where friendly, enemy and neutral elements intermingle, where the terrain – often urban – is complex, and where intentions become increasingly difficult to decipher, it will be, more than ever, the commander on the ground who will have the best feel for the truth.'

British post-invasion experiences in Afghanistan and Iraq also delivered important operational lessons on approaches to counterinsurgency; lessons that resonated with the experiences of the colonial era (Cousens, 2006: 59;

Marston, 2005: 19). Operation Telic and ISAF have added further weight to the necessity to tailor capability acquisition to the scenarios outlined in Krulak's vision of 'Three Block Warfare'. These conclusions are, as Chapter 1 highlights, clearly elucidated within British Defence Doctrine (August 2008), the changes instigated by Joint Doctrine note 01/09 'The Importance of Culture to the Military', within Joint Doctrine Publication 01 'Campaigning' and JDP 3-40 'Security and Stabilisation: The Military Contribution' (Kiszely, 2007: 13–14).[24]

The resonance of past approaches with contemporary challenges

The British colonial experience of COIN operations embodied both limited revolts and wider, more protracted military campaigns: the Second Boer War in South Africa (1899–1902); Iraq (1919–39); Palestine (1930–48); the Dutch East Indies (1945); Indo China (1945–6); Kenya (1953–60); Cyprus (1955–60); Aden/South Yemen (1964–7); Malaya (1948–60); Brunei (1962–4); Ireland (1919–21) and Northern Ireland (1969–) (Cassidy, 2004: 45–54; Cousens, 2006: 55; Crawshaw, 2007: 12–16; Kiszely, 2006: 16–21). The implications of these operations were codified in 'Keeping the Peace' – the Army's Tactical Doctrine Manual, published in 1963 – and in 'Counter-Revolutionary Warfare', published in 1969 which formed the foundation for the modern British approach to COIN (Cassidy, 2004: 134; Crawshaw, 2007: 11–12; Kiszely, 2006: 18).

In his detailed review of British COIN doctrine, Dixon (2009: 357–61) identifies four key features of the British approach to COIN. Firstly, the centrality of political will: the determination of the political elite to defeat insurgents and the concomitant necessity of close civil-military cooperation to ensure well-defined overall goals, and political and military aims (Dixon, 2009: 357–8). Secondly, 'winning the battle for hearts and minds': reducing support for the insurgents within the civilian population. This is a process that is designed to enable the military to more easily distinguish insurgents due to the willingness of the population to provide intelligence and the increasing isolation of insurgents (Dixon, 2009: 358–9). The 'battle for hearts and minds' will be won through three key aspects of COIN: good government and nation-building; psychological operations and the use of 'minimum force' (Dixon, 2009: 358–9). The third pillar identified as characteristic of the British approach to COIN is the importance of placing police and locally trained forces at the forefront of COIN (Dixon, 2009: 359–60). Finally, Dixon (2009: 360–1) points to the importance of ensuring the centralised coordination of action by civilian and military actors, a principle that dovetails closely with the principle of the 'comprehensive approach'.

The need to prepare for scenarios such as 'Three Block Warfare' and adopt a multi-agency, comprehensive approach to COIN is also articulated in a detailed study of British COIN doctrine and lessons-learned during the post-Cold War era, conducted by Michael Crawshaw, the former Senior

Editor of the UKDA Advanced Research and Assessment Group. Crawshaw (2007: 32) notes how the 'semi-formal'[25] approach to COIN during the British Empire and decolonisation period displays a strong level of convergence with the core attributes of the Comprehensive Approach and the concept of 'Three Block Warfare'. The study also highlights the importance of the 'strategic corporal' in irregular warfare.[26]

Crawshaw (2007: 11–12) identifies nine distinctive features of the 'British approach' to COIN that are outlined within Keeping the Peace and Counterrevolutionary warfare manuals which dovetail closely with the four features outlined by Dixon (2009: 357–61): 'Winning the political-strategic battle whilst containing the tactical level; the development of joint unified command structures that integrate the civil government, police and military'; intelligence-based operations; constant offensive pressure exerted by all arms of the security forces; small-unit, patrol-based offensive tactics with the support of a larger security force; utilising enemy defectors; the isolation of insurgents from the population through the control of resources; creating and securing large base areas to provide safe zones (stabilisation); psychological operations and winning the 'hearts and minds' of the local population (Alderson, 2007: 8; Cousens, 2006: 54–7).[27] These lessons, as Crawshaw (2007: 32) highlights, 'retain significant relevance to present-day situations'.[28]

Although the British approach to COIN is commonly understood as adopting the principle of the application of 'minimum force', this is a principle that is given little consideration in Crawshaw's report (Alderson, 2007: 6; Cassidy, 2004: 66–7; Crawshaw, 2007: 9). As Dixon (2009: 376) notes, an ambiguity exists in the British approach to COIN about the utility of the use of force in winning 'hearts and minds', leaving the principle of 'minimum force' open to interpretation. The British approach to COIN, informed like that of the French not only by colonial experiences, but crisis-management in the former Yugoslavia, places a much stronger emphasis upon the role of the application of kinetic effects that the German approach to Stabilisation. British COIN doctrine is, nevertheless, much more circumspect about the utility of force in COIN when compared to the US approach that has adopted a more aggressive approach in Iraq and Afghanistan (Rangwala, 2009: 505).

Crawshaw's report also highlights several distinctive features attributable to insurgency in the post-Cold War era: the networked, rather than hierarchical structure of insurgency forces; their lack of clear material goals; the ability of insurgents to act with a greater level of independence from the local population; the capacity of insurgents to use the media as a tool with which to gain support; the role of cyberspace as an arena for organisation and the increasingly broad range of actors (government agencies, NGOs and international organisations) involved in the conduct of COIN (Rutter, 2007). Yet these contemporary features of COIN, as well as the endurance of many of the characteristics of classical COIN have reinforced core principles at the heart of the British approach (Cousens, 2006: 49–63; Crawshaw, 2007: 18–28).

Crawshaw (2007: 21) notes how intelligence gathering remains critical and that principles of target identification and the identification of potential defectors now need to be applied not only in the territory of operation, but also within the 'electronic netwar battlespace' (Crawshaw, 2007). The broader range of actors involved in contemporary COIN bolsters the importance of achieving jointness and coordination with civilian actors and other arms of governments through the Comprehensive Approach. As in classical insurgencies, the establishment of legitimate, civil government structures with ownership over the COIN operations has emerged as a vital feature of successful operations in Iraq and Afghanistan. Medical aid, civil infrastructure projects and education have become even more important in winning the 'hearts and minds' of the population; whilst small, specialist units capable of low-high intensity conflict, particularly at the initial stages of a campaign remains critical, as does the coopting of local armed forces, police and auxiliaries as 'force multipliers' (Cassidy, 2007: 43–6; Nagl, 2005: xi–xvi; Rose, 2008: 11; Strachan, 2007: 8–11). Finally, Crawshaw (2007: 28) notes that lessons of post-Cold War insurgencies also point to the relevance of the British principles of restricting governance in nation-building to a small group of well-qualified individuals capable of exercising power with little oversight (Crawshaw, 2007: 18–28).

Recent experiences in Iraq and Afghanistan have also highlighted some of the deficits associated with existing British COIN practice, not least the increasing importance of intelligence (Chin, 2007: 213). As Crawshaw (2007: 23) highlights, a coordinated intelligence effort that is characterised by interagency trust and the dissemination of information is critical. In this area NEC embedded within the Comprehensive Approach can provide a means with which to ensure input from the tactical to the strategic levels. The importance of 'winning the media war' is also a key area of contemporary insurgency and has become increasingly vital in the dissemination of information and propaganda. This aspect was, however, neglected in previous British doctrine (Chin, 2007: 213; Crawshaw, 2007: 24).

Another lesson drawn from Afghanistan and Iraq is the centrality of training and education in the broad skills sets necessary for COIN (Kiszely, 2006: 20). As General Sir John Kiszely, Director of the UKDA (2007: 10–11) argues, whilst counterinsurgency requires some of the traditional characteristics of the 'warrior ethos' that forms a core element of British Defence Doctrine, it also necessitates the ability to deal with 'complexity, ambiguity and uncertainty...political interference, media scrutiny, the unfair constraints of user engagement' and calls, in particular, for qualities of 'emotional intelligence, empathy with one's opponents, tolerance, patience, subtlety, sophistication, nuance and political adroitness'. The 'adaptive foundation' that is embedded within the Future Land Operational Concept of 2008 and changes to cultural training outlined in Joint Doctrine Note 1/09 form important steps towards the establishment of balance between

OOTW training and the 'war-fighting ethos' that has traditionally stood at the heart of British Defence Doctrine (Constant, 2003: 44; Milton, 2001: 41–4). These changes reflects the lessons learnt from Operation Telic, in particular, from the British campaign in Basra, concerning the need for officers with training that would allow them to develop a deeper understanding of the political and social dynamics of insurgencies (RUSI, 2009).[29] Iraq also provided an emphatic lesson of the importance of planning for the post-invasion phase following initial entry, which led to a lack of suitable RoE and poor contingency plans which were ill-suited in dealing with lawlessness and insurgency (Rutter, 2007: 66–70). This lesson has added greater impetus to the need to further developing the 'Comprehensive Approach', not only at the national level, but at the level of the coalition/ Alliance (Rutter, 2007: 66–70).

There is also a broad recognition within the British military that any general guidelines on COIN should be treated with great caution. One of the key lessons drawn from COIN during both the colonial and post-Cold War eras is the difficulty of making general conclusions from operations conducted within different contexts. This problem is compounded by the way that contemporary insurgencies, such as Iraq and Afghanistan, blend both modern and classical features to different degrees (Crawshaw, 2007: 17–19; Melvin, 2002: 38; Rangwala, 2009: 511–12; Strachan, 2007: 9–10). As Strachan (2007: 9–10) pertinently argues: 'Iraq is ultimately not the same as Malaya or Northern Ireland, and it is also not the same as Afghanistan.' This caution reflects the broader principle of flexibility within British Defence Doctrine that emphasises how care should be taken not to 'overprescribe' doctrine (Cousens, 2006: 61; Melvin, 2002: 38; Milton, 2001: 43).[30] Consequently, Kiszely cites three factors that militated against an official updating of British COIN doctrine: the nature of each insurgency as *sui generis*; the increasing complexity of insurgency and advent of transnational insurgencies, making national doctrine increasingly irrelevant and finally, the 'amoeba-like', 'dynamic' and 'agile' nature of contemporary counterinsurgencies, which imply that doctrinal updates are likely to be superceded by the time of publication (Kiszely, 2006: 19; Kiszely, 2007).

These three factors played an important role in determining the temporality of British reexamination of its COIN doctrine – that had not been reviewed since 2001. The process of reexamination began in December 2006 and led to the release of a review in December 2007 that involved the updating, rather than rewriting, of British COIN doctrine. The piecemeal changes that the document outlined were highlighted by Colonel Alexander Alderson (2007: 9), Chairman of the Land Warfare Centre's Warfare Development Group, that, in cooperation with the DCDC, led up doctrinal evolution in COIN:[31] 'The message from the field was clear: nothing has changed so much that it invalidates the principles or the approach.'

The document blends analysis of past experiences, particularly the work of Callwell (1906), Galula (1964), Kitson (1971) and Thompson (1966) with the experiences of Afghanistan and Iraq (Alderson, 2007: 9–10). As Alderson (2007: 10) notes: Analysis of these approaches and experience from Iraq and Afghanistan shows that there are four paths to effective COIN. They are engagement with the local population, clearing insurgent-infected areas, holding those areas that have been cleared and building governance, confidence and stability. The fundamental strands of building and holding legitimacy and Information Operations will be woven through this basic idea of 'Engage-Clear-Hold-Build'. Whilst the manual validates a number of existing principles, it nevertheless also highlights the need to adapt the core tents of British COIN to areas of change in the nature of insurgency, several of which dovetail with the analysis of Crawshaw (2007): the increasingly global and complex characteristics of insurgency; the impact of Islamic societal structures on attitudes to violence and information; the increased importance of information operations and propaganda; the greater emphasis on Stability Operations as part of the handover process and the focus on the role of security sector reform in transition (Alderson, 2007: 9–10).

However, the inadequacies of COIN doctrine to deal with the increasingly complex challenge of stabilising failed states led to the development, under the leadership of the DCDC, of the joint operational-level doctrine JDP 3-40 'Security and Stabilisation: The Military Contribution' that was released in November 2009. Whilst recognising the utility of many of the UK's past colonial experiences to current operations, the document benefits from greater hindsight on the implications of missions in Afghanistan and Iraq for UK military doctrine than the December 2007 review of British COIN Doctrine.[32] The document should also be seen as response to the agenda set by the Cabinet Office in the March 2008 National Security Strategy that emphasised the increasingly serious implications of fragile and failing states for UK security and the importance of development and cross-government and international collaboration in tackling such challenges.[33]

JDP 3-40 points, therefore, to a wider set of weaknesses associated with British COIN and develops a broader approach to the Stabilisation of failed and failing states. It firmly situates COIN and the contribution of the military within a comprehensive, multiagency approach. The document notes a set of new challenges in the contemporary operational environment: state fragility, the increasing complexity actors involved in stabilisation operations, the more limited manpower that can be deployed in theatre, the global nature of the networks supporting insurgents and the increasing complexity and lethality of opposing forces.[34] JDP 3-40 identifies the need, in the context of these new challenges, for the military to deliver, assist and enable across three key Stabilisation tasks which are designed to enhance the influence of military forces within the host government, competing elites and wider population.

These three tasks are identified as: building human and national security;[35] fostering host government capacity and legitimacy[36] and stimulating economic and infrastructure development.[37]

The document also builds upon JDP 01 'Campaigning' (2nd Edition) that was released in December 2008, by focusing upon the key tenets of campaign analysis, planning, execution and assessment in Stabilisation Operations. JDP 3-40 pays particular attention to the human dimensions of intelligence;[38] political and social analysis[39] and cross-government, multi-agency campaign and military planning.[40] Furthermore, the doctrine also builds upon the 2007 revision to British COIN by emphasising the importance of executing operations within a 'population-focused activity framework' that is categorised into four main activities: shape, secure, hold and develop (a framework that is more likely to be applied in a sequential manner at the tactical than the theatre-level).[41]

Central to the 'Shape' activity is the development of a comprehensive understanding of the problems standing in the way of achieving the key stabilisation tasks through multi-agency planning, combined with offensive action to attain intelligence and disrupt the enemy.[42] At the strategic level, Shape activity involves the definition of objective and securing of resources. At the operational level the activity centres upon the establishment of a 'comprehensive campaign design' with key external actors. At the tactical level Shape involves the development of an improved understanding of the dynamics of the immediate conflict environment and assistance in the development of the governance structures which meet the requirements of the population.[43] 'Secure' activity refers to the 'delivery of security in a defined area' (446) – the neutralising and isolation of insurgents and irregulars.[44] The 'Hold' stage of activity is the point at which a 'semi-permissive' environment is created by foreign and indigenous forces (in the form of village militias), permitting OGDs, NGOS and IOs to assist with the development of basic governance, economic and security infrastructure.[45] 'Develop' activity involves the growth of local capacity in governance, particularly in areas such as the judiciary and legislature that cements stability over the long-term.[46]

JDP 3-40 adopts a highly-critical approach to the lessons of past experiences during the Colonial Era, the relevance of which are carefully distilled through the lens of post-Cold War crisis-management/stabilisation and COIN operations. This willingness to question long-held assumptions is evidenced by the broad base of expertise on which the document was developed, including input not only from a wide cross-section of the British military, but also from US military, the FCO, DfID and a number of academics.[47]

In summary, Miskimmon (2004), Thornton (2003), Frantzen (2005: 93) and Farrell (2008) correctly demonstrate that practices at the tactical and operational levels developed during the colonial era enjoyed a good degree of fit with the challenges of the post-Cold War security environment.

Embedded practices have formed, however, a repository of knowledge that has been critically applied in the light of operational experiences, rather than a set of cultural norms which have themselves determined policy responses. Hence the selective emulation of US EBO and NEC that emphasises the centrality of 'human factors', flexibility in command and control and the importance of a Comprehensive Approach is primarily a result of British operational experience and conformity to the imperatives of 'best practice', rather than the application of culturally-embedded norms.

Growing contestation on the precise implications of a balanced force for capability acquisition

The recent emphasis on COIN, Stabilisation Operations and 'Three Block Warfare' following the Iraq and Afghan deployments has not led to a full reprioritisation in favour of such operations, as evidenced by the decision in 2009 to renew Trident and by the commissioning of two new aircraft carriers (Cousens, 2006: 59). The importance of preparing for traditional state-on-state warfare is central to the updated British Defence Doctrine of August 2008[48] and the October 2008 Future Land Operational Concept that outlines how the Army must be ready to undertake major combat operations (MCO) and intervention/stabilisation missions 'both sequentially and simultaneously' (Dannatt, 2008: 59). Indeed, the vital necessity of retaining the capacity to conduct major MCO is pertinently demonstrated by Sir Richard Dannatt, Chief of the General Staff (2006–9): 'The Army does not subscribe to the point of view that MCOs are a thing of the past... Defence is about an insurance policy as well as the ability to conduct current operations – and we do not throw away our home insurance policies just because crime is down in our neighbourhood.'

The precise implications of the lessons of recent operational experiences for investment in capabilities and force postures over the medium-long term remain ill-defined, as highlighted by the May 2009 speech of Sir Richard Dannatt (the Chief of Defence Staff 2006–9) to Chatham House. Sir Dannatt argued that the British military should focus capability investment and force posture on tackling 'hybrid' circumstances (necessitating sustained campaigning in complex geographical and human terrain against a combination of state, non-state and proxy forces in asymmetrical warfare) at the expense of MCO (BBC, 2009a). The former Chief of Defence Staff attacked the resilience of an outdated 'Industrial War' mentality; a comment that implicitly threatens investments such as the Future Aircraft Carriers (BBC, 2009a).[49] These remarks therefore elicited a strong response from Admiral Sir Jonathan Band (First Sea Lord, 2006–) in favour of retaining key MCO capabilities and force postures (BBC, 2009a).

The comments of Sir Dannatt must be contextualised as part of the sharpening of the interservice battle for resources in an economic downturn and the increasing disjuncture between British strategic ambitions and financial reality (Cornish and Dorman, 2009). Sir Dannatt is certainly correct in high-lighting the urgent need to rebalance capabilities, force postures and training to cope with 'three block warfare' situations and the challenges of COIN and stabilisation and the need to move away from platform to investment in the more 'unglamorous' enablers such as strategic air lift, medium and heavy lift transport helicopters and C4ISTAR capabilities. The UK also faces significant problems of troop overstretch in manpower in the conduct of manpower-intensive COIN/Stabilisation operations, having significantly reduced the size of its infantry over the post-Cold War period (see Table 1.1). Yet as Sir Dannatt (2008) argued only six months previously, the possibility of a loss of relative power through the cancellation of the renewal of Trident, despite its estimated cost of £20 billion, or through the loss of power projection capa-bilities that would derive from the failure to invest in aircraft carriers, makes these projects imperative in what continues to be a highly-uncertain world. It is, therefore, likely that the SDR will adopt a 'Seacorn' approach to certain capabilities (such as anti-submarine warfare) retaining a very basic capability, but investing more heavily in the updating of doctrine, training and in the skill-base of the UK defence industry in these areas, in order to allow a more fulsome capability to be developed at relatively short-notice, should the requirement emerge.[50]

Hence although there is a strong-level of consensus about military 'best practice' over the short-medium term, the nature of conflict scenarios over the medium-long term remains contested and an arena for organisational politics. Such debates are highly-sensitive and politicised, particularly at the senior levels of the Single Services, whose leaders are keen to maximise the long-term budget share and influence of their Service. As a senior source within the UK MoD noted: 'There is a huge desire at the lower levels of the Services for a rational prioritisation of capability investment, but at the level of one star officer and above (Commodore, Air Commodore or Brigadier) career development depends upon how one delivers in defence of one's Service'.[51] Partly as a consequence of these pressures, the Army emphasises the need to prepare over the longer-term for complex land operations amongst the people as encountered in Afghanistan; the Navy draws attention to the potential for MCO and the need for Carrier Strike Groups, whilst the Air Force (despite recognising the requirement to focus on ground-support, investment in tactical air transport and helicopters over the short-term) continues to advocate investment in strike, attack and offensive-support aircraft.[52] Such contestation has important implications not only for investment in key platform capabilities, but also for areas such as ISTAR. There is a lack of clear guidance on whether ISTAR capabilities should, over the medium-long term, be focused on deployment in a permissive or contested operational environment.[53] Such debates high-light the increasingly urgent requirement for a new SDR that will take place following the General Election in 2010.

Managing military input into defence planning: Ensuring adaptability at the tactical and operational levels

As in the case of France, civilian leadership in structuring military input into defence planning has played an important role in ensuring adherence to the dictates of operational experience and 'best practice'. Having developed cross-party and MoD consensus behind the broad trajectory of UK reform through the SDR process, it was not necessary for the Government to consult broadly on the 2002 and 2003/04 Defence White Papers. Instead, the reviews were conducted in-house with a significant amount of input from the Policy Planning Directorate of the MoD, with conceptual development around NEC, EBAO/effects-based thinking emerging from a strongly 'bottom-up' process.[54] As the above section has demonstrated, this method of structuring military input to defence planning has been largely successful in identifying a model of military 'best practice' at the tactical and operational levels that is relevant to the short-medium term conflict scenarios that the UK is likely to face. This dynamism is, in large part, a consequence of the institutional protection provided by the JDCC and UKDA for the key principles of jointness and interoperability with alliance partners and the capacity of these institutions to foster an environment of experimentation and critical thought on doctrine and CD&E.[55] However, although the development of these institutions was also accompanied by a number of reforms to the capability acquisition process, these reforms have failed to adequately structure military input on questions of the detail of capability investment and have allowed organisational politics to prevail in the structures responsible for decision-making on capability acquisition and force posture. Capability procurement has, therefore, been characterised by overbidding and an underestimation of the real costs of major capability projects. As this section will outline, this situation has led to the consideration of more far-reaching plans for reform to UK capability acquisition and decisions on force posture which, if enacted, will further strengthen civilian control and the capacity to implement the forthcoming SDR.

The JDCC, established in the aftermath of the 1998 SDR has acted as a mechanism of institutional protection for 'transformation' process as the digitisation of the UK armed forces picked up pace and the requirement for jointness became increasingly pressing (Cornish and Dorman, 2009: 253; Frantzen, 2005: 107).[56] Together with the Advanced Research and Assessment Group at the UK Defence Academy (UKDA), the JDCC worked in partnership with the Warfare Centres of the Single Services to strengthen the objectivity of the 'lessons learned' process by distancing doctrinal development and CD&E from the bureaucratic politics of interservice competition.[57] In 2006 the JDCC was strengthened, becoming the DCDC and the central authority on doctrinal and conceptual work within the armed forces.

A set of reforms have also been instigated to the UK 'lessons-identified' process following operational experiences which have helped to develop a rigorous process of lesson-identification and follow-up on issues of doctrine, training and capabilities at the tactical and operational levels, particularly on issues relating to jointness and interoperability.[58] Whilst doctrinal development during the Cold War was relatively static, the experiences of the 1982 Falklands Campaign began the process of institutionalising lesson-identification within the warfare directorates of the three Services.[59] It was, however, not until 1996 that the process of lesson-identification received greater coordination through the establishment of the Permanent Joint Headquarters (PJHQ) as the operational environment became increasingly complex and the requirement for enhanced jointness and interoperability become increasingly pressing. The J7 Division of PJHQ, responsible for Joint Training has, since 1996, worked with the DCDC to draw together the Doctrinal and Warfare Centres of the individual services to collate the lessons of operational experience and enhance warfare joint development.[60] The PJHQ acts a 'service agnostic' node in lesson-identification and follow-up, determining which service will take the lead on implementing key joint lessons and works with the DCDC and Single Service Warfare Centres to identify the implications of operational experiences for doctrine and training.[61] The DCDC, in partnership with the Single Service Warfare Centre, heads up the interviewing of several levels of command upon the return of units from operation and distills and disseminates the key joint lessons.[62] The DCDC enjoys a good working relationship with the Single Service Warfare Centres which have, overall, been cooperative in developing a strong culture of jointness.[63] The DCDC is also active in identifying and communicating lessons-learned with Allies through NATO, particularly those lessons with implications for interoperability and enjoys close bi-lateral relationships with JFCOM and the Single Services in the US.[64]

Despite the lead role of the PJHQ and DCDC and the implementation of an IT system in support of the lessons-identified process, the system has received some criticism for its follow-up. The Single Services retain a strong level of authority in identifying and following-up the lessons of operations which are not perceived by PJHQ as having direct implications for jointness. Although the lessons-identified processes of the Single Services are viewed by the DCDC and other actors within the MoD as competent, the Single Services retain the capacity to erect a 'firewall' which hinders the ability to determine the extent of follow-up.[65] In short, there is a requirement for more neutral, centralised management of the lessons-learned process in Single Services issues. Furthermore, in contrast to France, the outsourcing of questionnaire development and workshops in the lesson-learned process is limited. This scepticism of external consultants derives from the perceived lack of military expertise in the private sector that is usually provided by retired military personnel, who are perceived as out of touch with the contemporary operational environment.[66] The lessons of operational experience do, however, quickly find their way into pre-deployment training, as Officers and Commanders who have had recent experience of deployment are closely involved in the development and delivery of the six-month pre-deployment training.[67]

Furthermore, in 1995 the Directorate of Operational Capability (DOC) was established under former Secretary of State for Defence Michael Portillo (1995–7). The DOC conducts audits in different areas of the operational capability as set out in the Defence Programme Directory (an internal MoD document that matches Defence Planning Assumptions to Force Structures and Capabilities) and gathers and exposes operational lessons. DOC reports directly to the Ministerial level, and is meant to act as an extra filter to sift out organisational politics between the Single Services.[68] The Vice Chief of Defence Staff takes full responsibility for ensuring that the problems identified are followed up and implemented and must answer to the Secretary of State for Defence. The ability of DOC to translate the lessons of operations into far-reaching change to the strategic direction of UK defence policy is, however, constrained by the broader direction to force postures delivered within the 1997/78 SDR, and 2002/04 White Papers, which the Single Services can invoke to justify the *status quo*.[69] The capacity of the Secretary of State for Defence to challenge fundamental assumptions on force posture and capabilities has been limited in recent years due to the potential negative implications of far-reaching change on the UK defence industry and the impact that this would have on the Labour Government's performance in the forthcoming General Election.[70]

The UK has also implemented the Urgent Operational Requirements (UOR) scheme that permits the military to quickly respond to the changing operational environment and is coordinated by PJHQ and the MoD. Since the inception of operations in Iraq and Afghanistan the scheme has involved an outlay of £3.6 billion that has been concentrated in the areas of force protection and ISTAR (MoD, 2009).[71] Financed by contingency funding from the Treasury, UORs are not subject to a budget limit, but must be fielded with 18 months of the ratification of a request. The scheme is largely self-policing by the MoD and PJHQ; a system that functions surprisingly well, as should the MoD use UOR scheme to request non-urgent equipment, it would threaten a valuable stream of revenue.[72] It has, however, been more difficult to push through changes to the formal equipment programme following the identification of UORs with medium-long term implications (for reasons explored below). This has led to problems in the area of ISTAR in particular, due to the need to reconfigure broader system architecture following the addition of UOR.[73]

Hence, despite some problems, this set of institutional reforms has been largely successful in promoting jointness and interoperability and in the identification of and conformity to 'best practice' at the tactical and operational levels. However, the 'bottom-up' dissemination of post-Cold War lessons-learned into more far-reaching changes to force postures and capability investment has been hampered by the impact of organisational politics at the higher-levels of the Single Services, that is manifested within DE&S and the Defence Board. This acts as a brake on the capacity of the military to respond to the rapidly changing security environment.[74] Yet, as the following section will demonstrate, it is not organisational politics itself that is the key variable in determining 'strategic drift'. Causality lies in the constraints in executive autonomy which have incentivised the temporal management of defence reform by the core executive. The impact of the electoral cycle dissuaded the core executive from conducting an SDR in 2007/08 when it became apparent that a rebalancing of capability investment and force posture to cope with the challenges of three block warfare/stabilisation operations was required.[75] An SDR that developed broad cross-party consensus on the precise force structures and capabilities of the 'balanced force' would have had the effect of compelling the Single Services to undertake far-reaching reform and negated the impact of organisational politics. This process has instead been deferred to the new Parliament in 2010.

Low executive autonomy and the temporal management of defence reform during the third term of the Labour government

Since the 1998 SDR the institutional structures underpinning defence capability acquisition have undergone a series of reforms as part of the 'Smart Acquisition' process.[76] These reforms were designed to ensure that major capability projects reflect as closely as possible the future conflict scenarios that the military will face, whilst being responsive to contemporary operational requirements and that projects are delivered on time and to budget. Major reforms included the development in 1998 of 'Initial' and 'Main' Gates in the Departmental decision-making process in order to ensure an accurate assessment of project cost; the transformation of the Procurement Executive into the Defence Procurement Agency (DPA) and development of the Defence Logistics Organisation (DLO) in 1999.[77] The SDR also created the Equipment Capability Customer (later termed the MoD Capability Sponsor) that drew the three services together in an attempt to form a more effective organ that could determine the capability needs of the forces as a whole more effectively.[78] The 2005 Defence Industrial Strategy (DIS) also attempted to communicate the key requirements of the MoD to UK industry and ensure the retention and development of skills and knowledge in key strategic areas. The DIS and Enabling Acquisition Change Report of 2006 (EAC) led to the merging of DPA and DLO into Defence Equipment and Support (DE&S) and to changes to acquisition patterns in strategic industrial sectors. In addition, the EAC spurred the development of the Through Life Capability Management (TLCM) plan, initiated in 2006, that has sought to enhance the coherence of the key Defence Lines of Development (DLoD) by adopting a broader strategic view of capability delivery by more closely considering the relationship between doctrine and capabilities and the implications for infrastructure and personnel.[79] TLCM has attempted to develop a more efficient defence

output by identifying the opportunities for the alignment and synchronisation of capability development across the services: to more closely balance
desired capabilities with available resources. Finally, in 2008 the Performance,
Agility, Confidence and Efficiency Programme (PACE) was initiated under the
Defence Acquisition Change Programme as an overall framework to optimise
the work of the organisation.[80]

These reforms have, however, met with only limited success in delivering capabilities on time, to budget, and in a prioritised manner. In order to
remedy this situation, former Secretary of State for Defence, John Hutton
(October 2008–June 2009) commissioned the independent Review of Acquisition for the Secretary of State for Defence, conducted by Bernard Gray (former journalist and advisor to the MoD), that was released on 15 October
2009. Gray's report points to a significantly 'overheated' procurement programme and concludes (from a sample of 40 defence capability programmes)
that the costs of programmes are on average 40 per cent greater than initially
planned and that programmes are delivered 80 per cent later than initial estimates.[81] This is a problem that is worsening, as highlighted by the increasing
need to rely on the supplementary budgets of the UOR to purchase Army
equipment for Afghanistan.[82]

The report highlights the difficulty of maintaining a balance between
MCO and expeditionary operations within current budgetary constraints
and the crucial requirement for a new SDR process to provide top-down
guidance on the exact balance necessary between MCO and 'Three Block
Warfare' tasks. Gray's Review also points to a lack of an accurate costing of
the capability requirements outlined in the SDR and DIS, a problem that
derives, in part, from ten planning horizons, despite some projects (such as
the acquisition of CVF) extending over a 30-year period.[83]

The Report demonstrates the negative impact of poor civilian control
of the acquisition process that has led to overbidding for capabilities
and underestimations of cost. This situation has, in large part, been a consequence of the structure and composition of the key organs which decide
on capability procurement and pass recommendations to Ministers. These
problematic institutional structures are identified as the MoD Capability Sponsor (composed of officers of the Single Services) and the Defence
Board (composed of the Chiefs of the Services who are not subordinate to
the Chief of Defence Staff and enjoy direct access to the Prime Minister).[84]
These organs, dominated by military input, are incapable of making a sober
assessment of priorities in military capability procurement and of forcing
through the reduction or cancellation of lower-priority programmes.[85] As
a confidential source within DE&S noted: 'The dominance of the Single
Services in decision-making on capability procurement is highly problematic as it is questionable whether a military figure rooted in his/her
Single Service has the necessary neutrality to balance requirements with
resources.'[86]

Gray's Report points to the utility of the 'Spiral Development Model' – that introduces a capability at 80 per cent of its full technological capability and is improved over time if necessary. This model permits capabilities to be introduced at an earlier stage and with a lower degree of risk.[87] However, Gray highlights a set of major changes to the process of defence planning which will be necessary to endow this model – and financial reality – with institutional protection.

Firstly, the Review recommends the introduction of regular Defence Reviews (modeled on the US QDR) to take place at five-year intervals, including a full costing of the implications of the Defence Review in order to provide clear and unambiguous guidance on broad pillars of Defence reform.[88] Secondly, the Review recommends that the MoD's budget cycles be shifted from short-term cycles to a rolling ten-year budget (modeled on the French LPM).[89] This rolling budget would include a stronger role for the Permanent Under Secretary (PUS) in the accounting process and make the PUS directly accountable to Parliament and annual external auditing processes. The Review also identifies an urgent need for the PUS, DG Finance and Chief of Defence Material of DE&S to be held accountable for failing to balance the capability procurement budget in each financial year.[90]

The third recommendation of the Report proposes reform of the Defence Board and MoD Capability Sponsor in order to ensure that capability plans reflect budgetary reality. These changes include the creation of an Executive Equipment Committee of the Defence Board that strengthens the role of DG Finance and the PUS. The Executive Equipment Committee would be responsible for proposing a plan for a 'balanced and affordable' equipment plan to the Defence Board that is rejected or approved as a whole in order to negate the ability of the individual services to 'cherry pick' the plan.[91]

In order to avoid cost over-runs due to the changing requirements and specification of capability procurement and the ability for industry to increase costings the fourth recommendation of the report centres upon reforms to the Capability Sponsor and DE&S in order to more clearly delineate their roles in the acquisition process and create a stronger customer-supplier relationship.[92] These changes also involve the enhancement of the role of DCDS Capability to act as a single point of contact within the MoD. Fifthly, the Review points to the need to improve the decision-making process for approvals associated with the Initial and Main Gate approval process by strengthening of the role of the MoD DG Finance to allow it to Chair the Investment Approvals Board (IAB) and by introducing independent cost estimates.[93]

Whilst praising the goals of the TLCM, the Review's sixth recommendation is for changes to the execution of TLCM in order to improve the availability of equipment to front-line soldiers.[94] As a confidential source within DE&S noted: 'The TLCM programme has the right song, the problem is getting people in tune and delivering a coherent melody.'[95] The programme has faced difficulty in implementation due to the lengthy period of time it has had to devote to planning and consultation, leaving it constantly playing a game of 'catch-up' in assessing the possibilities for the exploitation of opportunities for collaboration across DLODs. Consequently the harmonisation of defence output has been reduced to a series of 'crash diets'.[96] Hence the Gray Review points to the need to improve the financial and programme data sets on which decisions of the Programme Boards[97] are made. The Report also argues risk that TLCM will undermine the gains in accountability attained through the changes of the Smart Acquisition Process, as well as the potential for TLCM to increase short-term spending. Consequently, the Review recommends an independent review on the provision of in-service support, the simplification of the TLCM process, the enhancement of financial modeling skills and a more thorough investigation of the implications of TLCM for accountability.

The Review also lauds the creation of the DPA and DLO following the SDR and the recent merger of these two organs into the DE&S. It points, nevertheless, in its seventh recommendation to the need for the organisation to focus more explicitly on delivering new equipment and support. Gray also notes the importance of rebalancing the senior management structure of DE&S in order to reduce the influence of the individual services, strengthen independent cost estimation and increase the incentives for industry to provide accurate costings.[98] Furthermore, the Review points to the need to alter the recruitment of staff within DE&S who have, at times, been imposed on managers by the Single Services. The Report also recommends that line managers serve for a minimum of four years to allow DE&S to reap the benefits of experience.[99] In addition, the Review highlights the requirement for Common Operating System and Management Tools within the DE&S and identifies a common legal framework and an external review process for major contracts as vital in allowing the MoD to exert greater control over contractors.[100] In order to effectively institute these changes and marginalise opponents, the Review's final recommendation is that the DE&S become a Government-Owned, Contractor-Operated (GO-CO) organisation, that will give the DE&S greater independence from the MoD.[101]

Whilst Gray's Report was highly embarrassing for the Labour Government, it has acted to imbue reforms to the acquisition process with gravitas and impetus.[102] The key recommendations of the review, apart from the Go-Co initiative, were broadly accepted by the Secretary of State for Defence, Bob Ainsworth.[103] Gray's proposals have also found support within the Defence Acquisition Reform Project Team (DARPT), led by Lord Paul Drayson (former Minister of State for Defence Equipment and Support, May 2005–November 2007) (AOF, 2009). DARPT is currently developing a more detailed Strategy for Acquisition reform that will be published in early 2010, alongside the Green Paper on defence in the build-up to a new SDR process that will take place following the 2010 general election (AOF, 2009).

A number of reforms are also planned which will strengthen the capacity of the Directorate General (DG) Strategy of the MoD to deliver the core goals identified by the forthcoming SDR process. The DG Strategy is responsible for strategic assessment and fleshing out the baseline for force postures set out within the 2003/2004 Defence White Papers. The DG Strategy works closely with the DCDC Defence Intelligence Staff, and other government intelligence Departments in the development of the Strategic Assessment, a classified document that outlines key areas of insecurity over a 15–20 year period.[104] Indeed, in the years since its establishment, the DCDC has become an increasingly important actor in providing input to the future conflict scenarios developed by DG Strategy, to the point that the DCDC has been described as the 'Fourth Floor of the MoD'.[105]

The DG Strategy plays an important role in the Studies Assumption Group that approves the key operational scenarios which are used to define capability requirements and produces Defence Strategic Guidance (DSG).[106] The Strategic Assessment is used to produce Part One of DSG that fleshes out the key threats outlined in the UK National Security Strategy through a detailed analysis of developments within and between different regions of the globe, including demographic, environmental, economic and resource trends, the likelihood of interstate warfare, the implications of shifts in the global balance of power and the evolution of regional and international institutions.[107] The DSG, in turn, forms the basis for the Defence Planning Assumptions (a document that defines the likely scale of operations, military tasks and concurrency of operations over the short-medium term). The implications of the DPA for force attributions (manpower, equipment, training and support) are then outlined in detail within the Defence Programme Directory.[108]

The DG Strategy is particularly 'civil servant heavy' in order to attempt insulate these processes from the agendas of the Single Services.[109] However, the capacity of the DG Strategy to overcome the 'status quo' on delivering policy into programme has been hampered by the yearly planning rounds which acted to provide 'post-facto justifications for existing force structures' and by the capacity of the Defence Board to block major change, leaving the Directorate constantly playing a game of 'catch-up'.[110] As a consequence of this problem the yearly planning rounds will, following the forthcoming SDR, be replaced by a new process of policy implementation.[111] Defence Strategic Direction (DSD) will supercede Defence Strategic Guidance and form a more concise, longer-term (15–20 year) resource-informed vision of key priorities in Defence. The DSD will be accompanied by a Defence Plan that outlines how this DSD will be realised over the near-term (five years) and is divided into a set of ten substrategies for delivery.[112]

The problem of finding the appropriate balance between the 'bottom-up' military input to defence planning and 'top-down' civilian leadership is an enduring problem throughout history (Imlay and Toft, 2006) and the

British case is an instructive example of the ongoing struggle that civilian figures face in attaining an accurate picture of key requirements in defence. The reforms to the MoD that accompanied the 1998 SDR and 2002/04 Defence White Papers were largely effective in ensuring a focus on jointness and in fostering an environment that has been conducive to debate and critical analysis about future threats and the tactical and operational-level implications of ongoing operational experiences and the experiences of others. The creation of the DCDC and UKDA have helped to ensure that operational experience across the 'continuum of conflict' during the 1990s and early 21st century, combined with observation of the application of US capabilities and doctrine have formed the key drivers of reform at the tactical and operational levels since the instigation of third-order change in 1998. Emulation of the US-led RMA in the form of NEC and EBAO/effects-based thinking is therefore based upon scepticism of the capacity of technology to transform the nature of warfare. British emulation of the RMA is focused on the delivery of operational effects across the 'continuum of conflict' through the embedding of NEC and EBAO/effects-based thinking within the Comprehensive Approach. At the same time, the lessons drawn from the post-Cold War operational environment have acted to attenuate the dominance of the 'war-fighting' ethos within the British military and have led to a focus on cultural-generic and cultural-specific training that delivers an 'adaptive foundation' in preparation for the conduct of 'three block warfare' and COIN/Stabilisation tasks.

A key contextual factor determining the process of British decision-making on force structures and doctrine is the potential cost to British relative power of a faulty assessment of the operational challenges. The contemporary operational environment, particularly in the aftermath of September 11, has generated increasingly pressing challenges for Britain's expeditionary forces. The threat of defeat in the ongoing operations of Iraq and Afghanistan has acted as a powerful incentive to ensure the correct are drawn from recent experiences and observation of the US-led RMA. The centrality of the objective lessons of operational experience and the threat of defeat as drivers of military innovation and emulation are alluded to by Farrell (2008). Hinting at the decline of EBO that was about to take place in the US and of European EBAO as an emergent model of best practice in effects-based thinking Farrell (2008: 797–8) states: 'It may even be that the pressure of operations is leading to cultural change in the US military, with some field commands beginning to appreciate the British EBAO.'

However, when translating these operational lessons into broader strategic decision-making on capability acquisition and force attributions the threat of defeat becomes diluted by organisational politics. The 'bottom-up' dissemination of the lessons of operational experience has been blocked by competition between the Single Services that has been manifested most strongly within DE&S and the Defence Board. The absence of a correct balance between civilian and military input to defence has fostered, if not completely inaccurate capability plans, then overbidding, inaccurate cost assessments and the inadequate prioritisation of projects. As Bernard Gray highlights, the majority of the capability initiatives which comprise the UK's 'overheated' capability procurement programme are in line with the requirements of the international security environment: 'Most of the equipment being proposed is useful, and it is desirable to have it. In an ideal world one would acquire it all...the real question is not whether any particular piece of equipment has utility but how it ranks against other possible defence uses of that money.'

It is, therefore, crucial that institutional protection is provided for financial constraints and that civilian actors strictly control the process of capability acquisition and provide clear guidance on priorities.[113] The Gray Report clearly demonstrates the weakness of the reforms undertaken as part of 'Smart Acquisition' in channeling interservice competition into a positive force and the incapacity of MoD structures to make difficult decisions about capability programme prioritisation and adhere to tight budgetary constraints. Many of the problems identified by the Gray Report have, to the credit of the Labour government, been recognised by Bob Ainsworth and DARPT. The 2010 SDR and reforms to the capability procurement process and role of DG Strategy should provide strengthened mechanisms allowing for more sober judgments to be made on the precise capabilities which should accompany a 'balanced force' and empower the capacity of the MoD to implement the key outcomes of the SDR.

The root cause of the current strategic drift in UK defence policy lies, however, in the constraints of decreased executive autonomy. It is broadly recognised within the MoD that an SDR process was required in 2007 as the imperative of striking a more accurate balance between current requirements in Afghanistan and future conflict scenarios became apparent.[114] UK defence reform has, therefore, been subject to temporal management since 2007 that has slowed the speed with which the UK military is able to converge around the dictates of military 'best practice'. At such a late stage in the life of the current Parliament the Labour government is acutely sensitive to the potential for 'bad news' in terms of jobs lost within the UK defence industry (that supplies 10 per cent of UK manufacturing jobs and is 75 per cent dependent on MoD expenditure). The Government is therefore unable to implement an SDR in advance of the General Election.[115] As a senior figure within the UK Defence Ministry noted: 'The current drift in UK Defence Policy is a consequence of the impact of electoral cycles: no government would be in a position to implement a resource-driven SDR process at any other point than the first two years of a new Parliament.'[116]

The institutional forums of British defence policy: Reflecting systemic imperatives

Although British armed forces reform is a case of 'third-order' change – to the objectives and instruments of defence policy – this has not been accompanied by a fundamental shift of institutional forum. Despite playing an important role in the development of intergovernmental initiatives such as the 1998 Saint Malo Accord, 1999 Helsinki Headline Goals and 2003 ESS and an incremental shift towards the embedding of British defence policy within ESDP, UK defence and security policy remains firmly anchored within NATO (Dorman, 2001; Dover, 2005; Dunne, 2004: 908). Although the December 2003 White Paper contains five references to ESDP, it only once refers to ESDP without 'ring fencing' this through reference to NATO or the US (Edwards, 2006: 12). Nevertheless, the December 1998 Saint Malo Accord, 2002 Helsinki Headline Goals and 2003 ESS represent a series of important, albeit gradual, steps towards the embedding of British defence policy within ESDP and a recognition that Europe has to be capable of autonomous military action in cases of US disinterest (Dorman, 2001: 187–8; Dover, 2005; Jones, 2007: 55).

According to normative approaches, British 'Atlanticism' and preference for routing defence cooperation through NATO is a consequence of the culturally-bounded and institutionally-embedded lessons drawn from the Second World War and the Suez Crisis about the utility of the US security guarantee in helping the UK 'punch above its weight' and the result of elite socialisation processes during the Cold War (Miskimmon, 2004: 90; Smith, 2005; Wallace, 1992). The sequencing and temporal location of changes to the 'settings' of British institutional forums (following changes to the objectives and instruments of policy) is therefore viewed as a result of the depth of Atlanticism in British security culture, acting as a powerful normative constraint on the willingness of British policy-makers to sanction any policy that might threaten the Atlantic Alliance (Miskimmon, 2004: 90; Quinlan, 2001: 36).[117] The British lead on the St. Malo initiative was, therefore, according to Howorth (2004: 221), a result of the normative entrepreneurship of key figures and officials within British defence and security policy subsystem, who provided the ideational impetus that pushed Blair across the European 'rubicon'.

Neoclassical realism, however, provides a more accurate explanation of the temporality of changes to the institutional venues of British defence policy. The temporal location of the incremental shift towards the development of a stronger European military capability (the Saint Malo Initiative of October 1998) was the product of the increasing clarity of the implications of uni-polarity for the institutional forums of British defence policy in mid-late 1998 (Dorman, 2001: 195–6; Rynning, 2005: 91). Change was spurred by the fear of 'abandonment' by the US in the run-up to the 1999 Kosovo conflict, that brought home to British policy-makers the uncertainties of the US security guarantee.[118] Indeed, it is interesting to note how cultural approaches to the Europeanisation of British defence policy cannot account for the temporality of Britain's emergence as a leader on ESDP without recognising the primary causal role played by systemic pressures. As Howorth (2004: 220–1) notes, a stronger defence and security arm for the EU was, by late 1997, being proclaimed by the US as the only means with which to rescue NATO from impotency and irrelevance. This was an event that, in tandem with the growing crisis in the Balkans, acted to 'galvanise British security cultural thinking' (Howorth, 2004: 221).

ESDP serves, therefore, a dual purpose in British defence policy that is consistent with the thesis of 'reformed bandwagoning' and the view of NATO and ESDP as mutually reinforcing (Dorman, 2001: 195; Howorth, 2007: 53; Moens, 2003: 26; Reynolds, 2007: 361; Rynning, 2005: 91; Sloan, 2002: 56), rather than the first signs of 'soft' balancing behaviour (Posen, 2006: 170). On the one hand, ESDP was promoted by the British as an 'insurance policy' that will permit autonomous European action within its geopolitical neighbourhood in cases of US disinterest. On the other hand, whilst the SDR identified the 'arc of crisis from North Africa to the Middle East' as the likely geographical boundaries of military deployment, the uncertainties of the international security environment also threw into sharp relief British dependence upon US assets for deployments further afield. This was an imperative that was later reinforced by British participation in ISAF and UK reliance on the US was codified in the 2004 Defence White Paper (Dorman, 2006: 164).[119] Consequently, the British impetus behind ESDP at the St. Malo Initiative served a secondary and equally vital function, as the development of an institutional framework that, in tandem with capability initiatives under the auspices of NATO, would enhance the relevance of the UK and Europe as an alliance partner to the US (Howorth, 2007: 53).[120]

A secondary, though important, factor determining the temporality of the incremental Europeanisation of British defence policy was the identification of ESDP by Blair as a means with which to help remedy Britain's increasing lack of influence within the EU, countering German influence though EMU, compensating for the British decision not to join in the first wave and for early French leadership on ESDP (Dorman, 2001: 194–5; Dover, 2005: 511–12). These systemic imperatives combined with high levels of executive autonomy to determine the quick pace of changes to the 'settings' of British policy on institutional venues (Barnathan, 2006; Croft et al, 2001: 63; Dorman, 2001: 194; Dover, 2005: 513).

Hence in contrast to Germany, and in line with France, 'executive autonomy' facilitated a stronger focus by British policy leaders on the 'national interest', rather than the domestic political ramifications of 'allied cooperation'.

British security culture: A readily deployable instrument

Existing British 'security culture' formed a versatile tool with which to frame the 'third-order' change to the British military that was outlined in the SDR.[121] The new expeditionary focus of British defence policy was firmly located within the three tenets of British security 'culture' identified by Miskimmon

(2004). Reform was portrayed as critical in order ensure Britain's continued capacity to 'pack a punch in the world'[122] and to fulfill the special responsibilities which derived from the United Kingdom's history as a colonial power: 'Our economic interests and our history give us other responsibilities...our national security and prosperity thus depend upon promoting international stability, freedom and economic development. As a Permanent Member of the UN Security Council and as a country both willing and able to play a lead role internationally we have a responsibility to act as a force for good in the world.'[123]

The SDR was also accompanied by strong strategic leadership on 'allied cooperation' and the third pillar of British security 'culture': Atlanticism. Both Blair and Robertson used NATO and the trans-Atlantic relationship as mechanisms within which to frame and embed the new role and structure of the military.[124] Although Robertson outlined radical reform, he also emphasised Labour's commitment to NATO as the key institution of British and European Security and framed military reform as a means with which to renew the Atlantic Alliance and ensure US engagement in Europe, helping to bind the Conservatives to the reform agenda (Dorman, 2001: 195; Miskimmon, 2003: 15).

These core principles of British security 'culture' were brought together and reshaped to form a key element of Blair's overarching narrative on international security: the 'Doctrine of the International Community' that was outlined at a speech to the Economic Club of Chicago on 24 April 1999. This doctrine formed an important rhetorical tool legitimating UK participation in Operation Allied Force (Frantzen, 2005: 105; Howorth, 2004: 226–7). However, following the September 11 attacks (in which 67 British citizens lost their lives) policy leaders within the UK core executive were endowed with the tool of an enhanced sense of 'public vulnerability' to direct attack – not only upon the values of the UK, but also upon its territory. Public vulnerability was manipulated as Freedman (2004: 7–50) notes, to 'hoodwink national and international opinion' and provided an important context that elite figures were able to exploit in order to mobilise support behind conflict in Afghanistan, Iraq and a global expeditionary role for the British military (Becker, 2009; Freedman, 2004). Whilst the core principles of British security culture – Britain's responsibility to her Alliance partner the US, and burden as a global player to promote the values of freedom and democracy – were also invoked as part of this process, they formed secondary arguments (Becker, 2009: 349–50).

The incremental change that took place to the institutional venues of British defence policy through the October 1998 St. Malo Initiative was sold to a dubious and largely anti-European public by remoulding existing Atlanticist discourse. Blair framed a lead role in St. Malo as a means with which to strengthen the Atlantic Alliance (and thereby Britain's relative standing within NATO) by building up the Alliance's European pillar. As

Miskimmon notes: 'The discourse which Blair uses is almost exclusively centred around the idea that European capabilities will strengthen the trans-Atlantic link.'

Howorth (2004: 221–3), however, makes the interesting observation that Britain's new lead role in ESDP was accompanied by a particularly thin level of 'communicative discourse'. Howorth credits this to the complexity of the construction of discourse in this area to the lack of an overarching British European policy and a desire not to draw attention to the crisis within NATO. Howorth (2004: 221–3) highlights the difficulty of deploying culture as an instrument in this instance due to the need to develop parallel and somewhat contradictory discourses at the European, trans-Atlantic and domestic levels. One must, however, also factor in the important role of executive autonomy. With a large parliamentary majority and elections far over the horizon, Blair – unlike his Conservative predecessors – was in a strong position to engage in strategic innovation on the institutional forums of British defence policy, reducing the need to use the tool of British security culture as an instrument. This autonomy was further enhanced by the impending threat of the outbreak of another conflict in the Balkans that demonstrated the importance of St. Malo to the British public.[125]

Furthermore, unlike German security 'culture' and French Gaullist ideology which were tools requiring significant remoulding by elite figures in order for them to become effective instruments, the British security 'culture' and 'identity' that had become cemented as the appropriate response to systemic incentives over the course of the post-war period embodied elements which dovetailed closely with the expeditionary requirements of the post-Cold War era. It does not however, follow from this that culture was the key factor in determining the temporality and outcome of British reform. Whilst 'culture' was a more convenient tool to wield for figures within the British core executive than it was for German policy leaders and ossified practices within the British military dovetailed more closely with the requirements of the post-Cold War security environment; the high level of executive autonomy in defence policy that was enjoyed by the 1997 Labour government was the decisive variable in determining the temporality of 'third order' British defence reform.

The narrowing of executive autonomy during the mid-1990s disincentivised the pursuit of 'third order' reform by the Conservatives as systemic imperatives began to clarify (Howorth, 2004: 217). However, the domestic opportunity structure that faced Blair and Robertson in 1997 induced strategic innovation and the use of culture, identity and the manipulation of 'public vulnerability' to frame adherence to the dictates of international structure. Gordon Brown's capacity to provide a compelling narrative to 'sell' the war in Afghanistan has come under great criticism during 2009 (TG, 2009). It is, however, the reduction of executive autonomy deriving from the threat of electoral defeat in the forthcoming 2010 general election and unpopularity

Table 6.1 Neoclassical Realist and Cultural Explanations of the Temporality of Military Reform

	Britain	France	Germany
Cultural Explanations of the Temporality of Reform	**Location:** 1997–98 shift to crisis-management and restructuring facilitated by resonance with institutionally/societally embedded beliefs concerning role of military in fighting small wars of varying intensity outside Europe during the colonial era. Given such resonance the late location of convergence when compared to France is perplexing. **Pace:** 14 month reform process surprising given resonance of changes with British security culture. **Sequencing:** Reform to objectives, instruments followed by incremental Europeanisation, consequent upon depth of Atlanticism within British security culture.	**Location:** 1994–96 shift to crisis-management/professional forces due to roles of Balladur and Chirac as 'norm entrepreneurs' overcoming path dependent commitment to conscription. **Pace:** 32 month reform consequent upon path dependent commitment to conscription. However, this fails to capture domestic material factors restricting executive autonomy. **Sequencing:** Reform to objectives and institutional forums preceding reform to instruments due to Balladur/Chirac's role in identifying ESDP with idea of France as 'third force' and 'Europeanisation of French Exceptionalism'; impact of path dependent commitment to conscription.	**Location:** 2003 shift to crisis-management due to deeply embedded culture of anti-militarism, resistant to change. **Pace:** Path dependent commitment to conscription and citizen in uniform'. Laggard role of Defence Ministry on ESDP due to post-war socialisation processes, leading to Atlanticised institutional culture. Difficulties in explaining six month reform to objectives, given societally/institutionally embedded norms concerning objectives and instruments of German defence policy. **Sequencing:** Path dependency and impact of German security culture leading to stasis on policy instruments.

Table 6.1   Neoclassical Realist and Cultural Explanations of the Temporality of Military Reform   – *continued*

	Britain	France	Germany
Neoclassical Realist Explanations of the Temporality of Reform	**Location:** Opacity of systemic power shift in early 90s; reduction in executive autonomy for Conservatives in mid-90s due to internal disunity and forthcoming 1997 Parliamentary elections. High executive autonomy enjoyed by Labour Government in May 1997 (unitary state, high parliamentary majority and weak links between defence, social and budgetary policy subsystems).	**Location:** High executive autonomy and 'state power' due to nature of Defence Policy as 'reserved domain' of the President, unitary state and ability of President to implement base closures and weaker links between social, defence and budgetary policy subsystems.	**Location:** Low executive autonomy and 'state power' due to dispersal of formal competencies on defence policy within core executive; federal state leading to heightened sensitivity to politics of base closures; interlinked social, defence and budgetary policy subsystems due to system of *Zivildienst*. 'Culture' not causal but a tool in temporal and political management of reform.
	Pace: Configuration of domestic power relationships; linkages between budgetary and defence policy –Treasury's wish that SDR did not precede Comprehensive Spending Review.	**Pace:** Nature of military policy as 'shared domain' during cohabitation (1993–95) and lack of support from Finance Ministry for reform to policy instruments during cohabitation; impact of forthcoming Presidential elections in May 1995.	**Pace:** Six month reform (May–October 2003) due to SPD concern with implementing base closures consequent upon the downsizing of the armed forces by 35,000 troops in advance of the next Federal elections and to close down possibility for macro-political debate on conscription.
	Sequencing: Incremental shift towards ESDP following SDR due to realisation of threat of abandonment by US in late 1998.	**Sequencing:** Reform to institutional forums preceding objectives and instruments due to French focus on balancing German power through EMU by lead role on 'defence Europe'; impact of cohabitation upon reforms to policy instruments.	**Sequencing:** Temporal manipulation of reform incentivised by low executive autonomy.

of the Labour Government that forms the main causal variable impacting on Brown's ability to deliver a bold and compelling policy narrative. Tellingly, Defence Secretary Bob Ainsworth has operated under clear instructions from the Cabinet Office to 'keep Defence as quiet as possible in the run-up to the general election'.[126] These constraints on executive autonomy have also impinged on the capacity of the government to deliver a new SDR process in a timely manner and provide unequivocal 'top-down' guidance on the precise force structures and capabilities which should characterise a 'balanced force'.

7
Conclusions: The Empirical and Theoretical Implications

This chapter spells out the key empirical and theoretical lessons which can be drawn from the study. In doing so it outlines the practical implications of the book, in particular, for the structuring of military input to decisions on doctrine, capability investment and force structures. It also engages with the implications for the academic community, notably for theoretical debates on defence reform and European security cooperation. The section will also examine the strengths and weaknesses of the empirical and theoretical material and set out the main agendas for future research.

Neoclassical realism and defence reform: Matter over mind

Neorealism provides only a partial explanation of convergence and divergence in defence reform. Through its focus on the role of the competitive nature of the international system in forcing states to organise for war as effectively as possible, neorealism neglects the extent to which domestic power relationships can incentivise a short-medium term preoccupation with domestic political interests rather than 'systemic imperatives', leading to the political and temporal management of reform (Christensen, 1996: 20; Farrell and Terriff, 2002: 271; Zakaria, 1998: 40).

Although the strength of the shift in the systemic distribution of capabilities following the end of the Cold War is driving Britain, France and Germany towards convergence in the instruments, objectives and institutional forums of defence policy, the analysis presented demonstrates how the policy implications of systemic power shifts are not always immediately clear to figures within the core executive (Morgenthau, 1966: 154; Rose, 1998: 153). The opacity of systemic imperatives forms an important initial intervening variable that impacts upon the temporality of reform over the short-term by incentivising policy-makers to 'err on the side of caution' by adhering to existing policy responses rather than taking risky decisions under conditions of extreme informational uncertainty. It is also important to note that whilst 'broadly similar' in material capabilities and 'external vulnerability', attention should also be paid to nuances in British, French and German 'external vulnerability' stemming from geographical loc-ation. Hence, as the analysis has demonstrated, French preoccupation with relative power *vis-à-vis* Germany impacts upon the scope and pace of change to the institutional forums of French defence policy. This helps to explain why, despite high levels of 'executive autonomy' in both the UK and France, changes to the institutional forums of their defence policies took place at divergent temporal locations (1994 and 1998 respectively).

In the initial years following the seismic shift in the systemic distribution of capabilities precipitated by the fall of Communism, Britain, France and Germany faced the common challenge of decision-making on the objec-tives, instruments and institutional forums of their defence policies under conditions of intense uncertainty; in particular, uncertainty about the nature of conflict scenarios over the short-medium term (Imlay and Toft, 2006). The post-Cold War constellation of friends and foes soon became apparent: in a uni-polar world European states would continue to bandwagon on US power, whilst crises in the Balkans and the Gulf demonstrated that the European Great Powers would have to be prepared to deal with instability in their geopolitical neighbourhood as well as deploy forces further afield as part of shifting coalitions.

However, assessing the nature of war proved a more tricky process: would conflict predominantly involve stand-off precision strike warfare against near-peer competitors, as the Kosovo conflict and Gulf War appeared to suggest, or complex crisis-management operations of varying intensity, necessitating the substantial commitment of ground forces, as hinted by operations in Somalia and Bosnia? The early 1990s also failed to answer the related question of the full implications of uni-polarity for the precise extent of the US commitment to European security. It remained unclear what balance of capabilities would be necessary in order to follow a policy of 'reformed bandwagoning'; of how to remain useful partners of the US, whilst simultaneously filling the gaps left in the provision of security within Europe's geopolitical neighbourhood.

The opacity of the nature of conflict was magnified by the risks for 'sec-ondary' powers which were associated with faulty choices in defence policy. The resource endowment of the US allowed it the luxury of experimenting with a strategy of innovation in military capabilities and doctrines in the form of the RMA. However, the status of West European Great Powers as 'sec-ondary' states has reduced the 'margin of error' and predisposed these states to a more careful approach of the identification of 'best practice' and obser-vation of the failures and successes of others. At the same time, Britain, France and Germany enjoyed the advantage of a short-lived 'peace dividend' and bandwagoning on the US security guarantee through NATO in the immediate post-Cold War era. This allowed these states a measure of breathing space to adjust to the extreme uncertainty and flux of the new security environment and to begin the process of settling on a model of military 'best practice'.

The broad trajectory of reforms emerged in the mid-to-late 1990s as the strategic imperatives of the post-Cold War era began to clarify. However, the risks of faulty emulation were such that it was only in the early 21st century that the West European Great Powers have converged around a specific model of 'best practice' in force structures, capabilities and doctrine that will be relevant to conflict scenarios over the short-medium term. This has taken the form of modular, expeditionary forces, focused upon the simultaneous delivery of both kinetic and non-kinetic effects in complex stabilisation and 'three block warfare' situations supported by NEC, EBAO and the Comprehensive Approach. At the same time, reforms emphasise the need to retain a balance in force structures and capabilities which will ensure a continued capacity to undertake MCO.

Furthermore, as Colin Bennett (1991: 19) reminds us, convergence is 'process of becoming rather than being alike'. Some national differences continue to persist, particularly in military doctrine. It is, however, possible to identify convergence around the importance of the principles of 'mission command' and the 'manoueverist approach' in the conduct of 'three block warfare' as part of Stabilisation/COIN operations. Doctrine and training are increasingly focused on developing the capacity to simultaneously deliver effects across the conflict spectrum. Hence French, and particularly, British Defence Doctrine and training emphasises the need to attenuate the 'war-fighting ethos' with a focus on the cultural skills and doctrine necessary to undertake 'wars amongst the people'. German military doctrine and training is, on the other hand, gradually increasing its emphasis on the kinetic. The gradual and incremental convergence of doctrine reflects the complexity of strategic and operational learning under conditions of uncertainty and the legacy of nuances in external vulnerability. This is evidenced in the case of the Federal Republic of Germany whose lack of experience of the maintenance and dissolution of Empire over a sustained period of time and post-WW2 restrictions on the role of the *Bundeswehr* has made adaptation to the challenge of Three Block Warfare more difficult by delivering only a thin repository of doctrine on which to draw. It is also important to note the impact of continued political interference in German doctrinal development.

Indeed, despite the broad commonalities enjoyed by the West European Great Powers in terms of their external vulnerability, Britain, France and Germany undertook a temporally uneven adaptation to the requirements of the post-Cold War international security environment. 'State power', impacting upon the ability of the core executive to 'extract and direct the resources of their societies', emerges as the crucial intervening variable in explaining temporal divergence (Rose, 1998: 161). The book has examined in detail the nature of the 'transmission belt', whereby systemic pressures are translated into domestic policy responses. Its findings challenge not only the literature on strategic culture, but also the literature on transitional military norms of conventional warfare (Farrell, 2005b: 38–9; Goldman and Eliason, 2003). This study finds that there is a predominantly material dynamic at work, not only at the systemic level, but also in the 'transmission belt' at the domestic level. The inducements of the international system – the balance of power, balance of threat and pervasive uncertainty – create powerful socialisation pressures of a material nature driving states of common size, material power and geographical position towards convergence. At the same time, executive autonomy at the domestic level determines the timing of a state's response to the international security environment.

The book has demonstrated the important impact of the institutional structure of the state and domestic material power relations on 'state power'. It finds that 'executive autonomy' in the sphere of defence policy – a determinant of the degree of centralisation/decentralisation of the state, the constitutional powers of the core executive and linkages between social, finance and defence policy subsystems – is the key intervening variable in shaping the temporality of reform. It does so by impacting upon the ability and willingness of Presidents/Prime Ministers and Defence Ministers to undertake 'strategic innovation' and provide 'institutional protection' to new objectives and instruments of defence policy. The extent of 'executive autonomy' in defence policy also informs the degree to which 'allied cooperation' through NATO/the EU will reflect the 'domestic' or 'national' interest over the short-medium-term. Convergence is, therefore, a non-linear process, proceeding in fits and starts, and is dependent upon fluctuations in executive autonomy. The British case between 2007 and 2010 provides an excellent example of how the position of the electoral cycle can incentivise the temporal management of reform by the core executive. This has delayed a much-needed rebalancing of the force posture and capabilities of the UK military. In short, 'matter' triumphs over 'mind' at both the systemic and domestic levels.

Planning for the unexpected: The imperative of the balanced force in the post-Cold War era

> 'Uncertainty remains one of the few certainties for contemporary military planners' (Imlay and Toft, 2006: 4).

The powerful effects of uncertainty have led military planners in post-Cold War Europe to 'hedge their bets' and invest in capabilities that will permit both the conduct of 'three block warfare' operations across the conflict spectrum in stabilisation situations, whilst retaining the capacity to undertake MCO (Imlay and Toft, 2006: 254). Although the Cold War era began with an MCO, the experience of diverse expeditionary crisis-management – including peacemaking, peace-keeping, post-conflict reconstruction as well as stabilisation and COIN – have demonstrated the need to invest in doctrine, structures and capabilities tailored to scenarios such as 'three block war' and 'wars amongst the people'. Despite the low likelihood of major interstate conflict over the short-term, history teaches both civilian and military figures the importance of preparing for the unexpected. As Imay and Toft (2006: 1, 253–4) note: 'prudence alone dictates that states and their militaries plan for interstate war...During peacetime, military forces should strive, within financial and other limits, to develop an array of weapons systems, doctrines, and force structures, accepting that some of them may turn out to be less useful than expected in a future war.' Such a position is also adopted by Benbow (2009: 30): 'The assumption that there will be no significant state-on-state warfare...resembles a piece of wish fulfillment. If it were true it would represent a complete turnabout in a fundamental pattern of modern history.'

This throws into sharp relief the arguments of those who suggest that the militaries of Europe's secondary powers should concentrate their energies on peacekeeping, COIN and even the challenges of 'Fourth Generation Warfare'[1] (Hammes, 2005: 189–221). Such arguments have been expressed in the recent debate on the renewal of UK nuclear weapons systems and criticism by the IPPR of British capability acquisition policy. It is undeniable that some rebalancing of UK procurement will be necessary to free-up resources for 'Three Block Warfare/Stabilisation' scenarios and ongoing requirements in Afghanistan. However, to sacrifice projects such as the Future Aircraft Carrier for a predominant focus on COIN/Stabilisation would have two very serious potential consequences. Firstly, it would alter the relative power balance within the Atlantic Alliance, leaving European states ever-more subject to US hegemony and dependent upon American power in managing the reemergence of powers such as China and Russia as global and regional players. Secondly, a major sacrifice of conventional warfare capabilities for COIN/ Stabilisation would constitute a significant risk that outweighs the benefits of moving away from the 'balanced forces' approach as it would leave the UK vulnerable to shifts in the balance of power and to the outbreak of 'state on state' warfare in what remains a highly-uncertain world over the medium-long term.

Although some within the British military (such as Sir Richard Dannatt) have advocated a focus on asymmetric warfare, the assessment generated by the DCDC in 2007 (Global Strategic Trends Programme 2007–36) highlights the threat of interstate war during the next 20 years as a result of an increased competition for resources caused by climate change, dwindling oil reserves and population growth.[2] The reduction of some MCO programmes, following a careful consideration of future conflict scenarios will be necessary in order to meet today's challenges effectively and permit further investment in C4ISR and strategic mobility. However, a 'Seacorn' approach that reduces certain capabilities but retains strong investment in training, doctrinal development and maintains skills within the UK defence industry, would be strongly advisable.

Managing uncertainty and organisational politics: Organising military input to defence planning

'A balance of civilian and military input is indispensable for effective planning under conditions of uncertainty' (Imlay and Toft, 2006: 250).

In accordance with the arguments of Posen (1984) actors from the core executive have emerged as central in defining the grand strategic visions which underpin defence reform and in ensuring that reforms to military structures, doctrines and capabilities are broadly capable of helping states respond to the strategic imperatives identified. This was particularly evident in French Defence Reforms of 1994–6 and the British 1997/98 SDR, in which broad consensus was achieved around the core pillars of 'third order' change. As Imlay and Toft (2006: 250) note, military planners are 'especially effective when it comes to the military aspects of planning, but less skilled when it comes to working out the broader grand-strategic and political implications of war planning'.

There is a strong 'bottom-up' dynamic to doctrinal change and capability acquisition and decisions on force structure. The military establishments of the West European Great powers have played a central role in adding flesh to the bones of third-order change outlined in the 'third order reforms' of the UK and France. Although civilian leaders identified a selective emulation of the RMA as vital in meting the core strategic imperative of retaining interoperability with the US as part of the process of 'reformed bandwagoning', the knowledge generated by European militaries has been central in determining the precise detail of this emulation, notably by providing the expertise behind the development of NEC and EBAO and doctrine on COIN and Stabilisation.

For the French, and in particular, the British, the challenges of the post-Cold War security environment – not least stabilisation/COIN – dovetailed with embedded practices consequent upon their diverse and extensive operational experience of OOTW during the establishment, maintenance and dissolution of Empire (Cousens, 2006: 56–7). As contemporary insurgencies embody a set of characteristics common to the experiences of the former European colonial powers, this placed Britain and France at a distinct advantage to Germany by forming a repository of knowledge for the development of post-Cold War doctrine on COIN and on the delivery of both kinetic and non-kinetic operational effects in Stabilisation operations. Nevertheless, modern insurgencies also display a number of important new characteristics. The key challenge for France and in particular, the UK (given its comparatively heavy involvement in COIN in Afghanistan and Iraq), was not to allow 'culture' or 'path dependency' to determine doctrine, but to recombine old knowledge in new forms and ensure a sober assessment of the applicability of existing doctrine takes place during and following operational experience. As Chapters 4 and 6 have demonstrated, the British and French approaches not only to COIN doctrine but also to networking and EBAO/effects based thinking have been tested in the crucible of their own and others' experiences.

Civilian intervention emerges, however, as critical in ensuring objective lessons-learned processes emerge from operational experience, countering the argument of Stephen Rosen (1991) who emphasises the importance of 'military mavericks' as entrepreneurs of change. The empowerment of Joint Staffs and institutions such the DCDC and UKDA in Great Britain and the DGA and CICDE in France has played an important role creating an environment conducive to critical analysis and debate within and between the individual Services (McNerny, 2005: 206).[3] Whilst these institutions have acted to provide institutional protection for the principles of jointness and interoperability and work to identify likely future conflict scenarios, they have also ensured that the 'bottom-up' process of military input into defence planning from the individual services has not been overly clouded by interservice competition, particularly at the tactical and operational levels. The capacity of the European Great Powers to adapt their doctrine, capabilities, force structures and training to a constantly changing security environment and stay abreast of 'best practice' has also been enhanced by the reforms undertaken to the process of lesson-identification and follow-up after military operations. As Imlay and Toft (2006: 7–8) note: 'Whether this process [of competing interests] can result either in paralysis or in a beneficial give and take dynamic – or something in between – will depend on the extent to which there exists a culture of honesty and experimentation within a military service that encourages hard questions, the testing of assumptions, and the willingness to view mistakes as learning experiences rather than failures.'

However, despite the presence of dynamism at the tactical and operational levels, it is vital that adequate institutional protection is delivered to financial control and that civilians are able to channel organisational politics into a force for good. Whilst military input is crucial in capability acquisition, it is equally important that civilians take the key decisions on which procurement projects should take priority and that civilians are able to structure the process by which specific capability proposals are developed in order to verify information gathered from the single Services. It is, of course, impossible to completely strip the distribution of financial resources between the Services from bias and from the logic of organisational politics. No state is perfect in this regard. Nevertheless, in France stricter civilian control over the process of defence procurement more closely links defence acquisition to financial reality. In Germany and the UK the defence procurement process has been less than capable of finding the appropriate balance between military and civilian input to the process of capability acquisition.

However, as Chapters 4–6 demonstrate, organisational politics is not a stand-alone variable in explaining temporal divergence with the dictates of international structure and the operational environment. Although the threat of defeat is an important dynamic compelling greater civilian intervention in defence planning (Posen, 1984: 77), executive autonomy forms the key variable determining the capacity of civilians to provide compelling top-down guidance on the precise implications of post-Cold War operational experience for military capabilities and force postures. It does so by impacting on the willingness and ability of the core executive to conduct defence reviews with serious implications for base closures and job losses in the defence sector during particularly sensitive periods of the electoral cycle.

The balance between civilian and military input to defence planning can also swing too far in favour of civilians. The case of Germany is one in which civilians – under conditions of low executive autonomy – have enjoyed excessive influence over military doctrine. Even today the German core executive deliberately attempts to block lesson-learning on conscription and COIN doctrine under ISAF. This has reduced the effectiveness of the *Bundeswehr* in meeting the challenge of 'Three Block Warfare', particularly at the higher-end of the conflict spectrum. Nevertheless, as neoclassical-realism suggests, these domestic factors emerge only as intervening variables. As the pressure for Germany to play a more active global military role in conflict across the conflict spectrum has grown, so the *Bundeswehr* is gradually moving towards the capabilities and doctrine that will allow it to undertake COIN and 'Three Block Warfare'. Germany has taken important steps in the acquisition of NEC capabilities and in the development of thinking on NetOpFue and EBAO. Convergence is also evidenced by the gradually-waning influence of 'non-offensive' ideas within the *Bundeswehr* and the recognition of the need for greater emphasis on the development of a 'warrior ethos' and 'character/resilience' as core qualities of the land forces. Other, more long-standing elements of German doctrine, such as *innere Fuehrung* and *Auftragstaktik*, which have proved appropriate to the challenges posed by 'Three Block Warfare', have prevailed. The capacity of the *Bundeswehr* to adapt to the contemporary operational environment will also be reinforced by the ongoing reforms to the German process of *Einsatzauswertung* and the increasingly prominent role of the BTC and Operational Command within the *Bundeswehr*.

The contradictory imperatives of structural realism and European defence cooperation

The study also allows us to draw some tentative conclusions about the potential scope of European security and defence cooperation. As a model of military best practice has emerged and European states, subject to largely similar systemic pressures – particularly the threat of abandonment and entrapment by the US – have begun to converge around a common selective emulation of the RMA, so the incentives for cross-national cooperation have increased.

In her account of post-Cold War European Defence Cooperation, Matlary (2009: 79) notes 'realist power balancing appears to be very far from political realities in Europe'. This paints, however, a rather uni-dimensional picture of the possible responses to a uni-polar international system (Paul, 2004: 1–17). In focusing on refuting the 'soft balancing' thesis Matlary (2009: 77–9) sets up Realism as something of a 'straw man'. Realist thought has much to say about the scope and form of European defence cooperation and cannot be jettisoned so easily. Indeed, the study highlights that it is exaggerated to claim, as Howorth (2004: 230) does, that 'Neorealism would suggest that the ESDP project was always fatally flawed.' Chapter 2 demonstrates how structural imperatives – the convergence of European states around 'reformed bandwagoning' on US power and emergence of a model of military best practice (NEC, EBAO embedded with the Comprehensive Approach) – have provided the impetus for a wide range of joint procurement projects and force generation initiatives. The emergence of ESDP does not, therefore, represent the emergence of a 'European strategic culture', but the conformity of European states to the powerful socialisation pressures invoked by the balance of power and threat. The current economic crisis may also provide a further, though very much secondary, incentive for the pooling of capabilities under the auspices of ESDP.

Whilst not fatal, a significant flaw exists, nevertheless, in the logic underpinning ESDP. The Alliance Security Dilemma forms an important countervailing systemic pressure impacting on the scope and depth of cooperation in defence policy (Snyder, 1984: 461–95). Policy-makers must balance two contradictory imperatives: the gains that can be accrued from cross-national capability procurement and the risks associated with a decrease in national strategic autonomy. Dependence on the military capabilities of the US through NATO is unavoidable in a uni-polar world and a risk worth taking to deal with common foes. However, dependence on other geographically-proximate secondary states of equal relative power runs the risk of placing one's national strategic autonomy in jeopardy and a loss in relative power to close potential competitors, should they fail to deliver on their promises. The potential loss of national defence industrial capacity in key strategic areas also heightens the risks associated with such projects.

Consequently, the avoidance of duplication through comprehensive national specialisation in military capabilities and a shift from intergovernmental cooperation to supranational integration under ESDP is unlikely to occur, as policy-makers seek to balance the potential risks and gains of cooperation in defence. Given the uncertainty that exists even within Alliances, a level of duplication is far from 'unnecessary' (Matlary, 2009: 179); it is instead a logical and rational strategy. The main culprit for the slow progress on ESDP and differentiation between European states cannot, therefore, be found through an analysis of domestic factors (Matlary, 2009: 79). Domestic factors, in the guise of material power relations, emerge as important intervening variables in determining the differentiated temporality of cooperation through NATO and ESDP and bi-pluri-lateral capability procurement and force generation initiatives. It is, however, in the competitive and uncertain nature of the international system where the greatest impediments to European defence integration lie.

The Alliance Security Dilemma is magnified for the states at Europe's Eastern borders, which are particularly sensitive to the threat posed by a resurgent Russia. The sensitivity of such states to Russian power has been enhanced by the invasion of Georgia in the summer of 2008. Furthermore, recent Russian military reforms are focused on the development of networked, precision-strike capabilities that will endow it with an enhanced expeditionary power projection capacity in its geopolitical neighbourhood (BBC, 2009b).

Exposure to Russian power creates a predicament for CEE states. On the one hand, the Alliance Security Dilemma suggests that these states should retain a strong capacity for territorial defence. To rely only on the US security guarantee would be folly – indeed, history is replete with examples of the capricious nature of military alliances, not least for CEE states. On the other hand, these states are aware that defending their borders alone will be a tall order. Hence a resurgent Russia also incentivises burden-sharing by CEE states in order to prove their worth as Alliance partners by contributing forces to its expeditionary crisis-management operations.

This quandary is pertinently demonstrated by the Open Letter to the Obama Administration penned by former CEE policy-makers and intellectuals on 15 July 2009: 'NATO must reconfirm its core function of collective defence even while we adapt to the new threats of the 21st century. A key factor in our ability to participate in NATO's expeditionary operations overseas is the belief that we are safe at home.'[4] Matlary (2009: 183) suggests that 'only a military that will never be used can continue an old-fashioned mobilisation defence', citing Finland as a key example of 'Cold War thinking'. This is an argument that is based on the assumption that the contemporary security environment necessitates a focus solely on expeditionary crisis-management by all European states. Such a perspective neglects the variance in external vulnerability in Europe, particularly to Russian power and the unacceptable risk of a dramatic loss in relative power that is associated with failing to prepare for the unexpected.

The invocation of culture, nationalism, ideology and exploitation of public vulnerability on behalf of internal and external balancing

A systematic examination of the impact of nationalism and ideology was beyond the scope of this book. The study focuses instead on the concept of 'culture' that encompasses a number of the core features of nationalism and ideology. The book provides strong evidence of the role of the core executive as the 'gatekeeper' of culture and identity formation in the sphere of defence and security policy. Culture emerges as a malleable tool that is used selectively in the process of both internal and external balancing. Two particularly striking examples of the selective and paradoxical use of culture emerged: German security culture and French Gaullist ideology.

German historical memory and identity was selectively invoked by successive policy leaders within the core executive in an ever-more 'hollowed-out' form to frame the increasingly militarised global role of the *Bundeswehr* and the process of reformed bandwagoning on US power. Yet German security culture was concurrently employed in the temporal management of reform under conditions of low executive autonomy and used to justify the retention of territorial defence as the core objective of German defence policy until 2003. It continues to be utilised to legitimate policy stasis on the issue of conscription. The Federal system does, however, place constraints on the capacity of the core executive to use culture as a resource, by increasing the sensitivity of policy leaders to public opinion. These constraints incentivise a salami-slicing approach to changes to defence policy, particularly when conflict (such as the ISAF mission) is not associated with a sense of immediate threat.

In France, Gaullist ideology was invoked to legitimate processes that contravened its core tenets. Whilst the framing of allied cooperation through ESDP from 1994 onwards contravened the principle of national strategic autonomy that lay at the heart of Gaullism, the Europeanisation agenda first outlined by Balladur overlapped, nevertheless, with another key tenet of Gaullist ideology: the retention of independence from US hegemony. ESDP was also framed as the dissemination of Republican principles at the European level: as the 'Europeanisation of French Exceptionalism'. The high-level of executive autonomy in defence allowed Sarkozy room for manoeuvre in redefining the institutional forums of French defence policy. Gaullism was, therefore, invoked in a highly 'hollowed-out' form to justify France's reintegration into NATO's military command structures as part of the process of attaining public support for reformed bandwagoning on US power and marginalising parliamentary opposition. In contrast to France and Germany where culture was a more difficult tool to employ or required significant reshaping by policy leaders, the embedded policy narratives in Britain that had been generated as part of responding to post-World War Two security challenges proved to be more readily deployable tools.

Although we must look to structure (executive autonomy) rather than agency as the root-cause unit-level variable that provides the incentive for the promotion of short-medium term temporal lag with systemic imperatives, this does not fully negate the impact of specific instances of domestic reform management in determining patterns of change and continuity in military policy (Rynning, 2001–2: 114). A focus on the ability of policy leaders to successfully manage the three aspects of change – strategic innovation, institutional protection and allied cooperation – is certainly a significant factor in determining the temporality of military reform. This is most evident in Germany, from the mid-late 1990s onwards, as the inadequacies of a conscript *Bundeswehr* oriented towards territorial defence became increasingly evident (Dyson, 2007: 187–91). The ability of Rühe, Scharping and Struck to control the flow of ideas and learning within the Defence Ministry, policy subsystem and at the macropolitical level had an important impact upon the success of the promotion of 'policy "stasis"'.

The study suggests, therefore, important implications for theories of Securitisation and cultural approaches to defence and security. The analysis presented in this book confirms Securitisation theory's conception of defence policy as an 'exceptional realm'. It also highlights the capacity of figures within the core executive to refashion culture. This does not, however, equate to a strong role for agency and form a validation of the internalist 'Derridian' take on securitisation that emphasises the performative power of the speech act. Neither does it validate the highly 'externalist' account of securitisation offered by the concept of strategic culture. The analysis of the detail of strategic leadership presented in the book sheds doubt upon the utility of culturalist approaches as stand-alone explanations of policy change by drawing attention to the selective use of 'strategic culture' by policy leaders. It highlights how 'culture' is not so much a cause of action as instrumental and a tool in the domestic political and temporal management of military reform (Johnston, 1995: 39–41; Klein, 1988: 136).

The 'securitisation' of issues takes place as a consequence of a combination of material forces, both at the international and domestic levels: the balance of power and threat (the intensity of the security dilemma) combined with the constraints and opportunities offered by domestic material power relations (executive autonomy). Buffeted by these forces, politicians within the core executive deploy culture to frame either the temporal management of defence reform or a more timely adaptation to systemic pressures.

There is, however, another potent weapon that is used in the maximisation of state power: the exploitation of public vulnerability. As highlighted in Chapters 4–6, after the attacks of September 11 'public vulnerability' to direct attack – by terrorists or 'rogue states' equipped with nuclear weapons – has formed an important tool that policy leaders in France, Germany and in particular the UK, have been adept at exploiting when drawing resources from society on behalf of convergence with the imperatives of the international security environment. This has formed an important mechanism in mobilising and sustaining public support behind the global deployment of troops in long-term expeditionary missions like ISAF and the attack on Iraq, which come at significant cost, both in lives and material. As Chomsky and Raj (2002: 189) note: 'The US-led war against Iraq has been a propaganda war. Politicians and Generals alike realise that securing the home front is a critical element in fighting wars.'

The open-ended nature of 'wars amongst the people' means that the skill of actors within the core executive to exploit public vulnerability, ideology, nationalism and culture will emerge as an increasingly vital factor in the conduct of successful military campaigns. Hence agency may, over time, develop into an increasingly important variable determining state power.[5] As outlined by General Sir Richard Dannatt in the Future Land Operational Concept of November 2008: 'The development and delivery of persuasive strategic narratives will be essential elements of any successful discretionary operation.'[6] Furthermore, as the current example of the Brown Government in the UK demonstrates, it is important to note the limitations imposed on the capacity of unitary states to engage head-on with such sensitive issues in the context of the reduced executive autonomy that derives from looming general elections.

The limitations of the book and avenues for future research

Although neoclassical realism has emerged as a theory of great utility in shedding light on a number of the key systemic and domestic-level dynamics determining the content and timing of European defence reforms, it leaves other areas in relative shade. Further research is required on the organisation of military input into defence planning and the relationship between civilian and military figures in the development of doctrine, capability procurement, force postures and CD&E. The limitations of a single monograph have restricted the extent to which the book has been able to explore this issue in the depth it deserves. More focused, in-depth, single case study research is required on the decision-making processes which have underpinned major capability procurement projects, doctrinal developments and on the impact of the recent reforms which have taken place to the 'lessons learned' processes in Britain, France and Germany.

The constraints imposed by a single monograph have also curtailed the extent to which the book has been able to undertake a systematic examination of the instrumental use of ideology and nationalism across all three case studies. Another key area for future scholarship is, therefore, thorough and nuanced single case studies of the instrumental use of ideology and nationalism by political elites in Europe. In particular, further work is needed to explore the interplay between variance in external vulnerability and the constraints imposed by electoral cycles on the ability of the core executive to deploy culture as a resource on behalf of internal and external balancing. Such studies would go a long way to providing a much more accurate and detailed picture of differentiation in the objectives, institutional forums, instruments and temporality of the defence policies of European states.

Notes

Introduction

1 The book disaggregates temporality according to the three categories outlined by Schedler and Santiso (1998): temporal location (when reform takes place); sequence (in what order reform is enacted) and pace (the speed at which reform takes place).

2 See Barnathan (2006); Howorth (2007); Hunter and Farley (2002); Jones (2007); Hyde-Price (2007); Meyer (2006); Posen (2004, 2006); Riecker (2005) and Sloan (2005).

3 See also Riecker (2005) on the Europeanisation of Security Identities in Nordic States; Miskimmon (2007) on the Europeanisation of German Foreign and Security Policy and Dover (2007) on the Europeanisation of British Defence Policy.

4 On 'international structure' and ESDP, see also the valuable contributions of Barry Posen (2004) and (2006) and Barnathan (2006). It is important to recognise the excellent empirical contributions made by the edited volumes of Gänzle and Sens (2007) and Howorth and Keeler (2003), the works of Hunter and Farley (2002), Salmon and Shepherd (2003), and Sloan (2005) to understanding the development of ESDP and its relationship to the Atlantic Alliance, but which do not adopt a fixed theoretical position.

5 There are several important texts analysing the processes and outcomes of national military reform processes, but no book that systematically and rigorously compares and contrasts reforms in the three major European NATO/EU states (Britain, France and Germany) since 1990. The majority of studies on Germany focus on the Federal Republic as a testing ground for cultural and historical institutionalist (path dependency) approaches to military change. These include Berger (1998); Dalgaard-Nielsen (2006); Duffield (1998) and Longhurst (2004). Whilst Utley (2000) and Gregory (2000) provide important empirical analyses of French military reforms, Rynning (2001) highlights the utility of neoclassical realism in understanding military change in France from 1958–2000, emphasising the important intervening role played by instances of policy leadership in managing processes of policy change. This study does not deny that the quality of leadership can be an important variable, however, it builds upon Rynning's argument by demonstrating the centrality of 'executive autonomy' in conditioning the *ability and willingness* of policy-makers within the core executive to provide strategic leadership on behalf of systemic power shifts. The work also builds upon work of Adams and Ben-Ari (2006) who provide a detailed account of the capability gaps within the Atlantic Alliance. The book does so by analysing the contributions of neorealist, neoclassical realist and cultural approaches to understanding the process of European military reforms and their selective emulation of the US-led RMA.

6 On the decline of realist analyses in British and European IR scholarship see Mearsheimer (2005): 139. On neoclassical realism see (Rose, 1998). See also Charles Glasner (1994–5) on the potential for the construction of multilevel analyses guided by structural realist theory.

7 For more on neoclassical realism and executive autonomy please see Chapter 3.

8 J. Glenn et al (eds) (2004) test the explanatory power of neorealism and strategic culture in understanding military change across a global range of contemporary (post-Cold War) case studies, whilst Farrell and Terriff (2002) test the utility of cultural and neorealist approaches by analysing a set of case studies from a variety of historical periods. Forster (2006) also provides important empirical account of the transformations that have taken place in European militaries since the end of the Cold War, but does not test cultural and realist accounts in a systematic manner or seek to develop a theory of military convergence, innovation and emulation, focusing instead on issues of armed forces-society relations. This book will also critically engage with the work of Elizabeth Kier (1997), who emphasises the role of organisational culture as an intervening variable between civilian decisions and military doctrine in her study of interwar British and French military reforms.

9 See Table 2.6.

10 A policy subsystem refers to a 'group of people and or organisations interacting regularly over periods of a decade or more to influence policy formulation and implementation within a given policy area/domain' (Sabatier and Jenkins-Smith, 1999: 135).

11 According to Dalgaard-Nielsen (2006: 13) central beliefs are 'abstract beliefs and basic assumptions about the international system...rarely questioned and stable'; 'operational beliefs' relate to the 'efficacy of different policy instruments and strategies', whilst 'peripheral beliefs' are 'more transient and concern concrete issues and objects'. Longhurst (2004: 17) terms the three layers of beliefs of which strategic culture are composed 'foundational elements', 'security policy standpoints' and 'regulatory practices', whilst Sabatier and Jenkins-Smith (1999: 133) also argues that advocacy coalitions are structured by three layers of beliefs: 'deep core', 'policy core' and 'secondary aspects'.

12 Barry Posen (2006: 156) classifies Britain, France and Germany as second-rank, 'consequential' states, of similar relative material power, that combined with their similar geographical location leads to a comparable level of 'external vulnerability' (Taliaferro, 2006: 467).

13 This approach contrasts to *Innenpolitik* perspectives, which attach causal weight to domestic politics in driving foreign and defence policy (Hobson, 1938; Kehr, 1973; Snyder, 1991; Zakaria, 1991: 180–1).

14 Peter Hall defines three levels of policy change: 'first-order change' in which the settings of policy instruments are changed, while the overall goals and instruments of policy remain constant; 'second-order change' in which both the instruments and settings of policy are altered, while the goals of policy remain unchanged and finally 'third-order change', in which all three components of policy (settings, instruments and the hierarchy of goals) are transformed (Hall, 1993: 278–9).

15 Although, as the analysis will demonstrate, the opacity of systemic imperatives emerges as an important additional factor determining the initial short-term temporal lag between systemic power shifts and military reform in states with high levels of executive autonomy (Morgenthau, 1966: 154; Rose, 1998: 153).

Chapter 1

1 As Waltz (1979: 124) recognises, military convergence will not 'proceed to the point where competitors become identical'.

2 It is important to note that despite French withdrawal from NATO's integrated military commands the Ailleret-Lemnitzer and Valentin-Feber Accords of

1966–7 outlined far-reaching French cooperation with NATO states in the context of European conflict (Gregory, 2000a: 15; Menon, 1995: 19).

3   On the core post-Cold War security threats identified by EU and NATO member states, see 'A Secure Europe in a Better World: European Security Strategy', Brussels, 12 December 2003, 1–5; 'Riga Summit: A Reader's Guide', Brussels: NATO, 6 July 2007 4; see also Cottey (2008: 73) and Hyde-Price (2007: 112). Although as discussed in Chapter 3, the objectivity of these security threats is challenged by the literatures on securitisation and strategic culture. On securitisation, see Balzacq (2005): 171–205; Buzan et al (1998); Stritzel (2007: 357–83). On strategic culture and the subjective and nationally-specific normative and discursive processes which determine whether issues are identified as security threats, national defence policy objectives, appropriate policy instruments, and capability investment, see Dalgaard-Nielsen (2006), Johnston (1995) and Longhurst (2004).

4   A frequently-cited definition of the RMA is provided by Krepinevic (1994: 30) 'It is what occurs when the application of new technologies into a significant number of military systems combines with innovative operational concepts and organisational adaptation in a way that fundamentally alters the character and conduct of conflict. It does so by producing a dramatic increase – often an order of magnitude or greater – in the combat potential or military effectiveness of armed forces.' For further definitions see Cohen (2004: 395).

5   As Boot (2006: 325–7) recognises, the Vietnam War spurred the development of a range of new technologies including radiation-seeking missiles, electronic jamming equipment, thermal and electro-optical sensors and satellite navigation. The Vietnam conflict also witnessed the deployment of the first laser-guided bomb (the Paveway) by the US.

6   The idea of revolutionary changes in military affairs has been invoked on several occasions throughout history, for example upon the advent of gunpowder and professional standing armies in Europe during the 16–18th centuries; during the industrialisation of warfare in the early mid-20th century and following the development of nuclear weapons at the end of WW2.

7   Marshall enjoyed a close relationship with Defence Secretary Donald Rumsfeld (2000–06) and other prominent figures within the administration of George W. Bush, such as Vice-President Dick Cheney and Deputy Secretary of Defence, Paul Wolfowitz.

8   A 'stand-off' advantage is one that allows the projection of military force without the threat of being targeted by an opponent's defence system.

9   Admiral William Owens argued that the RMA coheres around three major technological developments: Intelligence Collection, Surveillance and Reconnaissance (ISR); Command, Control, Communication, Computer and Intelligence Analysis (C4I) and Precision Guided Munitions and Stand-Off Weapons (PGM) (Bratton, 2002: 88).

10 'Transformation Planning Guidance' (TPG), US Department of Defense, 2003, p. 5.

11 Rapid decisive operations were defined by General William F. Kernan, Commander in Chief of the US Joint Force Command, as: 'a rapid series of relentless strikes by a full-spectrum joint force operating in an inter-agency context to defeat a regional power' (Stone, 2004: 418).

12 Metz (2006: 4) cites a Pentagon study that stated: 'our supremacy will rapidly diminish over time if we do not continue to enhance our military prowess'. See also TPG, 2003, p. 5.

13 See also: TPG, 2003, p. 3.

14 See Neal (2003) for a detailed discussion of the concept of 'transformation' and its various definitions.

15 As Farrell (2008: 22) highlights, EBO is a revival of WWII and interwar American Air Power Theory, developed by the Air Corps Tactical School, elucidated in the US Air Army Corps Air War Planning Document 1 of 1941 and put into practice in US attempts to disrupt the German war economy by destroying key industrial targets. Ho (2005: 170–1) traces the roots of EBO back to Sun Tzu, Carl von Clausewitz, Liddell Hart and Giulio Douhet. Aaron Frank (2004: 70–1) also notes how EBO builds upon theories of 'strategic manipulation', notably, Hans Delbrueck's 'strategy of exhaustion' involving the application of precise, focused and limited force against key instruments of national power: economic, political and informational, as well as military targets, in order to manipulate an enemy's strategic calculations.

16 'The capabilities-based model focuses more on how an adversary might fight rather than specifically whom the adversary might be or where a war might occur. It recognises that it is not enough to plan for conventional war in distant theatres. Instead the US must identify the capabilities required to deter and defeat adversaries who will rely on surprise, deception and asymmetric warfare to achieve their objectives.' 2001 'Quadrennial Defense Review' (QDR), US Department of Defense, Preface, iv.

17 *Ibid*, p. 30.

18 On the pillars of transformation, see *Ibid*, p. 32.

19 As Kagan (2006: 285) highlights, the OFT was instructed to 'evaluate the transformation efforts of the military Departments and promote synergy by recommending steps to integrate ongoing transformation activities'.

20 The Afghan Model is an 'indirect' approach to counterinsurgency, applied both in Afghanistan and Iraq, in which indigenous forces were backed up by US advisors, Special Operations Forces and supported by precision air-strikes in the hope of minimising cost and risk to US forces.

21 TPG, 2003, p. 3.

22 *Ibid*, p. 5.

23 *Ibid*, p. 3.

24 *Ibid*, p. 1.

25 'Army Transformation Roadmap', Department of the Army, 2004, p. 13, quoted in Metz (2006: 16).

26 It is important to note, however, that the emphasis on 'jointness' has its roots in the reforms to US command structures outlined by the Goldwater-Nichols Defence Reorganisation Act of 1986 that built upon the perceived lessons of the 1980 Iran hostage rescue operation and 1983 invasion of Grenada. The Act established the Chairman of the Joint Chiefs of Staff (with a staff comprising of over 1,000 officers) as the main advisor to the President and Defence Secretary and streamlined the chain of command through the establishment of six geographically-defined commands, each under the authority of a single General. In 2002 these commands were joined by the Joint Forces Command (that prepares forces for conflict through joint concept development and experimentation; joint training; joint capabilities development and acting as a joint service provider); the Strategic Command (that acts as the military's command and control centre responsible for command and control, communications, surveillance, intelligence and reconnaissance (C3ISR)); the Transportation Command (responsible for fulfilling the logistical requirements of the armed

forces) and the Northern Command for Homeland Defence. See Boot (2006: 334) and Kagan (2006: 162).

27   According to the US Department of Defence *Dictionary of Military and Associated Terms* NCW is defined as: 'an information superiority-enabled concept of operations that generates increased combat power by networking sensors, decision-makers, and shooters to achieve shared awareness, increased speed of command, higher tempo of operations, greater lethality, increased survivability, and a degree of self-synchronisation. In essence, NCW translate information superiority into combat power by effectively linking knowledgeable entities in the battlespace' (Reynolds, 2006: 453–4).

28   Frank (2004: 78) defines operational effects as those which 'hinder the adversary's ability to conduct military operations and perform organisational processes for accomplishing assigned tasks' and defines strategic effects as those which 'target the adversary's political feedback mechanisms, and compel its leadership to ultimately sue for peace by forcing the adversary to reexamine relations between desired ends and available means'.

29   Farrell (2008: 793) defines three forms of strategic effect. 'First-order' effects are those effects 'directly caused by an activity' whilst second- and third-order effects are the extended effects of an activity and reflect the distance of an effect from the original activity.

30   EBO were defined by the 2002 US Joint Forces Command 'Rapid Decisive Operations' White Paper as 'a process for attaining a desired strategic outcome or "effect" on the enemy through the synergistic, multiplicative and cumulative application of the full range of military and other national capabilities at the tactical, operational and strategic levels' (Echevarria, 2002: 131).

31   The concept of DBK was first elucidated by Admiral William Owens in 1995; see Kagan (2006: 212). Jordan et al (2008: 110) define DBK as: 'a decisive information advantage that would allow the US to maneuver and apply massive force, rapidly and with greater precision, while denying the enemy the possibility to do so'.

32   DoD Directive 3000.05 of 28 November 2005 defines stability missions as 'a core US military mission' to be given 'priority comparable to combat operations' and forms an important turning point in the transformation process. See also the 2005 National Security Strategy (pp. 2–3).

33   Dixon (2009: 356) defines COIN as embodying three key characteristics: 'A war waged by governments against a non-state actor; the aim of counterinsurgents is to remove the government or an occupation; counterinsurgency may be distinguished from counterterrorism by the substantial popular support for counterinsurgents.'

34   The concept of operational art is defined by Milan Vego (2000: 1) as: 'to soundly sequence and synchronise, or, simply stated, to orchestrate the deployment of military forces and nonmilitary sources of power to accomplish strategic or operational objectives in a given theater'.

35   For example the Global Information Grid, integrating US military and Department of Defence into a single super-network that costs $20 billion and will be fully-developed by 2020 (Reynolds, 2006: 450).

36   Williams (2001: 50) also highlights how the Kosovo Conflict illuminated the potential vulnerability of Command and Control Warfare to attack from low-cost electronics and weapons systems. As Gray (2006: 46) states: 'A defence transformation will flatter to deceive if the transformed military instrument performs well against an incompetent or severely disadvantaged enemy.'

37   Ho (2005: 177–8) highlights how the operational dimensions of EBO and network-centric warfare were tested only to a limited extent in Operation Iraqi Freedom

as the 4th Infantry Division – at that time, the most networked division in the US military – was not employed. On the development of US targeting models for EBO see Ho (2005: 177–8) and Frank (2004).

38 Please see below for a more detailed discussion and definition of 'Mission Command'.

39 See, in particular, the arguments of Gray (2002) and Smith (2006).

40 In seeking to build a consensus definition of 'small wars' Hoffman (2005: 915) draws upon the definitions offered by Charles E. Calwell and Colin Gray, describing them as 'campaigns in which at least one side of the conflict does not employ regular forces as its principle force and does not fight conventionally'. See Hoffman (2005: 915–16) for a more fulsome discussion of the various categories of conflict that are encompassed under the term 'small wars'.

41 See Malkasian (2008) for an in-depth account of the advantages of a 'clear-hold-build' approach, involving large numbers of ground troops in Iraq. See also Biddle (2005/6: 161–76) and Anders et al (2005/6) for a detailed discussion of the factors that determine the success of an 'indirect' approach to counterinsurgency. See also 2006 QDR, pp. 10–11.

42 Lebovic (2008: 11–21) highlights a set of factors which combine to limit the effectiveness of US military force: The nature of military power as asymmetric endowing the 'weaker' side with considerable advantages; the incomplete and uneven military dominance enjoyed by the US; constraints on the ability of the US to project power inland; the compromises necessary to project global power; dependence upon other governments for military support; the inflexible and exhaustible nature of US military power and finally, the 'inert' nature of power.

43 These lessons also dovetailed with those learned form the last major conflict in which the US was involved (Vietnam) and the consequent commitment within the US military and civilian leadership to the decisive defeat of its adversaries (Stone, 2004: 417).

44 As President Bush stated in December 2001, following the initial stage of Operation Enduring Freedom: 'The conflict in Afghanistan has taught us more about future conflict than a decade of blue-ribbon panels and think tank symposiums…When all of our military can locate and track moving targets – with surveillance from space – warfare will truly be revolutionised' (Reynolds, 2006: 456).

45 The Outgoing Commander of NATO's International Security and Assistance Force (ISAF), US General Dan McNeil (February 2007–June 2008) noted that should counterinsurgency guidelines be strictly followed, NATO would require 400,000 ground troops in order to stabilise Afghanistan. 'The Taliban Kills More Civilians Than NATO', *Spiegel International*, 24 September 2007.

46 'Future warriors will be as proficient in irregular operations including counter-insurgency and stabilisation as they are today in high-intensity combat', 2006 QDR, pp. 42–3.

47 Corum (2007: 131) cites a senior US Army Commander in Iraq, Major General Chiarelli, who stated in 2005: 'Our traditional training model, still shuddering from the echo of our Cold War mentality, has infused our organisation to think only in kinetic terms.'

48 General Krulak argued that the development of smaller, more flexible units would require Non-Commissioned Officers (NCOs) with a more developed skill-set and tactical, operational and strategic awareness (Terriff, 2007: 148–9). The 'strategic corporal' should demonstrate 'independence, maturity, restraint and judgement at the lower levels of hierarchy' (Ho, 2005: 182–3).

49   General Petraeus would later replace General George Casey as Commanding General of the Multi-National Force in Iraq, serving from 10 February 2007 to 16 September 2008.

50   The Centre for Lessons Learned at Forth Leavenworth, Training and Doctrine Command (TRADOC) was quick to address the tactical lessons of the US experience in Iraq and integrate these improvements into FM 3-07.22 (Corum, 2007: 131–2).

51   'FM 3-24 Joint Army/Marines Counter-Insurgency Doctrine Field Manual' (FM 3-24), Department of the Army, 2006, pts. 3-20–3-51.

52   FM 3-24; pt. 7–6.

53   FM 3-24 pts. E1, 23–24; 1, 21–23. 'Western militaries too often neglect the study of insurgency. The falsely believe that armies trained to win conventional wars are prepared to win small, unconventional ones.' FM 3-24, pt. ix.

54   FM 3-24, pt. 1–22.

55   FM 3-24, pt. 1–148.

56   Fm 3-24, pt. 1–153.

57   FM 3-24, pt. E3, 1–128.

58   'The Hobbled Hegemon', *The Economist*, June 27, 2007.

59   FM 3-24, pt. 2–40.

60   FM 3-24, pts. 2–26–38. Nora Bensahel (2006) and Donald Dreschler (2005) highlight how 'dysfunctional inter-agency processes' were a key factor in the problems faced by US in post-conflict reconstruction in Iraq.

61   The troop increases were officially much larger: an increase of the Army by 65,000 and the Marines by 27,000. However, increases were in reality smaller as the Army and Marines had already exceeded the limits set in the 1997 QDR (482,000 and 175,000 respectively) (Conetta, 2007: 3). Army and Marine troop numbers have also been boosted through the 'Integrated Global Presence and Basing Strategy' that frees up 60,000 Army and Marine personnel for deployment and DoD's 'business transformation' that has increased the number of troops available for active deployment by 15,000.

62   See: 'The Significance of Culture to the Military', Joint Doctrine Note 01/09, UK Ministry of Defence, 2009, pt. 5b10.

63   In particular, to assist with the 'shift from major combat operations, to multiple, irregular, asymmetric operations'. For a comprehensive list of the major changes in emphasis, see: 'QDR', 2006, preface vi–vii.

64   'Commander's Appreciation and Campaign Design', Pamphlet 525-5-500, TRADOC, Virginia, US, January 2008, pt. 1.1.

65   *Ibid*, pt. 1.1d.

66   FM 3-24, pt. 2–57.

67   Neal (2003: 81) notes that the costs of the top five most expensive weapons systems in the US increased in cost from $281 billion to $512 billion between 2001 and 2006.

68   The 1993 Statement on Defence Estimates prioritised territorial and alliance defence as the core objective of the armed forces. 'Out of area' crisis-reaction/prevention and humanitarian missions in support of the UN were afforded the lowest priority (Dorman, 2001: 192).

69   Defence Diplomacy is defined by Colin McInnes (1998: 836–7) as 'activities falling short of military operations designed to prevent or diffuse crises'. Defence diplomacy formalised the role of the military in conflict prevention and management (Dorman, 2006: 154). The SDR outlined three main Defence Diplomacy missions: arms control, outreach (involving visits, military assistance, joint exer-

cises and training programmes, in East Central Europe) and finally, a similar set of activities in other areas of the globe.

70 'Strategic Defence Review', UK Ministry of Defence, 1998, p. 174.

71 SDR, 1998, p. 178.

72 'The Comprehensive Approach', UK Ministry of Defence, 2006, pt. 102.

73 *Ibid.*

74 'Delivering Security in a Changing World: Defence White Paper', UK Ministry of Defence, 2003, pt. 1.5.

75 'NEC has emerged as the UK's term for the capability enhancement achieved through the effective linkage of platforms and people through a network. It replaces the expression Network Centric Capability used in the SDR New Chapter.' 'Delivering Security in a Changing World', 2003, pt. 1.4, fn.2.

76 'Delivering Security in a Changing World: Future Capabilities', UK Ministry of Defence, 2004, pts. 2.1–2.3. See also 'Network Enabled Capability', JSP 777, edn. 1, UK Ministry of Defence, p. 10.

77 Interviews, DCDC, Shrivenham, 18 November 2009.

78 The British Defence Doctrine (2008) and 'The Comprehensive Approach' (2008) defines the Comprehensive Approach as embodying four core aspects: the proactive engagement of actors across Whitehall, preferably preceding a crisis; the development of a shared common baseline of understanding on the basis of which common risk assessments, judgements and decisions can be made; outcome-based thinking (basing planning and activity on the extent of progress towards the government's strategic objectives) and collaborative working (including increased collaboration, trust and transparency supported by more efficient systems of data management). See 'British Defence Doctrine', UK Ministry of Defence, 2008, pt. 137, 'Campaigning', JDP 01, Second Edition, UK Ministry of Defence, 2008, pts. 237–8 and 'The Comprehensive Approach', Joint Discussion Note, 4/05, UK Ministry of Defence, 2006, pt. 112.

79 On centrality of the 'comprehensive approach' to future land operations see: 'Future Land Operational Concept', Development, Concepts and Doctrine Centre, UK Ministry of Defence, 2008, pt. 153. On the Comprehensive Approach, see also: 'Campaigning', 2008, pt. 229; 'The Comprehensive Approach', 2006 and 'Security and Stabilisation: The Military Contribution', Joint Doctrine Publication 3–40, UK Ministry of Defence, 2009, pt. 1.

80 'Delivering Security in a Changing World', 2003, pt. 3.4. On the delivery of non-kinetic effects, see 'Incorporating and Extending the UK Military Effects Based Approach Joint Doctrine', 7/06, Development Concepts and Doctrine Centre, Shrivenham, UK Ministry of Defence, September 2006. See also 'The Comprehensive Approach', 2006, pt. 116.

81 'British Defence Doctrine', 2008, pt. 201.

82 A fulsome definition of Mission Command is provided in 'British Defence Doctrine', 2008, pt. 508: 'The fundamental guiding principle is the absolute responsibility to act, or, in certain circumstances to decide not to act, within the framework of a superior commander's intent. This approach requires a style of command that promotes decentralised command, freedom and speed of action and initiative, but which is responsive to superior delegation when the subordinate overreaches himself'. See also 'Army Doctrine Publication' (ADP), Volume 2 Command, Army Code 71564 UK Ministry of Defence, 1995, paragraph 0210.

83 See 'British Defence Doctrine, 2008, point 511.

84 On the need to prepare for conflict that can quickly shift from low to high intensity, see 'The Future Land Operational Concept', 2008, pt. 112.

85   The Manoeuvrist Approach is defined British Defence Doctrine (1996) as: 'One in which shattering the enemy's overall cohesion and will to fight, rather than his material, is paramount'. As Sir John Kiszely (1998: 37) notes of the Manoeuvrist Approach: 'it focuses on the deceptive, illusive, scheming adroitness which causes someone to be forced, driven or manipulated out of something'. Whilst the majority of the literature on the Manoeuvrist Approach contrasts the approach to 'Attritional Warfare', it is important to note the arguments of Owen (2008: 67), who posits that rather than in competition, these two forms of warfare should be viewed as complementary: 'The purpose of manoeuvre is to gain a position of relative advantage to an opponent. This advantage may be used to deliver overwhelming violent attrition.'

86   See 'British Defence Doctrine', 2008, pt. 521. This approach to operations was reinforced by post-Cold War missions, particularly at the higher end of the conflict spectrum, which required precisely these attributes (see Chapter 6).

87   See 'British Defence Doctrine', 2008, pts. 205–25.

88   'Network Enabled Capability', p. 3. On the importance of tempo to contemporary military operations across the 'continuum of conflict' and the consequent reinforcement of the utility of Manouever Warfare and Mission Command, see Kiszely (1999: 37–41) and Chapter 6.

89   These capabilities built upon improvements in precision-guided munitions since the SDR which included the acquisition of the Storm Shadow (SCALP EG cruise missile), Brimstone (anti-tank missile) and Maverick (air-surface tactical missile) Precision Guided Missiles. The Tornado F3 had also been equipped with medium (AMRAAM) and short-range missiles (ASRAAM).

90   These acquisitions built upon the maritime capabilities acquired following the SDR which included the development of two amphibious assault ships, the HMS Albion and HMS Bulwark, which entered into service in 2003. Delivering Security in a Changing World: Future Capabilities also outlined the acquisition of eight new Type 45 destroyers (to be fitted with the Principal Anti-Air Missile System and the capacity to be fitted with a land-attack missile capability) though eventually, only six were ordered.

91   'Delivering Security in a Changing World: Future Capabilities', 2004, pts. 2.11–2.18. The restructuring of the Army involved changing a Challenger 2 regiment to an armoured reconnaissance regiment; the creation of three light armoured squadrons in support of FRES and changing three AS90 Batteries to Light Gun in support of the light brigade. See 'Factsheet 2 Future Capabilities: Capability Implications', UK Ministry of Defence, 2004.

92   The Future Land Operational Concept highlights the need to remain interoperable with the US and the capability to deliver two core attributes to coalitions of the willing involving the US: 'A manoeuver capability of some size under a divisional headquarters; and to put boots on the ground until overall campaign success is achieved' (Dannatt, 2008: 57).

93   In 2004 the UK and the US signed a bi-lateral interoperability agreement on Land Battlespace Systems to ensure a 'frequent and structured exchange of information' (Farrell, 2008: 803).

94   'Future Capabilities', 2004, pts. 2–11.

95   See: 'Campaigning', 2008, pt. 110.

96   'Future Capabilities', 2004, pt. 2.3.

97   'Defence Industrial Strategy: Defence White Paper', UK Ministry of Defence, 2005, pt. B8.41.

98   'Delivering Security in a Changing World', 2003, 4.22; 'Defence Industrial Strategy', 2005, B8.34.

99 'Defence Industrial Strategy', 2005, pt. B8.36.
100 *Ibid*, pt. B8.38.
101 *Ibid*, pt. B8.43.
102 *Ibid*, pt. B8.40.
103 'Future Capabilities', 2004, pt. 2.3.
104 'Defence Industrial Strategy', 2005, pt. B8.39.
105 On the imperative that US technological innovation places upon the British to invest in military capabilities and structures ensuring continued interoperability with US forces see: 'Future Land Operational Concept', Development, Concepts and Doctrine Centre, 2008, point 159; see also Dorman (2006: 158).
106 'Conflict and the associated Land Forces response to it will continue to occur across a spectrum of activities, from humanitarian and disaster relief through stabilisation operations to major combat operations.' 'Future Land Operational Concept', 2008, pt. 111.
107 See, for example, 'Campaigning', 2008, pts. 237–8; 410c.
108 See, for example, 'Joint Air Operations: Interim Joint Warfare Publication 3–30', Joint Doctrine and Concepts Centre, UK Ministry of Defence, 2003, pt. 506.
109 'The primary challenge is to fully incorporate the human dimension into the development of NEC.' See, 'Network Enabled Capability', 2005, p. 9. See also 'The Future Land Operational Concept', pt. 159: 'ISTAR will provide situational awareness, but commanders will still require other human factors to deliver situational understanding.' The Future Land Operational Concept also notes that with the increasing importance of the Comprehensive Approach to operations and the swift variance in conflict intensity 'more attention will have to be paid to the coordination, training and operating aspects of environmental seams, with sufficient, integrated, joint and combined inter-agency training opportunities scheduled to improve collective awareness, performance and understanding'. See: 'Future Land Operational Concept', 2008, pt. 157.
110 'Effects Based Operations: Implications of Recent JFCOM Commander's Guidance', DG, DCDC, 24 September 2008.
111 Effects Based Operations: Implications of Recent JFCOM Commander's Guidance', 2008; Interviews, DCDC, Shrivenham, 18 November 2009; Interview, UK Ministry of Defence, London, 20 November 2009.
112 Chapter 3 – Influence: The Central Idea in 'JDP 3–40, Security and Stabilisation: The Military Contribution', pt. 301–2.
113 'Even within individual operations they [the armed forces] will often be faced with several tasks at once,' 'Delivering Security in a Changing World: Defence White Paper', 2003, pt. 4.9. It is, however, noted that 'striking the right balance of capabilities to meet all eight strategic effects will not be easy'. 'Delivering Security in a Changing World: Defence White Paper', 2003, pt. 4.9. See also 'Campaigning', 2008, pt. 120, pt. 125.
114 'British Defence Doctrine', 2008, pt. 403e.
115 'Future Land Operational Concept', 2008, pt. 120.
116 The Army Culture and Language Capability Paper of December 2008 outlines for levels of cultural training: cultural awareness, cultural understand, cultural competence and bespoke. For information on the 'target audiences', see: 'The Significance of Culture to the Military', 2009, pt. 5–1, Annex 5A.
117 'The Significance of Culture to the Military', 2009, pt. 507.
118 The 2004 Defence White Paper did, however, reduce the number of Type-45 Destroyers to be ordered from 12 to six.
119 'Shared Responsibilities: A National Security Strategy for the UK', Institute for Public Policy Research, London, June 2009.

120   As Cornish and Dorman (2009: 259) note: 'Gordon Brown has indicated the defence is not immune from future government cutbacks'. Indeed, the rising costs of key projects (rising at up to 10 per cent), increasing Urgent Operational Requirements expenditure and the £550 million expenditure on service accommodation, raises the possibility that a core equipment programme will face cancellation (Cornish and Dorman, 2009: 260).

121   'Review of Acquisition for the Secretary of State for Defence', 15 October 2009, p. 6.

122   Whilst acknowledging the importance of a 'balanced' military and the need to retain a potential to respond to threats in a uni-lateral manner, the March 2008 National Security Strategy provides no substance on the implications for force posture and capabilities. See: 'The National Security Strategy of the United Kingdom', Cabinet Office, London, 2008, pp. 9, 56.

123   Spending on the nuclear deterrent was cut from 38 billion Francs in 1990 to 19 billion Francs by the late 1990s (Bratton, 2002: 93)

124   During the Gulf War the French were able to mobilise only 14,000 expeditionary troops from an active force of 280,000, in comparison to the 35,000 troops deployed by the British who could only call on a pool of around 140,000 troops (Bratton, 2002: 92).

125   See also 'Manuel D'Emploi des Forces Terrestres En Zone Urbaine', French Army, French Ministry of Defence, 2005, pt. III.7.

126   The PR4GVS4-IP radio set was also introduced to infantry forces in 2004 and permits the simultaneous transmission of voice and data at a rate three times faster than the existing system. The French Army is also equipped with the FELIN system that allows land forces access to map databases, imagery from UAVs and enhances the internal coordination of combat units (Wasielewski, 2004: 19).

127   Knowledge and Anticipation is understood as covering five core areas: intelligence, the knowledge areas of operation, diplomatic action; analysis of future trends (horizon scanning) and information management. The White Paper places a particular emphasis upon the role of intelligence (notably from space based capabilities) in ensuring that commanders and civilian decision-makers are in a position to take informed action. 'The French White Paper on Defence and National Security', French Ministry of Defence, 2008, p. 2.

128   Strengthening the capacity of French public authorities to respond to civil emergencies through communication, information and civil warning systems and close communication between the military, security services and civilian agencies emerge as critical in the protection of the French population.

129   The 2008 DWP outlines how future French military operations are likely to be one of (or a mixture of): civilian operations (humanitarian relief or civil reconstruction); civil-military operations in which military forces provide a secure environment for civilian agencies to operate in support of local authorities and finally high-intensity operations, such as peace enforcement. 'The French White Paper on Defence and National Security', 2008, p. 11.

130   *Ibid*, p. 6.

131   *Ibid*, p. 12.

132   *Ibid*, p. 2.

133   'French White Paper on Defence and National Security', 2008, p. 11. The 'Crisis-Management Concept' (Chapter 1) notes the importance of adapting to the 'non-linear nature of conflict, operations in built up areas, fighting among the people, against an irregular opponent, and the problems of communication and information'. 'Crisis-Management Concept', 2007, Chapter 1.

134 French White Paper on Defence and National Security', 2008, p.11.
135 On the capacity to conduct conflict that can vary rapidly in intensity, see 'Crisis-Management Concept', 2007, pt. 3.2.
136 *Ibid*, Chapter 1.
137 'Winning the Battle Building the Peace: Land Forces in Present and Future Conflicts', FT-01 (ENG), *Centre de Doctrine d'Emploi des Forces*, French Army, French Ministry of Defence, Paris, 2007, pt. 1.1. On the need to rapidly shift operational modes and synchronise effects see: 'Manuel D'Emploi des Forces Terrestres en Zone Urbaine', French Army, French Ministry of Defence, Paris, 2005, pts. III.6–III.8.
138 'Winning the Battle Building the Peace: Land Forces in Present and Future Conflicts', 2007, pt. 1.1.
139 *Ibid*, pts. 1.1–1.2.3.
140 *Ibid*, pt. 2.1.2.
141 *Ibid*, pts. 4.1–4.3.
142 *Ibid, pts*. 1.1–1.2.
143 *Ibid*, pts. 2.2.1–2.2.3.
144 *Ibid*, pts. 3.1.2, 3.2.2, 3.4.
145 The Crisis-Management Concept also outlines the need to attain the correct balance between force protection and the maintenance of contact with the local population, highlighting how this: 'is most often the vital element of the military contribution to the resolution of crises'. 'Crisis-Management Concept', 2007, pts. 4.1, 4.5.
146 The DWP outlines the further development of the high resolution optical satellite programme (MUSIS, also known as Helios) that will be operational from 2015. The DWP also promises investment in Electronic Intelligence Satellites (ELINT) including the deployment of the CERES system by 2015 and a ballistic missile detection system by 2020. See 'French White Paper on Defence and National Security', 2008, p. 3. The focus on space-based assets will be supported by organisational changes, notably the development of a Joint Space Command managed by the Air Force and under the authority of the Chief of Defence Staff. These initiatives will be accompanied by an increase in funding for space applications from 380 million Euros to 740 million Euros. See 'French White Paper on Defence and National Security', 2008, p. 14.
147 $300 billion has been earmarked for investment in new capabilities between 2008 and 2020. This will be financed by the reduction in civilian and military posts by 54,000, combined with an increase in the defence budget at 1 per cent above inflation from 2012.
148 See: 'Manuel D'Emploi De Forces Terrestres en Zone Urbaine', 2005, pt. III.5; see also 'Winning the Battle', pt. 3.2.1.
149 'Winning the Battle', 2007: 2.2.3, 2.3.2, 3.2.1.
150 'Crisis-Management Concept', Defence Staff, CICDE, French Ministry of Defence, 2007, pt. 4.6.
151 'Military operations of the future will increasingly be conducted for and within the population, generally within an urban environment...peace operations are increasingly lethal.' See: 'French White Paper on Defence and National Security', 2008, p. 5. Restructuring was also designed to free up 26 billion Euros over 12 years that could be directed towards capability investment (Breuer, 2006: 213).
152 'French White Paper on Defence and National Security', 2008, p. 5.
153 'Interview zur Zukunft der *Bundeswehr* und zur weiteren Weiterentwicklung in Irak', 24 April, 2003 (BMVG, 2003).

154   'Verteidigungs Politische Richtlinien' (VPR), German Federal Ministry of Defence, 2003, Chapter V.2, pt. 57.
155   The Operational Command Headquarters, created in July 2001 and based in Potsdam, is responsible for the planning and conduct of all overseas operations (Ruwe, 2004: 52).
156   *Ibid*, Chapter V.2, pt. 57.
157   *Ibid*, Chapter V.2, pt. 58.
158   *Ibid*, pt. 57.
159   *Ibid*, Chapter VIII, pt. 95.
160   *Ibid*, Chapter II, pt. 15.
161   'White Paper on German Security Policy and the Future of the *Bundeswehr*', German Federal Ministry of Defence, 2006, pp. 5, 9.
162   'The transformation of the *Bundeswehr* covers all aspects of the Armed Forces and their administration: capabilities, strengths, structures, stationing, personnel, material, equipment and training. It puts an end to static force planning and establishes a continuous process of adaptation', 'German Defence White Paper', 2006, p. 74.
163   On the internal organisation and competencies of the different sections of the three key Divisions of the BTC see: 'Bundeswehr Transformation Centre', Bundeswehr Transformation Centre, Federal German Ministry of Defence, 2007.
164   'White Paper on German Security Policy and the Future of the Bundeswehr', 2006, p. 76.
165   *Ibid*, p. 85.
166   *Ibid*, p. 77.
167   *Ibid*, p. 78.
168   It is, of course, important to recognise that the principle of Mission Command has been long embedded within the German armed forces, deriving from the *Auftragstaktik* developed by the Prussian Military Staff. The *Auftragstaktik* received a great deal of attention by British and American military figures in the post-war era following its successful application by the *Wehrmacht* and formed the basis for William Lind's concept of 'Manoeuvre Warfare' that was became influential within the British military during the 1980s.
169   On NetOpFü as a 'force multiplier' see 'Sicherheitspolitische Zukunftsanalyse: Ausblick auf 2035 Trends und Entwicklungen', 2007, p. 16.
170   'Abschlussbericht zur Studie SFT 21-2040 Mensch in Transformation Workshop Z' (Report on the Study: The Human Being in Transformation Workshop), Bundeswehr Transformation Centre, German Federal Ministry of Defence, 2006, p. 13.
171   See also: 'Sicherheitspolitische Zukunftsanalyse: Ausblick auf 2035 Trends und Entwicklungen', 2007, p. 16.
172   See: 'Abschlussbericht zur Studie SFT 21-2040 Mensch in Transformation Workshop Z', p. 13; see also: Vernetzte Operationsfuehrung (2009).
173   'White Paper on German Security Policy and the Future of the *Bundeswehr*', 2006, p. 78.
174   'It is not possible to guarantee security with armed forces only...what is called for, rather, is an all-embracing approach that can only be developed in networked security structures'. *Ibid*, p. 22. The concept of Networked Security is itself embedded within an overall concept of 'Civilian Crisis-Prevention, Conflict Resolution and Post-Conflict Peace Building' that is focused on preventing the structural causes of crises. *Ibid*, p. 23.
175   *Ibid*, p. 120.
176   Interviews, German Defence Ministry, Bonn, 12 October 2009.

177 *Ibid*, pp. 81–4.
178 'White Paper on German Security Policy and the Future of the *Bundeswehr*', 2006, p. 85.
179 *Ibid*, p. 82. These systems build upon the development of the Autoko-90 (*Automatisiertes Korpsstammnetz*) digital wide area communication network that was launched in 1995 and became fully operational in 2002 and the acquisition of Tactical Digital Information Links (Link 11) by the *Luftwaffe* (Billy, 2003: 57).
180 'White Paper on German Security Policy and the Future of the *Bundeswehr*', 2006, p. 90. The 'Sicherheitspolitische Zukunftsanalyse: Ausblick auf 2035 Trends und Entwicklungen' points to the growing importance of space-based assets (and their protection from disruption and destruction) and to the importance of Germany's ability to deploy NetOpFü at the global level in response to conflict and crisis. The report also highlights the future importance of developments in nanotechnology for the *Bundeswehr* in the areas of networking, robotics, space technology and medicine, explosives, materials and force protection. It is recognised that in order to minimise cost, quicken the pace the development of deployable systems costs, partnership with civilian space technology ventures and regional cooperation will be critical. See 'Sicherheitspolitische Zukunftsanalyse: Ausblick auf 2035 Trends und Entwicklungen', 2007, pp. 16–19.
181 The establishment of the CSW COE follows the commitment of NATO members at the 12–13 June 2003 Ministerial Meeting of NATO's Defence Planning Committee and Nuclear Planning Group to establish 'multi-national and nationally sponsored CoEs to test doctrine, improve interoperability and assess new concepts'. Germany is also the location for the NATO Joint Air Power Competence Centre COE and the Military Engineering COE. For further detail on these and other COEs, see: COE (2008a).
182 'White Paper on German Security Policy and the Future of the *Bundeswehr*', 2006, pp. 95–7.
183 *Ibid*, p. 98.
184 *Ibid*, pp. 7, 54.
185 *Ibid*, p. 79.
186 'White Paper on German Security Policy and the Future of the *Bundeswehr*', 2006, p. 75; 'Abschlussbericht zur Studie SFT 21-2040 Mensch in Transformation Workshop Z', 2006, pp. 68–9.
187 'Abschlussbericht zur Studie SFT 21-2040 Mensch in Transformation Workshop Z', 2006, pp. 50–1, 68–9.
188 The 2003 Defence Policy Guidelines recognise that basic service conscripts will be unable to contribute to the 'reaction forces' or the 'stabilisation forces'. 'VPR', 2003, Chapter VII, pt. 80. The high level of training needed to operate the systems associated with NetOpFü hinders the Air Force to make use of their quota of conscripts in functions other than administration. Interview, German Defence Ministry, Bonn, 12 October 2009.

Chapter 2

1 A focus on smaller 'third rank' European states is vital in understanding the patterns of regional (through NATO and ESDP) and subregional (through bi-pluri-lateral arrangements outside NATO/EU frameworks) cooperation which are being promoted by the European Great Powers.

2   However, the Partnership for Peace Programme (PfP), initiated in 1994 and European Atlantic Partnership Council, launched in 1997, provide a mechanism for non-NATO states in Eastern Europe, the Caucuses, Central Asia, Scandinavia and Mediterranean region to draw upon the expertise of NATO in military reform, to cooperate on common security issues and contribute to NATO operations on a case by case basis.

3   This chapter follows the typology of differentiated international cooperation outlined by Koelliker (2009: 6). 'A la carte' cooperation refers to instances in which the participation of outsiders is dependent upon their own willingness to join an arrangement; in 'variable geometry' arrangements, outsiders may not participate in cooperation under any condition; 'multiple speed' cooperation refers to arrangements in which outsiders may participate following the fulfillment of specific criteria.

4   It is also important to recognise the roles of the WEU and OSCE in European Security and Defence cooperation. However, the Western European Union's (WEU) capabilities and functions have been largely incorporated into the EU. The OSCE deals primarily with 'softer' security issues (including human, politico-military and economic-environmental security concerns) and provides an important forum for pan-European dialogue. Consequently, the OSCE is characterised by broader membership than NATO and the EU and includes both Russia and the US (see Table 2.1).

5   Sweden and Finland have recently announced their intention to contribute to the NATO Response Force (that also includes the participation of other PfP nations).

6   Denmark secured an opt-out on matters of security and defence at the Edinburgh European Council in December 1992.

7   However, both Turkey and Norway contribute to EU Battlegroups.

8   'Delivering Security in a Changing World', UK Ministry of Defence, 2004, pt. 3.3.

9   *Ibid*, 2004, pts. 2.18–2.19.

10   On the 'Atlanticisation' of British defence and security policy see Dover (2007: 88); Dunne (2004: 893–911); Farrell (2008: 781–2); Jones (2007: 223) and Miskimmon (2004).

11   On the 'Europeanisation' of French defence and security policy see Brenner (2003); Irondelle (2003a); Lungu (2004b); Menon (1995) and Sutton (2007: 307–11).

12   On Germany's 'bridge role' see Dyson (2005: 373) and Hyde-Price (2000).

13   The 1992 Petersburg Declaration bolstered the operational role of the Western European Union (WEU) to include humanitarian and rescue tasks, peacekeeping and peacemaking.

14   The PSC is an Ambassadorial-level committee that provides political controland determines responses to international crises; the EU Military Committee composes the Chiefs of Staff of EU member states and is advised by the Committee for Civilian Aspects of Crisis Management; the EU Military Staff consists of civilian and military experts drawn from national member states and performs an early warning, situation assessment and strategic planning role.

15   'European Security and Defence Policy: The Civilian Aspects of Crisis Management', EU Council Secretariat, 2007.

16   The initiative permits the contribution of troops not only to humanitarian and rescue and peacekeeping tasks, but also to higher-intensity combat forces in crisis-management operations. See 'Headline Goal 2010', pt. 2.

17 The Civilian/Military Cell consists of an Operations Centre, whose permanent staff consist of five Officers and three NCOs and a Strategic Planning Staff consisting of eight military and seven civilian experts that includes two officials of the European Commission. See: 'Remarks to the European Parliament Sub-Committee on Security and Defence by Brigadier General Heinrich Brauss, Director Civilian/Military Cell', Brussels, 1 March 2007.

18 The NRF also includes contributions from non-NATO members Finland and Sweden as well as PfP states.

19 'The principle threats to the Alliance are international terrorism and the proliferation of weapons of mass destruction and their delivery systems, as well as instability caused by failed or failing states; regional crises; misuse of new technologies; and the disruption of the flow of vital resources.' 'The Riga Summit: A Reader's Guide', NATO Public Diplomacy Division, 6 July 2007, p. 4.

20 'Riga Summit Declaration', 26 November 2006, pt. 10; 'The Riga Summit: A Reader's Guide', pt. 16 h-l.

21 *Ibid.*

22 On the similarities shared by the NRF and Battlegroup concepts see Kaitera and Ben-Ari (2008: 7–8).

23 'A Secure Europe in a Better World: European Security Strategy', European Council, Brussels, 12 December 2003, pp. 1–5.

24 Whilst the EDA's 'Initial Long-Term Vision for European Capability and Capacity Needs' notes the necessity for a 'more characteristically European approach' to NEC 'different in ambition and character (for example with a strong emphasis on civil-military interoperability, and on the tactical level)' it notes that efforts must 'ensure interoperability with the leading efforts of the US in this area' and 'nested within NATO conceptual frameworks and standards'. 'Initial Long-Term Vision for European Capability and Capacity Needs', Brussels, European Defence Agency, October 2006, pp. 20–1.

25 These include at a minimum of two meetings at the level of Foreign Ministers; three meetings at Ambassadorial level per semester; two meetings at the level of Military Committee per semester and regular routine meetings at the committee and staff level.

26 In contrast to the NRF, the EU Battlegroups are only land based and lack dedicated airborne and maritime capabilities and the NRF is focused not only on crisis-management operations, but collective defence (Kaitera and Ben-Ari, 2008: 7).

27 The civilian dimension of ESDP, launched at the June 2000 European Council, has been bolstered by the Civilian Headline Goal 2008 and 2010.

28 NATO support for the AU Peacekeeping Mission in Darfur involves the provision of air transport for peacekeepers and training for AU officers; the NATO Training Assistance Implementation Mission in Iraq is focused on training Iraqi Security Forces.

29 Several lesser-rank European states are also investing in C4ISR, particularly the Netherlands and Sweden, Italy, Spain, Norway and Finland (Adams and Ben-Ari, 2006: 12–17; Flournoy and Smith, 2005: 91; Shepherd, 2000: 23–4).

30 The EDA builds upon the Western European Armaments Group (WEAG), a subsidiary of the WEU that was established in 1976 to facilitate armaments cooperation, and Western European Armaments Organisation (WEAO) that was launched in 1996, and ceased activity in 2006, following the absorption of its functions by the EDA. On WEAG and WEAO see Adams and Ben-Ari (2006: 116–18).

31 The DCI was launched at the April 1999 Washington Summit in an attempt to ameliorate the growing technological gap within NATO between the Europeans and the US.

32 The EDA builds upon the work of the European Commission, that has sought stronger competence in armaments policy and championing a European Defence Equipment Market in the 'STAR 21 Report' of 2002 and 2003 'Communication on Armaments Policy' which pointed to the need to harmonise military requirements and procurement to achieve operability both within Europe and between Europe and the US.

33 Of European NATO member states, all but Denmark and Turkey are represented in the EDA (Norway signed a cooperation agreement with the EDA on 7 March 2006). Input into decision-making on EDA projects is determined by whether a state is making a financial contribution to the initiative. This mechanism for 'a la carte' differentiation inside the EDA provides a means with which to overcome the problems encountered by NATO's Research and Technology Organisation (RTO) that operates on the principle of the equality of nations. Such institutional design disincentivises cooperation and leadership by the European great powers within the RTO by giving net security consumers decision-making powers over projects largely funded by net security providers.

34 ECAP had identified eight areas of improvement necessary to develop Europe's NEC: UAVs for target surveillance and acquisition; deployable communications modules; headquarters; theatre surveillance and reconnaissance air picture; strategic ISR imagery intelligence (IMINT) collection; UCAVs; early warning and distant detection at the strategic level (Adams and Ben-Ari, 2006: 112).

35 HHG 2010 outlined a set of milestones including the full capacity in strategic lift and compatibility in terrestrial and space based networking capabilities by 2010.

36 'An Initial Long Term Vision for European Defence Capability and Capacity Needs', European Defence Agency, Brussels, October 2006, pp. 25–8. The Long Term Vision (pt. 34) also notes that: 'the EU will increasingly utilise a comprehensive approach combining its hard and soft power instruments and coordinating civilian, military, governmental and non-governmental bodies to achieve the necessary political effects'.

37 See Table 2.2. Each of these project areas is at a different stage of development and involves the voluntary participation of different EU member states. For further details, see: EDA (2008a).

38 States involved in the Maritime Surveillance Network initiative have withheld information on their participation from the public realm.

39 See: EDA (2008a).

40 Participating nations include Austria, Belgium, Cyprus, the Czech Republic, Estonia, Finland, France, Germany, Hungary, Ireland, Italy, the Netherlands, Norway, Poland, Portugal, Slovakia, Slovenia, Spain and Sweden.

41 For details on the first JIP-FR projects, see: EDA (2008b).

42 Participating states include: Cyprus, France, Germany, Greece, Hungary, Italy Norway, Poland, Slovakia, Slovenia and Spain. See: 'EDA Press Release: EDA Establishes New Joint R&T Programme On Disruptive Defence Technologies', European Defence Agency, Brussels, 26 May 2008.

43 'Network Enabled Capability Pre-Study, Public Executive Summary', Western European Armaments Organisation Research Cell, 12 June 2006. See also 'RTP 9.12, Miracle Project Final Report: Project Overview: Research and Technology Project on Micro-Satellite Cluster Technology', Kongsberg Spacetech, Norway, 12 July 2007.

44 However, as Terrence Guay and Robert Callum (2002: 763) note, it is difficult to determine what level of consolidation constitutes the 'optimum level of efficiency' at which the appropriate balance between competition and consolidation is reached.

45 ESA members include Austria, Belgium, Denmark, Finland, France, Germany, Greece, Ireland, Italy, Luxembourg, the Netherlands, Norway, Portugal, Spain, Sweden, Switzerland and the United Kingdom. Canada takes part in projects under a Cooperation agreement. Hungary, Poland, Romania and the Czech Republic participate under a European Cooperating State (ECS) agreement. Estonia (June 2007) and Slovenia (May 2008) have signed cooperation agreements with the ESA.

46 See Gordon Adams and Guy Ben-Ari (2006: 126). See also ESA (2008a).

47 'White Paper on Space: A New European Frontier for an Expanding Union: An Action Plan For Implementing the European Space Policy', European Commission, Brussels, 11 November 2003.

48 Cooperation is most clearly evidenced in the development of the Tactical Imagery Exploitation System (TIES) that will put in place a workstation for intelligence imagery analysis. See 'EDA Press Release: EDA, EU SATCEN Demonstrate Potential for System to Integrate Intelligence Imagery', European Defence Agency, Torrejon, Spain, 20 February 2008.

49 'Final Report on the Civilian Headline Goal 2008', 19 November 2007, Doc. 14807/07, p. 2.

50 CHG 2008 outlined a set of aspects for further consideration by the CHG 2010 process including improvements in mission and procurement planning; the development of closer 'synergy' between the civilian and military capabilities of members states; enhancing cooperation with other international organisations and NGOs; the need to institute a regular 'reality' check on ESDP capability development to update future 'illustrative scenarios' (virtual planning scenarios) and required capabilities. See 'Final Report on the Civilian Headline Goal 2008', Section 5, pp. 5–7.

51 The development of instruments under CHG 2010 includes the Civilian Capability Management Tool, information exchange requirements in the form of an integrated inter-service civilian-military project, developing the management mechanisms for a civilian lessons-learned process and finally, improving mission security and intelligence capabilities. See 'Civilian Headline Goal 2010', 19 November 2007, Doc. 12843/07, Section 3, pp. 3–5.

52 For further details on the NATO C3 Agency, see also: (NC3A, 2008).

53 It is important to note, as Joyce (2007) highlights that the RTO suffers a 'constitutional disadvantage' when compared to the EDA, as input into decision-making is equal. This disincentivises action by the larger member states, whose influence over projects for which they are acting as paymasters is diluted. Within the EDA a memorandum of understanding ensures that only nations that are making financial contributions to projects are able to influence their attributes.

54 On the main activities of these six panels see: 'Targeting Tomorrow's Challenges', pp. 5–22. For information on the panels organised by the RTO since 1998, see: RTO (2008a).

55 *Ibid*, p. 3.

56 On member state involvement in each of these initiatives see: RTO (2008a).

57 On the restructuring of NATO command structures see: NATO (2008a).

58 For information on the 17 CoEs, see: COE (2008a); COE (2008b) and Ben-Ari (2005: 2).

59   The DCI outlined five core capability improvement areas: deployment and mobility; sustainability and logistics; survivability; effective engagement; consultation, command and control.

60   The PCC includes intelligence, surveillance and target acquisition; air to ground surveillance, command, control and communications; combat effectiveness and precision guided munitions and suppression of enemy air defences; strategic air and sea-lift; air to air refueling and deployable combat support and combat service support units. 'The Prague Summit and NATO's Transformation: A Reader's Guide', NATO Public Diplomacy Division, Brussels, 2002, p. 11.

61   The Prague Summit also established a Multinational Chemical, Biological, Radiological and Nuclear Defence Battalion. 'NATO Briefing: Operational Capabilities', NATO Public Diplomacy Division, Brussels, October 2006, p. 4.

62   See: NATO (2008c).

63   'NATO Briefing: Operational Capabilities', p. 7.

64   'The Riga Summit: A Reader's Guide', 2007, p. 42.

65   'MAJIIC Introduction', NATO C3 Agency, October 2006.

66   TMD is a project with deeper roots than the 2002 PCC. The 1999 Strategic Concept recognised the need for work of NATO missile defence systems. 'NATO Press Release NAC-S (99)65: NATO Strategic Concept', 24 April 1999, pt. 56.

67   Members of the consortium includes Raytheon, EADS Astrium, Thales, Thales Raytheon System Company, IABG, TNO, Qinetiq, DATAMAT and Diehl.

68   Interview, UK Defence Ministry, London, 20 November 2009.

69   See: Eurofighter (2008).

70   The Meteor is also compatible with the French Rafale, JAS-39 Gripen and US Joint Strike Fighter.

71   See: KMWeg (2008).

72   On OCCAR and the projects coordinated under its auspices, see: OCCAR (2008).

73   The COBRA system has, for example, proved critical in the provision of indirect fire support in French crisis-management operations (Tarle, 2004: 23).

74   Germany has ordered the UHT multirole fire support version of the Tiger; the French have ordered the HAD multirole combat and HAP combat support versions; the Spanish have ordered the HAP combat support version.

75   FREMM builds upon the structures established by the Horizon Frigate, a joint initiative of DCN (France) and Orizzonte (Italy); two frigates each were delivered between 2005 and 2008.

76   For further information on ISL research projects see: ISL (2009).

77   Membership is dependent upon the subjective willingness of 'outs' to participate (Koelliker, 2010: 6).

78   See: Pleiades (2008).

79   See: SAR (2008).

80   A number of European states also participate in the Multinational Standby High Readiness Brigade for UN operations (SHIRBRIG). This initiative was launched by Denmark in 1994 and now includes Argentina, Austria, Canada, Denmark, Finland, Italy, Ireland, Lithuania, the Netherlands, Norway, Poland, Portugal, Romania, Slovenia, Spain, as full members; Sweden and Chile, Croatia, Czech Republic, Egypt, Jordan, Latvia and Senegal as observer members.

81   Austria, Greece, Poland and Turkey integrated staff into Eurocorps HQ on 2002–3. See: Eurocorps (2008).

82   Leading to the transfer of soldiers from other NATO states (including the US, Denmark, Norway, Spain, Italy and the UK) to the Corps. See: GMF (2008).

83   See: EAI (2008).

84 See: EAG (2008).
85 See: SCC (2008).
86 Since October 2003 the EAC and SCC have been listed in the Helsinki Forces Catalogue.
87 The SCC holds quarterly coordination boards including representatives of the NATO HQs, NATO Planning Boards and the EUMS.
88 See: EAC (2008).
89 Open to participation by any 'willing nation'.
90 See: MCCE (2008).
91 Membership is dependent upon 'demonstrated willingness, competence and capability' to act as lead nations in multinational expeditionary operations.
92 See: MIC (2008).
93 The MIC also signed a statement of cooperation in September 2001 with the Combined Communications Electronics Broad (CEEB) that includes Australia, Canada, New Zealand, the UK and US. CEEC's origins lie in WW2. The organisation establishes working groups to coordinate military communications between the C4 systems of its members.
94 Membership is dependent upon planned or existing development of C2IS; new member states are first granted observer membership, transition to full membership is dependent upon conformity to C2IS interoperability. 'Multilateral Interoperability Programme Management Plan' (MPMP), Multilateral Interoperability Programme, 22 April 1999, Annex B.
95 See: NORDCAPS (2008).
96 See: BDC (2008).
97 The concept of a balanced military refers predominantly to balance between heavy, medium and light capabilities, but also balance between combat and command and control and logistical support capabilities and between division and brigade units (Constant, 2003: 47).
98 It is important to note limitations imposed upon the *Bundeswehr's* capacity to undertake MCO by its poor naval and air capabilities.
99 However, as section 3 of the book demonstrates although Britain and France can be characterised as cases of 'third-order change' the capacity of states to fully translate the lessons of operational experience into changes to force posture and capability investments has been hampered by the impact of organisational politics. This problem has been particularly manifest in the UK where the electoral cycle has incentivised the temporal management of reform by the core executive and the deferment of a much-needed SDR process to 2010. Chapter 6 demonstrates how low executive autonomy has allowed organisational politics between the Single Services to have an undue impact on decisions surrounding force structure and capability investment.
100 As Farrell (2008: 792–3) highlights, in the case of Britain 'the term EBAO was adopted to indicate the British perspective that what had changed was not operations themselves, but rather the approach to operations. In contrast, for the Americans EBO provided the possibility for the profound change in the very character of military operations.'

Chapter 3

1 The term 'security dilemma' was first coined by John Herz (1950: 157–80) and refers to a situation in which states attempting to attain security become involved

in a vicious circle of power accretion due to the anarchic context within which they are situated.

2 On the core premises of Waltzian neorealism, see Donnelly (2000 82–103); Hobson (2000: 18); Kolodziej (2005: 135–9); Little (2007: 167–85) and Schmidt (2005: 523–49).

3 It should be noted that there are significant limits on 'rational' action due to the structural uncertainty of the anarchic international system that creates an incentive for states to exaggerate or underplay their strength, magnifying the problem of imperfect information (Mearsheimer, 1994/95: 10; Resende-Santos, 2007: 58–9).

4 Whilst Waltz argued that the ultimate goal of states is security and can be thought of as a defensive realist: 'The first concern of states is not to maximise power but to maintain their positions in the system', he was ambiguous on how much power guaranteed security, opening the door to offensive realists who maintain that his emphasis on the anarchy and uncertainty of the international system creates an imperative for statesmen to engage in power maximisation.

5 For a more fulsome discussion of defensive realism see Labs (1997: 7–11) and Zakaria (1991: 190–6).

6 Prominent 'offensive' realists include: Eric Labs (1997), John Mearsheimer (1994/95), Hans Morgenthau (1946) and Joao Resende-Santos (2007), though rather than prioritising system level factors in determining expansion, Morgenthau emphasises the 'will to power' (*animus dominandi*) inherent in human nature. Niccolo Machiavelli (1997 [1531]: 206) also recognised the necessity of expansion in order to survive in the international system.

7 'The system forces states to behave according to the dictates of realism, or risk destruction' (Mearsheimer, 1995: 91); 'States are forced to think, and sometimes act offensively because of the structure of the international system' (Mearsheimer, 1994–5: 10).

8 Defensive Realism's focus on the domestic sources of foreign and defence policies has left the approach open to criticism that it is simply restating the arguments of the Liberal *Innenpolitik* tradition (Legro and Moravcsik, 1999: 25).

9 As Resende-Santos (2007) argues, one should not view socialisation as an independent variable leading to the internalisation of norms, but as 'rational behavioural adjustments and adaptation to external constraints and inducements'.

10 These concepts are discussed in the following analysis in greater detail.

11 For definitions of 'balancing' and 'bandwagoning', see below.

12 Bi-polarity is the most stable distribution of power, in which two superpowers enjoy relative equality in material capabilities. Both powers are able to regulate their spheres of influence in the international system, hence as long as neither state declines in its ability to maximise 'state power', the approximate symmetry between the capabilities of the major powers in the international system leads to a fragile and short term balance of power and a basis for international (and particularly regional) order, as demonstrated by the Warsaw Pact and NATO Alliances during the Cold War.

13 For a detailed discussion of neorealism and the 'balance of power' see Richard Little (2007: 191–209).

14 For a system to be considered uni-polar it is not necessary for one state to enjoy global hegemony. An international system is uni-polar when one state has the military capacity to stem the rise of balancing behaviour by other great powers who may seek to challenge its dominance. A uni-polar leader may enjoy hegemony over its geopolitical neighbourhood, but act as an 'offshore balancer' in other regions, intervening only to stymie potential challengers or to deal with

threats to its vital strategic interests (Hyde-Price, 2007: 42; Mearsheimer, 2001: 4).

15 Transformation Planning Guidance, 2003, p. 5.

16 See also Altmann (2004: 65–6) on US research and development in the field of military nanotechnology.

17 See also Wohlforth (1999: 20).

18 Williams (2001: 50) also highlights how the Kosovo conflict also illuminated the potential vulnerability of Command and Control systems to attack from low-cost electronics and weapons systems.

19 According to the indices of Waltz (1979: 131) Britain, France and Germany are balanced along the main indices of population, resource endowment, geographic size and competent government.

20 Buckpassing refers to a situation in which great powers attempt to pass the responsibility for balancing and the development of a new balance of power to other great powers in the international system, hoping to benefit from the increase in relative power they accrue, as the other power devotes substantial resources to balancing.

21 Bandwagoning is defined by Waltz as 'aligning with the stronger party to a conflict'; see below for a more fulsome discussion of bandwagoning.

22 As Hyde-Price (2007: 50) notes, states are also able to counter a rising hegemon though aggressive, preventative war.

23 Defined by Pape (2005: 15) as 'rearmament or accelerated economic growth to support eventual rearmament'. Internal balancing against the US by any of the European great powers is of course a futile exercise given the overwhelmingly large disparity in relative power between Britain, France, Germany and the US.

24 Defined by T.V. Paul (2004: 3) as: '...tacit balancing short of formal alliances. It occurs when states generally develop ententes or limited security understandings with one another to balance a potentially threatening state or a rising power. Soft balancing is often based on a limited arms build-up, *ad hoc* cooperative exercises, or collaboration in regional or international institutions; these policies may be converted to open, hard-balancing strategies if and when security competition becomes intense and the powerful state becomes threatening.' See Layne (2006: 14) on the viability of balancing strategies against the US.

25 The 'soft balancing' thesis also neglects the high risk associated with such strategy, not least the longer-term escalation of tension between nuclear powers.

26 Walt's work has been challenged not only by systemic approaches but those emphasising the domestic sources of alliances. See Schweller (1994: 76–9).

27 This does not imply agreement with Walt's (1985: 12) assertion that variation in states' *perceptions* of the offensive intentions helps to explain the absence of balancing behaviour, as this is inconsistent with structural realism (Layne, 2006: 15; Legro and Moravcsik, 1999: 37; Resende-Santos, 2007: 86). Rather, variance in US strategic interests (consequent upon its dependency on particular areas of the globe for resource extraction, or upon the inability of secondary powers to stem the rise of potential challengers to the US), combined with geographical differentiation in reach of US military power, leads to differentiation in 'aggressive intent' and willingness to use military force, by a US that is pursuing a policy of primacy.

28 'In addition to its overall capabilities the degree to which a state threatens others is affected by its geographical proximity, offensive capabilities and perceived intentions' (Walt, 1988: 280–1).

29   Vasquez (1997: 901) argues that the work of Walt is degenerative in the sense that it is 'characterised by the use of semantic devices that hide the actual content decreasing nature of the research programme through reinterpretation'.

30   On the consistency of the 'balance of threat' with the core premises of neorealism, see Donnelly (2000: 75); Resende-Santos (2007: 86); Sterling Folker (1997: 23) and Walt (1988: 281).

31   See, for example, the actions of North Korea and Iran, whose exposure to US strategic interests have led to an attempt to 'balance' US power through the acquisition of weapons of mass destruction (Walt, 2005a: 116).

32   Bandwagoning has also been described as 'predatory buck-passing': 'riding free on the offensive efforts of others to gain unearned spoils' (Schweller, 1994: 74 n.11).

33   Although Walt recognises that bandwagoning can be motivated by profit (Walt, 1985: 7–8) as Schweller (1994: 83) highlights: 'Walt identifies this motive but then overlooks it because the logic of his theory forces him to conflate the various forms of bandwagoning into one category: giving in to threat.'

34   This corresponds with Colin Elman's (1996: 28–9) distinction between manual and automatic expansion. States that are manual expanders deliberately strive for hegemony; automatic expansion refers to states that expand their power subject to the constraints and opportunities of the international system. See also Labs (1997: 12).

35   As Labs (1997: 15–16) notes: '[States] may not feel immediately threatened by the power which provides them the spoils or feel that the potential threat is more distant. In the context of an existing conflict, therefore, watching a friend gain power may not be completely comforting, but the short-term priorities of security demand that you gain now against your enemy and worry about the post-war balance of power with your friend later.'

36   As Pape (2005) and Hyde-Price (2007: 93) note, although a set of common issues and interests unite the US and EU, some differences exist in how best to tackle these issues. In addition, bandwagoning is associated with the risk that the regional hegemon/offshore balancer may pose a threat to its great power allies once it has eliminated other opponents (Hyde-Price, 2007: 50). Nevertheless, bandwagoning emerges as the most rational strategy open to European states in the context of the constraints and opportunities presented by the contemporary international system. It is the strategy of least risk and cost and a means with which to attempt to gain some, albeit limited, influence over US policy and share in the spoils of victory.

37   Wohlforth (1999: 7–8, 2002: 98–118) highlights how the relative power gap between the US and other great powers makes balancing a futile response.

38   Hence European powers are particularly concerned to ensure continued US involvement in matters of European security and a US troop presence in an attempt to avoid the risk that in the future the US will 'pass the buck' to the European great powers to balance against a potential hegemon (not least Russia and Iran).

39   'Binding' refers to the ability of smaller alliance partners to use existing institutional ties to restrain a larger alliance partner from pursuing uni-lateral policies and avoid 'entrapment' by a more powerful ally (Schweller, 1998: 70–1).

40   It is important to note that the uncertainty of the international security environment means that states can never be full certain from where the next threat will arise. Whilst the US may form a capricious partner, the potential recourse through NATO to a global full-spectrum power projection capability and nuclear umbrella forms an important insurance policy against the unknown.

41 On system 'punishment' see Waltz (1979: 89–93); Feaver et al (2000: 167); Hobson (2000: 21–2); Rathburn (2008: 317) and Sterling-Folker (1997: 19–20).

42 Policy stasis is closely linked to what Randall Schweller (2006: 10) terms 'under-balancing', in which a state fails to correctly respond to changing systemic imperatives and adopts imprudent policies, such as the retention of existing defence policy instruments, leading to a decline in its relative power. See also Rathburn (2008: 311).

43 When innovation is based on new technological knowledge, as is the case with the US-led RMA (Altmann, 2004; Paarlberg, 2004), it is likely to offer a sustained advantage due to the significant period of time and financial investment required to develop a scientific and engineering base (Horowitz, 2006: 12; Paarlberg, 2004).

44 Defined by Resende-Santos (2007: 63) as: 'The state's aggregate material and organisational resources, of which its productive base, organisational capacity and raw military assets are key components.'

45 As states are focused on maximising their security and relative power, economic prosperity matters in as much as it is critical in determining a state's military might and its standing in the international community (Mearsheimer, 1994–5: 5–49).

46 Whilst the uncertainty is an inherent feature of the international system, the problem of imperfect information is magnified following a dramatic shift in the balance of capabilities. States, as rational actors must become more acquainted with the opportunities and constraints presented by their new strategic environment (Hyde-Price, 2007: 32). See also Keohane (1986: 167) on the 'rationality assumption' and realist thought; see also Mearsheimer (1994); Grieco (1988); Lake and Powell (1999) and Iida (1993: 431–57).

47 For more detail on the lessons of operational experience and the emergence of 'best practice', see Chapters 4–6.

48 As Nick Whitney notes, it is difficult to establish the precise level of contribution to ESDP missions as there is no central record of who has contributed to operations so far. This is complicated by the withholding of data by member states of the EDA on participation in armaments and research and technology cooperation. See Whitney (2008: 23). On Europe's Great Powers as leaders of reformed bandwagoning, see Whitney (2008: 59–64). On the contribution of smaller states to Alliance 'burden sharing' see Ringmose (2009) and Kupchan (1988).

49 On bureaucratic politics see also Sterling-Folker (1997: 19–20).

50 As Chapters 4–6 demonstrate, although external threat forms the key driver of policy choices, executive autonomy forms an important intervening variable impacting on the capacity of the core executive to compel Single Service Chiefs to ensure that doctrine training, force posture and capabilities conforms to the dictates of the operational environment.

51 This argument contrasts with the arguments of Stephen Rosen (1988, 1991), who posits that major military innovation during times of peace is possible, without civilian intervention to assist 'mavericks'.

52 Posen (2006: 156) classifies Britain, France and Germany second-rank, 'consequential' states, of relatively analogous size and productive capacity, which combined with their similar geographical location leads to a comparable level of 'external vulnerability'. On 'external vulnerability' see Taliaferro (2006: 467, 479).

53 Europe forms the largest source of Foreign Direct Investment in Africa and Britain and France are the central trading partners on the continent. Jackson (2006: 358) highlights how Britain imported £14.6 billion in goods from Africa in 2005 and exported £10 billion, whilst during the post-Cold War era Africa has accounted for approximately 5 per cent of French external trade (Utley, 2002: 130).

54 On UK gas and oil self-sufficiency during the 1990s see 'EU Energy and Transport in Figures Statistical Pocketbook 2007–08', Office for Official Publications of the European Communities, Luxembourg, Section 2.6 'Country Energy Statistics', p. 83.

55 See Nicholas Pederson (2000, Section 1 and 10) who highlights how: 'when uranium was discovered in Niger and Gabon, both former French colonies, France now had a reliable source of uranium. France intervened militarily in these countries whenever French leaders felt their supply of uranium was in danger'. This is also noted by Utley (2002: 130) who states: 'France's [military] bases in Africa have proved valuable in the protection of France's wider commercial, military and strategic interests.' On French nuclear energy generation, see: Europa (2008a). See also Europa (2008b).

56 France will withdraw 1,100 troops from the Ivory Coast by summer 2009. See: PM (2009). France also announced a significant reduction of its military bases in Africa in the 2007 defence white paper. In line with the geographical shift in French strategic interests outlined in the DWP France opened a military (Navy, Air and Training Camp) base in the UAE in May 2009 to facilitate French power projection in the Gulf region and Asia.

57 From February 2008 France has also contributed 1,650 troops to the 3,500 strong EuFor Chad/CAR mission that provides support to the UN in the protection of refugees from Darfur (February 2008–present). In January 2009 the French Prime Minister Francois Fillon announced the intention to withdraw 1,000 of these troops by summer 2009.

58 It is however, important to note that the *Ostpolitik* of Chancellor Willy Brandt (1969–74) set in place a substantial increase in oil and gas imports from the Soviet Union. The USSR supplied the Federal Republic with 10 per cent of its natural gas requirements (1 per cent of her total energy needs) in the early 1970s. German imports of Russian gas rose to 16 per cent by 1980 and 28 per cent by 1990 (4 per cent of West Germany's total energy requirement) (Stent, 2003: 168, 213). In 2006 the Federal Republic imported 39 per cent of its natural gas needs from Russia (9 per cent of Germany's total energy consumption).

59 For statistical information on changing Germany energy production and dependency see 'EU Energy and Transport in Figures Statistical Pocketbook 2007–08', Section 2.6 'Country Energy Statistics' p. 61.

60 The urgency of reforms to French policy instruments was compounded by the difficulties the French faced in generating expeditionary forces during the 1991 Gulf War. The French were able to mobilise only 14,000 expeditionary troops from an active force of 280,000, in comparison to the 35,000 troops deployed by the British, despite a much smaller overall pool of around 140,000 troops (Bratton, 2002: 92).

61 As Howorth (1997: 35, 2004: 215, 2007: 45) highlights, France has not only sought to embed its defence policy within ESDP, but has also been a key contributor to NATO missions during the post-Cold War period. France also took a lead role in developing the NRF in order to ensure that NATO and ESDP are 'mutually reinforcing'.

62 See 'Balladur Sets Kohl Meeting and Orders Cabinet Frugality', *International Herald Tribune*, 1 April, 1994.

63 The French return to NATO's integrated command structure and its broader rapprochement with NATO is a process that can be traced back to the end of the Cold War, beginning with the September 1992 proposal of Defence Minister Pierre Joxe to actively involve France with the work of NATO's Military Committee on a case

by case basis (Sutton, 2007: 304). On the trans-Atlantic relations and French defence and security policy, see also R. Pauly (2005: 7–16).

64 See also Cindy Williams and Curtis Gilroy (2006: 110–11) on territorial defence and East European states/Finland.

65 Interviews, UK Ministry of Defence, London, 19–20 November 2009. The European Council's 2006 Capability Improvement Chart outlines how of the 64 capabilities shortfalls identified in 2002 only five had improved. See 'Capabilities Improvement Chart I/2006', Council of the European Union, Brussels, 2006.

66 As Whitney (2008: 24) notes, despite Finland's increasing focus on C4ISR capabilities for use in expeditionary power projection operations and willingness to contribute to operations under the auspices of ESDP, it retains Europe's largest heavy artillery. Similarly, whilst Poland is an increasingly willing contributor to ESDP, it retains a military that is focused more on defence of national territory than expeditionary operations, limiting its capacity to move from a net security consumer to security provider (Longhurst, 2002: 57–8).

67 Waltz (1979: 123) recognised the limitations of neorealism's analytical leverage: 'The theory explains why a certain similarity of behaviour is expected from similarly situated states. The expected behaviour is similar, not identical. To explain the expected differences in national responses, a theory would have to show how the different internal structures of states affect their policies and actions.'

68 State power is defined as 'the impact of the strength of a country's state apparatus and its relations to the surrounding society upon ability of the state to mobilise and extract resources from society' (Rose, 1998: 152).
    On 'state power' and neoclassical realism see Rathburn (2008: 302); Rose (1998: 152) and Taliaferro (2006: 479–80).

69 See Legro and Moravcsik (1999: 29).

70 Stefano Guzzini (2004: 356) also notes how 'realism's theory of action is based on a self-interest which is defined in a predominantly materialist way'. On realism's materialist core see also Krasner (2000: 131); Mearsheimer (1994–95: 41, 1995: 91); Wendt (2005: 410) and Williams (2005: 148–50). As Legro and Moravcsik (1999: 35) note: 'If any government acting on the basis of geopolitical national interest, *or* the aims of a particular interest group *or* ideationally induced strategies or misperceptions is in accord with 'realist' theory, what plausible constraints on state behaviour are excluded?' As a counterpoint to this argument, Rathburn (2008: 310–11), citing Sterling-Folker's (1997: 19) recognition that under realist theory states are 'free to die', argues that neoclassical realism can include a focus both on domestic material interests/politics, as well as ideational variables, as long as a state is ultimately punished for its deviation from structural imperatives by allowing domestic politics and/or ideology to dictate foreign, defence and security policy choices. On the effectiveness of states' responses to anarchy see also Waltz (1979: 71).

71 Underbalancing is defined by Schweller (2004: 159) as: 'Where threatened countries have failed to recognise a clear and persistent danger, or more typically, have simply not reacted to it, or more typically still, have responded in paltry or imprudent ways.'

72 See also Margaret Hermann and Joe Hagen (1998: 128–9) on the impact of fragmented authority on foreign, defence and security policy decision-making.

73 Weak social cohesion is a problem more often encountered by developing states and is less applicable to the European Great Powers. See Taliaferro (2006: 487).

74 On the other hand Van Evera (1994: 5–39) argues that particular forms of nationalism are a cause of conflict, whilst Christensen (1996) notes that nationalism can sometimes escape the control of the core executive.

75   See also Legro and Moravcsik (1999: 35); Snyder (1991: 41); Van Evera (1999).

76   The work on path dependency overlaps with the insights of cognitivist approaches. As Rathbun (2007: 534) states: 'In cognitivism information is complex and subjectively perceived because decision-makers possess limited cognitive capabilities. States and statesmen rely on a number of cognitive shortcuts to cope with complexity that often has the effect of misperception and error.'

77   This is also consistent with the position of Gideon Rose (1998: 151–2) who argues that: 'Neoclassical realists occupy a middle ground somewhere between structural realists and constructivists...the world states end up inhabiting, therefore, is indeed one of their own marking.'

78   As General De Gaulle noted: 'For a power legitimacy emerges from the feeling it arouses and the unity and national community it incorporates when the motherland is in danger' (Rynning, 2000: 64).

79   The malleability of identity and important role of political leadership in the generation of 'national doctrine' was also recognised by Niccolo Machiavelli. As Erica Benner (2001: 166) notes of Machiavelli's arguments: 'In seeking the material to constitute a viable modern state, then, Machiavelli looked both backward and forward, but mostly forward. While arguing that 'the raw material exists' for establishing a strong Italian state, he insisted that this material would only acquire a coherent, worthwhile shape through political craftsmanship.'

80   Posen (1993: 122) highlights how nationalism can emerge from 'apparent dormancy' at speed. See also Farrell (2005a: 456–7).

81   This view is supported by Taliaferro (2006: 491) who, despite according nationalism the status of an intervening variable, states: 'leaders deliberately inculcate nationalism primarily as a means with which to achieve societal cohesion against external adversaries' (Taliaferro, 2006: 491).

82   On the role of 'first-image' variables in realist theory, the difficulties of measuring the impact of individuals and possible avenues for future research see Byman and Pollack (2001), Hermann and Hagen (1998) and Parasiliti (2001). Byman and Pollack highlight how the development of a comprehensive account of the role of individuals in history would be a 'work of many lifetimes'. Resende-Santos (2007: 63) notes how competitive effectiveness 'may also comprise intangible factors such as skill and leadership'. See also Greenstein (1967).

83   When threat level is particularly high – for example, in the context of an immediate threat to a state's territorial integrity, unit-level variables are likely to have a reduced impact upon state power.

84   Whilst the concept of strategic culture was initially associated with nuclear strategy (Snyder, 1977; Gray, 1981). Johnston (1995: 46) provides a broader definition of strategic culture, relating to a state's grand strategy: 'an integrated system of symbols (e.g. argumentation structures, languages, analogies, metaphors) which act to establish persuasive and long-lasting strategic preferences by formulating concepts of the role and efficacy of military force in interstate political affairs and by clothing these conceptions in such an aura of factuality that the strategic preferences seem uniquely realistic and efficacious'.

85   On strategic culture and German defence and security policy, see Berger (1998); Duffield (1998); Dalgaard-Nielsen (2006) and Longhurst (2003, 2004).

86   On the concept of normative entrepreneurs see also Cerny (2000: 437–8) and Hyde-Price and Jeffrey (2001: 692–3).

87   As Dalgaard-Nielsen, Longhurst and Sabatier demonstrate, it is highly-difficult for policy actors to directly challenge 'central' (Dalgaard Nielsen, 2006: 13), 'foundational' (Longhurst, 2004: 17) or 'deep-core' (Sabatier and Jenkins-Smith, 1999: 133)

beliefs. However, they can, over time, alter 'secondary' and 'operational' aspects (Sabatier and Jenkins, 1999) – which Longhurst terms 'security policy standpoints' and 'regulatory practices' and Dalgaard-Nielsen terms 'operational' and 'peripheral' beliefs – contributing over the longer-term, to change to central, foundational or deep-core beliefs.

88   Securitising actors include political leaders, bureaucracies, governments, lobbyists and pressure groups (Buzan, Waever and De Wilde, 1998: 40), though in democracies, governments tend to enjoy an advantage, stemming from their legitimacy.

89   'Part of public policy, requiring government decision and resource allocations' (Buzan et al, 1998: 23).

90   Referent objects include 'things that are seen to be existentially threatened and that have a legitimate claim to survival' (the state, national sovereignty, ideology, national economies, collective identities and habitats) (Buzan et al, 1998).

91   Defined by Buzan et al (1998: 23) as 'the move that takes politics beyond the established rules of the game'.

Chapter 4

1   Sabatier distinguishes between 'nascent' and 'mature advocacy coalitions. Mature coalitions have a 'line up of allies and opponents that are rather stable over a period of a decade or so', sharing common 'policy core' beliefs (Sabatier and Jenkins-Smith, 1999: 136).

2   For a detailed overview of the membership and work of the *Comite Strategique* see Gregory (2000a: 90–1).

3   Such a *laissez-faire* approach to force structure contrasts markedly to Germany, where the federal system and powerful regional politicians promote an acute concern with the detail of force structures and spatial targeting of troop reductions in order to minimise the political impact of base closures (Dyson, 2007: 63–4).

4   The DGA also established a working group on the implications of battlefield digitisation for 'contact' missions in 1998 that would deliver the concept of the 'Air-Land Bubble' in 2003 (Chevalier, 2003: 37).

5   Operations in Bosnia also underpinned the necessity to retain the capability to conduct deep operations from maritime platforms, a lesson imparted by Operation 'Balbuzard Noir' to rescue French hostages that was conducted from 27 May to 3 June 1995. The importance of such operations was further reinforced by the deployment of forces under EUFOR RD Congo (2006) and the deployment of the combined arms task force GITA-LECLERC to Lebanon in support of UNFIL (2006). See: (Allard, 2008: 82–5).

6   The EU mission to oversee the implementation of the Ohrid Agreements in Macedonia (Operation Concordia, March–December 2002) involved low-intensity tasks and the maintenance of a reputation of impartiality. However, participation in the Operations Field Liaison Teams highlighted to the French military the necessity to prepare for a potential deterioration in the security situation and the importance of the careful application of non-kinetic effects in order to ensure the maintenance of stability. See: Augustin (2006: 57–9).

7   To manage effects-based operations, particularly at the lower end of the conflict spectrum, including tasks such as disarmament, elections and security sector reform (LeCerf, 2008: 34).

8   See: 'Winning the Battle', 2007, pt. 1.2.

9 'Proceedings of the Fourth International Forum on Doctrine: Future Operations and Command Organisation', French Army Doctrine and Higher Military Education Command, French Ministry of Defence, 5 June, 2003, p. 14.

10 *Ibid*, p. 4. The importance of more decentralised command and control is also reinforced by Major-General Jean-Paul Lebourg (Deputy for Doctrine to the Commander of the Army Doctrine and Higher Military Education) who, in 2001, outlined that: 'We must move towards a common understanding of mission command to maximise our effectiveness in PSO...mission command is not a dogma to be adhered to slavishly. It is a philosophy to be applied intelligently'. 'Towards a European Vision for the Use of Land Forces?' Doctrine Forum, Army Command for Doctrine and Higher Military Education, French Military of Defence, June 15, 2001, p.60. On the 'greater freedom of action and extended responsibilities' for subordinates that accompanies battlefield digitisation, see: Nachez (2003: 21–5). On the lessons of the Algerian War of Independence for the importance of decentralised command and control and the resonance of these lessons with those learned from the observation of recent Israeli and Anglo-Saxon experiences, see Bezacier (2004a: 8).

11 Proceedings of the Fourth International Forum on Doctrine: Future Operations and Command Organisation', 2003, p. 45.

12 *Ibid*.

13 *Ibid*. As Major General Gerard Bezacier, Director of the Centre for Force Employment Doctrine noted: 'It should not be forgotten the general commanding the 1st armoured division (UK) never had the time to issue an order to seize Basra: three directives for the initial set-up, then conduct was left to brigades and battalions.' See Bezacier (2004a: 4). Furthermore, Bezacier (2004a: 8) notes: 'The best computer, connected to the best network in the world will not evaluate...the contingencies that still prevail in conflict. Only the present commander amongst his men can feel this immaterial element that he will find extremely difficult to describe and report to his superior.'

14 See: 'Manuel D'Emploi Des Forces Terrestres En Zone Urbaine', 2005, pt. III.5.

15 'Crisis-Management Concept', 2007, pt. 4.6; 'Winning the Battle', 2007, pts. 2.2.3, 2.3.2, 3.2.1.

16 'Winning the Battle', 2007, pts. 2.2.1–2.2.3.

17 On *'foudroydance'* see: 'Principes D'Emploi De La Fot Numerisee De Niveau 3', 2004, pt. II.2.2

18 'Ten French Soldiers Killed in Afghanistan as Taliban Attacks Grow More Audacious', *Guardian*, 20 August 2008.

19 *Aerocombat* is defined by General Vincent Desportes as: 'The coordinated and integrated maneuver of tactical level units operating on the ground and in an air-space close to the ground, under the direct responsibility of the Force's Land Component Commander.' See: Desportes (2008c: 6). On the historical antecedents of the concept of *Aerocombat* and the critical application of past French operational experiences see: Krugler (2008: 67–71).

20 See: 'Afghan Operations Highlight Need For Close Air Support', *Defense News*, 11 May 2009 (Defense 2009). The importance of integrated manoeuvre had also been demonstrated by deployments such as Operation Licorne and observation of US and UK combat operations in Iraq, in which combat helicopters proved critical in facilitating manoeuvre during the 'initial entry' stage of operations. These experiences pointed to the utility of the TIGRE HAP/HAD multipurpose attack helicopters which are fitted with short-long range precision-guided munitions facilitating the close support of land forces in urban environments as well as longer-range engagement on the battlefield. See: De Certaines (2003: 30–1).

21 As Brigadier General Vincent Desportes (2007: 8) stated of observation of the US in Iraq and Afghanistan: 'Each of us was able to observe that the military power could be bypassed...one must get prepared to the war we shall have to conduct...and we should know that the principles of irregular warfare, its politico-military grammar, are not affected by technological solutions.'

22 SIGNIT intelligence has also been crucial in intercepting enemy communication systems (Chereau, 2006: 28; Coppolani, 2006: 9).

23 The notion of the 'solider as sensor' refers to the role of the soldier in gathering accurate intelligence about the enemy in addition to environmental intelligence such as the cultural, social, religious and economic context. See: Coppolani (2004: 20); Desportes (2006: 3–4).

24 It is important to note, however, that the need to attain complementarity between technical and human intelligence collection capabilities was already embedded within the armed forces following the stabilisation missions in the Balkans and by France's colonial experiences (Blervaque, 2006: 32).

25 It is also important to note the lessons drawn by the French from the utility of technology in the context of asymmetrical conflict following observation of the Israeli attack on Lebanon in 2006 (Desportes, 2008a: 9; Desportes, 2007: 4). On the important role of civil-military cooperation (CIMIC) within the Mastery of Violence, see Fischer (2003: 35–6, 2004: 27). On the centrality of mastering the application of kinetic and non-kinetic effects, see: 'Doctrine D'Emploi Des Forces Terrestres en Stabilisation', 2006, pt. 1.2.

26 On the resonance of lessons-identified about the role of intelligence during the First Indo-China War with contemporary challenges, see Porte (2006: 100–2).

27 The emphasis on the importance of non-kinetic effects can be traced back even further to the French colonial experience of 'pacification' (a term that refers to the winning of trust amongst the occupied population) operations during the 19th century (Grintchenko, 2007: 102–5). See, for example, Savary de Beauregard (2007: 97–101) on the contemporary application of the doctrinal conclusions drawn from past colonial experiences in Tonkin and Madagascar (in particular, the work of Marechal Gallieni, Marechal Lyautey and General Pennequin).

28 On civil-military coordination in French military history, see: Hue (2007: 29–30).

29 Challe was, of course, not an isolated innovator within the French Military. The changes wrought by Challe in the Algerian War of Independence drew upon the work of a range of French theorists of 'revolutionary war' who came to prominence during the late 1950s, led by Colonel Charles Lacheroy, Head of the French Army's *Service d'Action Psychologique* (Roberts, 2008: 36).

30 France has also sought to learn lessons from the Israeli experience of combat operations in urban environments following the inception of the Intifada in September 2000. Key lessons-identified included the importance of manoeuvre, surprise and of pragmatism and flexibility in operating modes and command and control. See: Binnendjik (2004: 37–40).

31 The mixture of colonial experiences and observation of the experiences of others in determining the French approach to networking is illustrated by General Bezacier (2004a: 8): 'Let's recall the Algerian example of Lieutenant Colonel Bigeard conducting just by sight and voice an air-land battle of infantry companies, helicopters, direct support aircraft and artillery fires with a handful of radio sets around him. It is not necessary to rely on recent Anglo-Saxon engagements to state that the place of a brigade or a battalion commander is, in most places, up front. Information technology must be an aid and offer the commander the possibility to command at the heart of the action from a light and ultra-mobile tactical CP.'

32   Respondents included NCOs, Company Grade Officers, Former Company Commanders, Field Grade Officers with experience ranging from operations in Beirut in the 1980s to Afghanistan (Zbienen, 2004: 56–7).

33   'Doctrine' was preceded by the publication *Objectif Doctrine* that was first published in January 1999, although it was not until the edition of February 2001 that the French articles were accompanied by an English translation.

34   'Review of Acquisition for the Secretary of State of Defence', 15 October 2009, p. 215.

35   *Ibid*, pp. 220–1.

36   *Ibid*, p. 221.

37   *Ibid*, p. 221.

38   *Ibid*, p. 221.

39   *Ibid*, p. 222.

40   *Ibid*, p. 222.

41   *Ibid*, p. 222.

42   *Ibid*, p. 223.

43   *Ibid*, p. 223.

44   'Sarkozy Unveils Plans for French Return to NATO Command', *France 24*, 11 March 2009. See (France24, 2009).

45   'Sarkozy to End France's 40 Year NATO Feud', *Guardian*, 11 March 2009.

46   'Sarkozy Announces French Return to NATO After 43 Years', *Daily Telegraph*, 11 March 2009.

47   France24 (2009).

48   'Sarkozy Announces French Return to NATO After 43 Years', *Daily Telegraph*, 11 March 2009.

Chapter 5

1   Post-Cold War unity amongst both 'catch-all parties' the SPD (German Social Democratic Party) and CDU (Christian Democrats)/CSU (Christian Social Union) on the 'citizen in uniform' as a key element of *Innere Führung* makes it difficult to apply Kier's analytical framework, for despite this civilian unity, international threats and opportunities appear (until 2003) to play a lesser role in shaping military doctrine than in France and the UK. See: Dalvi, 2004; Dyson, 2005: 374–5; Kier, 1997: 4; Longhurst, 2003.

2   In the year 2000, a *Zivildienstleistende* (conscientious objector) cost the state DM 14,000, whilst a professional would have cost DM 50–70,000. See: 'Brennpunkt Zivildienst', *Focus* no. 22, 2000. In the late 1990s over 140,000 *Zivildienstleistende* were on active duty each year (Dyson, 2007: 77).

3   German Basic Law, Article 65a, 115b.

4   The Parliament has the power to prescribe the terms of engagement for the KSK, who, under ISAF, are restricted to deploying lethal force only when under attack and have therefore focused on reconnaissance tasks. The German Defence Minister is, however, required to inform only the Chairpersons of the Bundestag's Foreign and Defence Committees about KSK operations and retains the capacity to withhold 'classified information'. During confidential interviews in the German Defence Ministry it was acknowledged by an interview partner that the KSK have undertaken high-intensity operations in the South of Afghanistan.

5   The concept of *Innere Führung* was developed by Wolf Graf Baudissin. It took root in the *Bundeswehr* during the post-war period and, as outlined in the 2006

White Paper, 'promotes the capacity of the individual to act on his or her own responsibly in morally difficult situations'. See: 'White Paper on German Security Policy and the Future of the *Bundeswehr*', 2006, p. 71.

6 Whilst it is possible to make a broad generalisation about German security 'identity', it is important to note the presence of ideological divergence during the immediate post-Cold War era. On the 'freedom', 'peace' and 'pacifist' coalitions, see Dalgaard-Nielsen (2005: 344); Dyson (2007: 30–2) and Gutjahr (1994: 135–46).

7 Interview, *Fuehrungsakademie der Bundeswehr*, Hamburg, 22 October 2009.

8 Rühe's understanding of 'responsibility' contrasted markedly to the rhetoric employed by Foreign Minister Hans-Dietrich Genscher (1974–92) in the run-up to the 1990–91 Iraq War, in which 'responsibility' was associated not with military burden-sharing, but with a 'policy of good example' in the pursuit of a 'new culture of international coexistence' (Baumann and Hellmann, 2001: 61–82).

9 'Gemeinsam Rein, Gemeinsam Raus: Die Hilfe für den Zivilen Wiederaufbau hinkt der internationalen Friedensstreitmacht hinterher', *Focus*, no. 49, 1995. This policy narrative found strong support amongst foreign and security policy heavyweights within the SPD, such as Karsten Voigt, Rudolf Scharping and Guenther Verheugen and the 'Realo' wing of the German Green Party, which included figures such as Joschka Fischer and Waltraud Schoppe (Maull, 2000: 62–4). Ruehe also promoted a visit of Pacifist Green MPs to Bosnia (Dyson, 2007: 61).

10 'I don't need a professional armed force. I would only need one if I wanted to intervene worldwide in places like Haiti.' See: 'Zapfenstreich für die Wehrpflicht', *Focus*, no. 3, 1997.

11 'Wirklichkeit mit Tarnkappe', *Focus*, no. 16, 1999. Chancellor Gerhard Schroeder also emphasised Germany's 'historical responsibility to prevent mass murder with all necessary means' (Baumann and Hellmann, 2001). Baumann and Hellmann (2001) highlight how German intelligence leading up to the Kosovo conflict did not support claims of an impending genocide of ethnic Albanians. On the role of Foreign Minister Joschka Fischer in mobilising support for German participation in Operation Allied Force amongst the German Green Party and Left, see Hyde-Price and Jeffrey (2001: 704–7).

12 See also Breuer (2006: 209); Dalgaard-Nielsen (2005: 347–8); Hyde-Price and Jeffrey (2001: 707).

13 The discourses of responsibility, multilateralism and '*Berechenbarkeit*' were employed by elite voices within the German core executive in order to sell troop deployment in Afghanistan. As Chancellor Schröder stated in the parliamentary debate before the final vote on 16 November 2001: 'This is about the reliability of our policies in the eyes of our citizens, our friends in Europe and our international partners...By making this contribution, united and sovereign Germany is taking account of its increased responsibility in the world.' 'German Troops on Alert After Schröder Scrapes Crucial Confidence Vote', *The Independent*, 17 November 2001.

14 'Scharping, der unverdrossene Verteidiger', *Spiegel*, 7 April 2002. See also 'Krach zwischen Trittin und Scharping', *Spiegel*, 25 April 2002. Scharping also received the support of other elite figures in the dissemination of this discourse, including Chancellor Schroeder, see: 'Schroeder und Scharping halten an Wehrpflicht fest', *Handeslblatt*, 3 April 2002 and 'Schroeder fuer Wehrpflicht: Basta, es bleibt dabei', *Spiegel*, 8 April 2002.

15 'Interview zur Zukunft der *Bundeswehr* und zur weiteren Weiterentwicklung in Irak', 24 April 2003. See: BMVG (2003). On the extension of the geographical scope of deployment see: 'Verteidigungspolitische Richtlinien', 2003, p. 5.

16   'The defence of human rights, freedom, democracy and the rule of law are not abstract concepts, they are living tradition in the *Bundeswehr*. These values are, and will always be, a core orientation for any soldier on deployment.' See 'Rede des Bundesministers der Verteidigung, Dr. Peter Struck, an der Führungsakademie der *Bundeswehr*', 23 May 2003, Hamburg, Germany. On the link between *Wehrdienst* and *Zivildienst* see 'Interview zur Zukunft der *Bundeswehr* und zur weiteren Weiterentwicklung in Irak', 24 April 2003. See: BMVG, 2003. On the utility of conscripts in crisis-management operations, see: 'Wir müssen die Landesverteidigung neu definieren', *Süddeutsche Zeitung*, 4 February 2004.

17   See, for example: 'Den Super-Gau Denken', *Welt am Sonntag*, 9 November 2003. On the role of 'public vulnerability' in the mobilisation of societies behind conflict see Becker (2009: 357).

18   Struck legitimated the 2003 reform to policy objectives by framing it as a redefined form of territorial defence. See: 'Wir müssen die Landesverteidigung neu definieren', *Süddeutsche Zeitung*, 4 February 2004. See also: Verteidigungspolitische Richtlinien', 21 May 2003, p. 3.

19   'Rede des Bundesministers der Verteidigung, Dr Peter Struck, an der Führungsakademie der *Bundeswehr*', 23 May 2003, Hamburg, Germany.

20   As Breuer (2006: 216) notes: 'Today German democracy is very stable and it is doubtful if the "democratic and civil control" argument supporting conscription is still valid.'

21   See: 'Scharping, der unverdrossene Verteidiger', *Spiegel*, 7 April 2002.

22   See: 'Interview zur Zukunft der *Bundeswehr* und zur weiteren Weiterentwicklung in Irak', 24 April 2003 (BMVG, 2003).

23   See: 'Ende mit Schrecken', *Spiegel*, 17 March 2003, p. 50.

24   Rühe's and Scharping's unwillingness to alienate powerful regional figures within their parties due to their personal political ambition of the Chancellorship circumscribed their willingness to push through radical base closures and contributed to the careful spatial targeting of base closures and avoidance of large-scale closures in *Länder* with forthcoming elections (Dyson, 2007: 104, 108, 173). The sensitivity of the politics of base closures and the abolition of conscription made the Defence Ministry something of a political graveyard and an unattractive ministerial position, gaining a reputation as a '*Schleudersitz*' (ejector seat) (Dyson, 2007: 229).

     On Rühe and constitutional constraints see Dyson (2007: 59–61); on Rühe, the Bundestag and the deployment of troops see Dyson (2007: 61); on Struck and the negotiation of constitutional constraints, see Dyson (2005: 376–7).

25   See also: 'Verteidigungsminister Jung und Afghanistan', *Die Welt*, 12 September 2009.

26   *Ibid.*

27   'Out of Erbach', *Spiegel*, 46, 12 November 2007.

28   This sense of public vulnerability was present following the events of September 11 2001 and helped to mobilise the public on behalf of the initial deployment of the *Bundeswehr* under Operation Enduring Freedom. See for example, 'Den Super-Gau Denken', *Welt am Sonntag*, 9 November 2003.

29   This window of opportunity is, however, narrow, as the CDU faces an important election in May 2010 when it will attempt to retain control of Germany's most populous and economically-powerful State, North-Rhine Westphalia.

30   As a source within the Defence Ministry noted of the impact of resource constraints on the nature of Germany's emulation of the RMA: 'If we had a hammer, we too might see a nail'. Interview, German Defence Ministry, Bonn, 12 October 2008.

31 Interview, German Defence Ministry, Bonn, 12 October 2008.
32 'White Paper on German Security Policy and the Future of the *Bundeswehr*', 2006, pp. 70–2; Interview, *Fuehrungsakademie der Bundeswehr*, Hamburg, 22 October 2009.
33 Interview, *Fuehrungsakademie der Bundeswehr*, Hamburg, 22 October 2009.
34 Interviews, German Defence Ministry, Bonn, 12 October 2009.
35 Afghanistan reinforced the centrality of interoperable, secure tactical communication equipment and reconnaissance systems. 'Battlefield Lessons Show Network Centric Way for Germany', *Signal*, May, 2009; interviews Defence Ministry, Bonn, 19 October 2009.
36 Interview, German Defence Ministry, Bonn, 12 October 2009.
37 Interview, *Fuehrungsakademie der Bundesswehr*, Hamburg, 22 October 2009.
38 'White Paper on German Security Policy and the Future of the *Bundeswehr*', 2006, p. 72. On the key competencies of the Stabilisation Forces and *Eingreifskraefte*, see: 'SFT 21-2040 Mensch in Transformation Workshop', pp. 68–9. Germany placed emphasis on the importance of cultural awareness at an early stage. For example, care was taken to ensure that HUMINT teams on deployment under KFOR were not only endowed with linguistic skills, but that they also included members from the religious background of the local population. Interview, German Defence Ministry, Bonn, 19 October 2009.
39 Interview, Fuehrungsakademie der Bundeswehr, Hamburg, 22 October 2009; Interviews Bundeswehr Transformation Centre, Strausberg, 26 November 2009.
40 Interviews, Germany Defence Ministry, Bonn, 19 October 2009.
41 Interview, *Fuehrungsakademie der Bundeswehr*, Hamburg, 22 October 2009.
42 *Ibid.*
43 *Ibid.*
44 Interviews, Bundeswehr Transformation Centre, Strausberg, 26 November 2009.
45 Interviews, German Defence Ministry, Bonn, 19 October 2009; interview, *Fuehrungsakademie der Bundeswehr*, Hamburg, 22 October 2009; interviews, Bundeswehr Transformation Centre, Strausberg, 26 November 2009.
46 'SFT 21-2040 Mensch in Transformation Workshop', pp. 68–9. 'More technical, language, social and communication skills are needed in the armed forces. In the foreseeable future the traditional warrior qualities will also be necessary.' See: 'SFT 21-2040 Mensch in Transformation Workshop', pp. 50–1.
47 The KSK also participated in higher-intensity combat operations under Operation Enduring Freedom (Noetzel and Schreer, 2008b: 214).
48 See also: 'Afghanistan und die *Bundeswehr*: Viel Verstaendnis', *Sueddeutsche Zeitung*, 11 September 2009.
49 Interview, *Fuehrungsakademie Der Bundeswehr*, Hamburg, 22 October 2009.
50 'Mensch in Transformation Workshop', 2006, p. 40.
51 *Ibid*, p. 41.
52 *Ibid*, p. 69.
53 Interviewees within the Defence Ministry were keen to emphasise that Germany was now conducting counterinsurgency in the North of Afghanistan.
54 The notion of 'Three Block Operations' reflects the view that winning the support of the local population through the non-kinetic dimensions of irregular warfare must stand at the centre of operations.
55 See also: '*Bundeswehrverband*: Deutsche Soldaten sind in Kunduz im Krieg', *Frankfurter Allgemeine Zeitung*, 11 September 2009; Interviews, German Defence Ministry, Bonn, 19 October 2009; interview *Fuehrungsakademie Der Bundeswehr* Hamburg, 22 October 2009.

56 The *Heeresfuehrungskommando* conducted a military exercise in 2009 that focused specifically on how to shift operational modes at short-notice. Interview, *Fuehungsakademie der Bundeswehr*, Hamburg, 22 October 2009.
57 Interviews, German Defence Ministry, Bonn, 19 October 2009.
58 Interview, *Fuehrungsakademie der Bundeswehr*, Hamburg, 22 October 2009.
59 Interview, German Defence Ministry, Berlin, 10 November 2009.
60 Interview *Fuehrungsakademie der Bundeswehr*, Hamburg, 22 October 2009; interview German Defence Ministry, Berlin, 10 November 2009.
61 Interview, *Fuehrungsakademie der Bundeswehr*, Hamburg, 22 October 2009.
62 'White Paper on German Security Policy and the Future of the *Bundeswehr*', 2006, p. 77.
63 *Ibid*, p. 11.
64 Interview, *Fuehrungsakademie Der Bundeswehr*, Hamburg, 22 October 2009. See also Laupert (2008: 8).
65 'White Paper on German Security Policy and the Future of the *Bundeswehr*', 2006, p. 78.
66 'Sicherheitspolitische Zukunftsanalyse: Ausblick auf 2035 Trends und Entwicklungen', 2007, p. 16. Interviews, Defence Ministry, Bonn, 12 and 19 October 2009; Interview, *Fuehrungsakademie der Bundeswehr*, Hamburg, 22 October 2009.
67 Interviews, Defence Ministry, Bonn, 12 October 2009; Interviews, Bundeswehr Transformation Centre, Strausberg, 26 November 2009.
68 Interviews, Defence Ministry, Bonn, 12 October 2009.
69 Interview, Defence Ministry, Bonn, 12 October 2009.
70 Interviews, Defence Ministry, Bonn, 12 and 19 October 2009.
71 Interviews, Bundeswehr Transformation Centre, Strausberg, 26 November 2009.
72 Interview, *Fuehrungsakademie der Bundeswehr*, Hamburg, 22 October 2009.
73 Interview, Defence Ministry, Bonn, 12 October 2009.
74 Interview, *Fuehrungsakademie der Bundeswehr*, Hamburg, 22 October 2009.
75 *Ibid.*
76 *Ibid.*
77 *Ibid.*
78 Interviews Defence Ministry, Bonn, 19 October 2009; Interview, *Fuehrungsakademie der Bundeswehr*, Hamburg, 22 October 2009.
79 Interviews, Defence Ministry, Bonn, 12 October 2009.
80 Interview, Defence Ministry, Bonn, 12 October 2009; Defence Ministry, Bonn, 19 October, 2009.
81 Interviews, Defence Ministry, Bonn, 19 October 2009; *Fuehrungsakademie der Bundeswehr*, 22 October 2009.
82 Interviews, Defence Ministry, Bonn, 19 October 2009; interview Defence Ministry, Berlin, 10 November 2009.
83 *Ibid.*
84 Interview, Defence Ministry, Berlin, 10 November 2009.
85 *Ibid.*
86 Interview, *Fuehrungsakademie der Bundeswehr*, Hamburg, 22 October 2009.
87 Interview, Defence Ministry, Berlin, 10 November 2009.
88 *Ibid.*
89 Interview, *Fuehrungsakademie der Bundeswehr*, Hamburg, 22 October 2009.
90 Interview, Defence Ministry, Berlin, 10 November 2009.
91 Interview, Defence Ministry, Bonn, 12 October 2009.
92 Interview, Defence Ministry, Berlin, 10 November 2009.
93 *Ibid.*

94   *Ibid.*
95   *Ibid.*
96   Interview, Defence Ministry, Berlin, 10 November 2009; interviews Bundeswehr Transformation Centre, Strausberg, 26 November 2009.
97   Interview, Defence Ministry, Berlin, 10 November 2009.
98   *Ibid.*
99   *Ibid.*
100 Interviews, Defence Ministry Bonn, 12 October 2009; interviews Defence Ministry, Bonn, 19 October 2009.
101 Interviews, Bundeswehr Transformation Centre, Strausberg, 26 November 2009.
102 Interviews, Defence Ministry, Bonn, 12 October 2009.
103 Interviews, Bundeswehr Transformation Centre, Strausberg, 26 November 2009.
104 Interviews, Defence Ministry, Bonn, 12 October 2009; interviews, Defence Ministry, Bonn, 19 October 2009.
105 Interviews, Defence Ministry, Bonn, 12 October 2009.
106 Interviews, Defence Ministry, Bonn, 12 October 2009; Interviews Bundeswehr Transformation Centre, Strausberg, 26 November 2009.
107 Interviews, Defence Ministry, Bonn, 12 October 2009.
108 *Ibid.*
109 *Ibid.*
110 Interviews, Defence Ministry, Bonn, 12 and 19 October 2009; Interviews, Bundeswehr Transformation Centre, Strausberg, 26 November 2009.
111 *Ibid.*
112 Interviews, Bundeswehr Transformation Centre, Strausberg, 26 November 2006.
113 *Ibid.*
114 *Ibid.*
115 *Ibid.*
116 *Ibid.*
117 *Ibid.*
118 Interviews, Bundeswehr Transformation Centre, Strausberg, 26 November 2009; Interview, Defence Ministry, Berlin, 24 November 2009.
119 Interview, Defence Ministry, Berlin, 24 November 2009; Interview, Bundeswehr Transformation Centre, Strausberg, 26 November 2009.
120 Interview, Defence Ministry, Berlin, 24 November 2009.
121 *Ibid.*
122 Interview, Bundeswehr Transformation Centre, Strausberg, 26 November 2009.
123 Interview, Defence Ministry, Bonn, 24 November 2009; Interviews Bundeswehr Transformation Centre, Strausberg, 26 November 2009.
124 A 'core Europe' on ESDP also raised the specter of a loss of regional influence amongst East Central European states (Dyson, 2005: 376). See: 'Interview with Defence Minister Peter Struck', *Der Tagesspiegel*, 13 April 2003. On the 'indispensable' role of the US in German Defence and Security Policy see: 'Interview with Peter Struck: The Relationship with the United States and the *Bundeswehr* of the Future', *Hamburger Abendblatt*, 5 April 2003. See also 'White Paper on German Security Policy and the Future of the *Bundeswehr*', 2006, p. 6.
125 Including a force of 15,000 on permanent standby for the NRF; a commitment of 18,000 troops to the Battlegroups and 1,000 troops for the UN Standby Arrangement System. See 'White Paper on German Security Policy and the Future of the *Bundeswehr*', 2006, p. 35.
126 The 2003 VPR outline how 'armaments cooperation within a European and Trans-Atlantic framework will be given priority over the realisation of projects

under national responsibility'. See: 'Verteidigungspolitische Richtlinien', 2003, p. 5. The 'Future Threat Analysis 2035' also recognises that European cooperation – both with industry and other governments – will be critical if Germany is to develop space based ISR assets (in particular secure broadband data connections for UAV deployment). See 'Sicherheitspolitische Zukunftsanalyse: Ausblick auf 2035 Trends und Entwicklungen', 2007.

127   Interview, *Fuehrungsakademie der Bundeswehr*, Hamburg, 22 October 2009.
128   Interview, *Fuehrungsakademie der Bundeswehr*, Hamburg, 22 October 2009.
129   *Ibid.*
130   Interview, Bundeswehr Transformation Centre, Berlin, Germany, 25 September 2009 (conducted by telephone).
131   Interview, Defence Ministry, Bonn, 12 October 2009; Interview Defence Ministry, Bonn, 19 October 2009; Interview, *Fuehrungsakademie der Bundeswehr*, Hamburg, 22 October 2009.
132   Interview, *Fuehrungsakademie der Bundeswehr*, Hamburg, Germany, 22 October 2009.
133   *'Bundeswehrverband*: Merkel soll Afghanistan zur Chefsache machen', *Sueddeutsche Zeitung*, 11 September 2009.

Chapter 6

1   Kier's focus on organisational culture and civil-military relations would lead us to the conclusion that the smooth response to changing threats and opportunities at the international level is more a reflection of British civil-military relations and political consensus on the domestic role of the armed forces, than of the broader 'national security culture'.
2   On informational uncertainty following systemic power shifts and the risks associated with imprudent strategic choices see Rathburn (2007: 534, 2008: 317) and Rose (1998: 153).
3   As Howorth (2004: 217) notes, executive autonomy was a significant factor determining Tory policy towards the institutional forums of defence policy in advance of the 1997 general election: 'Limited thinking on European defence issues...was predicated upon the perceived electoral necessity of distancing the UK from the dangerous and heretical theories being spun in Paris.'
4   Conservative opposition to Labour's reform proposals was mitigated by the Tory legacy of cuts to the defence budget and the internal disarray within the Conservative Party following their emphatic electoral defeat in 1997. Labour's large parliamentary majority strengthened the competencies of the core executive in defence policy *vis-à-vis* the House of Commons Parliamentary Select Committee on Defence (Dover, 2005: 516).
5   'Strategic Defence Review', Essay 1, Point 19, UK Ministry of Defence, 1998.
6   'Strategic Defence Review', Essay 1, UK Ministry of Defence, 1998.
7   Blair and Robertson had originally intended the review process to last only six months (McInnes, 1998: 829).
8   'British Defence Doctrine', 2008, pt. 531.
9   The approach to defence reform that followed the 'third order' change of the SDR was as Cornish and Dorman (2009: 252) highlight, a form of 'recalibration'. See also Hollinshead (1998: 60–1). As the 2002 'New Chapter' noted: 'Whilst the work has examined some fundamental issues, we have not started from a blank sheet. The SDR...set us firmly on the right track...the emphasis on expeditionary operations, usually working with our allies, has enabled the UK to have a key role in

shaping the international security environment.' See: 'Strategic Defence Review: A New Chapter', 2002, p. 4.

10 On continuing contestation within the British military concerning the utility of the Manoeuvrist Approach, see Owen (2008: 62–7).

11 See: 'The Comprehensive Approach', UK Ministry of Defence, 2008.

12 The need to remain prepared for Major Combat Operations is demonstrated by the DCDC Strategic Trends Programme that highlight how: 'The risks of interstate war may increase beyond 2020 when intensifying competition for resources, particularly energy and possibly food, and continued population growth result in higher tension.' 'The DCDC Global Strategic Trends Programme 2007–2036', Development, Concepts and Doctrine Centre, UK Ministry of Defence, 2006 p. 68. See also: 'The Future Land Operational Concept', 2008, point. 114, b and Kiszely (2007: 13). On UK leadership of medium-sized operations, see: 'Future Capabilities, Factsheet 1: The Policy Baseline – Why We Need to Change', UK Ministry of Defence, 2004.

On the implications of post-Cold War military operations for the maintenance of interoperability with the US, see also 'Operations in Iraq: Lessons for the Future', UK Ministry of Defence, 2003, points 7.7–7.8.

13 See Geoff Hoon, House of Commons Debate, 11 December 2003, *Hansard*, vol. 415, p. 1209. See also: Chapter 6, 'Key Defence Capability Issues and Joint Lessons', in 'Kosovo: Lessons from the Crisis', UK Ministry of Defence, 2000.

14 See 'Kosovo: Lessons from the Crisis', Chapter 6.

15 *Ibid.* As Corelli Barnett (2000: 60) notes, rather than vindicating stand-off precision strike capabilities and air power, the Kosovo conflict demonstrated that 'it will be the threat, or the use of, land forces which alone will be decisive'.

16 The significant differences between the British and US approaches to the potential of stand-off, precision strike capabilities were already evident in the aftermath of the Kosovo conflict. As Vice Admiral Sir Jeremy Blackham noted in December 2000: 'This new capability is not the mythical silver bullet...the proposition that precision engagement can, by itself, particularly when conducted solely or mainly form the air, determine the political outcome of events, is a dangerous simplification' (Blackham 2000b: 67).

17 The Iraq conflict highlighted the flexibility and adaptability, extension of reach, role in target acquisition and force protection delivered by the UK Phoenix. The conflict also threw into relief a number of weaknesses with UAV systems, notably the need to boost interoperability between US UAV systems and UK land forces (Burridge, 2003: 18–23).

18 Interviews, DCDC, Shrivenham, 18 November 2009.

19 'The Comprehensive Approach', 2006, pt. 102.

20 This danger of senior commanders being dragged down to the tactical level was also noted by Air Marshall Brian Burridge, Commander in Chief, Strike Command in the immediate aftermath of Operation Telic (Burridge, 2003: 22) and by Vice Admiral Sir Jeremy Blackham, Former Deputy Chief of the Defence Staff (Equipment Capability) who also notes how human factors and training are critical to the successful exploitation of the digitisation of battlespace (Blackham, 2002: 29).

21 See also Gray (2000: 60–2).

22 See: 'Chapter 3: Communications and Information Systems', 'Operations in Iraq: Lessons for the Future', 2003. The initial phase of Operation Telic did, nevertheless highlight several areas of command and control requiring improvement: a need to reduce the size of deployed HQs, streamline HQ processes and focus on permitting a more efficient flow of information and to focus training on the

execution of operations under temporal and informational constraints. See: Rollins (2004: 62).

23　See: 'Chapter 3: Communications and Information Systems', 'Operations in Iraq: Lessons for the Future', 2003.

24　See: 'Campaigning', JDP 01, Second Edition, UK Ministry of Defence (2008: pt. 108–9).

25　As Rollins (2006: 87) highlights the experiences of 'small wars' were not codified in official doctrine, but were instead disseminated through 'a body of unofficial but influential writings'.

26　As Sir John Kiszely (2007: 15) notes, in contemporary British COIN: 'relatively junior commanders are making very senior decisions'. On British Defence Doctrine, see Milton (2001: 41–4). Major General John McColl (2004: 53) also cites the concept of 'Three Block War' as the conceptual framework within which NEC should be developed.

27　Air Marshall Sir Glenn Torpy (Chief of Staff, RAF) notes how doctrinal developments based upon the experiences of the RAF in COIN operations during the interwar period have largely been reinforced by contemporary operational experiences (Torpy, 2007: 18–22).

28　See also Cousens (2006: 56–7) who notes that whilst British peacekeeping doctrine draws heavily on the past, colonial experiences are in large part highly relevant to present day COIN and the challenges of Three Block Warfare.

29　Interviews, DCDC, Shrivenham, 18 November 2009.

30　See also: 'British Defence Doctrine', 2008, pt. 1.

31　Interviews, DCDC, Shrivenham, 18 November 2009.

32　Interviews, DCDC, Shrivenham, 18 November 2009.

33　'National Security Strategy of the United Kingdom: Security in an Interdependent World', Cabinet Office, London, pp. 13–14, 55–60.

34　'JDP 3-40 Security and Stabilisation: The Military Contribution', 2009, pts. 226–34.

35　Including Addressing the Drivers of Insecurity (focusing, in particular, on identifying and engaging with the decisive actors in a stabilisation operation (both friend and foe); understanding shifting allegiances; developing tailored approaches to engaging other actors in the operational environment); Establishing Human Security (focusing on protecting the populations; proving humanitarian assistance and developing secured areas); Security Force Capacity Building and Countering Adversaries (focusing on attention to the impact of the reactive and offensive use of force, the use of money and detention). *Ibid*, pts. 501–35.

36　Including Addressing Critical Governance Functions (the protection of civilians; restoration of essential services; engagement and conflict resolution; supporting elections; anti-corruption activities and building local capacities) and Reforming the Security and Justice Sectors (through a set of specific military tasks which will facilitate the development of accessible security and justice: the initial generation of indigenous forces; management of indigenous forces; education; disarmament, demobilisation and reintegration; host government and ministry reform; developing indigenous police services; the restoration of judicial institutions; development of border forces; tracking of intelligence and security services activities and longer-term partnership development following the transfer of responsibility to the host nation). *Ibid*, pts. 605–38.

37　Including working with DfID and other national and international actors in Addressing Critical Development Needs (including Provincial Reconstruction Teams; assisting in the stabilisation of the economy; assisting in the reconstruction of essential infrastructure; the generation of employment; addressing the economic drivers of conflict) and organising Quick Impact Projects (short-term, small scale projects at the tactical level designed to foster economic and political development and establish confidence and consent for local government). *Ibid*, pts. 704–36.

38 For further details, see: *Ibid*, Chapter 8.
39 *Ibid*, Chapter 9.
40 *Ibid*, Chapter 10.
41 *Ibid*, pts. 1001–2.
42 *Ibid*, pt. 445.
43 *Ibid*.
44 *Ibid*, pt. 446.
45 *Ibid*, pt. 447.
46 *Ibid*, pt. 447.
47 *Ibid*, x.
48 See 'British Defence Doctrine', 2008, pt. 301
49 'A Perspective on the Nature of Future Conflict', Speech by General Sir Richard Dannatt, Friday 15 May 2009, Chatham House, London.
50 Interview, UK Defence Academy, Shrivenham, 18 November 2009.
51 Interviews, UK Ministry of Defence, London, 19–20 November 2009.
52 *Ibid*.
53 Interview, UK Ministry of Defence, London, 20 November 2009.
54 Interviews, DCDC, Shrivenham, 18 November 2009; interviews, UK Ministry of Defence, London, 19–20 November 2009.
55 *Ibid*.
56 *Ibid*.
57 The DCDC was also designed to provide the intellectual foundations which would strengthen British input into NATO CD&E under ACT as well as facilitate Britain's adaptation to a quickly-changing operational environment.
58 Interviews, DCDC, Shrivenham, 18 November 2009; Ministry of Defence, London, 19–20 November 2009.
59 *Ibid*.
60 Interview, UK Ministry of Defence, London, 19 November 2009.
61 Interviews, UK Ministry of Defence, London, 19–20 November 2009.
62 Interviews, DCDC, Shrivenham, 18 November 2009.
63 Interviews, DCDC, Shrivenham, 18 November 2009; UK Ministry of Defence, London, 19–20 November 2009.
64 Interviews, DCDC, Shrivenham, 18 November 2009.
65 Interviews, DCDC, Shrivenham, 18 November 2009; UK Ministry of Defence 19–20 November 2009.
66 Interviews, UK Ministry of Defence, London, 19–20 November 2009.
67 Interviews, DCDC, Shrivenham, 18 November 2009; Interview UK Ministry of Defence, 19 November 2009.
68 Interviews, UK Ministry of Defence, London, 19–20 November 2009.
69 *Ibid*.
70 *Ibid*.
71 Interview, UK Ministry of Defence, London, 20 November 2009.
72 Interviews, UK Ministry of Defence, London, 19–20 November 2009.
73 Interview, UK Ministry of Defence, London, 20 November 2009.
74 Interviews, UK Ministry of Defence, London, 19–20 November 2009.
75 *Ibid*.

76   Smart Acquisition was the first major reform of defence acquisition since the Managing Major Projects in the Procurement Executive Report of 1987.
77   'Review of Acquisition for the Secretary of State of Defence', 15 October 2009, p. 59.
78   *Ibid*, p. 59.
79   *Ibid*, p. 59; interview, DE&S, UK Defence Ministry, Bristol, 16 November 2009.
80   Review of Acquisition for the Secretary of State of Defence', 15 October 2009; p. 60; see also 'DE&S: An introduction', pp. 20–4.
81   'Review of Acquisition for the Secretary of State of Defence', 15 October 2009, p. 16.
82   *Ibid*, p. 21.
83   *Ibid*, p. 32.
84   *Ibid*, pp. 30–1; interview, UK Ministry of Defence, London, 20 November 2009.
85   Interview, Defence Equipment and Support, UK Ministry of Defence, Bristol, 16 November 2009.
86   *Ibid.*
87   Review of Acquisition for the Secretary of State of Defence', 15 October 2009, p. 31.
88   *Ibid*, p. 22.
89   *Ibid*, p. 26.
90   *Ibid*, p. 26.
91   *Ibid*, p. 34.
92   *Ibid*, p. 36.
93   *Ibid*, p. 37.
94   *Ibid*, pp. 12–13.
95   Interview, DE&S, UK MoD, Bristol, 16 November 2009.
96   *Ibid.*
97   The Programme Boards coordinate issues of military doctrine, support, training equipment, manpower and personnel relating to the deployment of a capability.
98   Review of Acquisition for the Secretary of State of Defence', 15 October 2009, pp. 42–4.
99   *Ibid*, p. 47.
100 *Ibid*, p. 49.
101 *Ibid*, pp. 49–50.
102 Interview, DE&S, UK Ministry of Defence, Bristol, 16 November 2009; Interviews, UK Ministry of Defence, London, 19–20 November 2009.
103 'Ministerial Statement Independent Review Defence Acquisition', 15 October 2009.
104 Interviews, UK Ministry of Defence, London, 20 November 2009.
105 Interviews, Ministry of Defence, London, 19–20 November 2009.
106 *Ibid.*
107 Interviews, Ministry of Defence, London, 19–20 November 2009; on the key security threats identified by the National Security Strategy, see 'National Security Strategy of the United Kingdom: Security in an Interdependent World', The Cabinet Office, London, 2008, pp. 10–25.
108 Interviews, UK Ministry of Defence, London, 20 November 2009.
109 *Ibid.*
110 *Ibid.*
111 *Ibid.*
112 *Ibid.*
113 Interview, DE&S, UK Ministry of Defence, Bristol, 16 November 2009.

114 Interviews, DCDC and UKDA, Shrivenham, 18 November 2009; Interviews, UK Ministry of Defence, London, 19–20 November 2009.

115 Interviews, UK Ministry of Defence, London, 19–20 November 2009. On the importance of the UK defence industry to the UK economy, see BBC (2009c).

116 Interviews, UK Ministry of Defence, London, 19–20 November 2009.

117 The British emphasis on the importance of the Atlantic Alliance is arguably based not so much on cultural factors, as it is upon high levels of intelligence sharing, close cooperation on nuclear strategy since the late 1940s and nuclear weapons systems development since the late 1950s that, as Frantzen (2005: 91) notes has created a 'technological dependence' on the US.

118 Howorth (2004: 221) attests to the centrality of the Kosovo conflict in spurring St. Malo: 'When Blair was first properly briefed in mid-1998 on Europe's seriously defective capacity to react to a hypothetical crisis in Kosovo, he was appalled.'

119 'Our Armed Forces will need to be interoperable with US command and control structures, match the US operational tempo and provide those capabilities that deliver the greatest impact when operating alongside the US.' See: Chapter 3, 'Delivering Security in a Changing World: Defence White Paper', 2003, pt. 3.5.

120 As Defence Secretary Geoff Hoon (1999–2005) later stated: 'What is important is that we engage with our European partners in improving their military capabilities. If we can do that through NATO, all the good. If we can also do that through the European Union that would be an extra benefit.' See House of Commons Debate, 21 June 2004, *Hansard*, vol. 222, p. 1063. As outlined in the Ministry of Defence Policy Paper on European Defence: 'As the lessons of Kosovo showed...the Europeans need to significantly improve their military capabilities. They should not continue to depend so heavily on the US in dealing with crises within and around Europe. Europe needs to improve its ability to act in circumstances where NATO is not engaged. This will, in turn, produce a better, more coherent and effective European contribution to NATO...The EU is not competing with NATO or duplicating its operational structure...EU efforts will complement and strengthen NATO'. See: 'Ministry of Defence Policy Paper: Paper No. 3 European Defence', UK Ministry of Defence, 2001, pt. 3.

121 Whilst changes outlined in the 2002 and 2003/04 Defence White Papers were not as radical as those embodied in the SDR, the 2002 Spending Review had outlined an increased level of resource extraction from UK society in the form of a £3.5 billion increase in the defence budget between 2002 and 2006 (1.5 billion of which would be invested in new capabilities). This increase in spending was facilitated by a high level of executive autonomy in British defence policy, not least the autonomy that derived from the unitary political system, allowing the core executive to distance itself from electoral punishment by instigating the hike in defence spending in the aftermath of Labour's convincing election victory in June 2001. Increases in defence spending and the 2002 New Chapter were accompanied by a public discourse that framed investment in new capabilities within a sense of heightened threat and the war on terror: the extra resources would allow investment to take place with 'the urgency that September 11th demands'. See: Section 7, 'Conclusions', 'Strategic Defence Review: A New Chapter', pt. 96.

122 See: 'Strategic Defence Review', House of Commons Debate, *Hansard*, Vol. 315, 8 July 1998, p. 1083.

123 See: Chapter 2, 'Strategic Defence Review', 1998, pts. 20–1.

124 In the House of Commons debate that accompanied the release of the SDR George Robertson stated: 'We take our treaty commitments enormously seriously and our deep and lasting continued friendship with the USA underpins a common view

that we have about many of the problems in the world today.' See: 'Strategic Defence Review House of Commons Debate', *Hansard*, vol. 315, 8 July 1998, p. 1083.

125   As Dover (2005: 511–15) highlights, the pace (six months) of the incremental changes to the 'settings' of British policy on institutional venues in 1998 was facilitated by a high level of executive autonomy – a concentration of power in the core executive (notably Blair, but also Robertson) and a lack of domestic opposition from within the Defence Ministry or from other actors within the broader defence and security policy subsystem. First-order change to the 'settings' of policy did not require the bi-partisan 'brokerage' that had accompanied the 'third-order' change of the SDR.

126   Interviews, UK Defence Ministry, London, 19–20 November 2009.

Chapter 7

1   Fourth Generation Warfare (4GW) is defined by Thomas Hammes (2005: 190) as warfare that 'uses all available networks – political, economic, social and military – to convince the enemy's political decision-makers that their strategic goals are either unachievable or too costly for the perceived benefit...4 GW does not attempt to win by defeating the enemy's military forces. Instead combining guerrilla attacks or civil disobedience with the soft networks of social, cultural and economic ties, dis-information campaigns and innovative political activity, it directly attacks the enemy's political will.'

2   'The DCDC Global Strategic Trends Programme 2007–2036', 2006, p. 68.

3   It is also important to note that the creation of these institutions was also spurred by the desire to maximise influence over NATO's process of concept development and experimentation following the creation of Allied Command Transformation.

4   'An Open Letter to the Obama Administration from Central and Eastern Europe', *Gazeta*, 15 July 2009.

5   The important role of 'first image' variables in managing the public's perception of threat is highlighted by Leo Bogart, quoted in Jowett and O'Donnell (2006: 5): 'Propaganda is an art requiring special talent. It is not mechanical, scientific work. Influencing attitudes requires experience, area knowledge and instinctive judge-ment of "what is the best argument for the audience". No manual can guide the propagandist. He must have a good mind, genius, sensitivity and knowledge of how that audience thinks and reacts.'

6   'Future Land Operational Concept', 2008, pt. 104.

Bibliography

ACCS (2008) http://www.nato.int/issues/accs/index.html, date accessed 5 October 2008.

G. Adams and G. Ben-Ari, *Transforming European Militaries: Coalition Operations and the Technology Gap* (Abingdon: Routledge, 2006).

C. Aguis, *The Social Construction of Swedish Neutrality: Changes to Swedish Identity and Sovereignty* (Manchester: Manchester University Press, 2006).

A. Alderson, 'Revising the British Army's Counter-Insurgency Doctrine', *RUSI Journal* 152, no. 4 (2007): 6–11.

J.C. Allard, 'Operation "Balbuzard Noir": An Operational Model for Future Crises?', *Doctrine* no. 14 (2008): 82–5.

J. Altmann, 'The Strategic Uses of Nanotechnology: Perspectives and Concerns', *Security Dialogue* 35, no. 1 (2004): 61–79.

C. Amelineau, 'Doctrine and Teaching: The Higher Staff Course', *Doctrine* no. 2 (2004): 9–12.

R. Anders et al, 'Winning With Allies: The Strategic Value of the Afghan Model', *International Security* 30, no. 3 (2005/06): 124–60.

D. Andrews (ed.), *The Atlantic Alliance Under Stress: US-European Relations after Iraq* (Cambridge: Cambridge University Press, 2005).

AOF (2009) http://www.aof.mod.uk/aofcontent/downloads/gray/review_of_acqn.pdf, date accessed 19 October 2009.

J. Arbuckle, *Military Forces in 21st Century Peace Operations: No Job For a Soldier?* (Abingdon: Routledge, 2006).

K. Armingeon, 'The Effects of Negotiation Democracy: A Comparative Analysis', *European Journal of Political Research* 41 (2002): 81–105.

C. Arora, *Germany's Civilian Power Diplomacy: NATO Expansion and the Art of Communicative Action* (Basingstoke: Palgrave Macmillan, 2007).

R. Art, 'Why Western Europe Needs the United States and NATO', *Political Science Quarterly* 111, no. 1 (1996).

R. Art, 'Europe Hedges its Security Bets', in T.V. Paul et al (eds), *Balance of Power: Theory and Practice in the Twenty-First Century* (Stanford: Stanford University Press, 2004): 179–213.

R. Art, S. Brooks, W. Wohlforth, K. Lieber and G. Alexander, 'Correspondence: Striking the Balance', *International Security* 30, no. 3 (2005/06): 177–96.

B. Athow and R. Blanton, 'Colonial Style and Colonial Legacies: Trade Patterns in British and French Africa', *Journal of Third World Studies* 19, no. 2 (2002): 219–44.

P. Augustin, 'Operation Concordia/Altair in Macedonia', *Doctrine* no. 6 (2006): 57–9.

H. Auriault, 'Looking for a "Maneuvering State of Mind"', *Doctrine* no. 1 (2003): 12–13.

H. Aust and M. Vashakmadze, 'Parliamentary Consent to the Use of German Armed Forces Abroad: The 2008 Decision of the Federal Constitutional Court in the AWACS/Turkey Case', *German Law Journal* 9, no. 12 (2008): 2223–36.

D. Avant, 'The Institutional Sources of Military Doctrine: Hegemons in Peripheral Wars', *International Studies Quarterly* 37, no. 4 (1993): 409–30.

D. Avant, 'From Mercenary to Citizen Armies: Explaining Change in the Practice of War', *International Organization* 54, no. 1 (2000): 41–72.

J. Bailey, 'The United Kingdom's Approach to Command: A Doctrinal Perspective', *Doctrine* no. 5 (2004): 47–50.

T. Balzacq, 'The Three Faces of Securitization: Political Agency, Audience and Context', *European Journal of International Relations* 11, no. 2 (2005): 171–201.

A. Baring, *Germany's New Position in Europe: Problems and Perspectives* (Oxford: Berg, 1994).

C. Barnett, 'The Fallibility of Airpower', *RUSI Journal* 145, no. 5 (2000): 59–60.

R. Baumann and G. Hellmann, 'Germany and the Use of Force: "Total War", the "Culture of Restraint" and the "Quest for Normality"', *German Politics* 10, no. 1 (2001): 61–82.

R. Baumann and W. Wagner, 'Macht und Machtpolitik. Neorealistische Außenpolitiktheorie und Prognosen über die deutsche Außenpolitik nach der Vereinigung', *Zeitschrift für Internationale Beziehungen* 6, no. 2 (1999): 245–86.

BBC (2008a) http://news.bbc.co.uk/1/hi/world/south_asia/7432700.stm, date accessed 3 June 2008.

BBC (2008b) http://news.bbc.co.uk/2/hi/science/nature/7419752.stm, date accessed 17 July 2009.

BBC (2009a) http://news.bbc.co.uk/2/hi/uk_news/8081969.stm, date accessed 3 June 2009.

BBC (2009b) http://news.bbc.co.uk/2/hi/programmes/newsnight/7947082.stm, date accessed 24 March 2009.

BBC (2009c) http://news.bbc.co.uk/2/hi/uk_news/8230910.stm, date accessed 24 November 2009.

BDC (2008) http://www.mod.gov.ee/static/sisu/files/baltic_co_2002.pdf, date accessed 5 October 2008.

P. Becker, 'Vulnerability and Nationalism: The Support for the War in Iraq in Five Established States', *Nations and Nationalism* 15, no. 2 (2009): 540–60.

M. Beissinger, 'Nationalisms That Bark and Nationalisms That Bite: Ernest Gellner and the Substantiation of Nations', in J.A. Hall (ed.), *The State of the Nation: Ernest Gellner and the Theory of Nationalism* (Cambridge: Cambridge University Press, 1998).

H. Belde, 'The Doctrine, Education and Training Synergy in Germany', *Doctrine* no. 2 (2004): 30–1.

T. Benbow, 'Irresistible Force or Immovable Object? The "Revolution in Military Affairs" and Asymmetric Warfare', *Defense and Security Analysis* 25, no. 1 (2009): 21–36.

G. Ben-Ari, 'C3 Interoperability in Europe: The Challenge Ahead', *Eurofuture* Winter (2005): 1–4.

T. Benbow, 'Irresistible Force or Immovable Object? The "Revolution in Military Affairs" and Asymmetric Warfare', *Defense and Security Analysis* 25, no. 1 (2009): 21–36.

N. Bensahel, 'Mission Not Accomplished: What Went Wrong In Iraq?' *Journal of Strategic Studies* 29, no. 3 (2006): 453–73.

E. Benner, 'Is There A Core National Doctrine?', *Nations and Nationalism* 7, no. 2 (2001): 155–74.

C. Bennett, 'Review Article: What is Policy Convergence and What Causes It?', *British Journal of Political Science* 21 (1991): 215–33.

T. Berger, *Cultures of Anti-Militarism: National Security Cultures in Germany and Japan* (Baltimore: John Hopkins University Press, 1998).

D. Betz, 'The More You Know, The Less You Understand: The Problem with Information Warfare', *Journal of Strategic Studies* 29, no. 3 (2006): 505–33.

D. Betz, 'Redesigning Land Forces for Wars Amongst the People', *Contemporary Security Policy* 28, no. 2 (2007): 221–43.

G. Bezacier, 'The Transformation', Doctrine no. 1 (2003): 4–7.

G. Bezacier, 'Command and Control and Modernity in the 21ˢᵗ Century', *Doctrine* no. 5 (2004a): 4–8.

G. Bezacier, 'Military Power and its Applicability (modernity) in the 21ˢᵗ Century', *Doctrine* no. 3 (2004b): 4–11.

G. Bezacier, 'Editorial', *Doctrine* no. 2 (2004c): 3.

G. Bezacier, 'I Did Not Think I Should Have to Do It, But...', *Doctrine* no. 2 (2004d): 4–5.

G. Bezacier, 'The Commitment of Land Forces in Operations', *Doctrine* no. 6 (2005): 4–8.

S. Biddle, *Military Power: Explaining Victory and Defeat in Modern Battle* (Princeton: Princeton University Press, 2004).

S. Biddle, 'Allies, Airpower and Modern Warfare: The Afghan Model in Afghanistan and Iraq', *International Security* 30, no. 3 (2005/06): 161–76.

M. Billig, *Banal Nationalism* (London: Sage, 1995).

L-C. Billy, 'The German Land Forces Future CIS', *Doctrine* no. 1 (2003): 56–9.

B. Binnendjik, 'The Battle of Nablus (3–20 April 2002): Antiterrorist Combat in a Built-Up Area', *Doctrine* no. 3 (2004): 37–40.

H. Binnendijk and F.A. Petersen, 'From Comprehensive Approach to Comprehensive Capability', *NATO Review*, March (2008).

J. Blackham, 'Handling the Digitised Battlespace', *RUSI Journal* 145, no. 1 (2000a): 33–37.

J. Blackham, 'The Apotheosis of 21ˢᵗ Century Warfare', *RUSI Journal* 145, no. 6 (2000b): 64–8.

J. Blackham, 'Battlespace Digitisation: Roads to the Future', *RUSI Journal* 147, no. 1 (2002): 28–30.

P. Blervaque, 'Collecting Intelligence Adapting Our Capabilities', *Doctrine* no. 6 (2006): 30–4.

G. Bloch, 'French Military Reform: Lessons for America's Army?', *Parameters: US Army War College Quarterly* 30, no. 2 (2000): 33–45.

BMVG (2003) http://www.bmvg.de/portal/a/bmvg/ministerium/geschichte_bmvg/vertei-digungsminister_seit_1955/drpeterstruck?yw_contentURL=/C1256F120060B1B/N264X9B2625MMISDE/content.jsp, date accessed 1 April 2010.

BMVG (2009) http://www.bmvg.de/portal/a/bmvg/kcxml/04_Sj9SPykssy0xPLMnMz0vM0Y_QjzKLd4k38TIGSYGZbub6kTCxoJRUfV-P_NxUfW_9AP2C3IhyR0dFRQCTRs58/delta/base64xml/L2dJQSEvUUt3QS80SVVFLzZfRF80SjM!?yw_contentURL=per cent2FC1256F1200608B1Bper cent2FN264X9B2625MMISDEper cent2Fcontent.jsp, date accessed 14 May 2009.

Boene, Nogues and Haddad, 'New Missions for the Armed Forces: New Training for Officers', *Doctrine* no. 2 (2004): 39–42.

B. Bohineust-Comalat, 'The Tactical Third Dimension: The Army Helicopter Battlefield', *Doctrine* no. 14 (2008): 8–11.

H. Bore, 'French Practice in Getting Prepared to Overseas Operations', *Doctrine* no. 9 (2006): 95–9.

M. Boot, *The Savage Wars of Peace: Small Wars and the Rise of American Power* (New York: Basic Books, 2002).

M. Boot, 'The New American Way of War', *Foreign Affairs* 82, no. 4 (2003): 41–58.

M. Boot, *War Made New: Weapons, Warriors and the Making of the Modern World* (New York: Gotham Books, 2006).

H. Born and H. Hänggi, 'Governing the Use of Force under International Auspices', in *SIPRI Yearbook 2005: Armaments, Disarmament and International Security* (Oxford: Oxford University Press, 2008): 199–222.

L. Boue, 'Implementing A2C2 Tactical Coordination', *Doctrine* no. 14 (2008): 32–4.

D. Bourantonis and P. Tsakonas, 'The Southeastern Multinational Peace Force: Problems of and Prospects for a Multinational Peace Agency', *Politics* 23, no. 2 (2003): 75–81.

J.P. Bourin, 'Collective Training and Intelligence: A New Organisation Framework', *Doctrine* no. 6 (2006): 38–40.

M. Boyce, 'Achieving Effect: Annual Chief of Defence Staff Lecture', *The RUSI Journal* 148, no. 1 (2003): 30–7.

P. Bratton, 'France and the Revolution in Military Affairs', *Contemporary Security Policy* 23, no. 2 (2002): 87–112.

M. Brenner, 'The CFSP Factor: A Comparison of United States and French Strategies', *Cooperation and Conflict* 38, no. 3 (2003): 187–209.

F. Breuer, 'Between Ambitions and Financial Constraints: The Reform of the German Armed Forces', *German Politics* 15, no. 2 (2006): 206–20.

S. Brooks and W. Wohlforth, 'Power, Globalization and the End of the Cold War', *International Security* 25, no. 3 (2000/2001): 5–53.

S. Brooks and W. Wohlforth, 'Hard Times for Soft Balancing', *International Security* 30, no. 1 (2005): 76–8.

S. Bulmer, C. Jeffery and W. Paterson, *Germany's European Diplomacy* (Manchester: Manchester University Press, 2000).

Bundeswehr (2009a) http://www.bundeswehr.de/portal/a/bwde/kcxml/04_Sj9SPykssy-0xPLMnMz0vM0Y_QjzKLd443cTQCSYGYxgEh-pEwsaCUVH1fj_zcVH1v_QD9gtyIckdHRUUATi3qcg!!/delta/base64xml/L2dJQSEvUUt3QS80SVVFLzZfQ180Q0w!?yw_contentURL=per cent2FC1256EF4002AED30per cent2FN264HU9R434MMISDE-per cent2Fcontent.jsp, date accessed 3 September 2009.

P. Buras and K. Longhurst, 'The Berlin Republic, Iraq and the Use of Force', *European Security* 13, no. 3 (2004): 215–45.

B. Burridge, 'UAVs and the Dawn of Post-Modern Warfare: A Perspective on Recent Operations', *RUSI Journal* 148, no. 5 (2003): 18–23.

B. Buzan, O. Waever and J. De Wilde, *Security: A New Framework for Analysis* (Boulder: Lynne Rienner, 1998).

D. Byman, 'Building the New Iraq: The Role of Intervening Forces', *Survival* 45, no. 2 (2003): 57–71.

D. Byman and K. Pollack, 'Let Us Now Praise Great Men: Bringing the Statesman Back In', *International Security* 25, no. 4 (2001): 107–46.

P. Byrd (ed.) *British Defence Policy: Thatcher and Beyond* (Philip Allen, 1991).

C. Callwell, *Small Wars: Their Principles and Practice* (London: HM Stationary Office, 1906).

S. Canby, 'NATO: Reassessing the Conventional Wisdom', *Survival* 21, no. 2 (1979): 164–8.

A. Caplain, 'The Contribution of the Armed Forces in the Stabilisation Process', *Doctrine* no. 12 (2007): 16–17.

E.H. Carr, *The Twenty Years' Crisis, 1919–1939: An Introduction to the Study of International Relations* (London: Macmillan, 1939).

E.H. Carr, *Nationalism and After* (London: Macmillan, 1945).

R. Cassidy, *Peacekeeping in The Abyss: British and American Peacekeeping Doctrine and Practice After the Cold War* (Westpoint: Praeger, 2004).

R. Cassidy, 'Regular and Irregular Forces Indigenous Forces for a Long Irregular War', *RUSI Journal* 152, no. 1 (2007): 42–7.

P. Cerny, 'Political Agency in a Globalising World: Towards a Structurationist Approach', *European Journal of International Relations* 6, no. 4 (2000): 435–63.

M. Chalmers, 'Bombs Away? Britain and Nuclear Weapons under New Labour', *Security Dialogue* 30, no. 1 (1999): 61–74.

M. Chalmers, 'The New Activism: UK Defence Policy Since 1997', *New Economy* 2 (2002): 206–11.

C. Chamas, 'A Comprehensive Approach to Crises', *Doctrine* no. 12 (2007): 22–4.

B. Charbonneau, *France and the New Imperialism: Security Policy in Sub-Saharan Africa* (Aldershot: Ashgate, 2008).

M. Charlier, 'The Reconstruction: A Strategic Know-How', *Doctrine* no. 1 (2008): 11–20.

B.G. Chereau, 'New Threats: The Challenge for Military-Orientated Intelligence', *Doctrine* no. 9 (2006): 26–9.

G. Chevalier, 'The Revolution of Force Systems', *Doctrine* no. 1 (2003): 37–9.

W. Chin, 'British Counter-Insurgency in Afghanistan', *Defense and Security Analysis* 23, no. 2 (2007): 201–5.

C. Cholley, 'New Techniques, New Threats', *Doctrine* no. 9 (2006): 13–15.

N. Chomsky and M. Raj, *War Plan Iraq: 10 Reasons Against War With Iraq* (New York: Verso, 2002).

T. Christensen, *Useful Adversaries: Grand Strategy, Domestic Mobilization and Sino-American Conflict: 1947–58* (Cambridge: MIT Press, 1996).

J. Cimbalo, 'Saving NATO From Europe', *Foreign Affairs* 83, no. 6 (2004): 111–20.

F. Ciută, 'Parting the Black Sea (Region): Geopolitics, Institutionalisation and the Reconfiguration of European Security', *European Security*, 16, no. 1 (2007): 51–78.

COE (2008a) http://transnet.act.nato.int/WISE/TNCC/CentresofE, date accessed 6 November 2008.

COE (2008b) http://www.c2coe.org/, date accessed 5 October 2008.

C. Cogan, 'From the Fall of France to the Force de Frappe: The Remaking of French Military Power 1945–1962', in T. Imlay and D. Toft et al (eds), *The Fog of Peace and War Planning* (London: Routledge, 2006).

E. Cohen, 'Change and Transformation in Military Affairs', *Journal of Strategic Studies* 27, no. 3 (2004): 395–407.

C. Conetta, 'No Good Reason to Boost Army, Marine Corps End Strength', *Project on Defense Alternatives* (Commonwealth Institute: Cambridge MA, 2007).

J-F. Coppolani, 'Intelligence', *Doctrine* no. 3 (2004): 20.

J-F. Coppolani, 'Ground Intelligence: Future and Stakes', *Doctrine* no. 9 (2006): 9–12.

P. Cornish and A. Dorman, 'Blair's Wars and Brown's Budgets: From Strategic Defence Review to Strategic Decay in Less Than a Decade', *International Affairs* 85, no. 2 (2009): 247–61.

P. Cornish and G. Edwards, 'The Strategic Culture of the EU: A Progress Report', *International Affairs* 81, no. 4 (2005): 801–20.

L-C. Constant, 'The British Army by 2010', *Doctrine* no. 1 (2003): 46–9.

J. Corum, 'Rethinking U.S. Army Counter-Insurgency Doctrine', *Contemporary Security Policy* 28, no. 1 (2007): 127–42.

P. Coste, 'Adaptation of Army Doctrine to Stabilisation', *Doctrine* no. 12 (2007): 9–12.

A. Cottey, 'NATO: Globalisation or Redundancy?' *Contemporary Security Policy* 25, no. 3 (2004): 391–408.

A. Cottey, *Security in the New Europe* (Basingstoke: Palgrave, 2008).

R. Cousens, 'Amristar to Basra: The Influence of Counter-Insurgency upon the British Perspective of Peacekeeping', in R. Utley (ed.), *Major Power and Peacekeeping: Perspectives, Priorities and the Challenges of Military Intervention* (Aldershot: Ashgate, 2006): 49–63.

CPG (2006) http://www.nato.int/docu/basictxt/b061129e.htm, date accessed 29 November 2006.

M. Crowshaw, 'Running a Country: The British Colonial Experience and its Relevance to Present Day Concerns', *The Shrivenham Papers* no. 3 (2007).

S. Croft et al, Britain and Defence 1945–2000: A Policy Re-Evaluation (Essex: Pearson, 2001).

G. Cumming, 'UK African Policy in the post-Cold War Era: From Realpolitik to Moralpolitik?', *Commonwealth and Comparative Politics* 42, no. 1 (2004): 106–28.

E. Dahl, 'Network Centric Warfare and the Death of Operational Art', *Defence Studies* 2, no. 1 (2002): 1–24.

A. Dalgaard-Nielsen, 'The Test of Strategic Culture: Germany, Pacifism and Pre-emptive Strikes', *Security Dialogue* 36, no. 3 (2005): 339–59.

A. Dalgaard-Nielsen, *Germany, Pacifism and Peace-Enforcement* (Manchester: Manchester University Press, 2006).

S. Dalvi, 'Germany', in J. Glenn et al (eds), *Neorealism Versus Strategic Culture* (Aldershot: Ashgate, 2004): 204–24.

A. Danchev, 'Liddell Hart and Manoeuvre', *RUSI Journal* 143, no. 6 (1998): 33–5.

R. Dannatt, 'The Future Land Environment: Moving Towards 2018', *RUSI Journal* 153, no. 4 (2008): 56–61.

J. Day, 'After Afghanistan: The Role of Air Power', *RUSI Journal* 147, no. 6 (2002): 38–43.

G. Day and C. Freeman, 'Policekeeping is the Key: Rebuilding the Internal Security Architecture of Postwar Iraq', *International Affairs* 79, no. 2 (2003): 299–313.

De Certaines, 'The Contribution of Helicopters to Land Actions in Built Up Areas', *Doctrine* no. 3 (2003): 30–1.

C. De Lajudie, 'Force Protection: A Deadlock to be Avoided', *Doctrine* no. 15 (2008): 114–17.

Defense (2009) http://www.defensenews.com/story.php?i=4083044, date accessed 9 June 2009.

A. De Lammerville, 'Training for Intelligence: Evolutions to be Expected for Army Officers', *Doctrine* no. 9 (2006): 41–3.

J. Deni, 'The NATO Rapid Deployment Corps: Alliance Doctrine and Force Structure', *Contemporary Security Policy* 25, no. 3 (2004): 498–523.

M. Desch, 'Culture Clash: Assessing the Importance of Ideas in Security Studies', *International Security* 23, no. 1 (1998): 141–70.

M. Desch, *Civilian Control of the Military: The Changing Security Environment* (Baltimore: John Hopkins University Press, 1999)

V. Desportes, 'Editorial', *Doctrine* no. 6 (2006): 3–4.

V. Desportes, 'From Transformation to Adaptation: A New Paradigm?', *Doctrine* no. 12 (2007): 4–8.

V. Desportes, 'Avant-Garde Armed Forces for an Advanced Defence', *Doctrine* no. 16 (2008a): 6–9.

V. Desportes, 'Editorial', *Doctrine* no. 14 (2008b): 3.

V. Desportes, 'The Army Fights in Three Dimensions', *Doctrine* no. 14 (2008c): 4–7.

V. Desportes, 'Interview With Major General Vincent Desportes', *Doctrine* no. 14 (2008d): 51–2.

Die Zeit (2009a) http://www.zeit.de/2009/38/Portraet-Franz-Josef-Jung?page=1, date accessed 12 September 2009.

K. Deutsch, *Nationalism and Social Communication: An Inquiry into the Foundations of Nationality* (Cambridge, Mass: MIT Press, 1966).

M. De Corbet, 'What System of Protection for Tomorrow?', *Doctrine* no. 15 (2008): 98–100.

P. De Saqui De Sans, 'Lessons Still Valid Ten Years Later: Combat Operations in Mogadiscio', *Doctrine* no. 4 (2004): 51–5.

P. De Villiers, 'Reconstructing the Military in a Post-Crisis Situation: The Afghan Example', *Doctrine* (2008): 59–61.

P. Dixon, 'Hearts and Minds? British Counterinsurgency from Malaya to Iraq', *Journal of Strategic Studies* 32, no. 3 (2009): 353–81.

J. Donnelly, *Realism and International Relations* (Cambridge: Cambridge University Press, 2000).

A. Dorman, 'Reconciling Britain to Europe in the Next Millennium: The Evolution of British Defence Policy in the post-Cold War Era', *Defence Analysis* 17, no. 2 (2001): 187–202.

A. Dorman, 'Britain and Defence Transformation: A Model of Success or a Warning of Its Dangers?', *Defence Studies* 6, no. 2 (2006): 150–68.

A. Dorman, 'Britain and Its Armed Forces Today', *The Political Quarterly* 78, no. 2 (2007a): 320–7.

A. Dorman, 'The British Experience of Low-Intensity Conflict in Sierra Leone', *Defense and Security Analysis* 23, no. 2 (2007b): 185–200.

R. Dover, 'The Prime Minister and the Core Executive: A Liberal Intergovernmentalist Reading of UK Defence Policy Formulation 1997–2000', *British Journal of Politics and International Relations* 7 (2005): 508–21.

R. Dover, *The Europeanization of British Defence Policy: 1997–2005* (Aldershot: Ashgate, 2007).

D. Dreschler, 'Reconstructing the Interagency Process after Iraq', *Journal of Strategic Studies* 28, no. 1 (2005): 227–32.

C. Dueck, *Reluctant Crusaders: Power, Culture and Change in American Grand Strategy* (Princeton: Princeton University Press, 2006).

J. Duffield, 'Political Culture and State Behaviour: Why Germany Confounds Neorealism', *International Organization* 53, no. 4 (1999): 765–803.

J. Duffield, *World Power Forsaken: Political Culture, International Institutions and German Security Policy after Unification* (Stanford: Stanford University Press, 1998).

D. Dunn, 'European Security and Defence Policy in the American Security Policy Debate: Counterbalancing America or Rebalancing NATO?', *Defence Studies* 1, no. 1 (2001): 146–55.

T. Dunne, 'When the Shooting Starts: Atlanticism in British Security Policy', *International Affairs* 80, no. 5 (2004): 893–909.

T. Dyson, 'Civilian Power and History Making Decisions: German Agenda Setting on Europe', *European Security* 11, no. 1 (2002): 27–48.

T. Dyson, 'German Military Reform 1998–2004: Leadership and the Triumph of Domestic Constraint over International Opportunity', *European Security* 14, no. 3 (2005): 361–86.

T. Dyson, *The Politics of German Defence and Security: Policy Leadership and Military Reform in the post-Cold War Era* (New York: Berghahn, 2007).

T. Dyson, 'Convergence and Divergence in post-Cold War British, French and German Military Reforms: Between International Structure and Executive Autonomy', *Security Studies* 17, no. 4 (2008): 725–74.

EAC (2008) http://www.defence.gouv.fr/defence_uk/enjeux_defence/la_defence_dans_l_europe/les_euroforces/cellule_europeenne_de_coordination_aerienne/cellule_euro-peenne_de_coordination_aerienne_eacc, date accessed 3 October 2008.

EAG (2008) http://www.euroairgroup.org/history.htm, date accessed 5 October 2008.

EAI (2008) http://www.defence.gouv.fr/defence_uk/enjeux_defence/la_defence_dans_l_europe/les_euroforces/l_initiative_amphibie_europeenne/l_initiative_amphibie_euro peenne, date accessed 5 October 2008.

A. Echevarria II, 'Rapid Decisive Operations: US Operational Assumptions Regarding Future Warfare', *Defence Studies* 2, no. 1 (2002): 127–38.

EDA (2008a) http://www.eda.europa.eu/genericitem.aspx?area=Organisation&id=115# Softwareper cent20Definedper cent20Radio, date accessed 18 June 2008.

EDA (2008b) http://www.eda.europa.eu/genericitem.aspx?id=370, date accessed 5 October 2008.

G. Edwards, 'Is There a Security Culture in an Enlarged European Union?', *The International Spectator* 41, no. 3 (2006): 7–23.

T. Edmunds, 'What Are Armed Forces For? The Changing Nature of Military Roles in Western Europe', *International Affairs* 82, no. 6 (2006): 1059–75.

C. Elman, 'Horses for Courses: Why *Not* Neorealist Theories of Foreign Policies?' *Security Studies* 6, no. 1 (1996): 7–53.

EMF (2008) *Germany Energy Mix Factsheet* http://ec.europa.eu/energy/energy_policy/doc/factsheets/mix/mix_de_en.pdf date accessed 24 November 2008.

Eurocorps (2008) http://www.eurocorps.org/history/eurocorps_history/, date accessed 5 October 2008.

Eurofighter (2008) http://www.eurofighter.com/news/chapter132.asp, date accessed 5 October 2008.

Europa (2008a) http://epp.eurostat.ec.europa.eu/portal/page?_pageid=1996,45323734&_dad=portal&_schema=PORTAL&screen=welcomeref&open=/t_nrg/t_nrg_price&language=en&product=REF_TB_energy&root=REF_TB_energy&scrollto=818, date accessed 5 November 2008.

Europa (2008b) http://ec.europa.eu/energy/energy_policy/doc/factsheets/mix/mix_fr_en.pdf, date accessed 5 November 2008.

ESA (2008a) http://www.esa.int/esaLP/SEMRRI0DU8E_LPgmes_0.html, date accessed 8 October 2008.

T. Farrell, 'Figuring Out Fighting Organizations: The New Organizational Analysis in Strategic Studies', *Journal of Strategic Studies* 19, no. 1 (1996): 122–35.

T. Farrell, 'Culture and Military Power', *Review of International Studies* 24, no. 3 (1998): 407–16.

T. Farrell, 'Transnational Norms and Military Development', *European Journal of International Relations* 7, no. 1 (2001): 63–102.

T. Farrell, 'Constructivist Security Studies: Portrait of a Research Program', *International Studies Review* 4, no. 1 (2002): 49–72.

T. Farrell, 'World Culture and Military Power', *Security Studies* 14, no. 3 (2005a): 448–88.

T. Farrell, *The Norms of War: Cultural Beliefs and Modern Conflict* (Boulder: Lynne Rienner, 2005b).

T. Farrell, 'The Dynamics of British Military Transformation', *International Affairs* 84, no. 4 (2008): 777–807.

T. Farrell and T. Terriff, *The Sources of Military Change: Culture, Politics, Technology* (London: Lynne Rienner, 2002).

A. Faupin, 'Defense Sector Reform: The French Case Study', in I. Gyarmati and T. Winkler (eds), *Post-Cold War European Defense Reform Lessons Learned in Europe and the United States* (London: Brasseys, 2002): 44–61.

P. Feaver et al, 'Brother Can You Spare A Paradigm? Or Was Anybody Ever A Realist?', *International Security* 25, no. 1 (2000): 165–93.

D. Fischer, 'Evolutions of the CIMIC Operational Function by 2010', *Doctrine* no. 1 (2003): 35–6.

D. Fischer, 'CIMIC', *Doctrine* no. 3 (2004): 27.

F. Fischer, *Reframing Public Policy: Discursive Politics and Deliberative Practices* (Oxford: Oxford University Press, 2003).

M. Flournoy and J. Smith, *European Defense Integration: Bridging the Gap Between Strategy and Capabilities* (Washington: Centre for Strategic and International Studies, 2005).

A. Forster, *Armed Forces and Society in Europe* (Basingstoke: Palgrave Macmillan, 2006).

P.K. Forster and S.J. Cimbala, *The U.S., NATO and Military Burden Sharing* (Abingdon: Routledge, 2007).

France24 (2009) http://www.france24.com/en/20090311-france-nato-command-structure-wider-role-troops-charles-de-gaulle, date accessed 11 March 2009.

France24 (2009a) http://www.france24.com/en/20091009-mcchrystal-troop-surge-afghanistan-strategy-obama, date accessed 10 October 2009.

A. Frank, 'Get Real: Transformation and Targeting', *Defence Studies* 4, no. 1 (2004): 64–86.

H. Frantzen, *NATO and Peace Support Operations 1991–99: Policies and Doctrines* (Abingdon: Routledge, 2005).

M. Freeden, 'Is Nationalism a Distinct Ideology?', *Political Studies* XLVI (1998): 748–65.

L. Freedman, 'Britain and the Revolution in Military Affairs', *Defense and Security Analysis* 14, no. 1 (1998): 55–66.

L. Freedman, 'The War in Iraq: Selling the Threat', *Survival* 46, no. 2 (2004): 7–50.

A. Friedberg, *The Weary Titan: Britain and the Experience of Relative Decline 1895–1905* (Princeton: Princeton University Press, 1987).

A. Friedberg, *The Weary Titan, 1895–1905: Britain and the Experience of Relative Decline* (Princeton: Princeton University Press, 1998).

C. Fruchard, 'The Meetings of Experience Feedback Players', *Objectif Doctrine* no. 26 (2001): 13.

J. Fuller, *On Future Warfare* (London: Sifton Praed, 1928).

J. Gaffney, 'France, the Use of Force and the Power of Strategic Culture', in K. Longhurst and M. Zaborowski (eds), *Old Europe, New Europe and the Trans-Atlantic Security Agenda* (London: Routledge, 2007).

D. Galula, *Counterinsurgency Warfare: Theory and Practice* (New York: Praeger, 1964).

S. Gänzle and A. G. Sens (eds), *The Changing Politics of European Security* (London: Palgrave Macmillan, 2007).

F. Gere, 'RMA or New Operational Art? A View From France', in T. Gongora and H. von Riekhof (eds), *Towards a Revolution in Military Affairs: Defense and Security at the Dawn of the 21ˢᵗ Century* (Westport: Greenwood, 2000).

B. Giegerich and W. Wallace, 'Not Such a Soft Power: The External Deployment of European Forces', *Survival* 46, no. 2 (2004).

R. Gilpin, 'No one Loves a Realist', *Security Studies* 5, no. 2 (1996): 3–26.

C. Glaser, 'Realists as Optimists: Cooperation as Self-Help', *International Security* 19, no. 3 (1994/95): 50–90.

J. Glenn, D. Howlett and S. Poore, *Neorealism versus Strategic Culture* (Aldershot: Ashgate, 2004).

GMF (2008) http://www.1gnc.de/, date accessed 5 October 2008.

K.H. Goetz, 'The Federal Executive: Bureaucratic Fusion vs. Governmental Bifurcation', in K.H. Dyson and K.H. Goetz (eds), *Germany, Europe and the Politics of Constraint* (Oxford: Oxford University Press, 2003): 55–72.

E.O. Goldman, 'Cultural Foundations of Military Diffusion', *Review of International Studies* 32, no. 1 (2006): 69–91.

E.O. Goldman and Leslie C. Eliason (eds), *The Diffusion of Military Technology and Ideas*, (Stanford: Stanford University Press, 2003).

E. Goldman and T. Mahnken, *The Information Revolution in Military Affairs in Asia* (London: Palgrave Macmillan, 2004).

F. Gombeaud, 'The Ground Space Management Function', *Doctrine* no. 1 (2003): 34.

T. Gongora and H. von Riekhof 'Introduction: Sizing Up the Revolution in Military Affairs', in T. Gongora and H. von Riekhof (eds), *Towards a Revolution in Military*

Affairs: Defense and Security at the Dawn of the 21ˢᵗ Century (Westport: Greenwood, 2000).

P. Gordon, *A Certain Idea of France* (Princeton: Princeton University Press, 1992).

P. Gordon. 'The Presidents Special Role in Foreign and Defence Policy', in J. Hayward (ed.), *De Gaulle to Mitterrand: Presidential Power in France* (London: Hurst, 1992).

P. Gordon and J. Shapiro, *Allies at War: American, Europe and the Crisis over Iraq* (New York: McGraw-Hill, 2004).

Y. Gouriou, 'Military Cooperation in Stabilisation: The Afghan Example', *Doctrine* no. 12 (2007): 93–6.

F. Gout, 'The Other Actors in a Stabilisation Phase', *Doctrine* no. 12 (2007): 13–15.

C. Gray, 'National Styles in Strategy: The American Example', *International Security* 6, no. 2 (1981): 21–47.

C. Gray, 'Strategic Culture as Context: The First Generation of Theory Strikes Back', *Review of International Studies* 25, no. 1 (1999): 49–69.

C. Gray, *Strategy for Chaos: Revolutions in Military Affairs and the Evidence of History* (London: Frank Cass, 2002).

C. Gray, 'Technology as a Dynamic of Defence Transformation', *Defence Studies* 6, no. 1 (2006): 26–51.

F. Gray, 'The Contribution of Air Power to Manoeuvre Warfare', *RUSI Journal* 145, no. 3 (2000): 60–2.

S. Gregory, *French Defence Policy Into the 21ˢᵗ Century* (London: Palgrave Macmillan, 2000a).

S. Gregory, 'France and *Missions de Souverainete*', *Defense and Security Analysis* 16, no. 3 (2000b): 329–42.

F. Greenstein, 'The Impact of Personality on Politics: An Attempt to Clear Away the Underbrush', *American Political Science Review* 61, no. 3 (1967): 629–41.

J. Gregoire, *The Bases of French Peace Operation Doctrine: Problematic Scope of France's Military Operations within the UN or NATO Framework* (Carlisle: Strategic Studies Institute, 2002).

S. Gregory, 'France and the War on Terrorism', *Terrorism and Political Violence* 15, no. 1 (2003): 124–47.

J. Grieco, *Cooperation Among Nations: Europe, America and Non-Tariff Barriers to Trade* (Ithaca, New York: Cornell University Press, 1990).

J. Grieco, *Understanding the Problem of International Cooperation* (New York: Columbia University Press, 1993).

J. Grieco, 'Anarchy and the Limits of Cooperation: A Realist Critique of the Newest Liberal Institutionalism', *International Organization* 42, no. 3 (1988): 485–507.

C. Griffin, 'French Military Interventions in Africa: French Grand Strategy and Defense Policy Since Decolonization', *Paper Presented at the International Studies Association Annual Convention*, February 28–March 3 2007, Chicago, Illinois, United States of America.

C. Grintchenko, 'Operation Alante (January–July 1954): The Last Pacification Operation in Indo-China', *Doctrine* no. 12 (2007): 102–5.

T. Guay and R. Callum, 'The Transformation and Prospects for Europe's Defence Industry', *International Affairs* 78, no. 4 (2002): 757–76.

L. Gutjahr, *German Foreign and Defence Policy after Reunification* (London: Pinter, 1994).

S. Guzzini, *Realism in International Relations and International Political Economy: The Continuing Story of a Death Foretold* (London: Routledge, 1998).

S. Guzzini, 'The Enduring Dilemmas of Realism in International Relations', *European Journal of International Relations* 10, no. 4 (2004): 533–68.

C. Gwynn, *Imperial Policing* (London: Macmillan, 1934).

E. Haas, 'What is Nationalism and Why Should We Study It?', *International Organisation* 40, no. 3 (1986): 707–44.

P. Hall, 'Policy Paradigms, Social Learning and the State: The Case of Economic Policy-Making in Britain', *Comparative Politics* 25, no. 3 (1993): 275–96.

P. Hall and R. Taylor, 'Political Science and the Three New Institutionalisms', *Political Studies* 44, no. 5 (1996): 936–57.

J. Hallenberg and H. Karlsson (eds), *The Iraq War: European Perspectives on Politics, Strategy and Operations* (London: Routledge, 2005).

T. Hammes, 'War Evolves Into the Fourth Generation', *Contemporary Security Policy* 26, no. 2 (2005): 189–221.

E. Harrison, *The Post-Cold War International System: Strategies, Institutions and Reflexivity* (London: Routledge, 2004).

K. Hartley, 'The 2004 Defence White Paper: An Economic Perspective', *Defence Management Journal*, 26 (2004): 17–19.

B. Hauser, 'The Cultural Revolution in Counter-Insurgency', *Journal of Strategic Studies* 30, no. 1 (2007): 153–71.

C. Hay, and D. Wincott, 'Structure, Agency and Historical Institutionalism', *Political Studies* 46 (1998): 951–7.

Headline Goal (2010) http://www.consilium.europa.eu/uedocs/cmsUpload/2010%20 Headline%20Goal.pdf, date accessed 4 September 2009.

G. Hellmann et al, 'De-Europeanization By Default? Germany's EU Policy in Defense and Asylum', *Foreign Policy Analysis* 1 (2005): 143–64.

M Hermann and J. Hagen, 'International Decision Making: Leadership Matters', *Foreign Policy* 110 (1998): 124–37.

J. Herz, 'Idealist Internationalism and the Security Dilemma', *World Politics* 2, no. 2 (1950): 157–80.

J. Ho, 'The Dimensions of Effects-Based Operations', *Defence Studies* 5, no. 2 (2005): 169–87.

J. Hobson, *Imperialism: A Study* (London: Allen and Unwin, 1938).

J. Hobson, *The State and International Relations* (Cambridge: CUP, 2000).

F. Hoffman, 'Small Wars Revisited: The United States and Non-Traditional Wars', *Journal of Strategic Studies* 28, no. 6 (2005): 913–40.

P. Hollinshead, 'ICS/ISTAR: Force Development Issues', *RUSI Journal* 143, no. 6 (1998): 50–61.

J. Horn, *The Path Not Taken: French Industrialisation in the Age of Revolution 1750–1830* (Massachusetts: MIT, 2006).

M. Horowitz, *The Diffusion of Military Power: Consequences for International Politics* Paper Presented at the American Political Science Association Annual Meeting, 31 August–3 September 2006, Philadelphia, United States of America.

C. Hood, *Explaining Economic Policy Reversals* (Buckingham: Oxford University Press, 1994).

M. Howard, *Clausewitz* (Oxford: Oxford University Press, 1983).

M. Howard, 'A Long War?', *Survival* 44, no. 4 (2006/07): 7–14.

J. Howorth, 'France', in J. Howorth and A. Menon (eds), *The European Union and National Defence Policy* (Abingdon: Routledge, 1997): 23–49.

J. Howorth, 'French Defence Reforms: National Tactics for a European Strategy?', in *Brassey's Defence Yearbook 1998* (London: Brassey's, 1998): 130–51.

J. Howorth, 'Foreign and Security Policy in the post-Cold War World', in A. Guyomarch et al (eds), *Developments in French Politics* (Houndmills: Palgrave, 2001): 156–70.

J. Howorth, 'Discourse, Ideas and Epistemic Communities in European Security and Defence Policy', *West European Politics* 27, no. 2 (2004): 211–34.

J. Howorth, *Security and Defence Policy in the European Union* (Houndmills: Palgrave, 2007).

J. Howorth and J.T.S. Keeler (eds), *Defending Europe: The EU, NATO and the Quest for Autonomy* (Houndmills: Palgrave Macmillan, 2003).

J. Howorth and A. Menon (eds), *The European Union and National Defence Policy* (Abingdon: Routledge, 1997).

HTS (2009a) http://humanterrainsystem.army.mil/overview.html, date accessed 27 August 2009

HTS (2009b) http://humanterrainsystem.army.mil/components.html, date accessed 27 August 2009.

B. Hue, 'What do CIMIC Activities Bring to Stabilisation Operations', *Doctrine* no. 12 (2007): 29–31.

M. Humbert, 'What is Left of the Transformation?', *Doctrine* no. 14 (2008): 106.

R.E. Hunter and D. Farley, *The European Security and Defence Policy: NATO's Companion or Competitor?* (Santa Monica: RAND, 2002).

A. Hyde-Price, *Germany and European Order* (Manchester: Manchester University Press, 2000).

A. Hyde-Price and C. Jeffrey, 'Germany in the European Union: Constructing Normality', *Journal of Common Market Studies* 39, no. 4 (2001): 689–717.

A. Hyde-Price, 'Continental Drift? Trans-Atlantic Relations in the 21st Century', *Defence Studies* 2, no. 2 (2002): 1–20.

A. Hyde-Price, *European Security in the 21st Century: The Challenge of Multi-Polarity* (Abingdon: Routledge, 2007).

K. Iida, 'Analytic Uncertainty and International Cooperation: Theory and Application to Economic Policy Coordination', *International Studies Quarterly* 37, no. 4 (1993): 431–57.

T. Imlay and M. Toft, *The Fog of Peace and War Planning: Military and Strategic Planning Under Uncertainty* (Abingdon: Routledge, 2006).

B. Irondelle, 'Europeanisation without the European Union? French Military Reforms 1991–96', *Journal of European Public Policy* 10, no. 2 (2003a): 208–26.

B. Irondelle, 'Civil-Military Relations and the End of Conscription in France', *Security Studies* 12, 3 (2003b): 157–87.

ISL (2009) http://www.isl.eu/Content/research.aspx, date accessed 15 May 2009.

A. Jackson, 'British-African Defence and Security Connections', *Defence Studies* 6, no. 3 (2006): 351–76.

R. Jervis, 'Cooperation under the Security Dilemma', *World Politics* 30, no. 1 (1978) 167–214.

P. Joana, 'The EU Advisory and Assistance Mission for Reform of the Security Sector in the Democratic Republic of Congo', *Doctrine* no. 1 (2008): 20–4.

A. Johnston, 'Thinking about Strategic Culture', *International Security* 19, no. 4 (1995): 32–64.

S. Jones, *The Rise of European Security Cooperation* (Cambridge: Cambridge University Press, 2007).

D. Jordan et al, *Understanding Modern Warfare* (Cambridge, Cambridge University Press, 2008).

G. Jowett and V. O'Donnell, *Propaganda and Persuasion* (London: Sage, 2006).

M. Joyce, 'Britain's Integration Into The EU', *Collaborations* no. 1649, May 2007.

F. Kagan, *Finding the Target: The Transformation of American Military Policy* (New York: Encounter Books, 2006).

J. Kaitera and G. Ben-Ari, EU 'Battlegroups and the NATO Response Force: A Marriage of Convenience?', *Center for Strategic and International Studies Working Paper*, April (2008).

M. Kaldor, 'Rethinking British Defence Policy and its Economic Implications' (Unpublished Paper, 1995). http://www.sussex.ac.uk/sei/documents/wp8.pdf

A. Kapiszewski and C. Davis, 'Poland's Security and Trans-Atlantic Relations', in T. Lansford and B. Tashev (eds), *Old Europe, New Europe and the U.S.* (London: Routledge, 2005):193–219.

S. Kaufman, 'Organisational Politics and Change in Soviet Military Policy', *World Politics* (April 1994): 355–82.

P. Katzenstein (ed.), *The Culture of National Security: Norms and Identity in World Politics* (New York: Columbia University Press, 1996).

E. Kehr, *Battleship Building and Party Politics in Germany, 1894–1901* (Chicago: University of Chicago Press, 1973).

D. Keohane, *Labour Party Defence Policy since 1945* (Leicester: Leicester University Press, 1993).

R. Keohane, 'Theory of World Politics', in R. Keohane (ed.), *Neorealism and Its Critics* (New York: Columbia University Press: 1986).

J. Kergus, 'Taking into Account Stabilization Specifities Within Preparation and Evaluation Exercises', *Doctrine* no. 12 (2007): 47–9.

W. Keylor, *The Twentieth Century World and Beyond: An International History Since 1900* (Oxford: Oxford University Press, 2006).

E. Kier, 'Culture and Military Doctrine: France between the Wars', *International Security* 19, no. 4 (1995): 65–93.

E. Kier, *Imagining War: French and British Military Doctrine between the Wars* (Princeton: Princeton University Press, 1997).

A. King, 'The Future of the European Security and Defence Policy', *Contemporary Security Policy* 26, no. 1 (2005a): 44–61.

A. King, 'Towards a Transnational Europe: The Case of the Armed Forces', *European Journal of Social Theory* 8, no. 3 (2005b): 321–40.

A. King, 'Britain's Vietnam? Learning the Lessons of Operation Telic'.

J. Kingdon, *Agendas, Alternatives and Public Policies* (New York: Harper Collins, 1995).

A. Kirchgaessner and S. Marahrens, 'NetOpFue: Faehigkeiten fuer Stabilisierungs und Eingreifkraefte', *Wehrtechnische Report* no. 6 (2008): 24–9.

J. Kiszely, 'The Meaning of Manoeuvre', *RUSI Journal* 143, no. 6 (1998): 36–40.

J. Kiszely, 'Achieving High Tempo New Challenges', *RUSI Journal* 144, no. 6 (1999): 47–53.

J. Kiszely, 'Learning About Counter-Insurgency', *RUSI Journal* 151, no. 6 (2006): 16–21.

J. Kiszely, 'Post-Modern Challenges for Post-Modern Warriors', *The Shrivenham Papers*, no. 5 (2007).

F. Kitson, *Low Intensity Operations: Subversion, Insurgency, Peacekeeping* (London: Faber, 1971).

B. Klein, 'Hegemony and Strategic Culture: American Power Projection and Alliance Defence Policies', *Review of International Studies* 14, no. 2 (1988).

KMWeg (2008) http://www.kmweg.de/frame.php?page=19, date accessed 24 July 2008.

C. Knill, 'Introduction: Cross-national Policy Convergence: Concepts, Approaches and Explanatory Factors', *Journal of European Public Policy* 12, no. 5 (2005): 764–74.

A. Kober, 'The Israeli Defence Force in the Second Lebanon War: Why the Poor Performance?', *Journal of Strategic Studies* 31, no. 1 (2008): 3–40.

A. Koelliker, 'The Functional Dimension', in K.H. Dyson and A. Sepos (eds), *Whose Europe? The Politics of Differentiated Integration* (Basingstoke: Palgrave Macmillan, 2010).

P. Kohn et al, 'Towards a New Type of Air-Land Combat', *Doctrine* no. 14 (2008): 86–9.

E. Kolodziej, *Security and International Relations* (Cambridge: Cambridge University Press, 2005).

T. Konstadinides, *Division of Powers in EU Law: The Delimitation of Internal Competence Between the EU and the Member States* (The Hague: Kluwer, 2009).

E. Krahmann, 'Security Governance and Networks: New Theoretical Perspectives in Trans-Atlantic Security', *Cambridge Review of International Affairs* 18, no. 1 (2005): 15–30.

S. Krasner, 'Wars, Hotel Fires and Plane Crashes', *Review of International Studies* 26 (2000): 131–6.

A. Krepinevic, 'Cavalry to Computer: The Pattern of Military Revolutions', *The National Interest* 37, Fall (1994).

A. Krepinevic, *Transforming the Legions: The Army and the Future of Land Warfare* (Washington D.C.: The Centre for Strategic and Budgetary Assessment, 2004).

U. Krotz, 'Parapublic Understandings of International Relations: The Franco-German Construction of Europeanization of a Particular Kind', *European Journal of International Relations* 13, no. 3 (2007): 385–417.

G. Krugler, 'Tactical Third Dimension in France', *Doctrine* no. 14 (2008): 67–71.

Kujat (2009) https://outlook2003.surrey.ac.uk/exchweb/bin/redir.asp?URL=http://www.zeit.de/2009/32/Kujat-Interview, date accessed 13 September 2009.

C. Kupchan, 'NATO and the Persian Gulf: Examining Intra-Alliance Behaviour', *International Organization* 42, no. 2 (1988): 317–46.

G. Kvistad, *The Rise and Demise of German Statism* (Oxford: Berghahn, 1999).

A. Kydd, 'Sheep in Sheep's Clothing: Why Security Seekers Do Not Fight Each Other', *Security Studies* 7 no. 3 (1997): 114–54.

E. La Maisonneuve, 'What Aim for Higher Military Education?', *Doctrine* no. 2 (2004): 36–8.

E.J. Labs, 'Beyond Victory: Offensive Realism and Why States Expand their War Aims', *Security Studies* 6, no. 4 (1997): 1–49.

R.F. Laird and H. Mey, 'The Revolution in Military Affairs: Allied Perspectives', *McNair Paper*, 60 (Institute for National Strategic Studies: Washington, 1999).

D. Lake and R. Powell, *Strategic Choice and International Relations* (Princeton: Princeton University Press, 1999).

T. Lansford, 'The Triumph of Atlanticism: NATO and the Evolution of European Security After the Cold War', *Journal of Strategic Studies* 22, no. 1 (1999): 1–28.

G. Lasconjarias, 'Helicopters During the Algerian War', *Doctrine* no. 14 (2008): 72–4.

S. Laupert, 'Vernetzte Operationsfuehrung in Transformationsprozess', *Wehrtechnische Report* no. 6 (2008): 6–8.

C. Layne, 'From Preponderance to Offshore Balancing: The Future of American Grand Strategy', *International Security* 22, no. 1 (1997): 86–124.

C. Layne, 'The Unipolar Illusion Revisited: The Coming End of the United States' Unipolar Moment', *International Security* 31, no. 2 (2006): 7–41.

P-Y. Le Bail, 'Experience Feedback: A Management System for Decision Makers', *Doctrine* no. 1 (2003): 72–4.

F. LeBot, 'Licorne or the Challenge to Reality', *Doctrine* no. 9 (2006): 111–14.

A. LeCerf, 'The Ivory Coast Republic: A Typical Example of a Stabilisation Operation?', *Doctrine* no. 1 (2008): 31–4.

X. Lecinq, 'The Technical Operational Laboratory', *Doctrine* no. 10 2007: 69–72.

J-J. Leclerc, 'Update on the Future Land Action Study', *Doctrine* no. 1 (2003): 8–9.

J. Legro and A. Moravcsik, 'Is Anybody Still a Realist?', *International Security* 24, no. 2 (1999): 5–55.

J. Lebovic, 'The Unipolar Illusion: Neglected Limits to US Global Military Capacity', Paper Presented to the International Studies Association Annual Convention, San Francisco, 2008.

B. Liddell Hart, *The Decisive Wars of History* (G. Bell and Sons: London, 1929).

W. Lind, 'Some Doctrinal Questions for the U.S. Army', *Military Review* 57, no. 3 (1979): 54–65.

J. Lindsay, M. O'Hanlon, C. Glaser and S. Fetter, 'Correspondence: Limited National and Allied Missile Defence', *International Security* 26, no. 4 (2001/02): 190–201.

A. Linklater, 'The Transformation of Political Community: E.H. Carr, Critical Theory and International Relations', *Review of International Studies* 23 (1997): 321–38.

K. Lisbonne de Vergeron, *France, European Defence and NATO* (London: Forumpress, 2008).

R. Little, 'The Balance of Power in Politics Among Nations', Paper Presented to the 47th International Studies Association Annual Convention, San Diego, United States of America, March 2006.

R. Little, *The Balance of Power in International Relations: Metaphors, Myths and Models* (Cambridge: Cambridge University Press, 2007).

S. Lobell et al, *Neoclassical Realism, The State, And Foreign Policy* (Cambridge: Cambridge University Press, 2009).

K. Longhurst, 'From Security Consumer to Security Provider: Poland and trans-Atlantic Security in the 21st Century', *Defence Studies* 2, no. 2 (2002): 50–62.

K. Longhurst, 'Why Aren't the Germans Debating the Draft? Path Dependency and the Persistence of Conscription', *German Politics* 12, no. 2 (2003): 147–65.

K. Longhurst, *Germany and the Use of Force: The Evolution of German Security Policy 1990–2003* (Manchester: Manchester University Press, 2004).

K. Longhurst and A. Miskimmon, 'Same Challenges, Diverging Responses: Germany, the UK and European Security', *German Politics* 16, no. 1 (2007): 79–95.

K. Longhurst and M. Zaborowski, 'The Future of European Security', *European Security* 31, no. 4 (2004): 381–91.

S. Lungu, 'Military Modernization and Political Choice: Germany and the US-Promoted Military Technological Revolution During the 1990s', *Defence and Security Analysis* 20, no. 1 (2004a): 261–72.

S. Lungu, 'The US Military-Technological Revolution and the "Europeanization" of the French Industrial Sector During the 1990s', *RUSI Journal* 149, no. 1 (2004b): 58–63.

E. Luttwak, 'The American Style in Warfare and the Military Balance', *Survival* 21, no. 2 (1979): 57–60.

E. Luttwak, 'The Operational Level of War', *International Security* 5, no. 3 (1980/81): 61–79.

T. Maechler, 'The Air Force and the Coordination in Land-Air Operations', *Doctrine* no. 14 (2008): 19–25.

N. Machiavelli, *Discourses on Livy* (Oxford: Oxford University Press, 1997).

T. Mahnken and J. FitzSimonds, 'Revolutionary Ambivalence: Understanding Officer Attitudes to Transformation', *International Security* 28, no. 2 (2003): 112–48.

MAJIIC (2008) 'MAJIIC Press Release' October 2006, http://www.nato.int/docu/update/2007/pdf/majic.pdf, date accessed 24 July 2008.

C. Malkasian, 'Did the United States Need More Forces in Iraq? Evidence from Al-Anbar', *Defence Studies* 8, no. 1 (2008): 78–104.

L-C. Mandille, 'The British Battlefield Digitization', *Doctrine* no. 1 (2003): 50–5.

E. Mannik, 'Small States: Invited to NATO – Able to Contribute?', *Defense and Security Analysis* 20, no. 1 (2004): 21–37.

M. Marcussen et al, 'Constructing Europe: The Evolution of British, French and German Nation-State Identities', *Journal of European Public Policy* 6, no. 4 (1999): 614–33.

S. Marsh, 'The Dangers of German History: Lessons from a Decade of German Foreign and Security Policy', *Perspectives on European Politics and Society* 3, no. 3 (2002): 289–424.

D. Marston, 'Force Structure for High and Low Intensity Warfare: The Anglo-American Experience and Lessons for the Future', *Discussion Paper, NIC 2020 Project* (Sandhurst: MOD, 2005).

K. Marten, *Engaging the Enemy: Organisation Theory and Soviet Military Innovation* (Princeton, NJ: Princeton University Press, 1993).

S. Martigny and Y. Cabon, 'The Doctrine, Training Synergy in a Branch School', *Doctrine* no. 3 (2004): 16–17.

G. Martin, 'Uranium: A Case Study in Franco-African Relations', *The Journal of Modern African Studies* 27, no. 4 (1989): 625–40.

M. Mastaduno, D. Lake and G.J. Ikenberry, 'Towards A Realist Theory of State Action', *International Studies Quarterly* 33, no. 4 (1989): 457–74.

J.H. Matlary, *European Union Security Dynamics: In the New National Interest* (Houndmills: Palgrave Macmillan, 2009).

J. Mattis, 'Commander's Guidance for Effects-Based Operations', *Joint Forces Quarterly* 51, no. 4 (2008): 105–8.

M. Matzken, 'German Army Stabilisation Forces', *Doctrine* no. 12 (2007): 71–4.

H. Maull, 'Germany and Japan: The New Civilian Powers', *Foreign Affairs* 69, no. 5 (1990/91): 91–106.

H. Maull, 'Germany's Foreign Policy post-Kosovo: Still a Civilian Power?' *Survival* 42, no. 2 (2000): 91–106.

H. Maull, 'Normalisierung oder Auszehrung? Deutsche Außenpolitik in Wandel', *Politik und Zeitgeschichte* (March 2004): 17–23.

R. Mayntz, 'Executive Leadership in Germany', in R. Rose and E. Suleimann (eds), *Presidents and Prime Ministers* (Washington: AEI, 1980).

A.J. McAdams, 'Germany After Unification: Normal at Last?', *World Politics* 49, no. 2 (1997): 282–308.

MCCE (2008) https://www.mcce-mil.com/, date accessed 5 October 2008.

J. McColl, 'Adapting Command Hierarchies', *RUSI Journal* 149, no. 1 (2004): 52–5.

C. McInnes, 'Labour's Strategic Defence Review', *International Affairs* 74, no. 4 (1998): 823–45.

C. McInnes, 'The British Army: Adapting to Change in the 1990s and Beyond', in B. Bond and M. Melvin (eds), *The Nature of Future Conflict: Implications for Future Force Development* (London TSO/Strategic and Combat Studies Institute, 1999): 66–76.

J.J. McKenna, 'Towards the Army of the Future: Domestic Politics and the End of Conscription in France', *West European Politics* 20, no. 4 (1997): 125–45.

M. McNerny, 'Military Innovation During War: Paradox or Paradigm?', *Defense and Security Analysis* 21, no. 2 (2005): 201–12.

J. Mearsheimer, 'Back to the Future? Instability in Europe after the Cold War', *International Security* 15, no. 1 (1990): 5–56.

J. Mearsheimer, 'The False Promise of International Institutions', *International Security* 19, no. 3 (1994/95): 5–49

J. Mearsheimer, 'A Realist Reply', *International Security* 20, no. 1 (1995): 82–93.

J. Mearsheimer, *The Tragedy of Great Power Politics* (New York: Norton, 2001).

J. Mearsheimer, 'Power and Fear in Great Power Politics', in G.O. Mazur (ed.), *One Hundred Year Commemoration to The Life of Hans Morgenthau* (New York: Semeneko Foundation, 2004): 184–96.

J. Mearsheimer, 'E.H. Carr vs. Idealism: The Battle Rages On', *International Relations* 19, no. 2 (2005): 139–52.

J. Mearsheimer et al, 'Roundtable: The Battle Rages On', *International Relations* 19, no. 3 (2005): 337–60.

F.J. Meiers, 'A Change of Course? German Foreign and Security Policy After Unification', *German Politics* 11, no. 3 (2002): 195–216.

J. Meiter, 'Network Enabled Capability: A Theory Desperately in Need of a Doctrine', *Defence Studies* 6, no. 2 (2006): 189–214.

M. Melvin, 'Continuity and Change: How British Army Doctrine is Evolving to Match the Balanced Force', *RUSI Journal* 147, no. 4 (2002): 38–44.

A. Menon, 'From Independence to Cooperation: France, NATO and European Security', *International Affairs* 71, no. 1 (1995): 19–34.

S. Metz, 'America's Defence Transformation: A Conceptual and Political History', *Defence Studies* 6, no. 1 (2006): 1–25.

H. Mey, 'The Revolution in Military Affairs: A German Perspective', *Comparative Strategy* 17, (1998): 309–19.

C. Meyer, 'Convergence towards a European Strategic Culture', *European Journal of International Relations* 11, no. 4 (2005): 523–49.

C. Meyer, *The Quest for a European Strategic Culture: Changing Norms on Security and Defence in the European Union* (Basingstoke: Palgrave Macmillan, 2006).

J.P. Meyer, 'The Potential Risks Across the National Territory Against Which the Army Might be Committed: The International Terrorist Threat', *Doctrine* no. 6 (2006): 10–11.

MIC (2008) http://www.jcs.mil/j3/mic/, date accessed 5 October 2008.

X. Michel, 'Law and Order and Peace Support Operations', *Doctrine* no. 6 (2005): 55–6.

C. Michon, 'Stabilization Operations and their Influence in Terms of Equipment', *Doctrine* no. 12 (2007): 43–6.

A. Michta, 'Modernising The Polish Military', *Defence Studies* 2, no. 2 (2002): 40–9.

A. Milton, 'British Defence Doctrine and the British Approach to Operations', *RUSI Journal* 146, no. 6 (2001): 41–4.

MIP (2008) 'Statement of Intent For the Multinational Interoperability Programme (The Ottawa Agreement)', Multilateral Interoperability Programme, 1 October 2001. www.mip-site.org/01-Atccis/mip_doc/MIP_SOI.doc, date accessed 5 October 2008.

A. Miskimmon, 'Continuity in the Face of Upheaval: British Strategic Culture and the Blair Government', *European Security* 13, no. 3 (2004): 87–113.

A. Miskimmon, *Germany and the Common Foreign and Security Policy of the European Union* (Basingstoke: Palgrave Macmillan, 2007).

A. Miskimmon and W. Paterson, 'The Europeanisation of German Foreign and Security Policy: On the Cusp Between Transformation and Accommodation', in K.H. Dyson and K.H. Goetz (eds), *Germany, Europe and the Politics of Constraint* (Oxford: Oxford University Press, 2003): 325–45.

A. Miskimmon, 'Falling into Line? Kosovo and the Course of German Foreign Policy', *International Affairs* 85, no. 3 (2009): 561–73.

MoD (2009) http://www.mod.uk/DefenceInternet/FactSheets/UrgentOperationalRequirementsuor.htm, date accessed 25 November 2009.

A. Moens, 'ESDP, the United States and the Atlantic Alliance', in J. Howorth and J. Keeler (eds), *Defending Europe: The EU, NATO and the Quest for European Autonomy* (Basingstoke: Palgrave Macmillan, 2003): 25–37.

P. Morgan, 'The Impact of the Revolution in Military Affairs', *Journal of Strategic Studies* 23, no. 1 (2000): 132–62.

H.J. Morgenthau, *Scientific Man vs. Power Politics* (Chicago: University of Chicago Press, 1946).

H.J. Morgenthau, *Politics Amongst Nations: The Struggle for Power and Peace* (New York: Knopp, 1966).

F. Moriniere et al, 'Stabilization: Even More Demanding as Regards Simulations', *Doctrine* no. 12 (2007): 50–2.

T. Mowle and D. Sacko, 'Global NATO: Bandwagoning in a Uni-Polar World', *Contemporary Security Policy* 28, no. 3 (2007): 597–618.

M. Nachez, 'The Impact of Battlefield Digitization on Staff Officers' Culture', *Doctrine* no. 1 (2003): 21–5.

J. Nagl, *Learning to Eat Soup with a Knife: Counterinsurgency Lessons from Malaya to Vietnam* (Chicago: Chicago University Press, 2005).

NATO (2008a) http://www.nato.int/issues/military_structure/command/index-e.html, date accessed 08 October 2008.

NATO (2008b) http://www.nato.int/issues/strategic-lift-air-sac/index.html, date accessed 5 October 2008.

NATO (2008c) http://www.nato.int/issues/ags/practice.html, date accessed 8 October 2008.

NC3A (2008) http://www.nc3a.nato.int/organisation/index.html, date accessed 8 October 2008.

D. Neal, 'Do We Really Understand What is Meant by Transformational Change for Defence?', *Defence Studies* 6, no. 1 (2003): 73–96.

B. Newsome, *Made Not Born: Why Some Soldiers are Better Than Others* (Westport: Greenwood, 2007).

F. Nicol, 'Training for Actions in Urban Areas', *Doctrine* no. 3 (2004): 28–9.

F. Nicol, 'A Joint Concept for Force Protection', *Doctrine* no. 15 (2008): 13–14.

R. Niebuhr, *Moral Man and Immoral Society: A Study in Ethics and Politics* (New York: Charles Scribner's Sons, 1932).

T. Noetzel and B. Schreer, 'Counter What? Germany and Counter-insurgency in Afghanistan', *RUSI Journal* 153, no. 1 (2008a): 42–6.

T. Noetzel and B. Schreer, 'All the Way? The Evolution of German Military Power', *International Affairs* 84, no. 2 (2008b): 211–21.

T. Noetzel and B. Schreer, 'Missing Links: The Evolution of German Counter-Insurgency Thinking', *RUSI Journal* 154, no. 1 (2009): 16–22.

NORDCAPS (2008) http://www.nordcaps.org/?id=81, date accessed 5 October 2008.

F.M. Nunn, *Yesterday's Soldiers: European Military Professionalism in South America* (Lincoln: University of Nebraska, 1983).

NYT (2009) http://www.nytimes.com/2009/04/07/us/politics/07defense.html?page-wanted=1&_r=2&hp, date accessed 20 October 2009.

OCCAR (2008) http://www.occar-ea.org/view.php?nid=72, date accessed 23 July 2008.

M. O'Hanlon, 'A Flawed Masterpiece', *Foreign Affairs*, 81, no. 3 (2002).

M. Otte and J. Greve, *A Rising Middle Power? German Foreign Policy in Transformation, 1989–1999* (New York: St. Martins, 2000).

W. Owen, 'The Manoeuvre Warfare Fraud', *RUSI Journal* 153, no. 4 (2008): 62–7.

W. Owens and E. Offley, *Lifting the Fog of War* (New York: Farrar Straus and Giroux, 2000).

R. Paarlberg, 'Knowledge as Power: Science, Military Dominance and U.S. Security', *International Security*, 29, no. 1 (2004): 122–51.

R. Pape, 'Soft Balancing Against the United States', *International Security* 30, no. 1 (2005): 7–45.

A. Parasiliti, 'Correspondence: The First Image Reversed', *International Security* 26, no. 2 (2001): 166–9.

G. Parker, *The Military Revolution: Military Innovation and the Rise of the West 1500–1800* (Cambridge: Cambridge University Press, 1988).

S. Pau, 'The EU in Africa: Complementarities and Limitations in Stabilisation Operations', *Doctrine* no. 12 (2007): 79–81.

T.V. Paul, 'The Enduring Axioms of Balance of Power Theory and Their Contemporary Relevance', in T.V. Paul et al (eds), *Balance of Power Theory and Practice in the Twenty First Century* (Stanford, California: Stanford University Press, 2004).

R. Pauly, 'French Security Agenda in the Post-9/11 World', in T. Lansford and B. Taschev (eds), *Old Europe, New Europe and the US* (Aldershot: Ashgate, 2005).

N. Pederson, *The French Desire For Uranium* (University of Illinois at Urbana-Champaign: Program for Arms Control, Disarmament and International Security, 2000).

F. Penska and W. Mason, 'EU Security Cooperation and the Trans-Atlantic Relationship', *Cooperation and Conflict* 38 no. 3 (2003): 255–80.

L. Perron de Revel, 'No Stabilisation Phase is Like Another, But All Have Basic Features', *Doctrine* no. 12 (2007): 85–8.

P. Pierson, *Politics in Time: History, Institutions and Social Analysis* (Princeton: Princeton University Press, 2004).

Pleiades (2008) http://smsc.cnes.fr/PLEIADES/, date accessed 5 October 2008.

PM (2009) http://www.premier-ministre.gouv.fr/en/information/latest_news_97/francois_fillon_announces_cuts_62563.html: date accessed 11 May 2009.

R. Porte, 'Intelligence in Indo-China', *Doctrine* no. 9 (2006): 100–2.

B. Posen, 'Nationalism, the Mass Army and Military Power', *International Security* 18, no. 2 (1993): 80–124.

B. Posen, *The Sources of Military Doctrine: France, Britain and Germany Between the Wars* (Ithaca: Cornell University Press, 1984).

B. Posen, 'Command of the Commons', *International Security* 28, no. 1 (2003): 5–46.

B. Posen, 'ESDP and the Structure of World Power', *International Spectator* 1 (2004): 1–17.

B. Posen, 'The European Security and Defence Policy: Response to Uni-polarity', *Security Studies* 15, no. 2 (2006): 149–86.

B. Posen and A. Ross, 'Competing Visions for US Grand Strategy', *International Security* 21, no. 3 (1996): 5–53.

E. Poucet, 'Human Intelligence: Expectations and Problems', *Doctrine* no. 9 (2006): 74–7.

G. Press-Barnathan, 'Managing the Hegemon: NATO under Uni-polarity', *Security Studies* 15, no. 2 (2006): 271–309.

G. Press, 'The Myth of Airpower in the Persian Gulf and the Future of Warfare', *International Security* 26, no. 2 (2001): 5–44.

J. Pretorius, 'The Security Imaginary: Explaining Military Isomorphism', *Security Dialogue* 39, no. 1 (2008): 99–120.

X. Previsani, 'UAV-Helicopter Cooperation: A Promising Course of Action', *Doctrine* no. 14 (2008): 15–17.

G. Quille, 'The Revolution in Military Affairs and the UK', *International Security Information Service Briefing* no. 73 (December 1998)

M. Quinlan, *European Defence Cooperation: Asset or Threat to NATO?* (Washington: Woodrow Wilson Centre Press, 2001).

D. Ralston, *Importing the European Army: The Introduction of European Military Technology into the Extra European World* (Chicago: Chicago University Press, 1990).

G. Rangwala, 'Counterinsurgency Amid Fragmentation: The British in Southern Iraq', *Journal of Strategic Studies* 32, no. 3 (2009): 495–513.

B. Rathbun, 'Uncertain About Uncertainty: Understanding the Multiple Meanings of a Crucial Concept in International Relations Theory', *International Studies Quarterly* 51, no. 3 (2007).

B. Rathburn, 'A Rose By Any Other Name: Neoclassical Realism as the Logical and Necessary Extension of Structural Realism', *Security Studies* 17, no. 2 (2008): 294–321.

S. Reicher and N. Hopkins, *Self and Nation* (London: Sage, 2001).

R. Renner, 'America's Asymmetric Advantage: The Utility of Airpower in the New Strategic Environment', *Defence Studies* 4, no. 1 (2004): 87–113.

J. Resende-Santos, *Neorealism, States and the Modern Mass Army* (Cambridge: Cambridge University Press, 2007).

C. Reynolds, 'Military Capability Development Within the ESDP: Towards Effective Governance?' *Contemporary Security Policy* 25, no. 2 (2007): 357–83.

K. Reynolds, 'Building the Future Force: Getting Defence Transformation Right', *Contemporary Security Policy* 27, no. 3 (2006): 435–71.

F. Richier and A. Morel, 'Conception and Conduct of a Stabilisation Phase at Departmental Level', *Doctrine* no. 12 (2007): 19–21.

T. Ricks, *Fiasco: The American Military Adventure in Iraq* (New York: Penguin, 2006).

P. Riecker, *Europeanisation of National Security Identity: The EU and Changing Identities of Nordic States* (Abingdon: Routledge, 2005).

P. Riecker, 'From Common Defence to Comprehensive Security: Towards the Europeanization of French Foreign and Security Policy?', *Security Dialogue* 37, no. 4 (2006): 509–28.

J. Ringmose, 'Paying for Protection: Denmark's Military Expenditure During the Cold War', *Cooperation and Conflict* 44, no. 1 (2009): 73–97.

N. Ripsman et al, 'Conclusion: The State of Neoclassical Realism', in E. Lobell et al (eds), *Neoclassical Realism, The State and Foreign Policy* (Cambridge: Cambridge University Press, 2009): 280–99.

V. Rittberger, 'Selbstentfesserung in kleinen Schritten? Deutschlands Aussenpolitik zu Beginn des 21. Jahrhunderts', *Politische Vierteljahrschrift* 44, no. 1 (2003): 10–18.

A. Roberts, 'Doctrine and Reality in Afghanistan', *Survival* 51, no. 1 (2008): 29–60.

J. Rollins, 'Command in Operations: The Lessons From the British Experience in Iraq', *Doctrine* no. 5 (2004): 59–62.

J. Rollins, 'Doctrine and Command in the British Army: A Historical Perspective', *Doctrine* no. 9 (2006): 85–94.

G. Rose, 'Neoclassical Realism and Theories of Foreign Policy', *World Politics* 51, no. 3 (1998): 144–72.

M. Rose, 'Afghanistan', *RUSI Journal* 153, no. 5 (2008): 8–13.

S. Rosen, 'New Ways of War: Understanding Military Innovation', *International Security* (Summer 1998): 134–68.

S. Rosen, *Winning the Next War: Innovation and the Modern Military* (Ithaca: Cornell University Press, 1991).

G. Rouby, 'The Joint Dimensions of Operations Command', *Doctrine* no. 5 (2004): 11–15.

E. Roussel, 'Command and Control', *Doctrine* no. 3 (2004): 18.

RTO (2008a) http://www.rto.nato.int/activities.aspx, date accessed 23 October 2008.

RUSI (2009) http://www.rusi.org/go.php?structureID=S433AC69DF0216&ref=C49F9BEE-224FA0., date accessed 15 July 2009.

J. Rutter, 'The Unwinnable War Defeating Popular Insurgency Lessons from the British Experience in Malaya', *Doctrine* no. 13 (2007): 100–3.

J. Ruwe, 'A Doctrinal Process: Towards A New Organisation of Command and Control in the German Army', *Doctrine* no. 5 (2004): 51–3.

S. Rynning, 'French Defence Reforms After Kosovo: On Track Or Derailed?', *European Security* 9, no. 2 (2000): 61–80.

S. Rynning, *Changing Military Doctrine: Presidents and Military Power in 5th Republic France: 1958–2000* (New York: Praeger, 2001).

S. Rynning, 'Shaping Military Doctrine in France: Decisionmakers Between International Power and Domestic Interests', *Security Studies* 11, no. 2 (2001/02): 85–116.

S. Rynning, *NATO Renewed: The Power and Purpose of Transatlantic Cooperation* (Houndmills: Palgrave, 2005).

S. Rynning, 'Transformation and Counter-Transformation in the French Army', Paper presented on Panel FB11 'Global Norms, Organisational Culture and Military Transformation' at the 49th Annual International Studies Association Conference, San Francisco, March 26–9, 2008.

P. Sabatier and H. Jenkins-Smith, 'The Advocacy Coalition Framework: An Assessment', in P. Sabatier (ed.), *Theories of the Policy Process* (Boulder: Westview, 1999): 117–66.

T. Salmon and A. Shepherd, *Toward a European Army: A Military Power in the Making?* (Boulder: Lynne Rienner, 2003).

H. Sapolsky, E. Gholz and C. Talmadge, *US Defense Politics: The Origins of Security Policy* (New York: Routledge, 2009).

SAR (2008) http://www.ohb-system.de/gb/News/presse/1912_06.html, date accessed 5 October 2008.

P. Savary de Beauregard, 'Pacification: The French School', *Doctrine* no. 12 (2007): 97–101.

SATCOM (2008) http://www.nato.int/issues/satcom/index.html date accessed 5 October 2008.

SCC (2008) http://www.nosu.no/sealift/, date accessed 5 October 2008.

A. Schedler and J. Santiso, 'Democracy and Time: An Invitation', *International Political Science Review* 19, no. 1 (1998): 5–18.

B. Schmidt, 'Competing Realist Conceptions of Power', *Millennium: Journal of International Studies* 33, no. 3 (2005): 523–49.

G. Schroeder, *Entscheidungen: Mein Leben in Der Politik* (Hamburg: Hoffmann and Campe, 2007).

B. Schwarz and C. Layne, 'A New Grand Strategy', *Atlantic Monthly* 289, no. 1 (2002): 36–42.

R. Schweller, 'Neorealism's Status Quo Bias: What Security Dilemma?', *Security Studies*, 5, no. 3 (1996).

R. Schweller, 'New Realist Research on Alliances: Refining Not Refuting Waltz's Balancing Proposition', *The American Political Science Review* 91, no. 4 (1997): 927–30.

R. Schweller, *Deadly Imbalances: Tri-polarity and Hitler's Strategy of World Conquest* (New York: Columbia University Press: 1998).

R. Schweller, 'Bandwagoning for Profit: Bringing the Revisionist State Back In', *International Security* 19, no. 1 (1994): 72–107.

R. Schweller, 'Fantasy Theory', *Review of International Studies* 25, no. 1 (1999): 147–50.

R. Schweller, 'Unanswered Threats: A Neoclassical Realist Theory of Underbalancing', *International Security* 29, no. 2 (2004): 159–201.

R. Schweller, *Unanswered Threats: Political Constraints on the Balance of Power* (Princeton: Princeton University Press, 2006).

J. Serveille, 'Experience Feedback (RETEX) Within KFOR', *Doctrine* no. 2 (2004): 47–8.

A. Shepherd, 'Top-Up or Bottom-Down? Is Security and Defence Policy in the EU a Question of Political Will or Military Capability?', *European Security* 9, no. 2 (2000): 13–30.

A. Siedschalg, 'Neo-Realist Contributions to a Theory of ESDP', Presentation at the Second European Security Conference, Innsbruck, Austria 30 September 2006.

Q. Skinner, *Machiavelli* (Oxford: Oxford University Press, 1981).

E. Sloan, *The Revolution in Military Affairs: Implications for Canada and NATO* (Montreal: McGill-Queens University Press, 2002).

S. Sloan, *NATO, the European Union and the Atlantic Community: The Trans-Atlantic Bargain Challenged* (Lanham: Rowman and Littlefield, 2005).

D. Smith, *Nations and Nationalism in a Global Era* (Cambridge: Polity, 1995).

M. Smith, 'Sending the Bundeswehr to the Balkans: The Domestic Politics of Reflexive Multilateralism', *German Politics and Society* 14 (Winter 1996): 29–67.

M. Smith, 'Britain: Balancing Instinctive Atlanticism', *Contemporary Security Policy* 26, no. 3 (2005): 447–69.

M.L. Smith, 'Guerrillas in the Mist: Reassessing Strategy and Low-Intensity Warfare', *Review of International Studies* 29, no. 1 (2003): 19–37.

R. Smith, *The Utility of Force: The Art of War in the Modern World* (London: Allen Lane, 2006).

G. Snyder, 'The Security Dilemma in Alliance Politics', *World Politics* 36, no. 4 (1984): 461–95.

J. Snyder, *The Soviet Strategic Culture: Implications for Limited Nuclear Operations* (Santa Monica, California: RAND, 1977).

J. Snyder, *Myths of Empire: Domestic Politics and International Ambition* (Ithaca: New York, 1991).

J. Sperling, 'Capabilities Traps and Gaps: Symptom or Cause of a Troubled Trans-Atlantic Relationship?' *Contemporary Security Policy* 25, no. 3 (2004): 452–78.

A. Stent, *From Embargo to Ostpolitik: The Political Economy of West German-Soviet Relations 1955–1980* (Cambridge: Cambridge University Press, 2003).

J. Sterling-Folker, 'Realist Environment, Liberal Process and Domestic Level Variables', *International Studies Quarterly* 41, no. 1 (1997).

A. Stigler, 'A Clear Victory for Air Power: NATO's Empty Threat to Invade Kosovo', *International Security* 27, no. 3 (2002/03): 124–57.

J. Stone, 'Politics, Technology and the Revolution in Military Affairs', *Journal of Strategic Studies* 27, no. 3 (2004): 408–27.

J. Storr, 'A Command Philosophy for the Information Age: The Continuing Relevance of Mission Command', *Defence Studies* 3, no. 3 (2003): 119–29.

H. Strachan, 'British Counterinsurgency: From Malaya To Iraq', *RUSI Journal* 152, no. 6 (2007): 8–11.

Streitkraeftebasis (2009a) http://www.streitkraeftebasis.de/portal/a/streitkraefte-basis/kcxml/04_Sj9SPykssy0xPLMnMz0vM0Y_QjzKLt4g3cQsBSUGYwfqRMLGglFR9b31fj_zcVP0A_YLciHJHR0VFACDw1Fg!/delta/base64xml/L2dJQSEvUUt3QS80SVVFLzZfOF8xMVBJ?yw_contentURL=per cent2F01DB040000000001per cent2FW272-Y9J8225INFODEper cent2Fcontent.jsp, date accessed 23 June 2009.

Streitkraeftebasis (2009b) http://www.bundeswehr.de/portal/a/bwde/kcxml/04_Sj9-SPykssy0xPLMnMz0vM0Y_QjzKLd443cQoASZnFO8abeprqR0IYljAxQzc_NDHneOOAEJAYRK-vR35uqn5QSqq-t36AfkFuaGhEuaMiANStdHQ!/delta/base64xml/L2dJQSEv-UUt3QS80SVVFLzZfQ180Qk8!?yw_contentURL=percent2FC1256EF4002AED30per cent2FW26N3JWU590INFODEper cent2Fcontent.jsp, date accessed 23 June 2009.

H. Stritzel, 'Towards a Theory of Securitization: Copenhagen and Beyond', *European Journal of International Relations* 13, no. 3 (2007): 357–83.

A. Stulberg, 'Managing Military Transformations: Agency, Culture and The U.S. Carrier Revolution', *Security Studies* 14, no. 3 (2005): 489–528.

Sueddeutsche (2009a) http://www.sueddeutsche.de/politik/335/486747/bilder/?img=9.0, date accessed 14 September 2009.

M. Sutton, *France and the Construction of Europe, 1944–2007: The Geopolitical Imperative*, (Oxford: Berghahn, 2007).

A. Swidler, 'Culture in Action: Symbols and Strategies', *American Sociological Review* 51, no. 2 (1986): 273–86.

A. Swidler, *Talk of Love: How Culture Matters* (Chicago: University of Chicago Press, 2001).

SWR (2009) http://www.swr.de/nachrichten/-/id=396/nid=396/did=5389428/1wdq8r5/index.html, date accessed 15 October 2009.

S. Szabo, *Parting Ways: The Crisis in German-American Relations* (Washington D.C.: Brookings Institution Press).

J. Taliaferro, 'Security Seeking Under Anarchy: Defensive Realism Revisited', *International Security* 25, no. 3 (2000–1): 126–61.

J. Taliaferro, 'State Building for Future Wars: Neoclassical Realism and the Resource-Extractive State', *Security Studies* 15, no. 3 (2006): 464–95.

T. Tardy, 'French Policy Towards Peace Support Operations', *International Peacekeeping* 6, no. 1 (1999): 55–78.

J. Tarle, 'Indirect Fire Support', *Doctrine* no. 3 (2004): 23.

B. Tashev, 'In Search of Security: Bulgaria's Security Policy in Transition', in T. Lansford and B. Tashev (eds), *Old Europe, New Europe and the U.S.* (London: Routledge, 2005): 127–51.

P. Ternynck, 'Operation Benga: Aerocombat for EU-led Military Expeditions', *Doctrine* no. 14 (2008): 75–6.

T. Terriff, 'Of Romans and Dragons: Preparing the U.S. Marine Corps for Future Warfare', *Contemporary Security Policy* 28, no. 1 (2007): 143–62.

H. Tewes, *Germany, Civilian Power and the New Europe: Enlarging NATO and the European Union* (Basingstoke: Palgrave, 2002).

TG (2009) http://www.telegraph.co.uk/comment/columnists/lizhunt/6541903/Afghanistan-Gordon-Brown-is-losing-the-battle-for-hearts-and-minds.html, date accessed 12 November 2009.

M. Thompson, 'Lessons in Counterinsurgency: The French Campaign in Algeria', Air Command and Staff College, Air University, Maxwell Air Force Base Alabama, 2008.

R. Thompson, *Defeating Communist Insurgency: The Lessons of Malaya and Vietnam* (New York: Praeger, 1966).

R. Thornton, 'A Welcome Revolution? The British Army and the Changes of the Strategic Defence Review', *Defence Studies* 3, no. 3 (2003): 38–62.

Thucydides, *The Peloponnesian War* (New York: New American Library, 1951).

R. Tiersky, 'French Military Reform and Restructuring', *JFQ* 1 (1997): 95–112.

Times (2009) http://www.timesonline.co.uk/tol/news/world/europe/article6833225.ece, date accessed 5 November 2009.

A. Toje, *America, The EU and Strategic Culture: Re-negotiating the Trans-Atlantic Bargain* (Abingdon: Routledge, 2008).

G. Torpy, 'Counterinsurgency', *RUSI Journal* 152, no. 5 (2007): 18–22.

C. Twomey, 'Lacunae in the Study of Culture in International Security', *Contemporary Security Policy* 29, no. 2 (2008): 338–57.

M. Trachtenberg, 'The Question of Realism: A Historian's View', *Security Studies* 13, no. 1 (2006): 156–94.

UK Defence Statistics (2007) http://www.dasa.mod.uk/modintranet/UKDS2007/c2/table207.html, date accessed 17 June 2009.

UK Defence Statistics (2008) http://www.dasa.mod.uk/UKDS2008/pdf/CHAPTER2.pdf, date accessed 17 June 2009.

S. Ulriksen, 'Requirements for Future European Military Strategies and Force Structures', *International Peacekeeping* 11, no. 3 (2004): 457–73.

R. Utley, *The French Defence Debate: Consensus and Continuity in the Mitterrand Era* (London: Macmillan, 2000).

R. Utley, 'Not To Do Less...But To Do Better: French Military Policy in Africa', *International Affairs* 78, 1 (2002): 129–46.

R. Utley, 'A Means to Wider Ends? France, Germany and Peacekeeping', in R. Utley (ed.), *Major Powers and Peacekeeping: Perspectives, Priorities and the Challenges of Military Intervention* (Aldershot: Ashgate, 2006): 63–81.

R. Utley (ed.), *Major Powers and Peacekeeping: Perspectives, Priorities and the Challenges of Military Intervention* (Aldershot: Ashgate, 2006).

T. Valasek, 'New Members in Europe's Security Policy', *Cambridge Review of International Affairs* 18, no. 2 (2005): 217–28.

G. Van der Giet and G. Schreiber, 'Moderne Informationsstechnik: Befaehigung zur Vernetzten Operationsfuehrung', *Wehrtechnische Report* no. 6 (2003): 20–3.

S. Van Evera, 'Hypotheses on Nationalism and War', *International Security* 18, no. 4 (1994): 5–39.

S. Van Evera, *Causes of War: Power and the Roots of Conflict* (Ithaca, N.Y.: Cornell University Press, 1999).

J. Vasquez, 'The Realist Paradigm and Degenerative Versus Progressive Research Programmes: An Appraisal of Neotraditional Research on Waltz's Balancing Proposition', *The American Political Science Review* 91, no. 4 (1997): 899–912.

M. Vego, *Operational Warfare* (Newport: US Naval College, 2000).

M. Vego, 'A Case Against Systemic Operational Design', *Joint Forces Quarterly* 53, no. 2 (2009): 69–75.

Vernetzte Operationsfuehrung (2009) http://www.bundeswehr.de/portal/a/bwde/kcxml/ 04_Sj9SPykssy0xPLMnMz0vM0Y_QjzKLd443cQoASZnFO8abeprqR0IYljAxQzc_NDHne OOAEJAYRK-vR35uqn5QSqq-t36AfkFuaGhEuaMiANStdHQ!/delta/base64xml/ L2dJQSEvUUt3QS80SVVFLzZfQ180QlA!?yw_contentURL=percent2FC1256EF4002-AED30percent2FW26N3JZ9540INFODEper cent2Fcontent.jsp, date accessed 23 June 2009.

C. Voute, 'The Process of Experience Feedback in the French Army', *Objectif Doctrine* no. 26 (2001): 5–7.

P. Vouteau and P. De Solages, 'Meeting the Operational Requirement Through the Reactive Adaptive Function', *Doctrine* no. 15 (2008): 100–5.

W. Wagner, 'From Vanguard to Laggard: Germany in European Security and Defence Policy', *German Politics* 14, no. 4 (2005): 455–69.

W. Wallace, 'British Foreign Policy after the Cold War', *International Affairs*, 68, no. 3 (1992): 423–42.

S. Walt, 'Alliance Formation and the Balance of World Power', *International Security* 9, no. 4 (1985): 3–43.

S. Walt, 'Testing Theories of Alliance Formation: The Case of South West Asia', *International Organization* 42, no. 2 (1988): 275–316.

S. Walt, *The Origins of Alliances* (Ithaca, New York: Cornell University Press, 1987).

S. Walt, 'The Progressive Power of Realism', *The American Political Science Review* 91, no. 4 (1997): 931–5.

S. Walt, 'The Enduring Relevance of the Realist Tradition', in I. Katznelson and H. Milner (eds), *Political Science: The State of the Discipline* (New York: Norton, 2002).

S. Walt, 'Keeping the World Off Balance', in J. Ikenberry (ed.), *America Unrivalled: The Future of the Balance of Power* (Ithaca, New York: Cornell University Press, 2002).

S. Walt, 'Taming American Power', *Foreign Affairs* 84, no. 5 (2005a): 105–20.

S. Walt, *Taming American Power: The Global Response to US Primacy* (New York: Norton, 2005b).

K. Waltz, *Man, the State and War* (New York: Columbia University Press, 1959).

K. Waltz, *Theory of International Politics* (Reading MA: Addison Wesley, 1979).

K. Waltz, 'Structural Realism after the Cold War', *International Security* 25, no. 1 (2000): 5–41.

D. Walz (ed.), *Drei Jahezehnte Innere Fuehrung: Grundlagen, Entwicklungen, Perspectiven* (Baden Baden: Nomos, 1987).

J-M. Wasielewski, 'Telmatics (CIS)', *Doctrine* no. 3 (2004): 19.

Die Welt (2009) http://www.welt.de/politik/deutschland/article4421894/USA-wollen-mehr-deutsche-Truppen-fuer-Afghanistan.html#vote_4422170, date accessed 16 October 2009.

A. Wendt, 'Anarchy is What States Make of It: The Social Construction of Power Politics', *International Organization* 46, no. 2 (1992): 319–425.

A. Wendt, 'Four Sociologies of International Politics', in R. Little and M. Smith (eds), *Perspectives on World Politics* (Abingdon: Routledge, 2005): 405–15.

R. Whitman, 'NATO, the EU and ESDP: An Emerging Division of Labour?', *Contemporary Security Policy* 25, no. 3 (2004): 430–51.

N. Whitney, *Re-energising Europe's Security and Defence Policy* (London: European Council on Foreign Relations, 2008).

C. Williams and C. Gilroy, 'The Transformation of Personnel Policies', *Defence Studies* 6, no. 1 (2006): 97–121.

M. Williams, *The Realist Tradition and the Limits of International Relations* (Cambridge: Cambridge University Press, 2005).

R. Williams, 'Is the West's Reliance on Technology a Panacea for Future Conflict or Its Achilles' Heel?', *Defence Studies* 1, no. 2 (2001): 38–56.

L-C. Winckler, 'The Desirable Contribution of Lessons Learned to The Future Land Action Study', *Doctrine* no. 1 (2003): 77–81.

W. Wohlforth, 'The Stability of a Uni-polar World', *International Security* 24, no. 1 (1999): 5–41.

W. Wohlforth, 'U.S. Strategy in a Uni-polar World', in G.J. Ikenberry (ed.), *America Unrivalled: The Future Balance of Power* (Ithaca: Cornell University Press, 2002): 98–121.

D. Yost, 'The U.S.-European Capabilities Gap and the Prospects for ESDP', in J. Howorth and J. Keeler (eds), *Defending Europe: The EU, NATO and the Quest for European Autonomy* (Houndmills: Palgrave Macmillan, 2003): 81–107.

N. Zahariadis, 'Ambiguity, Time, and Multiple Streams', in P. Sabatier (ed.), *Theories of the Policy Process* (Boulder: Westview, 1999): 73–97.

F. Zakaria, 'Realism and Domestic Politics: A Review Essay', *International Security* 7, no. 1 (1991): 177–98.

F. Zakaria, *From Wealth to Power: The Unusual Origins of America's World Role* (Princeton: Princeton University Press, 1998).

R. Zbienen, 'The Capazub: Study About the Capacities Needed by a Combined Arms Task Force to be Committed in Built-Up Areas', *Doctrine* no. 4 (2004): 56–8.

R. Zbienen, 'The Epidote Operation in Afghanistan', *Doctrine* no. 2 (2004):

M. Zimmer, 'Return of the Mittellage? The Discourse of the Centre in German Foreign Policy', *German Politics* 6, no. 1 (1997): 23–38.

P. Zimmermann, 'The French Navy and 3-D Space Management', *Doctrine* no. 14 (2008): 26–8.

K. Zisk, *Engaging the Enemy* (Princeton, N.J.: Princeton University Press, 1993).

Documents

'A Secure Europe in a Better World: European Security Strategy', European Council, Brussels, 12 December 2003.

'Abschlussbericht zur Studie SFT 21-2040 Mensch in Transformation Workshop Z' (Report on the Study: The Human Being in Transformation Workshop), *Bundeswehr* Transformation Centre, German Federal Ministry of Defence, 2006.

'An Initial Long Term Vision for European Defence Capability and Capacity Needs', European Defence Agency, Brussels, October 2006.

'Army Doctrine Publication' (ADP), Volume 2 Command, Army Code 71564 UK Ministry of Defence, 1995.

'Army Transformation Roadmap', US Department of the Army, 2004.

'British Defence Doctrine', UK Ministry of Defence, 2008.

'Bundeswehr Transformation Centre', Bundeswehr Transformation Centre, Federal German Ministry of Defence, 2007.

'Campaigning', JDP 01, Second Edition, UK Ministry of Defence, 2008.

'Capabilities Improvement Chart I/2006', Council of the European Union, Brussels, 2006.

'Commander's Appreciation and Campaign Design', Pamphlet 525-5-500, TRADOC, Virginia, US, January 2008.

'Crisis Management Concept', Defence Staff, CICDE, French Ministry of Defence, 2007.

'DE&S: An Introduction', DE&S Corporate Communications, UK Ministry of Defence.

'Defence Industrial Strategy: Defence White Paper', UK Ministry of Defence, 2005.

'Delivering Security in a Changing World: Defence White Paper', UK Ministry of Defence, 2003.

'Delivering Security in a Changing World: Future Capabilities', UK Ministry of Defence, 2004.

'Die Bundeswehr Sicher ins 21 Jahrhundert: Eckpfeiler fuer eine Erneuerung von Grund auf' (A Secure *Bundeswehr* in the 21st Century: The Cornerstones of a Fundamental Renewal), German Federal Ministry of Defence, 2000.

'Doctrine D'Emploi Des Forces Terrestres En Stablilisation', *Centre de Doctrine d'Emploi des Forces*, French Army, French Ministry of Defence, November 2006.

'EDA Press Release: EDA, EU SATCEN Demonstrate Potential for System to Integrate Intelligence Imagery', European Defence Agency, Torrejon, Spain, 20 February 2008.

'Effects Based Operations: Implications of Recent JFCOM Commander's Guidance', Letter, DG DCDC, 24 September 2008.

'EU Energy and Transport in Figures Statistical Pocketbook 2007–08', Office for Official Publications of the European Communities, Luxembourg, 2008.

'European Security and Defence Policy: The Civilian Aspects of Crisis Management', EU Council Secretariat, 2007.

'Factsheet 2 Future Capabilities: Capability Implications', UK Ministry of Defence, 2004.

'Final Report on the Civilian Headline Goal 2008', Approved by the Ministerial Capabilities Commitment Conference and noted by the General Affairs and External Relations Council on 19 November 2007 – doc. 14807/07, Council of the European Union, 2007.

'Financial and Economic Data relating to NATO Defence', Press Release, Public Diplomacy Division, NATO, February 2009, Communique PR/CP 2009 (09).

'FM 3-24: Counterinsurgency', Headquarters, Department of the Army, December 2006.

'Future Capabilities, Factsheet 1: The Policy Baseline – Why We Need to Change', UK Ministry of Defence, 2004.

'Future Land Operational Concept', Development, Concepts and Doctrine Centre, UK Ministry of Defence, 2008.

'Gemeinsame Sicherheit und Zukunft der Bundeswehr: Bericht der Kommission an die Bundesregierung' (Common Security and the Future of the Armed Forces: Report of the Commission to the Federal Government), German Federal Ministry of Defence, 2000.

'Incorporating and Extending the UK Military Effects Based Approach', Joint Doctrine Note, 7/06, Development Concepts and Doctrine Centre, Shrivenham, UK Ministry of Defence, September 2006.

'Initial Long-Term Vision for European Capability and Capacity Needs', Brussels, European Defence Agency, Brussels, October 2006.

'Joint Air Operations: Interim Joint Warfare Publication 3-30', Joint Doctrine and Concepts Centre, UK Ministry of Defence, 2003.

'Die Konzeptionelle Grundvorstellung der Luftwaffe zum EBAO' (Conceptual Basis of the Air Force on EBAO), Air Force Planning Staff, German Ministry of Defence, Bonn, 2007.

'Kosovo: Lessons from the Crisis', UK Ministry of Defence, 2000.

'Loi de Programme Militaire 2009–14', NOR: DEFX0821148L/Bleue-1, French Defence Ministry, 2009.

'MAJIIC Introduction', NATO C3 Agency, NATO, Brussels, October 2006.

'Manuel D'Emploi Des Forces Terrestres En Zone Urbaine', TTA 980, *Centre de Doctrine d'Emploi des Forces*, French Army, French Ministry of Defence, July 2005.

'Ministry of Defence Policy Paper: Paper No. 3 European Defence', UK Ministry of Defence, 2001.

'Multilateral Interoperability Programme Management Plan', Multilateral Interoperability Programme, April 1999.

'National Security Strategy of the United Kingdom: Security in an Interdependent World', The Cabinet Office, London, 2008.

'NATO Briefing: Operational Capabilities', NATO Public Diplomacy Division, NATO, October 2006'.

'NATO Press Release NAC-S (99)65: NATO Strategic Concept', NATO, 24 April 1999.

'Network Enabled Capability', (NEC), JSP 777, UK Ministry of Defence, 2005.

'Network Enabled Capability Pre-Study, Public Executive Summary', Western European Armaments Organisation Research Cell, June 2006.

'Operations in Iraq: Lessons for the Future', UK Ministry of Defence, 2003.

'Principes D'Emploi De La Fot Numerisee De Niveau 3', *Centre de Doctrine d'Emploi des Forces*, French Army, French Ministry of Defence, July 2004.

'Proceedings of the Fourth International Forum on Doctrine: Future Operations and Command Organisation', French Army Doctrine and Higher Military Education Command, French Ministry of Defence, 5 June 2003.

'Quadrennial Defense Review Report', United States Department of Defense, May 1997.

'Quadrennial Defense Review Report', United States Department of Defense, September 2001.

'Quadrennial Defense Review Report', United States Department of Defense, February 2006.

'Remarks to the European Parliament Sub-Committee on Security and Defence by Brigadier General Heinrich Brauss, Director Civilian/Military Cell', Brussels, 1 March 2007.

'Review of Acquisition for the Secretary of State for Defence', 15 October 2009.

'RTP 9.12, Miracle Project Final Report: Project Overview: Research and Technology Project on Micro-Satellite Cluster Technology', Kongsberg Spacetech, Norway, 12 July 2007.

'Security and Stabilisation: The Military Contribution', Joint Doctrine Publication 3-40, UK Ministry of Defence, 2009.

'Shared Responsibilities: A National Security Strategy for the UK', Institute for Public Policy Research, London, June 2009.

'Sicherheitspolitische Zukunftsanalyse: Ausblick auf 2035 Trends und Entwicklungen' (Future Security Analysis: Forecast 2035), Bundeswehr Transformation Centre, Federal German Ministry of Defence, 2007.

'Strategic Defence Review', UK Ministry of Defence, 1998.

'Targeting Tomorrow's Challenges', NATO Research and Technology Organisation, NATO, Brussels, January 2008.

'The Comprehensive Approach', Joint Discussion Note, 4/05, UK Ministry of Defence, 2006.

'The DCDC Global Strategic Trends Programme 2007–2036', Development, Concepts and Doctrine Centre, UK Ministry of Defence, 2006.

'The French White Paper on Defence and National Security', French Ministry of Defence, 2008.

'Verteidigungs Politische Richtlinien' (VPR) (Defence Policy Guidelines), German Federal Ministry of Defence, 2003.

'The Prague Summit and NATO's Transformation: A Reader's Guide', NATO Public Diplomacy Division, NATO, Brussels, 2002.

'The Riga Summit: A Reader's Guide', NATO Public Diplomacy Division, NATO, Brussels, July 2007.

'The Significance of Culture to the Military', Joint Doctrine Note 01/09, UK Ministry of Defence, 2009.

'Towards a European Vision for the Use of Land Forces?', Doctrine Forum, Army Command for Doctrine and Higher Military Education, French Military of Defence, 15 June 2001.

'Transformation Planning Guidance', United States Department of Defense, April 2003.

'White Paper on German Security Policy and the Future of the *Bundeswehr*', German Federal Ministry of Defence, 2006.

'White Paper on Space: A New European Frontier for an Expanding Union: An Action Plan For Implementing the European Space Policy', European Commission, Brussels, November 2003.

'Winning the Battle Building the Peace: Land Forces in Present and Future Conflicts', FT-01 (ENG), *Centre de Doctrine d'Emploi des Forces*, French Army, French Ministry of Defence, Paris, 2007.

Index